Creativity for Soul Healing

A mindfulness survival guide —
at home and work

*Unblock your creative endeavor
from Timefields © 2023 to find
joy and fun!*

Kirstin Labita

Moonflower

Creativity for Soul Healing

Copyright © 2025 by Kirstin Labita

All rights reserved. Published by Moonflower.
No part of this book may be reproduced or transmitted in any form or by any means, electronic or mechanical, including photocopying, recoding, or by any information storage and retrieval system, without written permission from the publisher.

All illustrations and designs, including the book cover are copyright © Kirstin Labita 2025.

Visit www.klabitahealing.com

This book is not intended to replace professional medical care. It is meant for creative endeavor and emotional awareness. Seek professional medical care for your ailments, either physical, mental, or energetic through the practitioner that works best for you.

The body of this book is set in 10 point Calibri font type for those who are curious and those who need a more open font, such as people who have dyslexia.

Description: Moonflower [2025] Includes bibliographical references.
Identifiers: ISBN 9798218613112 (paperback), ISBN 9798218613129 (ebook)

Dedication

My unending gratitude to everyone who supported me on this journey from distances near and far through their creative endeavor and leadership skills in business and life.

And for:

Carrie: *who ignited my creative spark*

Corinne: *my sister who started me on my new path and supports me when I'm feeling tone deaf*

Elizabeth: *my soul sister who tucks me under her wing when I need a creative shove*

Ethan and Norah: *my grounding bubbles and joy balloons*

Sarah: *who changed my life with two good reads and her quick-witted wisdom*

Starlight, Sunlight, to the Moon and back again
R O Y G B I V

For survivors of guilt, shame, PTSD
and other trauma who have not gotten their due
because of lack of attention.

And finally, for all who heal, including women like my mom, who survived the demanding work environment of an intensive care unit for 30 years.

Dedication	iii
Table of Contents	iv
Author's Note	
WAIT! STOP! This is a choose-your-own-adventure self-help book	
Welcome, come in!	1
First, a few words:	2
A New System of Healing Through Emotions	

Introduction: Stories and Resistance to Change, rewriting the terms of engagement

Enacting Change Through Inner Strength	
Begin Here: Press the Start Button	7
Gather Your Gear: Prepare for Your Epic Journey	8
Mindfulness Demystified	
Learning Through Your Nervous System	

Part 1: Creativity and the Creative Process

Chapter 1: Paring Down Definitions of Creativity	13
Creative Products	
The Design Connection	
How Our Minds Create	
Try It: Optimal Creative State Visualization	18
Level Up Your Creative Process	
Chapter 2: Creative Blocks	22
Emotional Blocks	
Freeing the Pools of Creative Energy	
Frequencies of Color and Light	
Unrequited Love Frequency	
Try It: Journaling Visualization: What's Your Color?	30
Language and the Sneak	
Try It: Reprogramming Through Awareness	34
Chapter 3: Focal Points and Creative Blocks	35
System Maintenance for Creative Well-Being	
Perfectionism as Creative Block	
Joining the Images of Perfection with Imperfection	
Try It: The Diagonal Line - Changing your perspective	41
Chapter 4: Typical Creativity Life Cycle	42
Cycling Through Creativity	
Marking the Seasons of Time	
Creativity in the Seasons: Equinoxes and Solstices	
Try it: Seasons of Change	47
Chapter 5: Creative Life Concept	49
Filling Your Creative Cup	
Nourish Your Creative Process Through Concept	
No Vision or Mood Boards!	
Be Inspired	
Research and Data Collection	

Don't Forget Your X-acto Blade
Let's Begin! Create your Creative Life Concept

Chapter 6: Creativity in the Workplace   57
Organizational vs. Individual Values + Identity
Brands: The Name's the Thing
The Elusive Creative Culture
Try It: Creative Values for the Group (NOT ORGANIZATION)   64
The Abraxas Effect
Office Politics and Walls of Behavior
A New Level of Teamwork
Brainstorming and Improvised Creativity
Try It: Group Critique   73
Play, Exploration, and Idleness
For Love or Paycheck?
Minority Roles and Mis-compensation in the Workplace
Women's Roles in Understanding
Pulling Up to the Table of Plenty
Arm Wrestling a Giant
Egos at Work and Play
Egos and Myth Busters
Try It: Enjoying Your Time at Work (What!?)   90
Tomorrow of Passion

Chapter 7: Leadership   93
Paracelsus and Air Fairies
Artificial Strategies
Leadership and Communication Styles
Women's Roles in Leadership
Generational Leadership Styles
'We Are the World', Gen X
Double Vector in Business
The Flying V and the Hive
New Perspectives on Change Agents
Forgiveness and Gratitude as a Leader

Part 2: Flow and Timefields

Chapter 8: Revisiting Flow   115
Finding Your Flow
The Descriptive Model of Flow Theory
Four Levels of Flow

Chapter 9: Timefields   120
Ecotones: A Descriptive Model of Overwhelm
Heartwalls, Moats and Fortresses
Solid vs. Void
Stagnant Waters
Speaking into the Void
Don't Avoid Your Creativity
Try It: Heal Behaviors through the Moon's Void-of-Course   129

Chapter 10: Energy Healing Techniques   130

Does This Stuff Really Work?
Science: Faraday's Field and Maxwell's Switch
The Energy Body
Energy Healing Techniques
Sublimation Techniques in Energy Healing
A Systems Approach to Healing
Mind-Heart-Gut Connection
Forgiveness and Unrequited Love
Using My Healing Techniques
Try It: Putting it All Together: 'Body Scan' Method — 150
Grounded Healing through Timefields
Try It: Steps for clearing a Timefield — 152

Chapter 11: Systems of Timefields — 155
Unrequited Love and Stacking of Timefields
Try It: Clearing Stacked Timefields — 157
Judging Teens
Past Lives and Timefields
Understanding Past Lives Through Quantum Physics
Healing Past Life Timefields
Collective Timefields
Try It: Source Cord Viz for Humanity's rising influence on Earth's grid — 164
Indigenous Cultures Past and Present
The Energetics of Sacred Places and Spaces
Nervous System Impacts from Our Environment
Transitioning Away from Established Systems

Part 3: The Energetics of Healing the Emotional Body

Chapter 12: Emotional Body Healing — 173
The K-Drama Family Tree
Resetting Rhythms of Behavior
Try It: Clear Behavioral rhythms — 176
Try It: Clear and Release Behavior Patterns — 176
Releasing Stuck Energies in Your Divine Life Force Connection
Try It: Integumentary System Clearing and Release — 178
Tattoos Parlors and the Earth's Charms
Hairnets and Belief Systems
Judgment Errors in Memory
Try It: Currents of Time and Energy — 184
Clearing Past Fears and Avoidance
Try It: Limbic System Response Release — 186
Quantum Physics, Play & Idleness
Bringing in the Future
A New Approach for an Age-Old Problem of Healing
New Age Healing for Time-Honored Results
Creative Anger and Doing the Right Thing
Try It: Dream Journals — 195
Resetting the Scales
I'm Hungry

Try It: Stop putting judgments in your body	*201*
Chapter 13: Timefields & Addiction/Addictive Behaviors	**202**
Defining Addiction	
Try It: Healing Emotions Related to Addiction	*206*
Try It: Be a Monk	*208*
Even More Science: Newton's Third Law of Motion	
Healing Through Self-Love	
Time and Waste	
Chapter 14: Past Life & This Life Healing	**214**
Past Life Emotional Energies	
Square Dancing	
Try It: Tidal Locking and Sequence Statement	*217*
Passion and Romance	
Healthy, Wealthy, and Wise	
Emotional Healing With a Creative Touch	
Parasympathetic Nervous System Release:	*225*
Chapter 15: The Body in Motion	**227**
Learning Your Body's Language	
Trip the Light Fantastic	
Postural Olympics	
Exercise and Weight	
Try It: Your Energetic Body Type	*233*
Body Healing for Women	
Wish Fulfillment and Sublimation	
Try It: Wish Fulfillment Statement:	*238*
Slow Your Roll: Bridging the Mindfulness Gap	
Try It: Slow Down to Let Your Mind Wander	*240*
Chapter 16: Other Energetic Healing Modalities	**241**
Healing from Astrological Birth Charts	
Intercepted Birth Charts	
Finding Your Life Line to be a Lifeline	
Try It: Clearing Interception Energy	*247*
The Swallowtail of Existence	
Tesseracts and the Nature of Reality	
The Shape of Love	
Healing Through Ley Lines	
Try it! Look at an Image of the Earth	*257*
Oceans, Rivers, and Lakes: Healing Currents of the Earth	
Dancing Light	
Chapter 17: Final Notes on Creativity and Healing	**263**
Creativity in All its Forms	
Guides and Channeling	
Energy Healing in our New Existence on Earth	
Play List	**268**
Bibliography	**269**
Healing Protocols Template	**272**
End Notes	**278**

Author's Note
Though I am not a doctor of medicine or a member of the psychiatry field, I believe in mindfulness. Please remember, as you work through these exercises, that they are not a replacement for a trained psychiatrist, psychoanalyst, or therapist to help you through your injuries, just as a doctor of medicine should be the one to help you with any physical injury or illness.

WAIT! STOP! This is a choose-your-own-adventure self-help book
This book is about enacting change by doing things. Even though it's over 260 pages, <u>**you don't have to read them all**</u>, besides some of them are charts and pictures. Just read the ones you want and that interest you. I know many of us get irritated with too much talking and not enough doing.

> "Can you please get to the point of this meeting?
> Can you stop talking so I can put the phone down and get my work done?
> I'm done listening to the yammering.
> Can we just get to the heart of the matter?"

I call it "talk-i-tecture" but we've all been in situations that cause us to fight the urge to sling something across the table (or internet) to stop the talking. I've already gone on too long about this, but know that I have done my best to edit it down because I, too, appreciate **economy with words.**

Creativity for Soul Healing

Welcome, come in!

We are dreamers and roamers, wishers and bridge builders, rule-breakers and non-conformists, nine-tailed foxes and fairy wood nymphs.

We are believers and doers.

We see beyond the ordinary but have practical magic that connects us to our work, ourselves, and others.

*We support each other and find ways to support ourselves.
We believe in the future and begin again to see
the light of our creative best.*

First, a few words:

flibity-jibit, houndstooth, and antidisestablishmentarianism...
...along with my grandma's favorite phrase:
"Throw the horse over the fence some hay."

As far as I know, flibity-jibit is my own word, houndstooth has nothing to do with dogs and everything to do with fashion, but the last word is purposely obtuse so I will strike it from the lexicon of this book, though it is a worthy spelling bee puzzle.

As for the horse, are we throwing it or the hay over the fence? In the end, does it really matter?

Perhaps to the horse.

These words and my grandma's phrasing show us that the words we choose and how we use them have power—the power to make us **laugh**, **wonder**, or feel overwhelmed.

But a picture is worth a thousand words. **A thousand!** As long as the words aren't as difficult as antidisestablishmentarianism, I'm good with that because it's hard to read, let alone say it.

That means every picture we create is worth 1,000 words, and the words the creator was thinking are probably not the words the person viewing it is thinking, making the possibility of the meaning of the picture **endless** — which can be way more interesting than one long word.

Let's say it takes about 10 minutes to read 1,000 words but only a few moments to look at a picture. The number of possible words generated by the picture quickly moves towards **infinity**, considering the number of pictures each person looks at every day on the internet and the number of people worldwide.

I have heard that the infinity symbol — the sideways, loopy-looking number 8 — can also be read as a unity symbol. Meaning, we are **infinitely united**.

This is why we **create** and why creating has **value** in our lives. The equation is about unification, infinitely united in our ability to create. Our true connection with each other is our creativity — in all the ways there are to be creative — around the globe, across space and time.

Enjoy - *Kirstin*

A New System of Healing Through Emotions

In its simplest form, mindfulness is about asking, "How are you?" We often answer with, "Fine," "Can't complain," or the response that makes my skin crawl — "It is what it is." These are automatic responses because we think people don't want to hear how we really feel. Maybe it's just pleasantries, or we feel exposed, but what if you asked yourself, "How am I feeling?" Your answer is most likely quite different than the one you spoke out loud. How we feel and answer our feelings internally is a form of mindfulness that gets at the heart of this book: **being real in all its forms.** Being authentic to yourself and others is how we live our best lives and is a form of mindfulness because, at its core, is about relating as humans who are a part of each other in ways big and small.

Our energies are intertwined with the Earth's natural systems, keeping us in real-time and in the rhythm of belief in humanity. Time and energy are woven together within cultures and societies that are made up of interconnected systems that can either lift us up or keep us down. Nature forms the backbone of many cultures around the world, but over time, it has been edited out — lost in time, making us feel out of time and out of mind. From natural to cultural systems to other more nefarious systems that are not as helpful, we can easily see how our bodies and minds are impacted daily. If we are to heal ourselves, we need a new level of healing, a new way of understanding time and emotion and incorporating it into the power of attention and intention. Other healing modalities that are in place in this current time are not enough to move out the old energies from a systems perspective.

Through my *Timefield* terminology and methodology, this book presents a new healing system and represents over three years of healing myself and others through a guided approach. It is stacked on top of previous systems and modalities that sparked light for myself and others I have healed. Through love, we will find this new system to be ever-evolving and never-failing. I know I am one of many working in this field of endeavor, so I hope you find something within these pages that works for you in your creativity and creative healing practice.

Introduction: Stories and Resistance to Change, rewriting the terms of engagement

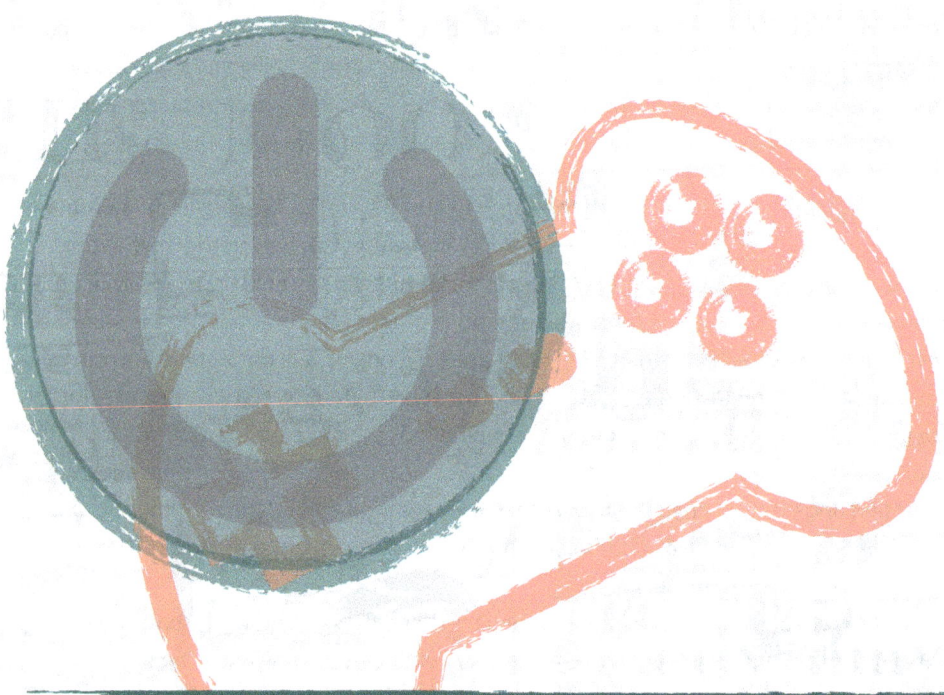

I am not a storyteller. I am a healer, designer, teacher, intuitive, and writer, but telling stories isn't my thing. Don't get me wrong I love a good story and good gossip because, at their best, stories can incite and enact change and transformation in our minds and hearts. But do we need to share the stories of the past to overcome our obstacles? Sometimes, other times, stories can cause us to rehash the past, keeping us down, stuck in a never-ending cycle of self-doubt and feeling unloved. As the journalist India Rakusen perceptively noted in her BBC podcast, *Witch*, "A story isn't about its words, it's about what you want to see" — or believe. We need to move on from those stories or risk being pulled back down into what we've climbed up and out of. But I admit that stories do help us connect. We find comfort in knowing that we share similar experiences and can relate to each other through the level of the story, even if what we see in front of us seems strangely different. I believe we should use stories to teach, heal, and create change within us, and as story-telling seems to be the thing of the moment, finding the right way to look at and feel a story is important.

Enacting Change Through Inner Strength

Our perception of strength comes through our superhero and gladiator stories that show us how having super human strength can take down the bad guys — more muscles and will power means more power within to enact change. Burn through that exercise routine! Pull down those structures around us! Tear up the world and leave a mess behind! I've often wondered who's responsible for cleaning up the destruction after the super heroes leave for the day. But as they are a force to be reckoned with, super heroes don't really care until the bad guys are in jail or some other form of incarceration. "You won't be needing this where you're going," they famously quip. And so the supervillains are sent to rot in jail, stew in their own juices and hopefully find some remorse while their freedom is taken away from them. No sense of justice for the villains, they're just bad guys and don't have an ounce of blood that's true.

But if we look at the superhero stories as metaphors for us as individuals, how we are both 'good' and 'bad', or light and dark, does that mean we need to shun the parts of us that are no longer acceptable? It doesn't make sense to me because as the saying goes, we are human and divine. How can we be both without acknowledging what is grabbing our attention to be freed?

This is what I mean by inner strength; it's not about being muscular or having the power to burn through rock with your eyeballs. It's about finding the *chutzpah,* as some would say, to look within and find the strength to know that you are both human and divine — not good and bad. Good and bad are value judgments on behaviors. While some are more pleasant than others, being human means you make mistakes, learn from them, take corrective action, and hopefully move on. Being divine means you see the beauty in all things, that you like all people and that you love the Earth, who guards and makes us feel safe. All of these aspects are true in our bodies, hearts, and minds. It's not one or the other, it's both-and — together. It's a dichotomy of existence that we are both our darkest truths and our lightest minds. We see it in each other and in ourselves and splitting hairs over who is better than the other is simply a waste of time because we are all one.

<u>We've All Been Through This Before</u>

We learned this fact quite literally during the pandemic as we watched a virus move like wild fire across our planet. We were free for a time, but then we were told to go into lockdown for our safety. Locked up like the superhero-villains we are to stew in our own juices and find the beliefs we hold to be self-evident. If we were fearful, it was amplified. If we were carefree, it was amplified. If we felt like fighting, it was amplified. All of those things happened during the pandemic in some shape or form and at different levels; in our own homes all the way up to the national and world stage. It was a superhero existence as 'ordinary' people did extraordinary things and we found that the villains were not so villain-y after all, or maybe more villain-y than we thought by being ungrounded in their natures, including leaders that took many missteps. But remember, we are all human and we are all divine.

So what does this all have to do with superheroes and enacting inner strength? To be honest, I don't know. I don't know how we got to being good and bad, strong and weak, inside or outside; we just arranged ourselves that way and the story has kept going for eons. So time for a different story. I'm bored with the superhero mystique — too many movies going over the same trope. I got it the first few dozen times, I don't need to see or experience it any more.

What about your story? I know you have one and it belongs to you just as we belong to each other in communities far and wide. Like a fairyland where each fairy has their special talent or interest and brings it to the group (except Smurfette, but we'll talk about patriarchy later), we all bring our talents to the table of justice in the aftermath of superheroes destroying our cities and towns. Maybe we can come together to enact change through our talents. To do that, we have to understand our creative endeavor, which is tied to our talent for making things. Even if you make math equations, line items on a spreadsheet, or make the discovery of a lifetime in the life sciences, we are all creative and have the vitality to move in the direction that allows us to be superhuman. We belong and we belong to each other, so let's band together and find a way to un-become superheroes and take on the villains of our memories to find out they are actually just wounded warriors like the rest of us.

Time for a new chapter in business that moves it toward an energy of civility. We no longer care if there is a right or wrong way to dress, act, or look in business as long as it is held accountable and actionable in love. I know love and business seem odd, but we are all people and business is made up of people, not suits. Let's find a way to be civil to each other in business and not make it about more or less, stronger and weaker, trimming off the 'dead wood' to make a profit. "The profit in what is, is in the use of what isn't" reads Ursula LeGuin's modern translation of the *Tao Te Ching*, our guide and centering aspect for leadership. Profit comes from our heart centers, which live in the hollows of our chests, an 'empty' space or void. The void is where we go to find serenity and healing; too little time spent there can be detrimental to our health and our lives.

Let's tear down the ideas of business and build them up again to be healthier by allowing people to be themselves and not conform to a standard that is way outside anybody's vision of what life is. We believe in each other and we find ways to support one another in business, not take down the rich bad guys or push out the poor. We'll find these truths to be self-evident as we look to bees and geese who fly around free and independent. Our Abraxas moment is waiting for us right outside the walls of discontent and so we hold others accountable for their own behaviors even as we work on our own.

All of these ideas will be covered in this book and we'll link it all back to creative endeavor and healing. It's not a nice-to-have anymore, it's imperative that we all take the time to understand who we are as individuals and see the collective hearts of the people around us who fit into our lives daily. I know we can do it because now is the time to start believing in ourselves as we look around at the systems that are being destroyed one by one. We know what they are, but we don't need to be dismayed. We can just say, "That worked for a while, but it's not working any more. Let's see if we can do it better next time." Just like prototyping and testing behaviors, we have the opportunity to make something new and better than the last time. But we can't do it alone, we need to come together in unity — be infinitely united — in our abilities, talents, and creativity to form a better world around us where all are equally supported and all are free.

Begin Here: Press the Start Button
To find out what comes next, remember your own story

So, let's start with a story, but not mine — it isn't different than any other story of someone who has gone through a difficult time. Instead, we'll begin with **your story** because it is by far the most important one to you. Once you've understood your story, you will change it, not by providing your medical history, which is one story, but by understanding your emotions, leading you on a new path. We can't be superhuman all the time; our energy needs time to heal so we can continue to thrive. The often repeated phrase "what doesn't kill you makes you stronger" brings up an image of a person — perhaps your favorite superhero or gladiator — lying on the ground in great pain and suffering. Let's reword that phrase to: **What HEALS you makes you stronger.** Meaning, let's focus on applying whatever healing modality works best for you. Let's not focus on the story but on the behavior that got us there and the behavior that will get us out of our pain and suffering.

But enough talking! **Time for action!** Press the start button.

Your Creative Backstory Map
Questing for positive behaviors from childhood

Relating is what we humans do best to heal and make sense of our world, and we often do this through stories. From Frodo Baggins in *The Lord of the Rings* to the gaming world of Nintendo's *Zelda*, epic journeys or quest stories mirror our lives. The journey of our lives takes us on one large adventure, with many side quests or mini-games. This path you're about to undertake is about you and you only. You get to uncover hidden treasure chests or bend toward true love's first kiss (if you're into that). It starts with one step and then another, finding your path of least resistance, and becoming familiar with your personal road map. If you think you don't have a road map, don't worry, I've got you covered.

Answer the questions below to find your own creative backstory. You might want a pen and a few pieces of paper. It's not a test, so have fun and enjoy a trip down memory lane.

- When I was a child, I liked to pretend to be _____ because....
- When I was a child, I wanted to be _____ when I grew up because...
- When I was a child, I was inspired by _____ because it made me feel...
- When I was a child, I had an imaginary friend whose name was _____. This friend made me feel…. (It's ok if you didn't have one, I didn't, either.)
- When I was a child, the fictional character I liked most was _____ because...
- Who is your favorite superhero? Why? _____

Feeling creative? Time to start on your path of uncovering your creativity's hidden depths. But first, you need to prepare for this epic quest.

Gather Your Gear: Prepare for Your Epic Journey
How do you communicate your creative process to yourself and others?
    Preparing for a journey requires preparation; every cell in your body needs to know it's time for something different. A hiker doesn't step onto the path without finding the right shoes, water bottle, backpack, food, and other provisions. Stepping onto the path also requires good communication between your heart, mind, and body. As you put one foot in front of the other on a new and exciting path, it's time to put on your upbeat playlist — plug in, tune out the world, tune into yourself, and set your mind to the task.

Creativity: Tools of the Trade
    We communicate our ideas using different tools. Coworkers, clients, friends, and family are all people that require different communication types. Whether it's a drawing, spectrometer, or recipe, the tools change depending on who we communicate with. But how you communicate with *yourself* is the most important aspect of this journey, requiring you to look deeper into understanding who you are. Your ability to do this will get you further than seems possible and it only takes a few thought starters.
    Where is your journey taking you? Not the end goal — the process. Set the scene for yourself as if you are in an **alternate reality**. You could be walking through a sci-fi reality like *Tron* or walking along the bottom of a lake. Or maybe you are on a spaceship jumping through hyperspace or gliding through a fairy forest. Once you know the place, select your mode of transportation: hoverboard, motorcycle, dragon — anything works. Be as fantastical as you want to be, and then make your grocery list of supplies:

- Write a list of at least **5 things** you will **bring** on board your vessel to support you on your journey.
- Write a list of at least **5 things** you will **find** on your journey to help you achieve success through your landscape.

Write about or draw a picture of discovery that helps you understand what **supports** you and what brings you **success**.

Healers: Tools of the Trade

Here is an alternative method for approaching your quest. We prepare ourselves as healers in different ways. Meditation, prayer, affirmations, or research are all methods of communicating with yourself to prepare for an inward journey. You can also set sail by using this affirmative visualization.

Imagine yourself on a boat far out at sea. You're not in danger, you're feeling peaceful. You could be there with your friends or in solitude. You may need a lot of snacks or your favorite armchair. Maybe the size of the boat grows to the size of an island. The point is to get the feeling of being supported in all the ways you need it. Make a list of items to support you on your boat ride.

- List at least **5 supportive** things that you **bring with you** on the boat.
- List at least **5 supportive** things **you discover** on the boat or in the water that will help you achieve <u>success</u> on your journey.

Have fun with it! It doesn't have to make sense. If you think you need a bright blue stuffed animal, then that's what you bring or find.

Now that you've set yourself up for success, the real fun begins!
Oh, one more thing. Without a sidekick to bring the jokes and help you through the tricky spots, here is some advice.

Mindfulness Demystified
The unsaid and unseen during spa days

There's no one thing that everyone can do — or should do — to stay mindful. It's a mystique that's worth debunking. Just like life, mindfulness is an up-and-down course that's rarely straight ahead. The twists and turns can be disorienting, making us feel like we've lost our way. It's not easy, and it is not for the faint of heart. Being mindful isn't always about focusing on good behaviors; it's about learning from the stuck behaviors or behaviors that keep you down in repeat patterns. It certainly brings about changes, but to get to the joy, you have to wade through the swamp of sorrow, loneliness, and unloved-ness in your life. You can't go around it; you have to go through it to heal.

We all have our sorrows, guilt, remorse, shame, and feelings of being unloved that we have to work through in our way. It's completely false to think that everyone should meditate or that everyone should take a 5-hour class that helps them tap into their deep, regressive wounds. Yes, those things can be part of it, but in my experience, being mindful takes years, not hours; it takes many different modalities, not one. In my experience, it takes research, understanding, curiosity, and being mindful <u>every moment of the day.</u> You have to be aware of all things that come up for you at all times — what the TV show you are watching is mirroring, what the conversation you just had with your friend symbolizes for you (or straight up tells you), what your body tells you through pain or illness, what your bank account says, and even what your house tells you. You have to be constantly aware and constantly mindful, because the Universe is constantly unfolding and changing.

Under the heading of "be careful what you wish for," mindfulness is about enacting change that causes — who knows what — to come up in your life. It's no walk on the beach. Well, maybe if it's during a storm… in the middle of winter… on a deserted island. That describes it best. Things can get turned upside down or right side up. The end goal is to find joy, love, or bliss, but getting there may make you feel like life is even crazier than you thought. More likely than not, your sense of self will dissipate only to be reborn into something new. Rebirth can be exhilarating, but it can also be painful and messy. Sometimes you want things to return to how they were, sometimes you wouldn't trade them for anything. The phrase 'dark night of the soul' will become your new favorite mantra as the energies within come up to make you walk through the darkness.

But, if you give yourself time to look back and see the changes that occur, you will find that though it feels untenable at times, everything is in your favor. Things like: "If I hadn't had that breakdown, I would never have accomplished…. X, Y, Z" will show up for you over and over. The synchronicities of being alive will happen over and over. Your life will balloon out in ways you never thought possible. You will believe in happiness and love again like you never thought possible. You will set a new standard of living that aligns with who you are, not who society says you should be. You will find love and healing on *your* terms, not someone else's. And you will find life magical again as if childhood has persisted all this time in an unending march toward believing, feeling, hearing, and seeing fairies and fairy dust, all-day rainbows, and the fog lifting just as the sun sets.

Joy is the ultimate way of living. We're not here to just exist and survive, we are here to thrive. Finding joy in what you do and how you live is how we should all live. It's easier said than done sometimes. But if we can see light in suffering, then we are on the right path to finding a way out — "joy inside my tears," as Stevie Wonder says. Mindfulness is not all scented candles and spa days. It takes perseverance and strength to go to the dark places in our psyches we would rather not see. But the goal of this book is to guide you, if even just a little way, on your journey of becoming more of who you are.

Learning Through Your Nervous System
Finding your path to understanding

There are many self-discovery books that have the same basic outline: follow this ONE WAY of doing things, and you will change. There also seems to be a formula for self-help books that include other people's stories to make a point. As creative people, we like choice in our actions. It irks us when we're lumped into a group like cattle, pushing us through a narrow gate to get to the same end goal as everyone else. And impatient readers have no qualms about skipping to the last page or chapter to get to the point. Besides, <u>this book is about you, not other people</u>.

In light of that, this book is designed as a field guide, so reading it cover to cover is <u>not necessary</u>. The interrelated sections are noted and I tell you to jump back or forward to connect to another section that underpins or builds on the current one. **Now that you know you don't have to read (much),** I hope you will give learning a try because the information is broken out into a choose-your-own-adventure style. It offers practical advice from a designer and healer who has found some good ideas to ease the path of creative healing. Feel free to skip around, but try to find something new to focus on, as this helps kick-start your creative process. Whatever your mood when you pick up this book, it's here to support you. Any topic you choose for the day, evening, or hour is right for you. You can make a game out of it and let the book fall open to any page and work through that topic as you wish. You can also read this book page by page. It's your creative journey, so have fun with it!

Everyone learns by doing, no matter your background, skill level, or nervous system type. So, if you are someone who processes the world differently than most, like ADD, PTSD, or dyslexia, I hope that you will give learning a try through the creative endeavor exercises I've included. Minimal reading is required in those sections with the hope of moving your creativity out onto a dance floor or baseball diamond. Finding the time to work through my suggestion points, journal topics, and healing practice moments is most beneficial. Allow the pictures to fill your mind's eye with discovery and feel the changes that occur, however subtle. For energy healers or people interested in this form of healing, once you become accustomed to how I approach healing, it will be easier to work through all the intervention points. Use them as a basis of design, or a starting point, to integrate with your healing modality. Take what works and leave behind the rest.

<u>Healing Through Creativity</u>

Creative expression comes in as many versions as there are people, and there is no set way to be creative or develop a creative process. *So why a guide for creativity?* First, I find that many people think they're not creative. They believe that creativity belongs to only the people who paint, do drugs to create, dance, draw, or whatever society dictates as creative. Can a spreadsheet be creative? Absolutely! Can a doctor or lawyer be creative in their professional field? Yep. Creativity is everywhere and yet we are cut off from it.

Second, there are many ways to say 'nope' in our lives: nope to self, nope to others' love, nope to living free. Conversely, our 'yes' is for working hard to eke out an existence for some and to keep up with the neighbors for others. It's a never-ending race to nowhere, and creativity gets shut out quickly, especially if you're too tired after a long day of work. True, some people have creative jobs, but even those jobs get tiresome, unrewarding, and stale. We are all creative at our core and need to express it.

Creativity exists in the change within. Much as a story finds its way into our hearts, creativity finds its way out of our hearts and onto the page, canvas, operating table, or any other creative expression. We begin with an understanding of creativity because healing is creative, and the creative act can be a healing modality. But to move further into healing, we need to be aware of our issues, our emotional baggage, and our overwhelm of feelings and thoughts. Part Two of this book presents this to you in a new and profound way to bring about healing through self-discovery and self-reliance. Part Three gets into some heady topics, such as understanding the body's systems, quantum physics, and tattoo parlors. Yes, it's all in here and ready for your discovery.

If you don't like the path you're on, begin again by finding a new one. It's ok to stop and start over. Find a new level of understanding your creative process by going with the Flow (another topic in this book) and not judging yourself if something isn't working for you. Not everything will work all the time and in all the ways you think. With that said, time to move on to creativity itself.

Part 1: Creativity and the Creative Process

Chapter 1: Paring Down Definitions of Creativity

> Researchers who study and write about creativity can present it in the most sterile way. It's not their fault, their creativity is staunched by being correct in their writing form. For example, the words "unique and useful" come up quite a bit in creativity research, but they never state for whom creativity should be unique and useful. They also distinguish between creative products, creativity, and the creative process, which tends to get a little cloudy. Full marks for setting out to define the indefinable, though!

But, sometimes personalities do break through the correctness, and a single line can be inspiring. In a 2010 report entitled *Creativity, Innovation and Arts Learning: Preparing All Students for Success in a Global Economy*, Sandra Rupert stated that creativity "requires building upon the capacity of one's **imagination** to visualize new possibilities for **human thought, action** and the use of **materials**." This three-pronged approach to defining creativity is the most comprehensive and inspiring definition because it sets us off on a path of discovery through space and time. It covers all aspects of how creativity happens. We see what other people are doing, which inspires us to imagine and find new possibilities within our way of doing things, with our version of the end result. In other words, our creativity inspires thought and action in others and it becomes a system to create change.

Creative Products
The materiality of creativity

Creativity is often defined through the result or product. The musician, entertainer, producer, writer, artist, and creativity connoisseur, Questlove, defines creativity this way: "Creativity sometimes results in products. But it is always a process." His book, *Creative Quest*, is aimed at people who work in traditionally creative fields, but he allows for different levels of creativity for people who don't earn their living in this way. For some, creativity exists only in producing "something original and useful."[1] Put another way, the result has "novelty and appropriateness"[2] — something that has never lived in the world before and provides a service. For example, the first iPhone was considered a creative product and continues to be today. At the time of its launch in 2007, almost everyone had a cell phone, and some even had a Blackberry, but the iPhone was unique in that it put a computer in our pockets, which was also a phone.

Are usefulness or appropriateness the only way to define a creative product? Is a painting hanging on the wall useful? I suppose we could parse that down to how beauty is useful. But does a copy of a piece of artwork lose its creativity because it's not unique? I'm not sure defining creativity through the end product is the way to go because there are as many opinions about what is creative as there are people. The great thing about it is that you can define it how you want. You are the creator, it is your process and your creative instinct, so find your own definition of a creative result.

Creativity: A Leveled Approach

Creativity and the creative process are even more nebulous with many definitions and ways of approaching both, with different types of endeavors. My favorite definition of creativity comes from 2009 research by James Kauffman and Ronald Beghetto, published in the *Journal of Psychology* as 'Beyond Big and Little: The Four C Model of

---

[1] S. Pfeiffer, *Serving the gifted: Evidence-based clinical and psychoeducational practice*, 2013
[2] Y. Wong & K. Siu, *A model of creative design process for fostering creativity of students in design education*, 2012

Creativity.' In this article, they used previously defined statements on creativity and developed a more comprehensive view.

- **Big C** represents the big eureka moments; flashes of inspiration that appear seemingly out of nowhere or just after the science lab blows up.
- **Little c** represents everyday, small moments of creativity, seeing a new pattern, or making a new thought connection to something you already know. Little c can lead you to a Big C moment.
- **Mini-c** is when we learn something new and apply the information — learning how to decorate a cake or fix a toilet, for example.
- **Pro-C** represents a seasoned professional with a minimum of 10 years experience. This is creativity at the expert level.

This multi-leveled description and approach to creativity gives us a deeper understanding of how we use and express creativity in our everyday lives and proves that we don't all have to be Albert Einstein or Santiago Calatrava, but we can learn from their work. We can find creativity in the everyday moments that bring us joy and connection to ourselves and others, exploring in the ways we see fit. When this happens, we find we can learn and grow from it, change it up, move it around, find new expressions — it doesn't matter because almost every moment can be about creativity if we look at it from the right angle. Creativity isn't just a precious moment that is coaxed out of thin air, it's also an every day occurrence that brings us closer to who we are as individuals and breaks us open into the wide world of seeing and believing in ourselves.

The Design Connection
Creativity heals and healing is creative

I'll stop right here and explain a little about myself — not my story, you understand, just a background check. Creativity has been part of my 'upbringing' as first a college student, then as a young interior designer in the retail design world, and finally as a highly trained and credentialed designer, managing projects and clients in teams and on my own. I returned to school later in my career to learn more about creativity, and much of the material in this section is from my master's thesis, expanded on and used as a method for mindfulness, with exercises based on the creative process I used on all of my projects.

I'll reference interior design a lot in this book as I was in the architecture profession for 25 years. The practice of interior design is fraught with many misconceptions, from "color picker" to "window dresser" to "pillow fluffer." These terms are demeaning to what an interior designer really does which is use both intuition and intellect to manage and interpret the cultural context, the client's goals, and the rules and regulations that keep people safe. Interior design has an involved creative process; it solves specific problems and, as Tim Greenlaugh wrote, "imagines remarkable experiences that touch all the senses in a way other design disciplines cannot. It stimulates impressions that move people emotionally in an instant, day to day or forever."[3] These emotionally charged experiences draw on culture, environment, psychology, and history. Just as the Pro-C level of creativity infers, a high level of creativity in interior design (and architecture) is hard to achieve, with ten years being a minimum amount of time to reach it.

Creativity is also the purview of healers because healing is a cooperative, creative experience and calls on all the same mental processes that we use for creative endeavor. The design connection is about being aware of what is happening in the moment, or mindfulness. When you're curious about how something is designed or made, you look at it differently and pay attention to the details. Same thing with healing; you stay curious in the moment and try to understand the process or energy that exists within a given framework. In this way we can get to the heart of the matter, or the skin of the matter, as you will learn later in the healing section. (This relates to our integumentary systems, which contain our heart center energy.) Let's continue our process of uncovering your creativity in all its forms and discovering life on your terms.

How Our Minds Create
The role of intuition and intellect

We use both intellect and intuition to be creative; the two cannot be separate. Intuition can often be subconscious — following your gut, for example. Bringing your intuitive knowledge to a conscious level creates the power to change your creativity. One of my favorite intuition quotes is from Clarissa Pinkola Estes, she says, "Like the wolf, it has claws that let you pry things open and pin them down, it has eyes that let you see through shields ... and ears that hear beyond the mundane range of normal human hearing."[4] In other words, intuition is your superpower. But don't dismiss your conscious mind in the act of creation. The poet and author Jane Roberts wrote: "The conscious mind is endlessly creative. This applies to all areas of conscious-mind thinking. It is also the organizer of physical data."[5]

Intuition's language is symbols, similar to the symbols you see in your dreams. Intellect's language is physical data. Our conscious minds sort and navigate between pure symbology and physicality. So, the information generated intuitively will then be organized into a pattern by your conscious mind. Your conscious mind, therefore, is only half of the equation. If you can't make sense of something, perhaps finding a different way of applying your mind will set you on the right path of understanding. We know this is true when we step away from something we've been working on for a while and then suddenly are inspired to act toward completing the creative picture. We feel it comes

---

[3] Tim Greenhalgh, *Disrupting Interior Design*, 2015
[4] Clarissa Pinkola Estes, *Creative Fire*, 1998
[5] Jane Roberts, *The Nature of Personal Reality*, 1985

out of nowhere, but our subconscious mind has been working on it, often in our sleep. This is why people wake up in the middle of the night and have to write an idea down, or wake up in the morning refreshed and ready to take action on the problem that was bothering them the day before.

The Creative Process

Sir Ken Robinson was an educator, writer, and creativity proponent who became popular from his TED Talk on how creativity has been squeezed out of kids through their schooling. He said that creativity *is* the process and that it should produce original ideas that have value.

"Creativity is the process of having original ideas that have value."

Breaking his statement down, he defines **process** as trial and error, or playing, making sense of the world around you by working through ideas and thoughts. These **ideas**, or thinking, can be original to you or the world; it doesn't matter which because it's a process that gets you to an end goal. The **value** relates to the judgments made by you in your process, not other people's judgments. You decide whether or not what you've created is good enough, needs to be tweaked, or should be discarded altogether. It's your value judgment, in other words, not the work of the collective. Other people may judge it later, but while it is in your hands as the creator, you have all the control. Be aware that there are different levels of how the group assigns value to the end product. For example, a child's drawing is no less creative than artwork in a museum, but we assign a value to it based on the Big, little, mini, and pro-C levels.

The following research shows how we can automatically turn what our subconscious does into a conscious act of understanding ourselves and, in the process, find a solution to any creative project taxing our brains. If this is a common occurrence, why not take more conscious control of what is happening subliminally and turn it into a focused behavior?

The 5 Rs: Complexity in a fluid state

As I tell my design students, being aware of your creative process gives you control. When you get kicked off your creative path, finding a way back is crucial to moving past the block. One way to be aware is through the *Five Rs of Sensational Thinking*. Developed in 1994 by researchers Sharon O'Neil and Doris Shallcross, the 5 Rs are a way to understand the innate levels of creative consciousness we move through.[6] This creative cycle description identifies transition phases between each step, which happens on a micro-level or day-to-day cycle that lives within the seasons of your creativity. It also highlights the link between a creative person's environment (physical and social)

---

[6] Sharon O'Neil & Doris Shallcross, *Sensational Thinking A Teaching/Learning Model for Creativity*, 1994

and their design decision-making, which is important because it outlines what we know intuitively: that our exterior environment impacts our creativity just as much as our internal processes.

The *5 Rs of Sensational Thinking* can help when you feel blocked by tuning into yourself and understanding where in your process the block resides. The authors note, "At each of these stages, mental imagery and external representation takes place in different proportions, and they are significant for understanding the creative process."[7] These steps are often intuitive and fluid. As you learn about each step, notice how you feel and what you are thinking about. Note that at the beginning and end of each step, there is a transition period of imagining and presenting. These transitions can be researching, brainstorming, sketching, list making — any form of outward expression that gets you to the creative or artistic form.

The 5 Rs are:
1. **Readiness**: when you let go and allow yourself to be open, like when you take a nap.
2. **Reception**: when you observe and experience the world around you.
3. **Reflection** is evaluating observations against the "problem."
4. **Revelation** is when you focus on patterns received, the solution is found.
5. **Recreation** is when the actual work gets done.

I like that the word 'recreation' is used for the final step. It shows that all the up-front work is in our minds, and when we finally ready to create, we're just dictating or in Flow. (See Flow in the Timefield Section of the book.) Imagery happens between the first and second steps — finding inspiration. Between steps two and three, you externalize your ideas by putting them down on paper or and finding the right notes. Between the third and fourth steps, you evaluate and chose. And between the fourth and fifth steps, a basic version of the final is created. Again, this is an intuitive, fluid process, but it's helpful to know the different steps and be aware of our abilities.

Try It: Optimal Creative State Visualization

Take a moment and think about a time when you've felt optimally creative. If you don't have a time, make one up — don't underestimate the power of imagination. Hold that time in your mind and re-create it through all your senses. What do you notice?
- Were you inside in your room, or outside on a hike, for example?
- Was your mind at that moment wandering or hyper-focused?
- Were you by yourself or with other people?
- Bring in all your senses to fully understand the moment.

---

[7] Ibid

Now, apply this to the difficult moment you're working through. For example, a piece of music you composed doesn't feel like it's your best work. You decide to step away from it and walk at your favorite park. (Readiness) As you walk, you observe the trees, birds, and other natural elements around you (Reception). You allow your mind to wander as you reflect on your composition. (Reflection) As you reflect, you discover a different way of organizing it that makes it more impactful. (Revelation) You head back home to make your edits. (Recreation)

Knowing what it feels like to be in your optimal creative state is important in understanding your process and can help when you're stuck. Knowing you're blocked is the first step. Finding a way to unblock is the next. To find your Flow again through this thought experiment, identify what's missing.

Level Up Your Creative Process
Design Thinking

Design Thinking, a method attributed to problem-solving, is a popular creative framework and has been researched and parsed out to examine its validity. It works in a step-by-step and cyclical manner and provides a framework for what to do next when you don't know. Because of its linear aspects, it can fit into processes already in place. Using design thinking is beneficial because it brings awareness, especially for those who struggle with any part of their creative instincts. A 2013 research report studied design thinking at professional design companies and defined it as "the transfer of the organization's design philosophy into design activities and outputs."[8] The philosophy is an "approach, which emphasizes … value through problem-solving"[9] and is impacted by many factors that guide the structured design thinking creative process, including end-users, organic organizational structures, brand image, and competitors.
Here are the basic steps:
1. **Empathize:** research through observing and understanding.
2. **Define:** state the problem. This seems obvious when written down, but it's often an overlooked step which can cause creatives to run in endless circles instead of circling around the solution. What problem are you trying to solve?
3. **Ideate:** or come up with ideas/brainstorm
4. **Prototype:** fast interpretations of your ideas that can be easily created
5. **Test:** put the prototype through the paces to see if it works

The key to this process is that you can circle back to a previous step at any point, proving that the linear process isn't all that linear. If your ideas don't seem to fit, you go back and redefine the problem or observe more. Likewise, if your test didn't work, you would return to the idea phase to make changes. It's essential to be aware that sometimes the

---
[8] S. Chen & A. Venkatesh, *An investigation of how design-oriented organizations implement design thinking*, 2013
[9] Ibid

path forward may be going backward for a while. I teach this process to my design students as a way to understand their creativity. As young designers who aren't used to non-linear thinking in their school work, they can often get frustrated. With grades constantly looming, going 'backward' seems like a waste of time to them, but it is part of the process and can leapfrog you to a new idea or position you may not have thought of before. This is the creative process in action! And there's no going forward if you're not feeling it or are blocked, so it's best to sit with it for a while until you can find the solution that gets you to your desired end goal.

Creative Decisions in a Spiral

Sometimes, as we plod along our path, new ideas fall into our heads, or we make a connection we didn't see before. It's not all about the slog through the marshy lands of indecision, it's also about moving past some places faster. This is explained in what I call the Zeisel Spiral and will serve as a better understanding of the 'aha!' moments that happen while working on creative endeavor. In his book, *Inquiry by Design*, John Zeisel describes the interior designer's — and I would add, any creative — decision-making process as a dynamic spiral that narrows down the choices until the solution is found. This description teases out details of the design thinking process and adds a level of awareness through examining the 'leapfrog' effect in creativity.

Activities such as imaging, presenting, and testing within the creative spiral help the designer make creative design decisions that narrow down the design problem, which helps them find specific solutions and form "a general, almost fuzzy, mental picture."[10] Concepts are presented as a way to communicate the design idea to others and include both variety reduction and an opportunity for expansion. Testing can be done through critiques or prototyping to ensure the design will work as intended. As they move through reductive decision-making, "designers look both backward and forward simultaneously" and adjust or improve their designs as required.[11]

Conceptual shifts happen when big jumps in understanding are made and can happen more than once during the process. These are the big moments that get us excited to change what we're doing. Where and when they come to us is a mystery, and it can feel divinely guided or appear as a magic trick — out of thin air. It is these magical times that provide us with the spark of understanding of who we are as creative individuals. We all know we're here for a purpose, but sometimes we don't know what that purpose is or how it's supposed to play out for us. These moments are like a hidden piece of that mystery revealed, and they feel electric. All of our senses are on board as our minds make new connections with new intuitions to guide us. Intuition is the guiding light for much of our creative process, and learning how we interact with it is crucial to understanding who we are as creatives.

---

[10] John Zeisel, Inquiry by Design, 2006
[11] Ibid

<u>Collective Individual Creativity</u>

Creativity is both an inner awareness and an outer realization brought on by our environment. If we see, hear, and feel the energy coming to us and then through us, we are well on our way to becoming something great. If we take a step back from how we think we're supposed to create or how we think we're creative, we may find that a new way shows up — out of the blue, with no strings attached, no smoke and mirrors. Our lives can be upended in the best way possible as we allow ourselves to take greater leaps of faith and understanding. Being creative touches all levels of our beingness and all aspects of our lives. It isn't just about writing or painting or working, it's also about being aligned with our environment and all the ways creativity shows up. When it appears in a way that hits us in our cores, we can push it out into the collective as an understanding of our who we are as individuals and our ability to help others. When we help others by doing what we love, we are at our creative best. We find ways to interact with the collective that are meaningful to us and bring about change and awareness through positivity that works in concert with our abilities.

We know who we are as individuals when we look out into the collective and see our faces and energies reflected back to us. Now is the time for you to let your voice be known so that others will be inspired through your reflection. When the same faces are shown over and over, it becomes stale, on a repeat loop pattern that says, "You're not good enough because you don't look, talk, or act like me." But if we were all contributing, nothing would be stale, everything would be fresh, and we would all feel welcome in our individuality. Find time to sit with that sentiment as you make your way through the rest of the book. Your time has come to spread your wings and fly out of the collective influence, not to put down other people, but to lift them up.

Creativity is the consciousness of all, not a select few, so believe in yourself as a creator and find the **ability** you want to be in the world, not necessarily the change — as discussed later, change just is. So strap on your seat belt, hook into the collective change that is happening across our planet, and begin again to see yourself as a creative individual, not just parsing out the techniques of people before you, but changing your ways to see how you fit in — or stand out — as the case may be for most. You have the ingenuity and drive to enact change, not just be. Find healing in your heart through your creative engine and drive home to yourself as you find new ways of understanding what it means to live in a world of an individual collective.

Chapter 2: Creative Blocks

Creativity is an awareness in the heart, mind and body. When these three systems or components of our energy are aligned, they keep us flowing in time. In this case, we no longer care about the ups and downs of our process because we know that we are in a moment and something will shake loose or show itself if we wait or keep going, depending on the behavior or our creative endeavor practice. But because we are both thinking and feeling people, creative blocks happen when too much or not enough emotion enters into our creativity. When we're overwhelmed or numb, we may not see the light of the matter, keeping us in the dark and disconnected from either our process, the engagement of others, or the final product.

Emotional Blocks
Feeling betrayed by unseen energies

    Now that we've defined creativity and the creative process, let's talk about how it can be blocked, starting with the biggest block: shame. Shame is a sneaky kind of fear that creates a sneaky kind of overwhelm. It shows up as fear of being ostracized, castigated on our truth, shunned by other people because of something we've said or done, or who we are as a person. Brene Brown is a well-known researcher, writer, and speaker on shame and vulnerability. She lists creative blocks, in the form of telling ourselves we are not good enough, as "one of the three most dangerous narratives."[1] The story of our shame keeps us down as the memory we hold in our body as we step into a *Timefield* of self-doubt. (Skip ahead to Part 2 for a Timefield definition.) Shame is a denigration pattern in an extreme sense because the words that are used against us or ourselves are then transformed into our bodies through guilt, causing us to feel less free. In other words, we don't feel free to be ourselves, so our bodies take on that understanding and act out in different ways to help us through awareness. But our minds tell us to hold on to the guilt and the non-understanding — for always, sometimes — and we find ourselves in a looping pattern of denigration that keeps us down in all the ways there are to be down.

    Beyond good and bad, shame is a powerful force in our lives because it is an aspect of feeling unloved, unworthy, and less than. All of these feelings push us down in our hearts and minds. They can manifest in our bodies through literally not growing to our fullest height, being in an unmet relationship in terms of needs, wants, and desires, and feeling our fullest when our bellies are really more than half empty. If you have ever said to yourself or others, "Why am I like this?" with a feeling of despair, then you are likely dealing with a deep-seated denigration pattern of shame that can show up as a life block. (This terminology is presented here, but can also be found in Chapter 16 under 'intercepted natal charts.')

Things like,
- not seeing love when it comes knocking on your door
- feeling afraid to step out into the unknown, even if the current situation is untenable
- being in an unawareness state related to relationships (denial)
- finding ourselves to be unreal in our bodies,

are all ways that the patterning cycle of denigration through shame keeps us from our authentic selves and lives, and are most likely life blocks. We see it all the time in other people, but can we take the time to see it in ourselves? It requires a level of unflinching awareness of self and the people in our lives that mirror both the positive and negative

---

[1] Brene Brown, *Daring to Lead*, 2018

aspects of who we are as individuals. For example, if you see shame or fear holding a sibling or coworker back, look to the ways a similar fear might also be holding you back. This is called mirrored consciousness and is a helpful way to start undoing the denigration patterns in your life. Once on this path, remember to give yourself love and grace of understanding where you were then and now. Don't be hard on yourself for past behaviors because we are all human and divine. Forgiveness is the power that keeps us in our hearts, minds, and bodies, so forgive yourself and others to step away from existing denigration patterns and stop new ones from forming.

Freeing the Pools of Creative Energy
Understanding the chakra system

Like other systems, energy can become blocked, and because it is in our bodies, we need to effect change through understanding. Chakras are described as pools or 'whirls' of energy and are a well-known and well-respected description of one of our body's energy systems. There are many chakras, but most people are familiar with the main seven that run up our spines. Though not contained within our bodies, they are visualized as part of the body's energetic system and work with other systems to keep us healthy. Like pools of connected water, gunk in the form of stuck emotions can block the entire system if one area of your life is blocked.[2] Conversely, releasing stuck energy in one can cause the others to release. If you are unfamiliar with chakras, here is a list of each with its recognized symbol, frequency color, and ability to affect change in our bodies' systems, perception understanding, and way of moving in the world.

The mycelial line is my addition and explains the energy within our bodies that forms a structure and can be likened to a tree root system or network pattern. The network effect of our lives is an incontrovertible truth as we all live in different collectives including the business or work network which helps us visualize the mycelial network within our bodies. A network is a pattern like denigration but is physical rather than behavioral and is about the beneficial aspects of life as reflected in our bodies' energetic systems. Mycelial energy is connected to the chakra system and takes on different aspects of our creative energy. As we connect to each other more and more, our mycelial systems are more impacted by each other, like a family tree or the internet.

<u>The Chakra System Explained</u>

The chakra system is like an electrical system for the energy body. When we're in Flow, energy moves freely through each chakra. The sacral chakra, the seat of our creativity, moves energy up through the solar plexus to the heart chakra. The heart chakra explodes outward into the world, pushing energy forward and backward from our chest area and up towards the crown chakra through our throat and third eye chakras.

---

[2] For an entertaining explanation of chakras, watch season 2, episode 18 of *Avatar, the Last Air Bender.*

	Root chakra clears your ability to connect to yourself in terms of feeling grounded in the Earth. It also connects us to the Source core of the Earth for healing and integration of energy.
	Sacral chakra is the seat of your creativity and clearing it helps you clear your creative powers and your connections to others through the Divine. It's considered your divine life force energy connection to and through others as well.
	Solar plexus is your point of power in the present moment, clearing it helps you step into your own power through your universal connection. It also connects you to the Source core of the Earth, an energy of love through the Divine.
	Heart chakra gets to the "heart of the issue" in terms of needs and wants. Also considered the 'heart center' which is an energetic component of your ethereal system, or the 'auric field.' Brings in energy and expands outwards, as we all know, through love and is our god-Source connection.
	Clearing the **throat chakra** clears your ability to speak your truth and not edit yourself. It expands your energy through the field of light, as in enlightening yourself through truth.
	Third eye clears your ability to see beyond what is in front of you and makes it easier to see what's happening internally as well as future sight, or your ability to see into the 'extended present' (a term coined by Albert Einstein).
	Clearing the **Crown** chakra clears "flibbity-jibbit" energy, or monkey mind and provides the ability to connect to sources outside our specific energy system (meaning Earth).
	Mycelial system, or basic grid*, creates a new form of energy in the body. Connects to all of the chakras and clears both systems in their entirety for residual energies. (*Note: refer to Donna Eden's book, *Energy Medicine* for more information on the basic grid, her term for the mycelial system.)

At our tailbone, the root chakra pushes energy down and up; down into the Earth and up into the sacral chakra, where we connect to Mother Earth and the Divine. Divine inspiration comes from above and below. The Earth connects us to our divine being-ness, while the crown chakra connects us to the divine of the cosmos, Universal Consciousness, and other divine sources outside our bodies. The chakra energies are connected through the mycelial system or 'basic grid.'[3] Like a web that intersects with

---

[3] Donna Eden, *Energy Medicine*, 1998

nodal points, the mycelial grid is an energetic system unto itself that moves energy throughout the energy body. Remember, this is all energetic, not biological or physical, but they impact the physical body because it's all connected through the force of our being on Earth.

During the course of a day, the energy in our bodies moves freely within these two systems, but I believe, maintains stasis during the night as we sleep. This brings our consciousness to a standstill, so to speak, and allows us to move into the dream state where we access our innermost thoughts through the subconscious. To access the subconscious while conscious, we need to have our chakra system flowing freely between the sacral, heart, and crown chakras. This awareness between the chakras allows our heart centers, minds, and bodies to be aligned, thereby freeing our nervous systems to feel safe to create. Nervous systems that don't feel safe look like being afraid to create our own lives in the manner that best suits us.

Creativity is energy and blocks will happen! We all need to find ways to unblock the gunk. Blocks can show up as literal writer's block, a fight with someone close to you, or just general over-tiredness, making you unable to focus. When you can recognize a creative block, applying tools to help you get back on track can be invaluable. (Skip ahead to the third chapter.) If all else fails, an Epsom salt bath does wonders to both calm your nerves and release energy. In fact, it's good practice to take a saltwater bath monthly or bi-weekly — bubbles and bath oil are encouraged. Think of them, or any other form of self-care, as a necessary tune-up, not a nice-to-have.

Frequencies of Color and Light
Moving into awareness through the color wheel

The combination of color and light is a conscious awareness at a certain frequency. Light and color are inextricably linked because that is how we experience the world around us. We can get caught in our own frequency of consciousness, which can produce tunnel vision where the light only occurs at one point in the distance or even a complete blackout of the love that is happening around us. Light filtered through a color expresses a specific type of awareness: rose-colored glasses, seeing green or red, feeling blue, having a black heart, etc. When someone shows their true colors, we now know who they really are because the color has been brought into the light.

<u>Color Frequencies</u>

If *"evening is the color of the soul,"* as one of my favorite bands, Big Head Todd and the Monsters sings, then color is our entry point into healing our emotional identities, and finding the right light color, or frequency, can get you there. Frequencies are often used as a healing modality as an auditory experience through singing bowls, listening to special music tuned just right, listening to natural sounds like a thunderstorm (which has the added frequency of lightening for extra power to heal and transform), or crickets and tree frogs at night. These are all frequencies that impact our well-being.

The opposite of these frequencies are man-made sounds and noises that can send us "up a tree" if it's irritating or even into emotional overwhelm if our nervous systems are already frayed. I'm talking about overly loud motorcycles, construction vehicles, etc. — all the high-octane frequencies, if you will. These sounds and noises have an impact on our consciousness and our well-being through our nervous systems. There's a reason why people don't want to live next to a highway or endure construction zones day and night! We are not aligned with the sounds, noises, and energies that emanate from those vehicles and industries. Though we may become accustomed to them, our nervous systems prefer nature's energies through our natural bodies.

Likewise, visual frequencies impact our well-being. In the US, 1980s beige will go down in history as the worst color choice possible. Of course, the 1980s are also linked to fluorescent colors on our jelly shoes and jelly bracelets (because as Cyndi Lauper sang, *"Girls Just Wanna Have Fun"*). The teal of the early 1990s has come up and around again, just tweaked a little for more contemporary palettes. The gray interiors that started in the early 2000s and persist to this day confound me, along with all-white interiors. While white and gray are colors and have their own frequencies, their monotone flatness and liberal use everywhere deny our eyes all the other frequencies our rich world has to offer. There is a term for this coined by artist David Bachelor — *chromaphobia*.[4] Yep, it's real. People are scared to show their true colors through their decor.

In interior design, we use color and light to transform an ordinary space into something magical and expansive. Color in pigment form is considered subtractive, color in light form is additive. As you may already know, color is not a physical part of objects we see, but is the effect of light waves bouncing off or passing through the objects that stimulates the photoreceptors in our eyes. All of the colors of the rainbow in pigment form make black. All the colors of the rainbow in light form make white. When light frequencies are added to an object or room, magic happens. Light wakes up a space, sets the tone or the mood, adds drama with highs and lows like in a restaurant, or flattens like a big box store. Gothic cathedrals feel mystical because the light is filtered through colored stained glass windows into a relatively darkened space, adding tons of drama. Reading scripture in a flat, white space would not have the same effect, for sure.

Metaphorically, light is conscious awareness. This notion is in our language: 'shedding light on an issue' and 'coming out of the dark' speak to our awareness. If you follow astrology, the sun, our constant light source that never goes out, represents consciousness itself. Adding light to a situation shifts our perspective, allowing us to see a new truth or a new sub-set of truths that brings our awareness to the forefront of our mind's eye. This could look like seeing a person in a new light and realizing they aren't as

---

[4] David Bachelor, *Chromophobia*, essay in *Intimus Interior Design Theory Reader*, 2006

you thought, or realizing that a childhood episode was not as bad as you remember when you discuss it with a friend. You finally see the light of the situation.

The Science of Light Frequencies

Isaac Newton is the man who is credited for understanding the frequencies of color and light. His development in the late 1600s and early 1700s of a new system of thinking about color and light led to later interdependent discoveries on the electromagnetic field and sunlight itself. We'll look at that later, but let's stay with Isaac, more than a hundred years before that discovery. He is noted for working with prisms that bend and refract light into its visible components, or the rainbow, which is made up of ROYGBIV - red, orange, yellow, green, blue, indigo, and violet. Violet is the predecessor to ultraviolet, which begins to move into areas of unseen frequencies by the unaided human eye in sunlight.

We now know there are many color and light frequencies we can't see, including gamma rays, x-rays, microwaves, and other forms of light radiation. Ultraviolet is the most magical of all these frequencies because it reveals patterns on butterfly wings and other insects, like viewing a secret message in invisible ink from a spy novel or movie. *Ultraviolet (Light My Way)*, from U2's 1991 *Achtung, Baby* album (their best, in my humble opinion) has the line "Your love was a lightbulb hanging over my bed," moving love into the spectrum of light, which can also be *Radioactive (*from the British rock band The Firm), or unstable.

Unrequited Love Frequency
Finding stability in love

Unstable love is not really love at all but feeling unrequited in love. Unrequited love is the most generated feeling on Earth and makes people feel stuck in their lives.* We have only to look at all the love poems, songs, and other forms of trying to release this energy from our consciousness to know the impact of this feeling. The stereotypical jilted love song that we listen to over and over after a big breakup is indicative of releasing unrequited love. However, unrequited love also comes from other relationships in our lives, such as parents and grandparents, siblings, friends, and so on. This frequency can impact your state of being on an hourly, daily, and even yearly cycle. We will dive into cycles later, but for now, understanding the state of love as a frequency is an important point.

The unrequited love frequency is a low vibration that does not allow us to seek our full potential as human beings. It keeps us in a stuck state of interdependence with other people and causes us to form habits related to drugs, alcohol, and other types of addiction. Not all unrequited love is to that level, but many people have the authority of their lives taken away from them. They feel stuck in a pattern that exists both in their minds and environment. It's a two-way street and it takes two to tango in these lessons so don't think you are alone in this feeling. If one person is feeling it, it's likely that the other person is, too. Feeling unrequited in love often begins in childhood and becomes a form of stuck energy in your body and energy field. Feeling picked on or left out is common, but leaves a mark and builds up over time. As we get older and mature in our life lessons, we may take stock of who we are as individuals and see the spectrum of possibility of being and seeing the source radiation of love. Being in love means moving outside our bounds of time and space, believing in our abilities, finding the inevitability in being in each other's arms, or orbits.

As you move into the next sections of this book, it's time to learn the lessons of releasing unrequited love from your life in all its forms and functions. Be aware of who you are as an individual, where you come from, who your people are, what your boundaries are, and when it is time to let people go who only serve to keep you in this state of being. To find more healing on boundaries, try Teri Cole's *Boundary Boss* book.[5] It's practical and to the point without clutter, with exercises to help you walk through your issues and programming from childhood and beyond. Now is the time to let go of those frequencies and let loose the love in your heart to open to a more stable, grounded, healing source of love. In fact, that is what we will be calling it for the rest of the book. As Source, love is the unifier of the Universe. It serves to protect us and heal us in all our creative endeavors.

Note: I first learned about unrequited love and unforgiveness energies through my healer, Ann, who sent me on a path of discovery through the powerful psychic and energy healer, Amy Jo Ellis, and her technique of the Full Court of Atonement. She has many unforgiveness protocols that can be used for a variety of things. If you want to learn more about how to heal unforgiveness, find her website at the back of this book under the End Notes section.

<u>Healing with Frequencies</u>

Frequencies can be used as a healing modality through the visual and verbal messages we send and can effect change in the body, mind, and heart. A specific frequency color as a form of energetic protection can be used if you're feeling stressed or unable to effect change without help. Ultimately, though, the healing comes from within ourselves and those frequencies come through both love and light. Love is the ultimate binder glue of the Universe; it creates change and allows us to see things beyond our normal vision just as light illuminates the dark. So love, as all energy, is a frequency and when we talk about love, it's through a level placement. Our love for another is deep, or we have fallen deeply in love and it is expansive and all-knowing. It creates a connection with another on a deeper level and provides us an understanding about ourselves. When we love, we know ourselves, our surroundings, and the people

---

[5] Terry Cole, *Boundary Boss*, 2022

we share those surroundings with.

Light as a frequency is a little easier to understand because we see it rather than feel it. We are "blinded by the light" or find someone's demeanor to be light and carefree. All the colors of the rainbow are appropriate for healing because that is what we see in our environment. We can bypass all of the specific colors and ask for the highest frequency, which is light. Light provides the maximum level of healing.

The healing statements below call up the frequencies of love and light, enacting a form of energy healing. Try it for yourself and see if it works for you. It's a simple statement and uses the power of your mind to effect change, rather than forces outside of you that can cause you to give away your authority or enact overwhelm. Remember, our minds are powerful. If our minds can cause illness through unconscious thought processes, then we can do the reverse and use it to heal ourselves. Here's the basic statement:

"I _____ [state your name] clear and release any and all energies that are causing overwhelm in my body, heart center, and mind through the deepest love and highest light."

This statement began with saying, "the most appropriate frequency," but I eventually decided to cut to the chase and ask for the highest and best of all frequencies. If you like using "most appropriate" in your healing practice, feel free to try it, how you want to work with it is up to you. Also, feel free to change the general statement to be more exact with what you are trying to heal. You will see later in the book that I use this phrase in many different ways. Also, if you want to visualize a specific color, do it! You may want to visualize the color surrounding you or going through your body's systems, or you can call it up and ask your mind and body to align with that frequency. Whatever you feel in the moment is the right thing to do. There are no right or wrongs in energy healing, just as there are no right or wrongs in your creative expression.

<u>Try It: Journaling Visualization: What's Your Color?</u>

For this visualization, ask yourself what color you are feeling in the moment. You can ask your mood color or, "What is the color of my soul?" as that gets to a deeper truth within yourself. The first color you think of is the right one, even if you have to stop for a moment to consider. Now that you have your color, pair it with its compliment that offsets your 'blue mood' or 'red anger.' Start with the color wheel and find the opposite, but if you want to be more specific, you can. For example, green is the compliment of red, but in the US and other countries, that might feel too much like Christmas, so maybe you want to go with candy-apple red complimented with lime-green.

I like the idea of bringing food into your color match because it feels like a food pairing at a fancy restaurant. "On today's menu, we have apples candied in a caramelized sauce with a squeeze of lime to add some tartness." Write about how those two colors make you feel individually and as a pairing. It might help you get to the heart of your issue or mood faster. And have fun with it! You don't need to be serious with colors or food.

Language and the Sneak
Moving past denigration patterns in language

Knowing how we use language subconsciously and consciously is essential to understanding how we move through our creative process. You have been learning about the creative process (or at least a few versions of it) through language, and each word you take in has been effective in creating new understanding or realizing old patterns in a new way. But before you move on, take a moment and understand how you use language against yourself and others. You may not be aware of it and that is the point. How do you dismiss your ideas or work product through the words you use? How do you enact change by being aware of the process? And conversely, how do you lift people and yourself in the same way? We know it impacts kids as they grow and learn. It's the same process for adults; we're just more used to it.

One word rises to the top for healing through a systems approach: denigration. Denigration is the form and function of how our bodies, minds, and hearts are kept in a behavior pattern that only serves to tamp us down. Many of the systems we live in today denigrate our minds, affecting our hearts and bodies. The denigration of a mind can turn us against ourselves and cause us to demean each other or live in a state that denigrates our very being-ness on Earth. It becomes a never-ending cycle of misuse and abuse.

The word denigration comes up a lot in this book, and you will see why as we move deeper into our understanding of creativity through healing practices. I consider denigration one of the worst — if not *the* worst — regulation practices to keep people down and "in their place." We not only denigrate each other, but we denigrate ourselves through put-down behavior. This is often done through verbal language, or words, that sneak into our nervous systems without our awareness and tamp us down, and sometimes stamp us out. Denigration is the behavior that keeps us from each other's hearts through our minds, whether it's put-down behaviors (in terms of who we love or don't love), or the lines we carry in our hearts that serve to keep us away from other people ("that person is crazy"), or even the choices we make at the grocery store with the foods we eat. Collecting, sorting, and putting each other in boxes by categorizing who we believe in and who we don't, or typecasting and stereotyping people based on looks or social behaviors keep us from believing in each others' capacity for love and accomplishment. Being 'that sort' of person means you might even take on those behaviors inadvertently and become the person you never thought you would be as a child or young adult.

We have the capacity to both accept through love and denigrate through admonition. As the 1980s pop band INXS sang, *What you do and what you say, do you know the difference any way*? The choice is ours to first understand how language affects us daily and then move away from these behavior patterns to feel joyful with one another and ourselves. When we are welcoming through our language, people feel the opposite of denigration. We can find this fact to be true with the Southern word 'y'all, a form of 'you' and 'all.' One little word includes everyone! As the stand-up comedian, Hannah Gadsby says, "Ya'll is the best, most inclusive, second person, plural pronoun in the English-speaking world!"[6] It's the most welcoming word in our existence as people of the world who see each others' differences but bring them in despite — or because — of them. And when you say it with the lilting accent of a Southerner, it sounds even more welcoming.

Symbols and Symbolic Language

Symbols are another form of language and we can look to the past as a way to understand them. The hieroglyphics of the Egyptians and Mayans, for example, show us how one way of writing can bring us back to the phrase 'a pictures is worth a thousand words.' Symbols communicate effectively through the cultural awareness of the shape and form. When we collectively understand a symbol to mean something, it becomes a shorthand for "do this thing that way" or "we are this type of truth." We are surrounded daily by symbols included in our common day parlance, which is a funny word for people in the 21st Century, but I use it purposely to point out how language and symbols ebb and flow with the time. The graphic nature of our language is used everywhere and can either lift us up, as in a rainbow flag, or make us feel fear, like a swastika.[7] How we greet each other is also a symbol for our engendered belief systems. The handshakes of businessmen have become informal in US black culture (and now exported around the world) through the half handshake, half hug action. So far I have only seen men do this, which keeps women on the outside because the men are saying non-verbally, "You're in the club." Of course women have their own way of relating, but the simple hug gets extended to all people, not just between women.

The symbols of our environment come into awareness only if we take a step back and look at them from a different perspective and see how we are either inclusive or exclusive. We would never today, for example, inform our brothers and sisters that we are biologically aligned with being humans because we know that we all are. But the women's suffrage movement in the late 1800s and early 1900s had to point that out again and again to get the 'right' to vote, as if their thinking somehow varied from men's thinking. And this thought extends to other people who have been marginalized for their physical appearance. In reality politics — and as an extension business — is a highly emotional institution. The stock market reflects this well as the Dow Jones and other indices fluctuate depending on the emotional state of the investors. This is shown to

---

[6] Hannah Gatsby, *Douglas* (Recorded 2019, Netflix)
[7] I think it is well known that the symbol used for the swastika has ancient roots and means peace in other cultures.

hilarious effect in the movie, *The Hudsucker Proxy*, when an investor from Texas starts throwing punches over being called "yeller." If women are supposed to be the overly emotional part of our communities, then what does the stock market — employing mostly men — say about men's emotional state? Are their 'flux capacitors'[8] any different than women's? I hope not because we are all relating people and we need to be in each other's heart centers.

Avarice Redefined

Language is an understanding of our truth. We use language in many ways and each culture around the world has its own sayings and idioms to share a cultural value or understanding of a concept. Because of this, words have power. We all know this. It's a known fact through our speeches, our historical references, and the inscribed words on monuments, tombs, and other artifacts. We repeatedly return to words for cultural and individual awareness and our sense of being and belonging. It's a powerful statement to say, "I belong," because it is also a visceral statement that we feel in our bodies. Language forms the backbone of collective understanding through the specific words of the time. Our cultural era is filled with slang words and idioms that people from the past, in historical terms, would have no idea what we're talking about, and we have the same response when reading old texts. Sometimes, we can take a word out of context and not understand what the true meaning is. I found this to be true for the word 'avarice.'

Avarice is defined as 'extreme greed and desire,' which connects it directly to the Latin word '*avarus*,' but if you follow the etymology of the word, it came from other words such as the Latin '*avere*' which means 'to crave, long for, be eager.' It can also be traced through the Proto-Italic word '*awe*' which also means to be eager; from the word '*heu-eh*' meaning to 'enjoy or consume,' and the Sanskrit word '*avasa*' which means 'refreshment, food.'[9] So, the original meaning of the word avarice could have been: 'a lust for life and all its glories from enjoying the Earth's bounties and each other.' The Oxford English Dictionary has the earliest known use of the word in one of Chaucer's poems in 1386 CE,[10] linking it in time to the power and domination of Christianity and its supposed 'seven deadly sins.' Avarice became about the sin of deep greed for money and sexual desire, which the church patriarchy frowned on and still does. It's also been adopted into secular society as a moral teaching. But sin is about shame, and we now know through many different researchers that shame damages our hearts, minds, bodies, and relationships. Taking the shame out of the word avarice is a big undertaking as it resets our minds and hearts. It removes the denigration from the word, capitalizing on its aspects of energy healing through joy.

---

[8] I use this term, from the movie, *Back to the Future*, as a short hand for all heart center energies.
[9] Online Etymology Dictionary
[10] Online Oxford English Dictionary

Based on this little expedition into the meaning of one word, we see how we've been cut off from Earth's natural cycles through sneaky language. The hidden message is: "We must not lust, enjoy, or be greedy otherwise, we will die sinners." In reality, our joy and lust for life bring us closer to who we are as humans. This often subtle change of commonplace language causes us to be disconnected from our intuitive centers. Since learning this information about the word avarice, I started using it as a term in my energy healing practice to install the 'good vibes' of being in a body on Earth. But because the word is so programmed into our society as 'bad,' I switched to using the Sanskrit word 'avasa' as 'joy about living and a lust for life.' Saying the word out loud is fun, too, so it fits the description.

Try It: Reprogramming Through Awareness

Now that you know this information, try reprogramming the word avarice for yourself. Set aside how society defines the word and look within yourself about how you feel about living in enjoyment through lust and desire. If it helps, take the sexual connotation out of it for the moment and think about what being in desire means to you. Then, move back into your body and see how it feels. Are you able to sit with the energy of lust and desire? For some, it will be difficult to the extreme, but if you keep working on it, you may find that to desire is to live out loud, to be right and true in your body. To accept all that means you are living in a non-denigration energy.

Chapter 3: Focal Points and Creative Blocks

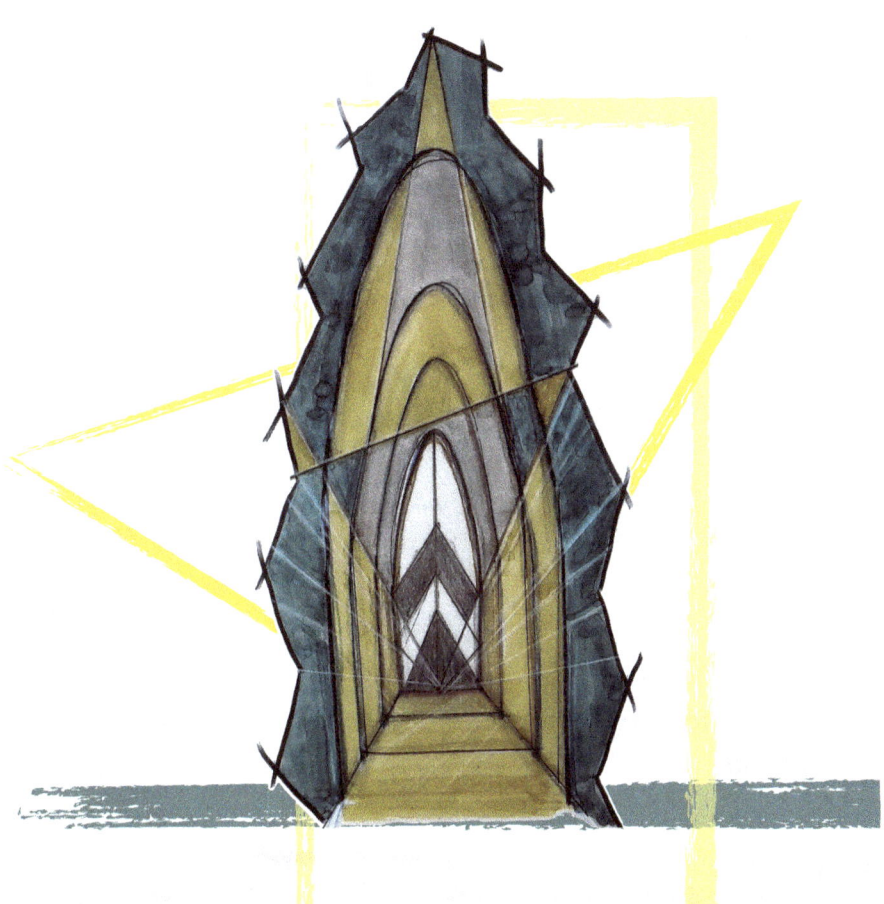

This is the first discussion on how the body reacts to the creative process. Emotions such as shame, fear, and anger can block us emotionally, causing us to abruptly stop or spin out, further disrupting our creativity. This can lead to a level of dis-ease if left for too long, so understanding and clearing your blocks is worth your time and effort. There is more detailed information about the body's systems in the third part of the book, but it's important to review a little now as you build on your understanding of your creative process and its impacts on your body's energetic systems.

System Maintenance for Creative Well-Being
Working through creative blocks so they don't become dis-ease

Creative blocks are tied to our creative endeavor through our energy systems. Blocks start with a single blip: not eating or sleeping enough, an argument with a friend or family member, a bad grade for students, or a difficult day at work. Blips are obviously not big issues, but they can collect and form a blockage over time. If the system isn't maintained with proper cleaning, gunk starts to build up in the form of stress, a type of emotional overwhelm, and we become blocked. If a block continues over a long time and the emotional overwhelm persists, it can turn into something I call a *Timefield*. (If you think you are dealing with more than just a block, skip ahead to Timefields to gain more information on what it is and how to get out of one.)

What Blocks Us:	What it Looks Like:
Fear	Over-tired
Shame (a form of fear)	Writer's block or other typical creative block
Feeling not good enough/unworthy	Arguments
Sadness	Unable to focus

There are three main focal points to be aware of in your creative energy system to keep blocks out and your system clear and clean:

Focal Point 1: Destress the Details

Blocks can be mitigated with awareness and attention to detail in our lives. Begin by understanding yourself and your stress points. Don't be afraid to pull at some frayed edges of your life, as those are typically where the blocks like to enter. For example, if you do not like to get up early on weekends, but your sibling always calls before 7 am on Saturday, review how that makes you feel and what you can do if it stresses you out.

Focal Point 2: Systems Check

Next, tap into your body's wisdom of what is going on as an essential step in mitigating what your mind might be pushing away subconsciously. Be aware of your inner processes that show up as a felt sense in your body. Are you flushed, overexcited, heated, down-and-out, tired, etc.? Take note of how you feel during the day while you experience the sensation. It helps to call your attention to what is happening beneath. Write down what you feel in the moment, even if it's just on a sticky note. When the day is over, review your notes and use them as a starting point to dig deeper into how you are feeling emotionally and what is below it.

Focal Point 3: Release for Change
    Finally, be kind to your nervous system by allowing the emotional energies to flow through you. Notice them, but don't hang onto them. You can even talk to them in your mind to encourage awareness and bring about change. For example, "I can feel my stomach turning into knots, which I know is fear. Fear, you don't need to stay in my stomach because I know you're trying to keep me safe." Release those energies into the Earth or the oceans as a visualization to help guide your mind away from the emotional overwhelm and into a clearer way of thinking that sees the feelings and bodily responses as activation points into understanding your inner processes, not as information to be avoided. It can be hard at first, but keep trying, and don't judge yourself if it doesn't work at first or if you miss seeing an activation point. There's always tomorrow and the next day to activate your healing process within.

Perfectionism as Creative Block
Stifling creativity through resistance to change
    If there is a 'big, bad wolf' of creative blocks, I consider perfectionism to be it. Perfectionism is a creative block that might start as uncertainty in what you are working on but then moves you into a state of fear, making every decision laborious. It stops your creative flow and burns you at both ends. You can't move forward, but you also can't let go of what you have done. Every little thing in your creative process becomes overly precious, and it takes time and consideration to make any change. 'Practice makes perfect' after all, and when perfectionism is the ultimate goal, you get hamstrung. This extends to our lives as well. Being perfect in our bodies, being perfect parents or perfect neighbors, which are perfect alibis for being stuck in your heart and mind. Perfectionism can be elevated to an art form where people are so rigid in their demands that they turn others away, making them shrink from their creativity, giving them performance anxiety. Being perfect becomes an irrational survival technique that says you have high demands for quality when, in reality, you are worried about your own level of creativity. The thought process goes along the lines of, "If I can't pull this off, then I'm a failure. If I fail, then no one will like me/hire me/think I'm good enough to be here."
    Perfectionism is a problem in the field of architecture. It's understandable, buildings cost a lot of money through materials, labor, maintenance, etc. But perfectionism starts in architecture school with a culture of pulling all-nighters to prove you're the best, ensuring every last keystroke or pen stroke is just right. Being perfect means you have worked hard to become the best of the best and can, therefore, charge more money for your services or get hired at a 'high-end' firm. Along with perfectionism, there is a strong sense of lack that runs through the architecture field — don't get me started on the poetic irony of the term 'value engineering.' But let's focus on one issue for now.
    Who holds the yardstick for perfection? The answer is that we all have our own

version of perfection, which means it's an unending process to be perfect, like a hamster running on a wheel — exhausting. To break perfectionism's hold, you have to learn to let go. "What!?," say all the architectural studios, "I can't let myself go! That means I'll become lazy, a slacker, and stop caring about my appearance! I'll get to go home for dinner, and then what will I do with my life?" Letting go doesn't mean we let go of ourselves and our bodies; it means we let go of the behaviors that keep us from realizing our fullness of life and creativity. To let go realizes the truth that we are not perfect and never will be, so enjoy life — and that includes your creative endeavor — as it is. Enjoying life means allowing time to not only rest, but also let creative energy move freely. That means you aren't slogging it out day after day, racing the clock to get it all done 'on time.' Time becomes the enemy when you feel you don't have much of it, and it's a double-edged sword when you are pursuing perfection.

    There is a tension between the phrases "let it go" and "work hard with effort" that, if understood, leads to changing behaviors that prohibit creativity. Many of us follow the sentiment that you must work hard to make a living, earn money, and live life. If you witnessed your parents or grandparents living this way, you likely took on their behaviors. Life is hard, so we have to work harder to be perfect, right? Not so much. This is a learned way of being, not a natural state. As a natural system, water flows downhill effortlessly through gravity; it finds a lower state to flow and move through. If not blocked or stagnated, it will eventually find its way to the oceans where the all-powerful energy exists to sublimate energies back to the Source core of Earth. Creative Flow, therefore, happens in a low state when you're not 'hyped up' or 'tensed up.' Too much effort requires too much force. Too much force means you are in a sense of lack because you don't believe the problem can be solved with ease. If you can stop yourself before the effort becomes too much, then you can move into a lower state allowing Flow.

<u>Finding Your 'Wei': Learning from the Tao Te Ching</u>

    When we are in free flow, we are not working hard; it is effortless creativity. 'Wu Wei' is a term in Taoism that translates into "do without doing" or "effortless effort."[1] It's a difficult concept to grasp, especially for Americans, who value hard work and lifting ourselves up by our bootstraps, which is a misnomer — we all help each other through the collective experience. Our sense of ease is replaced with a sense of "I've-gotta-get-it-done!" Wu Wei means we flow with the river and time and don't allow ourselves to get caught up in the turmoil of a rushing rapid. Let the rapid rush, it will carry us to our next mark or location. In the meantime, we can sit back and watch how what we do requires little to no effort and still gets done all the same. Sitting and waiting for the unknown to show itself can be difficult, but learning how to sit with an effort and letting it feel easy is the best way to catch a wave.

---

[1] I first learned about Wu Wei in the now classic book, *The Tao of Pooh* by Benjamin Hoff (yes, that Pooh).

Martial arts work to undo the behaviors of tense rushing by teaching people to work with the natural flow and momentum of the body. It is much easier to throw someone to the ground when they are coming at you, in motion, than when they are standing still like a rock. You also use leverage through your knees to get them up and over your shoulder rather than straining your back to haul them over like a sack of concrete. Working with the natural state of things means allowing flow to enter your beingness, and sometimes that flow will take you in a different direction. If you're a perfectionist, that direction may feel like a mistake. Perceiving the mistake as an error causes emotional overwhelm, which may result in a breakdown through anger, fear, or shame. This is when we start cussing, wreck what we've done in frustration, or give up altogether. But allowing the mistake to be more than a mistake — an opportunity or a possibility, for example — will transform the energy of frustration to a lower state of letting the outcome be exactly as it should be. It is a form of acceptance, but not an "it is what it is" type of acceptance, which is about giving up and not seeing the truth of the matter. The behaviors of a lifetime take time to undo.

Joining the Images of Perfection with Imperfection
How are the two made one?

If we allow ourselves to be in a state of effortless effort, we then allow that the unknown is ours to mold into what we want. We take a new perspective on time and our seeming mistakes or missteps and apply a new brush to them. Deepak Chopra calls this the *'Field of Potentiality'*[2] and relates it to an environment I envision as the primordial soup of life. We can take our projects, art, and lives into a new direction with a new perspective, molding it through metamorphosis into something completely new. This is not limited to our creative life — it also applies to our bodies and hearts through our minds' change of perspective.

When we create, the result can be a myriad of things related to what we see in our mind's eye. Sometimes, it is exactly as we imagined it, and we marvel at the miracle of it coming out just as planned. But more often than not, it doesn't go as expected. What happens when results don't show up the way we think they should be? Let's look at a creative interpretation through carpentry, or woodworking, as an example. A woodworker works with precision and takes the time to measure twice and cut once to get the desired results. But even with all the careful measuring and skill that goes into it, sometimes mistakes happen. Wood is a high-value product; when working with an extra special piece, it can't just be thrown away. Fixing that mistake takes another high-value concept to the level of an art form through joinery.

Woodworkers are known for creating different types of joints, and the terminology has made it into our everyday language. A dovetail is a common type of joint used in

---

[2] Deepak Chopra, *Seven Spiritual Laws of Success*, 1997

wood construction and is so-called because the shape looks like a bird's tail. If something dovetails together, it means it fits perfectly and with ease. There are also mortised and tendon joints, rabbet joints, tongue and groove, and miter joints, to name a few. All are used in specific locations and for specific types of projects. A skilled woodworker knows when and how to use these types of joinery methods with the added know-how of when to celebrate or camouflage them with stain or a different type of wood. All it takes is the method and knowledge to fix the mistake and move on. Some mistakes are happy accidents and provide a new level of understanding about the process or the material itself.

Metal workers also use different joining methods in their work. Soldering and welding join two pieces of metal of the same chemical makeup with a similar material that is melted at high heat to gain a tight bond. The solder or weld joint can be filed down to make it disappear, or it can be part of the design of the finished product. If the joint calls for connecting metal to another material, such as wood, a mechanical connection is made with a fastener like a bolt and nut. Because of the interest in bringing two disparate materials together, that mechanical fastener becomes a design detail. The connection point of the two materials creates interest, not the solid material. Our eyes automatically go to the corners or joints of rooms and objects, so making those moments artwork or an intentional part of the design can create a new perspective on what is viewed or experienced. Architects often play with the corners of buildings by joining glass at those locations rather than using a solid material. They create a field of pure potentiality by morphing the building into something unexpected.

Beauty in Imperfection

Sometimes, we create the unexpected — sometimes, it is forced on us. Either way, our perspective allows us to move into potential. If something is broken and needs fixing, there is often a noticeable seam or scar where the fix was made. Many will try to hide it, but others may leave it as a reminder of a job well done; something that was difficult to overcome. Others may even celebrate it by enhancing it. Japanese culture has a wonderful concept called *Kintsuki* — Golden Joinery — celebrating the imperfection in creative endeavor, whether in the process or the final product itself. It is often shown in pottery where a crack has run down the side of a pot. Instead of hiding it, it is painted gold to highlight it and show that there is beauty in imperfection. The gold adds drama and flare to something that otherwise would have ended up in the rubbish bin. It shows a level of perfectionism that is not focused on the outcome, but allows for a systems change in both the artist and the viewer. If a mistake or accident is unexpected, then there is beauty in it as well. Beauty is indeed in the eye of the beholder — can you let go to find the beauty from an ideal image in your mind to what is in front of you? And the beauty comes when our perspectives shift to find that perfection is also only in the eye of the beholder.

Try It: the Diagonal Line - Changing Your Perspective

Often times, we know when we're stuck, but still don't see a way through, even after cleaning off our desks and eating everything in the fridge. When we're aware but still can't move forward, a visual cue can sometimes push us back into creative territory. When I'm working on a design and I get stuck, I take a fat Sharpie and draw a diagonal line across my drawing. If I'm working digitally, I do the same. The line isn't there to represent failure — it's not an 'X'. It's my visual cue to tell myself to look at the design differently, change my perspective. It resets my brain by telling it to "Stop going down this path, find a new one." For me, the diagonal line represents something that is dynamic and cuts across what is expected and typical. If I'm struggling with a design, it's usually because I'm stuck in a rut and need to get out of it by *not* doing what I think is expected of me.

Find a visual cue for yourself that helps you stop and find another path when you are stuck. It doesn't have to be about abandoning what you've already started; deleting everything you just typed leaves you with another blank screen. Your cue could be an image, shape, or color that means something to you; a reminder that there are many solutions to one problem.

Chapter 4: Typical Creativity Life Cycle

The next two chapters mark the **basis of design** for all other healing modalities that come after. If you don't do any other activities in this book, try the next two because they are the most important in terms of discovery and healing and will often be referenced in other sections. Knowing your rhythms and cycles as well as your individual preferences as a creative and a healer is of utmost importance because they tend to impact each other. Find time and healing in these pages and it will be **worth your effort**.

I'm not the first person to say we are all born creative. Go into any preschool or kindergarten classroom and you will see creativity is everywhere. In our natural five-year-old state, we flourish with ideas and we don't care about being wrong, we just do it. Sometimes we play with the pasta and glue it to the paper, other times we eat it. Or the glue. Whichever. And other times we don't feel like doing anything at all; we throw it across the floor and take a nap.

Rediscover your inner five-year-old by equating your creativity with a trip around the sun. The Earth moves through seasons of growth, harvest, and entropy as it travels through its orbit. We are tied to the Earth through its seasons, which in turn, affects our own cycles. In her spoken word book, *The Creative Fire*, Clarissa Pinkola Estes describes it as a "life-death-life cycle"[1] where we each move through time and seasons on our own and through the collective that we all experience in unison. I've used her cycle words as a measure of creativity, but have added my own seasonal descriptions to dig deeper into understanding your individual creativity cycle. These terms are based on a four-season cycle. If you live in a part of the world that doesn't have deciduous forests or doesn't see snow, take that into account as you read and find how the cycles fit in with your own environment and the natural cycles you see around you related to time.

Cycling Through Creativity

1. **Quickening** (Late winter/early spring): We can feel things are changing. Temperatures are rising and we plant the seeds of creativity.

2. **Birth** (Spring): New ideas and new life are erupting from the fertile soil.

3. **Rising** (Summer): Growing and reaping the benefits of your creativity. There is an integration of what you learned through the process.

4. **Harvest** (late summer/early fall): The fruit of our labor is borne out and ready to be enjoyed. Time to celebrate! Feel good about a job well done and the satisfaction of sharing it with others.

5. **Decline** (Fall or Autumn): Settling down; no longer active; sitting down and resting.

6. **Death** (early winter): The creative energy you were using is no longer available; it has moved on to a different plane of existence or state of being.

7. **Incubation** (Winter): Something new is forming, often unconsciously, sometimes subconsciously. You are gathering information, synthesizing it into new patterns and forms, feeding the system, and keeping it warm.

8. **Quickening** (Late winter/early spring) Begin again....

---

[1] Clarissa Pinkola Estes, *Creative Fire*, 1995 and *Women Who Run with the Wolves*, 1992 a now classic book and uses the feminine archetype and stories to relate this sensation of going deeper into our understanding of our cycles.

The length of this cycle is different for everyone, from year to year or month to month, sometimes even day to day. Allowing yourself the space to breathe and accept that you can't always be 'up' and you can't always 'down' is critical to breaking out of your creative rut.

Death can be such a strong word for people, and I hesitate to use it, but it's important to move beyond the fear of it to understand the full natural cycle. Often when an energy is no longer available to us, it's because it has to make way for a new one coming in. That is the natural cycle of things on Earth. The real concern is when you think you are in a constant cycle of death and that there is no rising to the surface. This is a major energetic and creative block that takes deep unlearning. It sounds insurmountable, but it can be done. Although it's good to remember to be an uninhibited 5-year-old, imagine if you were still creating the same pasta and glue artwork you did then. Nothing would change, and you would be eating raw pasta and glue for the rest of your life!

Marking the Seasons of Time
Understanding your own processes

When we are feeling our best, we move in a synchronistic relationship with whatever season we're in. It is a harmonic and symbiotic relationship with the Earth. Harmony is love, symbiosis is a joy about living. When we find love and joy in living, we feel captivated by life itself. We mark the passing of the seasons on Earth through the Solstices and Equinoxes. The solstices are a change into either summer or winter. In the northern hemisphere, the longest day is the Summer Solstice and the longest night is the Winter Solstice — the opposite in the southern hemisphere. The equinoxes are about the balance of time — equal day, equal night — and occur during spring and autumn. These two axes are our truth about being on Earth related to change. In between these points, change and transformation happen both in the world around us and in our inner lives. Understanding our own processes can be converted into the time of year and season. The seasons of our lives are bound in time to our normal behaviors on Earth. We don't always notice them, but they are there, working in the background to bring about healing and transformation.

When we go to a party, where there are old and new friends, we find time to heal by reconnecting with familiar faces while meeting new people, new energies and feel uplifted by the energy around us. All the people in the room laughing and talking, sometimes very loudly, is a source of love that ricochets around, like a light fairy dancing around the room in enjoyment, making everyone tingle with each touch of her fairy dust. It's in enjoyment, therefore, that we find our light to be the brightest, the most fulfilled. We find healing in these moments because we enjoy seeing each other happy; it makes for good conversation, good connections, and we let go of the past in the moment. We might share our sorrows with each other, but we do it to let them go, not to hold onto them. We extend past that sorrow into an energy of love, which is the greatest connection of all.

Our connections with each other are also our markers of time. When we were in lockdown during the pandemic of 2020-21, we lost track of time. There was no wish fulfillment, or wishes coming true, because our calendars were empty. We had nothing to look forward to and nothing to hold onto as a way of being able to get through it. If we had a decided endpoint for how long we would be inside, it would have been easier because people would say to themselves, "I just need to get to this date and I'll be fine," like a runner who tells herself she needs to take the next step to get to the top of the hill. But the insurmountable worry, on top of not knowing how long, was excruciating for most and left us without a bucket to fill our desires. Sure, we saw each others' faces on screens through online meetings, but we were not sitting in each others' energy, which is exacting because we energize each other, just like at a party. The people we were in lockdown with may have been in deep sorrow, too, which held us to our belief that it was never going to end. So to be in joy and fulfillment is about sharing time with others.

I know that for some, spending time with others is difficult. That party situation may feel like it goes on forever because it is time out of mind for you. Your mind tells you it's time to go, but your heart may want to stay (or the opposite), so you hold on for dear life and hope that the right decision will present itself. It's a common party experience and leaves people feeling like party poopers if they have to leave. But, understand that your sorrow is not comprehensive, it's about the situation, not the party or the people there. In those moments, you are under a common belief that you are not worthy of the people there, that you somehow don't fit in. This could be a subconscious feeling that you are not fully aware of, so you find yourself feeling left out. When swallowed up by a whale, believe in yourself by either letting go or continuing to swim.

Creativity in the Seasons: Equinoxes and Solstices

The Fall, or Autumnal, equinox is about finding balance in our lives as we prepare to go inward. The Spring, or Vernal, equinox is about finding balance in our lives as we prepare to move out into the world. Along the way there are markers to help us with the movement inward or outward. For example, the Day of the Dead in Mexico happens in the Fall between the Autumnal Equinox and the Winter Solstice. This festival is about reconnecting to the people and ancestors who have passed on. People who celebrate this day find a connection to it by going inward and finding the memories that keep those people alive. Halloween is about being part of something larger than ourselves, and we extend out toward the possibility that ghosts and goblins do exist on another plane. We find the Earth's energy to be 'thin' during this time of year, where the veil of existence extends in both directions as we learn to cooperate with energies outside of ourselves, for good and ill. We light lanterns and enjoy the full moon because it reminds us that even in the darkness, we are bright lights and can have fun being with each other on All Hallow's Eve. (A hallow is an energy of love that begins in our sternums or heart centers, the cavity of our bodies, or rib cage, where our hearts reside. A hallow also protects us in the land, such as Sleepy Hallow, where the tale of *Ichabod Crane and the Headless Horseman* comes from.)

In the opposite time of year, Spring celebrations such as the Christian Easter and the Hindu Holi happen between the Vernal Equinox and the Summer Solstice. These celebrations are about moving outward, celebrating life itself, marking the days with plants, animals, and bright, vibrant colors that the Earth bestows on us. They are also about joy, rebirth, change, and letting go of the energies that no longer serve us to bring in the New. The breath of existence comes from our 'I am' energy and brings about change and transformation through the wonders of the birth canal as held in women's bodies. Women are the vehicle of change in the world as our bodies transform while pregnant and our lives transform once the baby is born. We find our lives to be irrevocably moved into the direction of feeding and being part of this little person's life, even if we didn't actually birth them (this goes for men, women, and any older siblings). Women are part of existence in terms of being the sole source of food for infants and belong in our rightful place as bearers of fruit for our countries. But, as we will discuss in the leadership section, we are not the moms of existence. We cannot tend to everyone's wounds and sorrows. We have our own children to take care of, and once they are grown, we take care of ourselves.

Solstices mean change and bringing in different energies. They bring to mind a passing of time or movement forward. Each solstice is marked by a single day, but we are actually in a season of change while we work on the creative endeavor attributed to the season. During the summer, we might work on the energy of being connected to others through the enjoyment of activities like family vacations, reunions, and sharing company with friends outside. During the winter, the party moves indoors, but we are also in a time of feeling our 'feels.' We might huddle under a blanket and watch a movie with our loved ones instead of going out on a cold night. Or we could also take a break from it all and not be sociable and use the weather as an excuse. Summer is a time to let our hair down and feel joy in the warmth of the time of year. Winter is a time to move indoors and feel the comforts of home.

It's easy to see change in summer while celebrating with friends and families, but how do we change during the winter when things go underground? Don't forget that incubation is part of this cycle and it is a form of winter change. It's slower and a little more discrete, but it marks a time when the energy has shifted from being outward to being inward. Inward energy looks like finding the time to be with ourselves and discovering an inner truth. Yes, there are the year-end celebrations to show us that we are not alone and that there is light in the darkness because this time can be difficult for many. But many people have difficulty with family traditions, too. How many rom-coms are there about going home to be with the family for the holiday season and pretending to have a boyfriend or girlfriend just to keep the parents' nagging at bay? So... many... rom-coms... So, the winter months are about change and discovery from within, deep in the Earth, and deep within ourselves.

The seasonal changes of the Earth are just one example of the many cycles that we move through as creative humans. The cycle is in constant movement and unending. It is good to remember that if we feel trapped or stuck, another season of change is on its way. We have only to look outside ourselves at nature and within to our inner nature for the clues that change is occurring, even if it doesn't feel like it.

Try It: Seasons of Change
How do you keep your life in balance while allowing change to occur? Engage with your own sense of time by following the journal prompts and writing about how the current season is impacting your ability to connect with yourself, or about a specific season or topic. Find the section that best suits you right now, or work through all of them in line.

<u>What kicks you off your path?</u>
1. **Entropy and Decline** are natural phases in creativity, but sometimes they can be forced onto us. Write about a time when your creativity was forced into decline by powers or events outside of you. What were you feeling?

2. **'Death'** in creativity usually means your cycle is complete and a new one is on its way. Dr. Estes calls it the life-death-life cycle that is inherent in all living things, including relationships. When our creativity experiences a death, we can lose our sense of direction, our sense of self. Write about a time when you felt creatively directionless, selfless, or even soul-less. Or write about how a creative death helped you move into a new phase of endeavor or similar aspect.

<u>Finding a new creative path</u>
3. **Incubation** helps set the stage for a new cycle of creativity. During incubation, we're preparing the soil, nourishing the seed. Write about how you usually ready yourself for a new project or creative cycle. How do you feel in your body, not just your mind and emotions? Do you have a ritual to help ready yourself? How do you begin the process of bringing in the new?

<u>Coming out of the dark</u>
4. **Quickening** is the beginning of something new. It's not fully formed, but it's just coming out of the ground. How do you feel when something new comes in? Excited? Fearful? Antipathy? Joy? Write about your experiences.

5. **Rising and birth** - As our ideas rise, we catch them from our subconscious and bring them to life through our bodies by creative endeavor. Whether it's dancing, writing, or playing music, releasing your ideas into the world comes through your body. Write about your favorite method of creating. As you describe it, notice how you feel in your body in that moment and write about it, too.
6. **Harvest** - Time to "party, fiesta forever," as Lionel Richey sings, "all night long" under the full moon, which is also the Harvest Moon (a good song by Neil Young, but check out the party mix by Poolside). All good project managers celebrate their team's success. How do you celebrate a job well done or the end of a cycle of creation? It's important to mark these occasions as they bring joy and love through sharing our abilities with others.

If you don't like where you are on your path of self-discovery, you have only to wait until the next season of change. I hate waiting, too, but if you need something to do until then, try the next episode of learning and discovery.

Chapter 5: Creative Life Concept

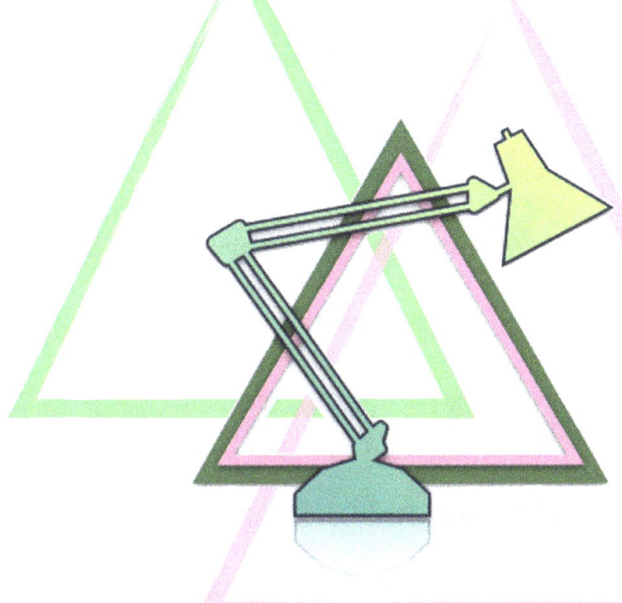

Creativity is the way we connect to ourselves, our inner light, and unconscious thoughts and memories. It's a crucial aspect of our lives and brings us into love, joy, and fulfillment in our life cycle of change. We are an energy of love and we extend it to others through our creativity and creative output. Creativity is a thinking and feeling experience that when we are in it, allows us to explore who we are as individuals and how we fit inside a collective. Moving from the creative life cycle into a process of joy and fulfillment is about understanding who we are, how we connect to others, and how we feel about ourselves. If we are always cut off from our inner selves, then we don't know who we are and how we feel. When we are in this state, we tend to project onto other people, making them fill our creative cup instead of finding the journey within to create our own.

Filling Your Creative Cup
The path of least resistance and other theories

Your cup could be paper mache or ceramic, it could be plain or ornate; it doesn't matter as long as it is aligned with who you are as an individual, so it is important to be true to yourself and not bring in what you think other people want you to be. Your creative process works the same way. Understand how you like to create, not how you think other people want you to create. This is a crucial statement because we often undergo an unheeded transformation in our creative process and output at work. We're asked to work harder, longer, and under tighter and tighter deadlines. If that fills up your creative cup, then you are on the right path. If you feel the squeeze and pressure of time, then it's time to look for a new path. You may want to switch careers, find another collective, or create in your own way. It's ok to take the time to sit with it and let it move through your body so that you feel joy about making the changes required.

Our creative lives require us to go within to find ourselves and the processes that align with our best selves, so we can create in the way that gives us joy. It doesn't matter the output, which is as varied as the number of people on this Earth — what matters is the look within. How do you connect to yourself on a daily, monthly, and yearly cycle? How do you find your creative spark and ingenuity? You have to go inward because that is your creativity's house, not on a piece of paper or a mechanical engine. Like any other house or mode of transportation, you have to take care of it, keep the wheels greased, maintain all the aspects of that energy. You can look at a person's house from the outside and know they are in a depressive state when you see that the house is in disrepair. They don't have the energy or drive to take care of the things that are in decay. When we walk into someone's house and see dishes piled up, smell rotting food or a general funk, feel the stagnation in the rooms themselves, we know that their inner life needs tending. It's a common theme used to great effect in storylines because it visually gives the cue to the viewer that something's not right.

Going within is connecting to your inner processes and how your creativity best suits you. It helps you see your life as a whole, rather than a mixed-up version of someone else's life. You are whole unto yourself and can find that creative spark by looking at your inner life, which is just as real as your exterior life — sometimes more. Once you know your creative values, you can see how you are a part of work, clubs, teams, and other relating experiences that call on our creative energy. So time to juice up the creative action on your inner processes. If there is an incongruence in your life, it could be that the way you relate to others is not aligned with who you are, or how you produce is not aligned with how you like to create. As with everything else in our lives, once you know, you know — and knowing is half the battle, as GI Joe used to say to me every day after school. If you feel you are battling at work, now is the time to take that into consideration and learn how to correct it. Once you know your creative values, you have the option to set yourself free and find those areas of life that will help you grow.

Nourish Your Creative Process Through Concept
How to find your path of least resistance

Using my design concept process as a framework, I developed the Creative Life Concept for myself as a roadmap for discovery and intention. It combines the creative design process with mindfulness exercises as a method to understand your creative life. First, let's define the word concept. A concept is an overarching idea or intention that is a big picture, also known as a Big Idea. Think of it as an umbrella that covers all of the little details. Details matter because they are in support of the overall idea and help bring to mind what the concept is. It's fully immersive. A creative concept is NOT about lifestyle. It is a way of conveying your creative life now and how you plan to use it as a road map for your future endeavors.

As I tell my design students, developing a strong project concept is the most critical step in design. I do my best to impress the importance of this beginning step because a project is directionless without a concept and can fall into chaos quickly, especially in design-by-committee situations. Learning how to create a strong concept separates the good designers from the great designers and allows for easy decision-making as the project progresses. How is a strong concept developed? Creativity and research. Something sparks an interest, but it has to be backed up with down-to-earth data that is collected from multiple sources. Learning to edit is also crucial and is part of the design process for any seasoned professional. Further definition of these steps are below, but first, let's start with a little rant.

No Vision or Mood Boards!

In interior design, you may be familiar with what's called a mood board. It's often pulled out on home improvement shows and has pretty pictures that inspire the project. They have become a popular way of self-exploration, self-expression, and life intention setting. I don't like the term 'mood board,' so please don't ever call it that and don't just grab pretty pictures off the internet — this is not research. You are developing a concept, so I prefer the term **'concept board'** because it sets an intentional aspect of the discovery process and requires you to really think about why you are selecting the idea, word, or image. Moods come and go, but your creativity and vitality are meant to be a structured aspect of your life.

This process you are about to undertake moves way beyond the mood board mystique and asks you to stop and consider your intention. Instead of an image board, you will create a full concept for your creative life using the tools I use to create strong and vital interior design concepts. We'll begin with descriptions of each step and then you will move on to your own creative life concept through step-by-step instructions.

Be Inspired

A strong concept begins with inspiration. The beginnings of an idea usually come from the project brief itself. The parameters in place provide a framework for exploration. Within this framework, inspiration happens. For example, your creative project may require a cultural reference. You may decide to present your culture, or explore a completely new one. We can find inspiration anywhere as long as it follows the project brief, or in this case, as long as it is true to your creative identity.

Research and Data Collection
The next step is research, collecting down-to-earth data from multiple sources. Knowing how the concept relates to other ideas, people, and connection points is important. For example, designing a restaurant takes considerable thought around aesthetics, functionality, and cultural aspects of dining in public — all molded together into an experience that will bring people back again and again. Parameters such as circulation for both patrons and servers, how the food is ordered, and how the look and feel communicate the design concept, all working together for a cohesive design. All of the details matter because they all point back to the concept. Research has to support the concept but sometimes it changes during this process, which is really what research is for. When someone has an idea, the data needs to fully support it. And sometimes, the data points to a new direction.

Don't Forget Your X-acto Blade
It's also important to learn to edit as you develop your concept. Narrow down the choices to one creative solution that works best for the design brief and the initial idea. Pie-in-the-sky is ok to start, but it's important to narrow it down to make it more impactful and effective. Too many ideas make for a confusing final design; it needs to be easily 'read' visually and viscerally. Editing is also the most difficult part of the process because we become attached to our ideas and don't know how to let them go. Learning how to edit down the need for everything to be perfect is difficult. Letting go can be difficult; learning it through creative endeavor gets you halfway to applying it to your own life.

Let's Begin! Create your Creative Life Concept
Now that you know the overall idea, time to move into researching your own creative life. Don't forget to have fun with it. Be endearing with yourself, not hard on yourself. Allow your mind to wander as you write and bring in all the good feelings about being a creative person. Let go of any preconceived notions about your creativity and let whatever comes to your mind first be your guiding path. You are here for a reason and that is to be creative, so find joy in that fact!

<u>Concept Step 1: Research yourself through creative values</u>
Note: This exercise is modeled after Brene Brown's 'Unlocking Us' worksheet on personal values.[1]
Remember, research is understanding from a grounded perspective. When we

---
[1] Brene Brown, *Daring to Lead*, 2018

research ourselves, we look inward to discover what is hidden or unclear. We move our focus from the outside world to the interior, my favorite place to be, because interior designers know that the space within can be shaped and molded with color, light, and texture. But it all starts with data collection.

Words have power. They bring to mind a certain connotation or intonation depending on our life experience and societal standards. For this reason, I start with words that resonate with me and the project brief. I simply make a list of words that bring a sense or feeling that relates to the topic at hand. Instead of words that describe a physical project, you will describe your interior life — how you find and maintain your creativity, how you see the world around you, or maybe how you react to what is happening around you. Let's define a few words for this exercise for agreement purposes, not because I want you to believe what I believe.

Belief - a subjective attitude that something is true (Example: "I believe grass is green." But grass can be many colors including red, purple, and yellow.)
Belief System - a set of ideologies comprised of beliefs that impact your reality. (The most common belief system is religion.)
Value - Truth (beliefs) and reality (belief systems) come together to form a value, but it is *your* truth and *your* reality, not the end-all-be-all of the Universe.

Your creative values represent what you relate to in your environment through your beliefs. Our beliefs have physical value and we feel physically aware of who we are through our belief systems. For example, if I value balance, then I believe that my creative life requires balance to be fulfilling or any other interpretation that aligns with me. If I feel out of balance in my creative life, then I will do what I can to find it. Being out of balance can look like being maligned by a coworker, having a difficult interview with a client, or having our creative work cut down and parsed into tiny pieces through denigration.

We feel disconnected from who we are as individuals when a person or situation sends us off in a direction of feeling not relatable. We may think, "How can they treat me this way, when I worked really hard on that _____?" But, if our creative work is praised, or our coworkers treat us with kindness and love, we feel right in our skin, in our bodies. All of these things impact our creativity and can be part of our belief systems.

Start your research exploration by circling or highlight all of the creative values that resonate with you in the table on the following page:

Creativity for Soul Healing

Adaptability	Environment	Legacy	Self-respect
Adventure	Equality	Love	Spirituality
Altruism	Excellence	Nature	Spontaneity
Ambition	Freedom	Openness	Stewardship
Authenticity	Generosity	Optimism	Success
Balance	Grace	Order	Support
Beauty	Gratitude	Patience	Tradition
Belonging	Growth	Peace	Trust
Collaboration	Harmony	Perseverance	Truth
Commitment	Heritage	Power	Understanding
Community	Honesty	Pride	Uniqueness
Compassion	Hope	Recognition	Usefulness
Confidence	Humor	Resourcefulness	Vision
Connection	Inclusion	Respect	Vulnerability
Independence	Integrity	Rigor	Wealth
Courage	Intuition	Risk-taking	Well-being
Curiosity	Joy	Security	Wisdom
Dignity	Knowledge	Self-discipline	Other:
Diversity	Learning	Self-expression	Other:

Now, select the **2 -3 values** that resonate with your creative endeavor the most. Engage with these values by writing why you selected them. Remember this is data collection, so the more you write, the more information you will have to hone in on your concept.

CREATIVE VALUE #1_____   CREATIVE VALUE #2_____

CREATIVE VALUE #3_____

Concept Step 2: House Visualization

This section relates to the Source Code in chapter 16. If you need further guidance on this topic, skip ahead to that section for an astrological view of this type of self-reflection.

Another form of personal data collection is to visualize or use **active imagination**, which was developed by the psychiatrist and psychoanalyst, Carl Jung. It's a common technique to help you tap into your inner voice more easily. This visualization helps you understand how your creative values impact your creative process through the symbology of a house, each room representing a different area that is important to you.

Sit with your eyes closed or allow your mind to wander as you imagine yourself walking through a house. It could be the house you live in now or your dream house, whatever feels right to you. As you walk through your life-house, bring in all of your senses as you see, hear, feel, smell, and taste your way through the house. How do you describe each room? Describing what you see is a start, but bringing your innate sense of feeling is really what we're trying to get at with this exercise. Consider using words such as warm, exciting, friendly, utilitarian, peaceful, etc., and then describe why.

What makes each room important in your creative life? Use your list of values to describe the rooms, focusing on the two main values you chose.

Kitchen:_____   Living Room: _____
Dining Room: _____   Bed Room: _____
Other: _____

Concept Step 3: Understanding the Concept Statement

Now that you have your data, it's time to create a concept. A concept is your Big Idea that informs all other areas; it's comprehensive and a grand gesture. A creative concept is NOT a lifestyle statement or aesthetic experience. It gets to the heart of the matter through your values. We typically communicate that idea through a concept statement. A concept statement succinctly describes your big idea. It is not a lengthy paragraph; it's a brief sentence or two — short and sweet.

Starting with the two to three values you chose in Step 1, write a BRIEF concept statement for your creative life, with 2 to 3 sentences at the most. If you're stuck, try beginning with the phrase "I am [your creative values] by…" and go from there. Focus on describing how you are the two values you selected. You can edit it later. Keep in mind this is a dynamic document and will change as you change.

Example:
My Creative Life Concept - Unique Courage
My Creative Life Concept Statement - *I am unique courage by finding my own path in life and not letting others' ideas and beliefs stand in my way from realizing who I am.*

Concept Step 4: Life Areas for Intention

And finally, now that you have your Big Idea, consider other areas in your creative life you want to bring attention to. Working with specific areas may also help you better define your concept statement if you feel it's not quite right. With your creative life concept in mind, write statements for each area of your life you want to set an intention for. Refer to your house visualization in Step 2 for inspiration. Common areas are listed below. Remember to be concise with your statement! No more than one or two sentences for each area!

- **Me:** (creative life concept from Step 3): *e.g., "I am Unique Courage by…"*
- **Creative Work:** *e.g., "I work courageously on my art by…"*
- **Creative Relationships:** *e.g., "I feel courageous in unique relationships by…"*
- **Abundance:** *e.g., "My courageous acts of abundance are unique to me…"*
- **Creative Partnerships:** *e.g., "I find courage in myself through unique partnerships…"*
- **Spirituality:** *e.g., "I am uniquely aligned with Spirit…"*
- **Other**

This is the final step but the beginning of your path to a new awareness of your creative life and creative process. Refer back to what you have written as often as you need to. I keep mine posted on my wall. Re-examine and rewrite your concept as often as needed, or write a separate one as needed—one for work and one for home, for example. The creative process is ever-changing because we are ever-changing.

Chapter 6: Creativity in the Workplace

Creativity in the workplace is a popular topic because it is linked to innovation. In the twenty-first century, innovation is a requirement to bring about significant change, whether as a product, service, or system. Innovation is a term we use to understand cutting-edge insights and other highly sought-after ways of creating something new that is unique and useful. This ties to the first chapter, so if you haven't read the definitions of creativity, you may want to jump back for a moment. Not all innovations are created equal, of course, and learning about the subtext is important. Often the insight required to innovate comes from within, and is dependent on a certain level of trust in the environment between individuals, teams, and inter-organizational relating. But before I get ahead of myself, we need to start with the basics. This chapter parses out the realities of the workplace through common aspects attributed to companies and organizations.

I have taken an opposite view of many current beliefs related to the office and working environment in terms of creativity. I don't present them as an end-all-be-all approach to 'how things are done' as there are too many of us and too many different organizations on the planet. But do try to reteach yourself by observing your own environment with my thoughts in mind and you might find room for change.

Organizational vs. Individual Values + Identity
Finding the Realness Underneath the Brand

Have you ever wondered why some companies thrive while others don't? Most people attribute it to the company culture — if there is just enough food, foosball tables, and other perks, the culture will follow suit and people will want to be there so much, they'll thrive and stay all the time. You will be surprised to know it's not the culture — it's how the space itself feels when you walk through the door. It's a welcoming aspect that gives the energy of liveliness, which is the <u>felt sense of the place</u> — not how trendy it looks, or if it's sporting the latest technology, or the 'values' assigned by upper management. If the <u>sensation</u> within the space feels open (not necessarily an open floor plan) and active, it feels alive, and people will want to be there. If it feels unwelcoming, closed, or 'dead,' then people feel awkward and leave — no one likes to hang out with a corpse. Talking in hushed tones, walking on eggshells or pins and needles, not greeting each other, and people not leaving their desks are all ways a workspace feels dead, and the behaviors show the felt sense of an organization. It's an act of hospitality that is extended to all employees at all levels within the organization. Like a house party, if people feel welcome, they'll stay. If they don't, they leave — simple as that. It's a feeling, not the culture or a value.

Some organizations use the term 'value' as a way of saying, "This is what we stand for," which is great, in theory. I often support companies that align with the things that I stand for, but I don't support them because of their values. Standing up for human rights isn't a value, it's a thing you do that supports your value of being a good person — supporting people who require it and loving all people because you are human. The value of the situation is love, not the corporate 'value' of human rights. Again, it's a felt sense. I can say I value human rights in my corporate statement, but then I send my product design to a third-world country to be made by daily wage earners. Or I can be all about Green Peace, but then I push through an entitlement that allows for bulldozers to remove wetlands. It's all a double standard, but it gets the value proposition off the table. If I truly value an energy's right to exist, I will do what I can to help <u>support that function</u>.

A mission statement is similar in that it states the company's purpose and goals. Goals are typically aligned with what the company stands for and what it is becoming. It may have a goal to bring a smile to everyone's face through a specific product or service, or it may have a goal to produce as many one type of product to make as much profit as possible without going into debt. That may seem obvious, but some companies don't state that as a goal and then wonder why they fail.[1] As reviewed under the design thinking section, it's necessary to state the function, desire, or 'problem' that needs to be solved — this includes how you're solving your particular style of business or organization. 'Loosey-goosey' doesn't work well for most organizations because people need to know what direction they're heading in their jobs, careers, and where that job brings them on a day-to-day and year-to-year basis. Clear and direct communication within the organization matters as much as the message sent to external sources. This aligns with presenting our best egos so that we can push our ideas, products, or services out into the world and understand, too, that what we do for ourselves matters. Note that the company's goals, not the individual's goals, are part of the mission statement. So, if an individual doesn't feel aligned with those goals, they may feel unwelcome and leave. If the individual dislikes the 'smile' approach to business, they will likely have a problem with it. Some people may have a snarky attitude, but in reality, they think it is inauthentic.[2]

Inauthenticity in Words: Describing What Matters

Describing a corporation's goals is good and part of the process of becoming something great. Corporate values, however, are bullshit. Values are aligned with people, not non-entities. You can't tell people what to believe. They have to live it, feel it, imagine it within themselves. A value is something we relate to in our environment that gives us a feeling of being alive. It's a sense in our skin that what we are doing, thinking, or feeling is aligned with who we are as individuals in our heart centers. In my estimation, the one and true umbrella value is love — everything else is a detail that supports it. (Skip backward for values in the Creative Concept section.) Only people have values because they are relational, not organizations, which are non-entities. People relate within a corporation, office environment, or across corporations, but the business itself has no emotional value, so it is not relatable. A company's assigned 'values' are often important to the founding members but may not be to employee number 8, 28, or 108. Before you say, "Well, then they shouldn't work here. That's why we come up with values," that's horse manure as well because, as of now, we hire people to perform a task or a function within a set hierarchy of rules and behaviors. We typically don't hire people because they value courage over tenacity, for example. We hire based on their skill sets and experience on their resumes — what they have done in the past that can set them up to be successful in the tasks they are to perform. So, values don't find their way into the corporate identity because they are individual to each person working or creating within the organization.

---

[1] For an entertaining take on workplace standards, watch *The Hudscuker Proxy*, a Cohen brothers and Sam Rami classic.
[2] The K-drama, *King the Land*, is the best at showing how smiles can feel inauthentic to some people.

Corporate vs. People Identity

Finding the corporate identity is essential to people as it is the lifeblood of the business. It explains who they are and who they want to be. A company's identity runs along the same lines as values. It's not something that you can brand or put a catchy slogan over; it has to be something that is felt authentically in the environment. Whether it's a retail store with multiple branches, a large institution, or a small start-up, people inhabit all of these places and we can easily sense if the identity is aligned with who we are as individuals. We can bring the fun and have people break dance on the tables if needed, but when all is said and done, we have our own sense of what is really happening under all the makeup. But let's be clear: **corporate identity does not equal people's identity**. People should not have to adhere to what corporations are because they are their own entity — people are their own identity. It's like asking you to take on the personality of your sister, brother, father, or mother because you live in the same house as they do.

The identity of a company or an organization is really its brand. Branding is the name, as discussed in the next section, but understand that your name belongs to you, just as the company's name is its only identity. When a company is started, it is mandated by your government organization that you don't have another company's name. Confusion ensues if you do, and you may find yourself constantly having to explain why you're not that other company, which leads to frustration, competition, and other negative aspects of business, just as identity theft is a real problem here in the United States, and I'm sure other countries. So, if the corporate identity is its name, then be careful in how you name it and take precautions to keep the authentic energy of the organization from seeping out into energy that puts profits or 'success' before the needs of the people. They put their energy into the company or organization, so it is their energy that provides the success and fulfillment, not the other way around. (Refer to 'For Love or Paycheck?' for more information.)

When companies or organizations fail, it's because they are not authentically aligned with the individuals who work there. We will explore this further in the leadership section, but for now, know that everyone has a pretty good built-in authenticity meter and can tell a fake rose from a real one, even if it's named differently.

Brands: The Name's the Thing
Branding from a different perspective

As first a retail designer and then a corporate designer for most of my career, I worked in the field of brands and creating visions under those names. I designed stores and stories that sounded good for the 'brand' and worked to uncover solutions that seemed insurmountable because of brand rules. What I discovered was that anything can be considered a brand. People started calling themselves brands! "What's your brand" is shorthand for, "Who are you as a person?" It's still taught to this day on social media and other platforms and to college students who think they need to create their own 'personal brand' to get hired, marking them as something different from everyone else. Of course they are different because we are all individuals, but the way it is presented is awkward and almost denigrating. To reduce an individual to a brand, like they are an object sitting on a shelf and not the multi-dimensional person they are, is antithetical to our accomplishments as creatives.

Branding is naming, just like cattle. The brand isn't the look or the color, it's the name. That's it. Short and sweet. It's not fonts, logos, contracts, or pledges — it's the name. There is no other word to describe it other than that which needs to be said. So, saying "brand name" is like saying "chai tea," which is really saying "tea tea." Just stick to 'brand' and you've covered it. Names are powerful, as we know in energy healing, so it is important to set the tone through the name. Saying things — language — is powerful. When you say your name, you are invoking power, and justice served to others comes through your name. "I am" is a powerful statement and when you put your name alongside it, it pulls in all your strength and power of being an individual.

The Dark Mark

As an example, let's look at the well-known brand of Batman. Through story manipulation, he has existed for nearly 90 years in our hearts and minds and is the exemplar of the perfect brand. The 'Dark Mark' is a well-known cultural logo worldwide through the export of this brand in different forms of media. This mark is Batman's name in image form of a stylized bat inside an oval, making it both a pretty picture and an adventure waiting to happen. The oval shape represents kinetic energy and is a marker for success, in my opinion. Ovals are essentially two circles overlapping, creating movement that's not as constant as a circle, making it exciting. The kinetic energy of this shape is seen in the orbits of the planets in our solar system, roller and ice skating rinks, track and field, and any other motion that brings the fun. Think of all the companies that use the oval in their insignia and you'll find a lot of sports teams and other motion-related companies. Toyota is another example that uses three ovals, making it one of the most perfect logos, in my opinion. When we sear the Dark Mark into a cow's backside, we've branded the cow as the property of Batman or the cow is now Batman himself, creating a gender-bending, cross-species version of this superhero. The cow now belongs to Batman and the story of him in some way. It doesn't matter the color, font, or the disciplinarian who put the mark there to begin with — the cow is now the brand.

The name of a company, therefore, invokes its power. You might remember when the pop icon, Prince, changed his name to a symbol as an act of defiance to take back ownership of his music from his record label. We weren't sure what to call him! It got confusing and people tripped over themselves trying to figure it out.³ He ultimately changed it back when he changed record labels because his name aligned with who he was as an artist. If my company's name includes the word 'innovative,' for example, that's what it is. If it's not innovative, people will hone in on that and feel if it's not right. Innovative sets up an expectation of being different, being alone in a matter, being outside the normal thought behaviors that are happening at the time. So innovation is an understanding that we are beyond expectations. What happens when we're not? We are all human; we can't always get it right. But we can be innovative in our solutions to those problems, the expectations we set for each other, and how we approach our problems — leadership style included.

Naming your company or organization after yourself has strong implications because it literally puts your name on the line. It requires a certain level of control, causing every little decision to be run past you before action is taken. If you like that control, maybe you think this is positive. But consider the people who may have to ask for even the smallest aspects of work. After a while, they don't feel free to make their own decisions or find clarity only from other people, not from their sovereignty, which sets up a denigration cycle. If the organization is built around your idea or profit, you may think that it's appropriate to have your name on the line. But consider office dynamics when, for example, the collective has argued and someone has to decide on the final word. That decision falls to the owner with the name on the door. If the work extends to the collective and requires other people to get it done, then it should be run that way, and the name should reflect it.

The Elusive Creative Culture
Creative talk through understanding your style

What does it mean to have a creative culture? Everyone wants it, but it escapes most organizations, even companies that provide design and creativity as a service. The answer to the question depends on the person. Being creative, while a universal trait to all humans, is an individual experience that cannot be dictated by the organization. A creative culture is a felt sense in the environment that allows people to be themselves and feel free to do the things they do best. So, the organization needs to support individuals who then turn to each other for support as an experience within the collective whole. Our relating sense creates the collective, not the other way around.

Creating a company with a felt sense that welcomes people is easy, but it isn't easy. Your heart center, where we all love, is the center of all things universal which includes companies because they are made up of people, not machines or AI. If I, as a member of an organization, feel cared for, seen, and secure, then I feel my best. My heart center is allowed to broadcast to others, allowing them to feel their best as well. Creativity

---

³ 'The Artist Formally Known As' will go down as the worst cover brand for an artist. I think even Price found it unacceptable which is probably why he changed it back. Symbols are relatable through visuals, not language. (See Language and the Sneak)

depends on three things: freedom, independence, and sovereignty. They may seem like the same thing, but there are differences to be analyzed. Let's work backward through the list.

Sovereignty is about having autonomy over your own life — your schedule, which includes the hours you work and how many, where you work, and how you work. What types of things you work on and how many also depend on your sovereignty. If your job dictates your creativity, you feel hamstrung in the way you express your sovereign right as an individual. Clients dictating the terms of your engagement impinges on your creativity — *not* the project's parameters, but how you express your creativity through it. There's a difference. Your right to be free comes from sovereignty and allows you independence of thought and action. It creates the critical thinking skills many university instructors search for in their students.

Independence is a sense of being autonomous unto yourself. You can independently work on something, or you can work in a group. You can be yourself because you do not need to comply with a corporate contract, dress style, or other myth-busting elements of "corporate culture." No, wearing jeans or a hoodie to work does not make you feel like slacking off; that's a myth that keeps you in your place and less comfortable in your environment. Your independence is your right to be free and sovereign in your creativity and creative expression. Independent thought and behaviors are mechanisms that keep us moving forward as individuals; ever learning and experiencing new things, new ideas, new abilities. Independence can mean feeling free to explore new cultures, new types of music, and new energies that move us toward expansion. Expansion of consciousness in our minds often, if not always, requires an expanded heart center, the area of expansion in our bodies; the two work together to give us our feelings of independence.

Freedom realizes the previous words in a way that expresses individuality from the whole. You feel free to be yourself in ways that suit you best and express yourself in ways that are about your independence and sovereignty (without hurting others deliberately). Freedom is the epitome of all things creative. We don't feel hampered or dragged down to create something in a style that is being dictated to us or is like someone else's. We feel fully engaged in our environment and can safely move through it without being restricted through our rights as sovereign, independent people. We feel trusted by others in our environment whom we relate to and can trust in return. Feeling trust means feeling freedom all in one go and it, too, is an expansive feeling in the body that is felt through love, or the heart center. Our existence on Earth depends on the trust and dignity of being trusted by others. If we don't feel trust, we feel denigrated and cut off from the whole and our hearts. Freedom of lack and need impact our ability to trust others. If I feel I don't need your approval, I can be free to be myself. However, when we are in a teamwork environment, approval is seen as a way of being accepted by the clan, so to speak. Being free is a function of accepting others' work and ideas and being accepted as an independent, sovereign person. Being free stems from all these aspects and is important to understand.

All three of these qualities add up to a person's style and, therefore, how they relate to other people in their workplace environment. Now, everyone is unique so it is essential to note each person's differences. That's where relating comes in. Asking someone how they feel free is a good start; understanding their individualistic desire to be creative is another. Ask what they feel when they are at their best — **not** "Where do you get the most work done?" or "How are you most productive?" These are questions for machines, not people. Save them for your next AI discussion because that's what algorithms do, produce. Your discussion should be led from the heart, so find a way to relate that works best for you and begin by understanding yourself. If you haven't done so already, I recommend returning to chapters 4 and 5 to understand your creativity cycle and values as a starting point. Use them, if you feel comfortable, to discuss with someone their creative freedom.

There are many variations of the performance aspects of foosball tables, ping pong tables, slides, and other types of theater companies use to sell their "fun and creative" work culture. The companies that support this type of culture do exist, but they are few and far between. Company culture is just a ham-and-potatoes approach to getting people to work harder and longer hours. Throw in the word 'family,' and you've got a setup for a confusing and possibly morally explicit work environment that denigrates instead of lifts up, causing people to feel fear and anger instead of freedom and independence.

I've worked with and been employed by businesses and corporations, big and small. From start-ups to large institutions, everyone wants the same thing: to be respected in their career goals, find the independence to thrive, and their own creative path to get there. The size of the company or organization doesn't matter, the 401k package doesn't matter (though it helps sometimes), and the coffee pumping through our veins doesn't matter, either (though it also helps). In my experience, it all hinges on those three components. You can't force-feed creative culture or values.

Try It: Creative Values for the Group (NOT ORGANIZATION)
The creative values worksheet can also serve as a discussion for a group. But remember, **don't ascribe values to the company or organization** as it is a non-entity and does not

have individual freedom of expression. If done as a group, find the relational points between people, the differences and similarities. It's not a personality test, as those are not helpful unless someone is there to help back up the information and work with each person on their preferences and desires. But creative values serve as an understanding of who we are and can help form a way that is individual to both people and the group.

The Abraxas Effect
A new way of understanding power struggles

Denigration is a power struggle between two people (and only two people) through a non-understanding of one person's truth over the other. The belief system of the person who doesn't understand wins out over the other, causing an unwelcome feeling. When denigrated, you feel unloved and exposed, so you create an energetic shelter by withdrawing into a shell or behind a wall. The shelter is made so you don't feel overwhelmed by anger, fear, hatred, etc. This type of energy greatly impacts the nervous system and deepens our emotional overwhelm through a feeling of non-understanding. Conversely, when we feel another person 'gets' us, we come out of the shell we are hiding in and expand into a creative consciousness; we are willing to share and be interactive. We see this behavior in teens as they retreat into their bedrooms with the phrase, "My dad (or mom) doesn't get me."

Denigration is an energy as old as the hills. We move in and out of it daily in our jobs, at home, at the store, and everywhere else we interact with another person with the potential to make us feel unwelcome through belief system power struggles. We know what they are; "You don't look like us, so leave," "You don't have the same morals as I do so you must not be right in the head, get out of town." These statements are ways we denigrate others, ourselves, or are the ones being denigrated. It starts in childhood and happens through all periods within a lifetime. Past denigration moves forward through the Abraxas Effect, a term I use to describe a deeply walled-off state of being. Please permit me a single quote from a story because it brings up other ideas later in this book.

> *"The bird fights its way out of the egg. The egg is the world.*
> *Who would be born must first destroy a world. The bird flies to God.*
> *That God's name is Abraxas."*
> Herman Hesse, *Demian*[4]

We create our own world by withdrawing into a shell or behind walls and end up dying there if we don't break out of the shell. The bird and the shell are not Abraxas, the god is. It is <u>our own ability</u> to break out of our shells and fly out to see the world as it is or should be in terms of love and enjoyment. As Michael Hutchence of INXS sang, "I told

---
[4] Herman Hesse, *Demian*, 1919

you, that we could fly, 'cause we all have wings, but some of us don't know why."

Depending on the reference, Abraxas is known as an angel, a demon, or a weird-looking monster that's a mash-up of different animals.[5] As an angel, it's the personification of the Eastern philosophy of yin-yang, where dark and light, good and evil exist together in unison within all of us. We all have shadows of shame and denigration, which pull forward through time because they also equal 'lessons learned' in today's language. Back in the day, it would be about 'wrestling with your demons' or the devil, also personified to get to the point of it being a human trait and not something that the land enforces on you like an earthquake or flood. So you see how all of these energies have been misconstrued through stories. If someone approaches me and I'm in fear, then they must be the devil. But in reality, I'm struggling with my own demons, my choices that have cost me or caused me to feel a certain way, usually not a happy way.

Office Politics and Walls of Behavior
Stride out confidently into the wilderness of self-appreciation

You know you've 'made it' in an office environment if you have four walls and a door while everyone else is in a cubicle. You can shut the door and find a level of privacy that others don't have, seek shelter from the constant din of other people's conversations, or not worry about people eavesdropping on yours. When I created floor plans for organizations, people often demanded that they deserve an office rather than a cubicle. It all came down to office politics and, as we all know, the best person always wins in politics, right? Of course they deserved to have their office. As stated earlier, we are sovereign individuals with a right to be independent and free, including how we like to work. But the machinations in the workplace, known as office politics, are denigrating to all but the top dogs. Constant jockeying for space reflects our innate need to have a piece of ownership or control, but we often don't feel that way at work.

It is a well-known factoid amongst interior designers that in modern culture, we spend as much as 85 - 90% of our time inside, keeping ourselves walled off from nature and the world outside, but people also innately like open space. It's freeing to wander, explore, and relate to others in the space and time that they like. Striding out into the landscape is like our souls finding their purpose in life. Ironically, cubicles are also called landscape furniture, making it seem like we're free to go out and wander around the office, but we're really meant to sit there and get work done. That's fine for many people who have a head's down approach, but others want and need collaboration, to move around, find their joy, and break out of their Abraxas lives. Both ways of working are appropriate and we often move between the two depending on our task. But forcing people to be one way or another is a difficult line to walk because as creatives we are sovereign, independent, and free.

---

[5] For the best and most comedic version of an Abraxas image, look to the new version of *My Little Pony* and the episodes with the character Discord, who is aptly named as a destroyer, but becomes a positive force of change by bringing a different perspective.

Walls serve to separate but also protect. We need to be careful about how we wall people and ourselves off, but sometimes boundaries and structure are good. We like to feel protected by walls behind us. Sitting down to eat, we'll position ourselves with our backs to the wall so that we can look out. But we don't like being backed into a corner, unable to move, and we may get sensitive about it, regressing to our past wounds and lashing out like a wounded wild animal. Find the balance in how you feel about being sheltered and walled off. Are you a person who prefers to see the open landscape? Or do you prefer shelter when you are thinking, perhaps off in a completely different landscape, or your own world? We look to nature to see how we're being fulfilled and to the forests, animals, sky, and stars to find our way. When we find it, we feel fulfilled and don't allow past hurts to minimize our behaviors and existence. But we also like to be sheltered when the winds and rains come; find protection from the storm.

I think office and work 'culture' serve as another version of the time when the land was being separated and segmented on Earth.[6] It was a time of deep walling off behaviors, "This is mine and that's yours. You can't cross the line of demarcation or I will shoot you, turn you in as a thief," and other separation tactics. We were told, "Don't go there; don't believe in that person, being, or life form because they don't belong to you. Don't go into the woods — a witch lives there and she eats children. Don't cross the border into the badlands. Find your way inside and stay there, or you will surely be eaten, destroyed, one and another — your children and your children's children." It was a defense mechanism to keep people safe, but in the end it damaged our culture through disbelief. Not knowing is deception. We deceive ourselves and others when we lack self-awareness but believe ourselves to be righteous in our actions, much like Robespierre of the 16th century, who spearheaded the 'Reign of Terror' that sent thousands of people to the guillotine in France because he believed himself the true thinker of all. We may start altruistically in helping others, but when we resort to violence or self-sacrifice, it becomes antithetical to our original beliefs. And life always seems to be outside, and there always seems to be more of it there — the grass is greener on the other side of the fence. But once you're there, now what? Cross the street and find out! Is there a chicken there or someone that just might turn out to be Punk Rock Spiderman[7] or the Black Panther? You don't know until you go, play, explore, have fun!

How We Get the Job Done

Of course, I'm writing in hyperbole to make a point. Many of us find our neighborhoods and surroundings comforting and familiar, while traveling can cause fear. We are all different in different ways. But the point I'm trying to make is that the Earth has been divided, sectioned off into one form after another, all the way down to the

---

[6] Silvia Federici, *Witches, Witch-Hunting and Women*, 2018
[7] From the movie, *Spider-man: Across the Spider-verse*, one of the most accurate portrayals of the Abraxas Effect in media.

individual unit of the house, which is essentially four walls and a door. As our office environments reflect this truth, maybe it's time for a renovation. The idea that office work is done in the office was dismissed during the 2020 pandemic. But people felt isolated and needed to refresh their lives while companies decided to refresh their offices to get people to come back, employing the age-old mantra, "If you build it, they will come." Perhaps, but will they keep coming back if they don't feel welcome? Freedom and sovereignty imply choice, choice of fulfillment and being in each other's energy. Notice how the pandemic and lockdown reflected this concept to us. We didn't have choices anymore; we had to stay home. We felt forced to get vaccinated — either by the fear of getting sick or the fear of being isolated. We were mandated to do so by our workplaces, or we couldn't return. There was nothing fun about the pandemic or lockdown except for some of the silly things we did to lift each other's spirits, which is another way of looking at it. In our isolation, we felt compelled to connect, to reach out to others we might normally disregard. Looking after each other is when we are in our best energy, in my opinion, and we saw it all over the place during lockdown.

Playing at Work

What if work is play? I know you're scoffing, but take a moment and imagine the wild possibility that being playful at work will help you feel more enlivened and more willing to stay if you need to. I'm not advocating for longer hours, so please don't take it that way. In fact, I think we should all work 20 hours a week OR LESS — the rest of the time, we should play and do the things we love. But if we love what we do at work or play, then there is a seamless existence between work and home life. We won't feel disgruntled when we get home, taking it out on our family. We will feel uplifted and ready to take on whatever task comes our way. We will feel joy, lighter on our feet, not trudging through the week as if some heavy load has been placed on our shoulders — oh wait, a heavy load has been placed on our shoulders in the dichotomy of existence between "do what you love and then do what you do." We're told to find a career that expresses who we are as individuals, find something that gives us a spark, makes our life tick in some perfect way, but when we get out into the 'real' world, we often find this isn't the case: get a job — any job — to support yourself, your family, your friends, who all demand something from you, whether it's time at the bar or restaurant, gifts, weddings, vacations, etc. All of these things take time and money, yet we are cut off from it because we are working to afford it. We buy nice houses to live in them, but we don't, really. We live at work, we sleep at home and sometimes eat. What's the enjoyment in that?

To find your joy, it's time to set out on a path that will get you to an Abraxas moment. Tear down the walls that keep you inside, but allow yourself the time to understand it. We do need structure and walls for safety, shelter, and time alone, but we also need to break down the walls that keep us eternally running on the hamster wheel of life. I know this is nothing new, we have been saying it to each other for what seems like eons at this point, but the first step is to break out and find a path of least resistance. Life shouldn't be hard, it should be easy and joyful, otherwise you're right back where you started. Yes, easier said than done, and that is probably the meaning of life for most — finding your joy and living in it. But believing in yourself shouldn't be impacted by others, it should be your own doing and way of being.

A New Level of Teamwork
Allowing trust in the workplace

Most of us come from pasts where being seen and heard, loved and appreciated didn't happen, or not how we hoped, and we carry that in our hearts. That wound can show up as fear, grief, sadness, and manifest as relationship issues. Corporations and businesses are essentially one big relationship where issues can arise. Many companies like to say that the relationship with their clients is what brings them success, but what do they really mean by that? Many of us experience messy personal relationships, faltering, or certainly not singing out with joy. How could that not carry over to workplace relationships?

Group mentality can have a strong influence in the workplace and beyond. But, the group is made up of people with their individual preferences and desires. When individuals share space and time, they start to take on each other's ideas and expressions just by being in each other's energy fields, and then the collective, or 'group-think,' becomes the driving energy in the room. This type of behavior is easily observed at home, in the office, on the sports field, and in any other cultural aspect of our lives. However, if we allow ourselves the freedom of expression we all desire, then relating at work will begin to take on a new tambour of feeling.

Trust is a comparison between two or more people. I allow you to take on some aspects that I'm working on because I trust you to get it done, do it 'right', and find the feeling that it belongs between the two of us, not just me. I trust you implicitly when your actions align with your words and your heart center is aligned with mine. For trust to flourish, I have to know who I am, as do you, and we have to agree that we are all one and individuals at the same time. If I trust you to take on aspects of me in my life, then I am giving you something and expect a reciprocal response, which is both thinking and feeling. Once again, it takes the tone of being hospitable towards each other, welcoming in a specific way that sets us both up for success because we believe in each other. The important part is that the actions align with love and you feel welcome. If the other person bites your head off when you ask them for help and doesn't think to apologize or work with you later when they're not stressed, then you are not required to trust because there is no requirement energy, or love, between you. (See 'Forgiveness and Unrequited Love' in chapter 10 for more information.)

For people who work in teams on projects, it's even more important for their heart centers to be clear to allow trust to flourish. If I care about you, I will help you if you need it, and you help me when I need it. We help each other to create something new. We find a connection point between ourselves that will serve as a pathway to success as defined by our group, not by the elders of the company or the boss. When we feel that success, we are up. When we don't, we support each other through words of encouragement or other means to help each other move past a disappointment, which is a moment in time, not the end of all things.

All of that positive energy permeates the space and the building and brings in a feeling of trust and accuracy in the form of an environment that supports, not an environment that denigrates and lives in the past because it doesn't need to. People exist in the 'now' in this type of environment and feel happy. They feel confident in their abilities to perform right now, which leads them to a sense of what they can do in the future; the future stems from the present. When a company is stuck in the past or overly nostalgic, it creates tension between the people who were there to experience "the good ol' days" and the newer people who bring in fresh ideas and fresh alternatives to the present moment. It negates the existence of the newer people and makes them feel stuck and unwelcome, creating a Timefield of separateness that permeates the space. The future sense of an organization depends on those whose life force energy is up and not tamped down. They feel free to create, to be themselves, which combines with the energies of the present to bring in a felt sense within the very walls of the workplace, which makes the future possible.

Being stuck in the past is a type of Timefield. Skip ahead to the discussion on Collective Timefields to learn more about how this can impact an organization's energy within the office space itself. Again, it begins and ends with people and their emotional overwhelm in the office.

Group-Think and the Individual

How we relate to each other individually impacts how we relate to each other as a collective. The collective invigorates the whole organization while bouncing back the activities of the individual. It's a mirrored process — let me explain. Our individual lives are sovereign and free according to the words described above. Often when we are in group settings, we find that we need to minimize our individuality in order to fit in. Some people call it being a chameleon, like the reptile that can change its color at will. But really, it's about camouflaging our individual expression. Sometimes we do this as a form of love, but it usually backfires on us when we hide our authenticity. The other person feels duped into believing you are one way when actually you are not. We see this scenario in sitcoms and movies, and the lesson is to always "be yourself." It's a hard lesson to learn when we, as a society, are told all day, every day that being ourselves isn't enough, through either patriarchal programming, our own belief systems, or other people around us who might 'poke fun' at our behaviors and even our looks.

This is a difficult situation to be in because the messaging is off. If *"I'm just being myself, cool as can be,*" sing Margo & Mac, how can that be when I don't know who I am or am told I'm not enough? Margo and Mac say, *"It's so easy. Get out your own way."* We carry wounds of unworthiness around with us, including the work environment where it's required to fit in and be part of the collective. The collective, however, is no more real than the energy that makes it up. Meaning, it can shift and bend with time as people show up or leave, as the seasons progress, or even as time bends, first one way, then another. (This relates to quantum physics and will be discussed later under sublimation.) If the energetics of the collective are unreliable, what is? The people who make up the collective are sovereign, independent, and free, so they are the energy that time bends around. But if they don't feel free, then the collective breaks down.

We've all seen this happen when people start whispering about someone else in an open office, have an obviously private conversation behind closed doors, and other behaviors that make people feel uneasy at best, denigrated at worst. The whispering people feel put down by something, otherwise they wouldn't be doing it, but their extended behavior creates an environment that pulls in the rest of the group by being open about their opaqueness. It becomes a vicious cycle that pulls people down, moves them into the past where they relate it to similar experiences, and causes them eventually to leave their job or the situation. I've seen it more times than I can count. When the whispering starts, havoc reigns. Begin again by seeing the light in each others' eyes, that we are all trying to be relatable, and that we all want what is best for ourselves and others. By and large, people want to succeed in a way that benefits the whole. We all know that teamwork works best and we all want to share in the success story.

What is Professionalism?

"Professionalism" can become a wall between ourselves and others in the workplace. Instead of showing up with open hearts, people are stony, emotionally unavailable, and afraid to show their true feelings. A frustrating meeting can send a person into overwhelm, but professionalism requires that they swallow their emotions and not say anything. Instead of trying to work out the issue, they go back to their desk, hands shaking, and try to calm down in silence. It goes the other way, too. We can be friendly to our coworkers but not overly friendly.

Relating at work is tricky because of the dichotomy of behaviors required to survive. Be yourself, but not too much. Be relatable, but not too much. Be aware, but not too much. Have fun, but not too much. Use your communication skills for business only, maybe sometimes for interpersonal stuff, but not too much and not when the boss is around. And make sure through all of it, you get your work done, are billable, reliable, and produce a profit for the company or participate in the organization's success in some way. It's not an easy environment for many, which is why workplace TV shows are so captivating! People showing their true feelings in the workplace is mesmerizing because we're told we can't do it. We are to maintain a constant, even-tempered existence at work that never veers off course, even though we are human beings who bring our own life experiences to every environment we enter, our perspectives and ways of doing things, and our personalities. It's no wonder many people come home from work every day and just collapse in front of the TV! We've been keeping our true identities, emotions, and lives, locked down and quiet all day — it's exhausting!

There is a dichotomy between bottom-line thinking and getting people to stay late for the 'family' feeling of it. Which is it? I also have to chuckle at the insistence of companies and organizations calling themselves a 'family' because there are SO MANY dysfunctional family situations out there.[8] Do you really want to recreate that in a work setting? Being a family to many means they're forced to sit at a table with people they don't like, and they wait for the moment when they can free themselves. But, there are also aspects to families that feel welcoming, where each member is treated with dignity and respect, which allows them the freedom to leave when they want, do what makes them happy, and feel how they want to feel when they are feeling it.

True relating in the office comes from respect for the other person's sovereignty. When you see others as truly individuals who have their individual right to freedom of expression, independent thought, and control over their bodies, then your individual expression will treat them with dignity and respect. They are no longer your meal ticket, your right to express your anger through sexual discourse, or by being overly domineering and impenetrably insolent. You drop the act of being the 'class clown,' so to speak, or the father/mother figure of the office. Instead, you treat your coworkers as individual adults who are there to express and give love through their divine life force energy, or creativity. This is not a nice-to-have, but a need-to-have if your company or organization is to thrive in a healthy, non-combative way. Your abilities mean nothing if you are not trustworthy. If you are not trustworthy, then your relating to others takes a hit, and the consequences can be far-reaching.

Brainstorming and Improvised Creativity
Working in creative teams

When you think about it, all creativity is improvised as we move through our decision-making process, but some creative endeavors stand out more than others. Jazz is the best example of this type of creativity. The musicians create a framework of a song and then improvise where the song will go in the moment, reducing the decision-making process to a split second. Each musician contributes their style, instrument's tone and tambour, and creative expression. Often the environment can impact the expression: is the audience engaged, are they playing in a small theater, or outside on a hot summer night? These things inform the creativity that is improvised in the moment, often never

---

[8] K-dramas are the best at showing this type of family dynamic, proving the world is smaller than we think.

to be heard that same way again (unless it's recorded, but still doesn't capture everything).

In 2009, group creativity and collaboration were studied by Sawyer and DeZutter using an interaction analysis method. "We use the term distributed creativity to refer to situations where collaborating groups of individuals collectively generate a shared creative product."[9] In this case, the creative product becomes improvisations acted out by various groups of people. This study is important to note because a type of improvisation occurs within the creative process as team members interact through brainstorming and other idea-generating steps; the dialog during this collaboration is channeled through improvisation. Improvisation requires each team member to be engaged, active, and collaborative. If one person carries the entire group, it's not creative improvisation — it's essentially dictatorship. This can show up as allowing only one person to create within the group while the others just 'support' that person's vision. In my mind, that's not really support, it's servitude. When we genuinely support each other, we allow others to actively participate, share their ideas, and incorporate them into the final product.

To examine this part of creative life at work, start asking questions. Here is a list to get your thoughts going:
- How do we support each other as a group to perform a task?
- Do you come to work to sit at a desk or a piece of machinery?
- Are my ideas heard **and** incorporated into the final creative product?
- Can I share my frustration or hurt in an open and caring environment?
- Am I required to work late or do things against my values because "we're family"?
- Do I trust my coworkers enough to share ideas even if they seem off the wall?

Try It: Group Critique
We often work with other people on group projects. This tool is similar to the 'Diagonal Line' tool but works best in a group setting. During a class critique, I tell my students they are not allowed to start comments with the phrase "I like...". Saying "I like" is the easy way out of giving feedback. I encourage them to use the following phrases to push them towards a mindset of providing constructive comments. "Yes, and.." "Did you think about...?" "What if...?" "Yes, and" keeps the original idea but builds on it. "Did you think about" proposes a new idea but uses what has already been created as a base. "What if" allows you to think wildly and go off the rails in a new direction. For example, "I know my paper topic is about Greek mythology, but what if I used my favorite food as a frame." The phrase 'what if' permits you to play.

Engaging Through Play

---
[9] Sawyer and DeZutter, *Distributed creativity: How collective creations emerge from collaboration*, 2009

Tom Kelly of the industrial design firm IDEO, published a book entitled The Art of Innovation: Lessons in Creativity from IDEO. In it, he calls for "coloring outside the lines" and states that, "the best companies recognize the value of talking — and listening — to kids." He recounts the well-respected design firm's creative and problem-solving process and advocates for learning how to "fail sooner and often in order to succeed."[10] Kids are great at improvising their creative endeavor. The improvised game 'Let's Pretend' bends, flows, and morphs into different shapes and angles as the participants come up with new ideas. They stay engaged by contributing their ideas and the rest of the kids either accept or deny their contributions. What happens when one child's ideas get rejected too often? "I'm not playing anymore! This is stupid!" Sound familiar? If the child doesn't feel respected or engaged with what's happening in the game, it's time to tap out. This is a form of acceptance that doesn't change when we get older, in fact, it moves into the work place. We need to have our ideas engaged with at a very minimum for a feeling of acceptance. As adults, we know that we're not going to have our ideas accepted all the time. But, we do need to have our ideas under thoughtful care and consideration by the group, our team members, or the company as a whole to feel respected, appreciated, and, yes, loved. Thoughtful consideration that is authentic, not just lip service, is an essential aspect of creativity in the office.

Sometimes, there is a performance around letting others contribute ideas, but in the end, only a single person's ideas appear in the final product. It's a sneaky, backhanded way of making people think they are valued, but really they're not. It messes with our hearts because the outward expression seems to be on par with our creative beliefs, but something in the back of our minds just isn't sitting right. It's the "do as I say, not as I do" form of behavior, or the performative aspects of trying to seem like a creative company. The ping pong table is in the break area, but it's collecting dust because no one dares use it or be shamed for slacking off, not being billable, or all the other turns of phrase that keep people from creative inspiration and expression.

Play, Exploration, and Idleness
The importance of doing nothing

Play and exploration are important in both the creative process and life. We all need to play and explore often as they change our perspective, create new connections, open our hearts, and let us feel joy. Stuart Brown, founder of the National Institute for Play says, "playing, being playful is the healthiest way to spend your time,"[11] underscoring how play is vital to our well-being and creative expression. Where I live, there is a museum dedicated to just play. All different types of play are part of the exhibits — from video games to dolls to books and pretending, they've got it all and encourage kids of all ages to interact with the exhibits, not just look at them. They take play seriously — so

---
[10] Tom Kelly, *The Art of Innovation*, 2001
[11] National Institute for Play, www.nifplay.org

seriously that they have a professional journal called *The American Journal of Play*. In one article, clinical psychologist Lynn Borenstein discussed the impact of lockdown during the 2020-21 pandemic on children's ability to play. She states that play and imagination are inseparable and that "imagination [underpins] visionary and creative thought."[12] As we get older, we may not explore as we did while we were kids. The fear and shame of failure set in, or grief may roll over you and keep you down, but exploring is a type of play and is vital to keeping our ideas fresh by understanding what blocks our sensibilities.

Additionally, idleness contributes to our creative imaginations and sometimes play *is* idleness. In the same journal, J.S. Russels's review of an essay on idleness says that through play, idleness can serve as an engine for more 'worldly' creativity.[13] Idleness is a form of play that brings us back to our creative center. Day dreaming, wandering mind, 'lost in space,' or 'zoning out' are all forms of spontaneous idleness. We all do it, and yet we also feel guilty about it. I believe it's because we view it as unproductive time, wasting time, not being efficient. Who cares!? Are we machines or are we humans? Seriously. Do you want to be measured by some artificial metric or do you want to be measured by your creativity? *Do you want to be measured at all? I don't.*

What does play look like for you: cleaning, solving math problems, woodworking, hiking, biking, laying on the grass looking at the stars, drawing/doodling? The point is to free your mind and body from the constraints you and others put on your creativity. Be curious about what you're feeling when you play, and this extends to your emotions. Many people find inspiration in the shower, while cooking, baking, gardening, etc. It's a 'moving meditation' because moving your body frees your mind to wander and find the intuitive connections, which can send us into Flow.

For Love or Paycheck?
The ultimate misconception of your divine life purpose

It's important to discuss money and creativity because many of us go into our chosen fields through a sense of purpose: serving our communities while fulfilling our creativity. This path is amazing when you are on it, but don't let the feeling of being fulfilled creatively, or even spiritually, lull you into a habit of not accepting money for your worth. You are worthy of a paycheck that supports yourself and your family in the way that you deem appropriate. Should I repeat that? You are *worthy* of a paycheck that YOU deem appropriate to support yourself and your family. Let's break this down into parts so you know I'm not just on a soapbox.

Creativity is the seat of our divine life force energy field through our sacral chakra. (Skip back to the Frequency section.) We feel our creativity through our oneness with others, nature, and the Universe. It is our divine right to be creative, in other words. Our

---

[12] Lynn Borenstein, *Imagination and Play in Teletherapy with Children*, 2022
[13] J.S. Russell, *Idleness as Play and Leisure*, 2022

individual preferences and desires around creativity make us unique and we use that expression in our gifts and talents in the form of 'products' and services. If our world were still on a bartering system, we would exchange goods and services evenly and make a value judgment each time we bartered. I may have a talent for weaving baskets, while you have a talent for fixing things. I approach you with the need to have something fixed and give you a handmade woven basket in return for your service. You then judge if you think the trade is appropriate for the level of service you provide. Maybe I have to throw in a couple of smaller baskets or some materials, but in the end, we find our terms. We each use our creative expression and share it with the world in both practical and artistic ways, but it is all creative and it is all divine because it comes from us.

Money replaced the intimacy of bartering and is the symbol for our divine life force energy exchange. As others have explained, the terms 'currency' and 'flow' to describe money are not random. Money must flow like river water to be appropriate to your life force energy. It feels esoteric until you look at it from the opposite point of view. In our society, 1% of people have stopped currency flow by hoarding it for themselves. We know this through the protests on Wall Street in New York City and other finance centers. During the 1980s in the US, then President Reagan sold the idea of "trickle down economics" which is a lie because we can look at the natural systems of the Universe and science to see that the flow of money follows the same laws as any other form of current. In other words, it's not a metaphor, it's a fact of physics because we live on planet Earth.

The Natural Flow of Currency

Think of a spring source for a stream or river. It's small and bubbles out of the Earth in a single spot. As it moves downhill, it gets larger, collecting other water as it flows, eventually moving into a larger body of water like a large river, lake, or ocean. The drop in the bucket starts the current windfall, which can explode outward. If the spring source is blocked, the rest of the stream will dry up. The 1% of people holding all the wealth in this country and around the world are damming up the flow of currency. They are hoarding it and drying up the system, therefore, nothing is trickling down. Well, it might be a trickle, but that's it, there is no flow. If money is to flow like the currency it is, then we should all be compensated fairly for our creativity, no matter what we do or the terms of employment. We are all a part of the Earth's natural systems, including the flow of money. Money in itself is worthless until we put a value on it. Because that value is tied to our divine life force energy, money's value skyrockets and you are deemed successful if you have a lot of it

You come to work to earn a paycheck doing something that interests you so that when you are done, you can feel proud of what you've accomplished and go home feeling positive about the day. Your paycheck expresses your divine life force energy, the creativity you have put out in the world. Remember that creativity is defined in many ways under many conditions, so you are still creative if you don't wield a hammer or mop bucket. Your creativity contributes to the whole of society and so should be returned in kind by a level of currency that you deem appropriate.

Minority Roles and Mis-compensation in the Workplace
The value proposition of divine life force energy

Because money is held back according to one task performed over another, its energy becomes negative in terms of caring and sharing. I'll explain. There are many organizations that have in place a hierarchy of people who support 'upper management.' Look at any organization chart to see who sits on top and who sits underneath. Even if your org chart isn't in the shape of a pyramid, there is typically one leader, maybe two, and the rest of the group is in a 'supporting role.' Who are the people that perform these support functions? Typically, women, people of color, and other marginalized people in society. From secretaries, admins, and office managers to janitors, bus drivers, and garbage collectors — all of these people do their jobs to support and be of service. A value is then placed on the position of 'support' as if the tasks involved in supporting are somehow less than those getting the support. The value says, "I am better than you because I do one thing and you do another. I deserve a larger paycheck than you because I lead and you follow," essentially.

This is not a new topic as gender, ethnic, and racial discrimination is a problem all over the world, even today. We see patriarchal rule happening everywhere, including our governments, education institutions, corporations, and down the line to the family unit. It's not new, but it is no less disconcerting. It is no secret that we are a patriarchal-ruled planet and the time has come to start breaking it down. This is not a male-bashing statement, it is a systems approach to healing our planet. We are not here to denigrate each other as the old systems will have us believe, we are here to lift each other up and be with each other in love and understanding. How did I get here on a topic related to money? Because it all fits together in a systems approach to living. If you are making changes in your creative life, it will affect other areas of your life including women and children, the topic of many public figures' speeches.

Women in the workplace gets to be a dicey subject, but I approach it from 25 years of experience and seeing who gets the promotions, who doesn't, who is happy to support, and who strives for a different role outside of their deemed appropriateness. As an interior designer in the architecture industry, I was considered 'support' on projects. Interior design is a predominantly female profession; architecture is predominantly male — the correlation isn't random. I was told once that as an interior designer (read: woman), I am not capable of being a project manager. My brain somehow couldn't handle managing people, projects, or budgets, yet I could manage all the work that goes into putting together a creative interior — from lighting, HVAC coordination with engineers, client expectations, building codes, finishes, furniture... all the way down to drawer pulls and flooring transitions, and then go home at night and make dinner, take care of my son, and manage all the household expenses as if they are different than a project budget.

Women in the workplace are denigrated. Period.

If we are to believe the status quo that we are less worthy than the men on the top rung of the ladder, then nothing changes. And women are *not* believing — in droves. The news reports that paint a doomsday picture of business because women are 'leaving' or only make up a small portion of the coveted C-suite numbers don't make sense to me. I see it as hopeful that women are stepping out to do their own thing, create their own jobs outside of societal rules, make their own version of business. And it makes *complete* sense that they aren't in the C-suite because that form of business is based on a patriarchal version of success. I respect the empowered women who can make it in that environment, but not everyone wants that. Across the US and in other countries around the globe, people are starting their own businesses. In the US, new businesses are formed at a high rate, with women entrepreneurs as the fastest-growing group, according to a January 2024 report commissioned by Wells Fargo.[14] New York leads the way in the US as the top state in the country for women-owned businesses, contributing to the 14 million — and rising — established businesses owned by women, generating $2.7 trillion in the US economy alone.[15] We are all sovereign individuals with independent rights to freedom of creative expression. So, who says the business world is 'lacking' because women have tapped out of the old version of success? It's all a matter of perspective. And perspective is what the business world needs including the energy and ingenuity from people of all races and ethnicities. In addition to women, minority-owned firms make up 26.4% of the businesses in New York, higher than the national average, with 17.6% of that number belonging to Asian-owned businesses. New York also leads the country in businesses owned by foreign-born people, pointing to our multi-ethnic, multi-cultural heritage as a country.

Across the US and around the world, people are seeing a new way of doing things as they learn about who they are as individuals and their right to freedom of expression in their own way that doesn't put down others, but lifts them up as a form of joy and respect. And it's catching not as a virus, but as a form of love that allows others to change their lives. From micro-loans and small grants to supporting each other in big and small ways on our journey to our version of success, people see that the top-down economics of business and life are an unsustainable system that doesn't allow for change, doesn't allow for love.

---

[14] Wells Fargo, *The Impact of Women-Owned Businesses*, 2024
[15] New York State Comptrollers Report, *New York State Business Owners* (March, 2024)

Women's Roles in Understanding
Believing in yourself beyond all measure of doubt

From a young age, girls and women are tightly controlled. From how we present ourselves in our dress or wear our hair, to how we exist and move in our bodies, to even how we communicate and spend time with friends, girls and women are held to a different standard than boys and men. We're constrained in our voices, our heart centers and our abilities as we try to navigate the many systems that keep us down on a patriarchal ruled planet. The control comes through different manipulative obligations:

- Don't stay out after dark (the most magical time), there's bad men out there.
- Safety in numbers: don't be by yourself, which extends to, don't live on your own. Get married to a man who will protect you from… more men? So we're being protected by the very type of person we're supposed to be afraid of?
- Help others in need: keep repeating the same behaviors that got you here in the first place. Help your dad, brother, grandfather and then your boyfriend, husband. (Note: if you are in a non-binary relationship, this idea could serve you as well.)
- Share and share alike: take all that is yours and give it away at all times, no ownership of our belongings or ourselves. While we're all taught to share as children, boys' and mens' egos are aloud to shine brightly while girls and women are told to be modest.
- Cooperate to set a standard for others: don't be yourself, tamp down any feelings that come up and when they do, you must be on your period because men are more rational, right? But they throw their anger around the house, work environment, internet, and anywhere that fuels their desire to be more. It's clear that anger is not a rational way to be on this planet anymore (if ever).
- Believe in yourself, but do it on your own time. When is it our own time?

Becoming someone's mother takes on a new tambour and tone as we're told to take care of this precious person, but also get work done, raise the family, make money, and embody the mighty religiosity of being a superhero at all times. Twenty-first century women must perform in the bedroom, in the boardroom and in the bored-room as we take on the responsibility of making sure everyone is happy. People-pleasing might be innate to many of us, but girls and women get the short end of this stick on this one. Stop suffering the consequences of other people's actions, and terms of endearment for yourself will show up in ways you will never expect.

To begin with, you have to find an understanding within yourself about who you really are and why you are here. It's hard to make that determination while serving someone else day in and day out. We are debilitated in our non-understanding of ourselves, our friends and neighbors, and the people we serve every day because, yes, that's what we do — we serve. We exist for the pleasure of others. As long as everyone else is happy, then all is well — but we also need to serve ourselves. Though this is not a book about stories, we need to understand ourselves at the level of story in this instance. We are on this Earth to serve ourselves and no one else. It's true. It's not selfish, it's pragmatic. We are the only sufferers of our 'fate,' or we are our own worst enemy, as the saying goes. We come into this world with ourselves and we will leave with ourselves. In between, we need to hold ourselves up for our own regard — not to be picture perfect, but to be real about how we are suffering and how we impact the world, not the other way around.

The Amorality of Justice

This is not a moral obligation. It is simply being in a relationship that has give and take. When one gives and the other takes, there is a rebound effect as a reflection of science that takes hold or control of the situation. If I know that a ball will bounce or a sound can ricochet off a stone wall, then I expect my movements and actions to do the same, including giving and receiving love. When one person does all the giving, and the other does all the taking, there is no moral obligation to stay in that relationship because it simply doesn't follow the basic laws of physics. For every action there is an equal and opposite reaction. So if my action is love, I expect the opposite reaction to be equal. <u>The opposite of love is not an absence of it, it is feeling fulfilled.</u> We feel fulfilled in a healthy relationship, and therefore, love is the energy that serves that purpose. It feels emotional, but it isn't — that's the story aspect. It's more of a thinking statement than a feeling one.

We are bounded by our truths in space and time. Feeling denigrated by someone else's reaction or inaction is not how we should live. When I share my reaction with you, you can either correct it or we come to an understanding. If the action (or inaction) of denigration is not corrected the way I expect, then I have the ability to move on. It doesn't have to feel negative, though it often does because of emotion and our physical response to that emotion. Allow yourself the time to calm down and see how you feel after a day or two. If you can't keep returning to the dry well of unmet needs and truths, then it's *"time to move on,"* as Tom Petty sings. *"She's an honest defector, conscientious objector, <u>now her own protector.</u>"* What a powerful statement! Tom Petty was truly one of the greats for distilling an idea down to a single line. Women, protect yourselves from these denigrating patterns of behavior!! It has been going on for way too long. We all know it's true — men and women. It's become the butt of jokes as if treating women shamefully is funny somehow. It's not. We can send out as many hashtags as we want on the internet, but without real change, it means nothing. Raising awareness was the first part, now we need to enact change. It starts with men realizing they have been taught to treat women this way and making conscious efforts to not do the same to their own mothers, sisters, wives, daughters.

Women, stick up for yourselves. It's hard even as we are denigrated daily, but you can do it. Stand in your power and tell yourself you are enough and you've had enough.

You will not be treated this way by your sons, brothers, husbands, fathers, boyfriends. It's not enough that your significant partner showers attention on you after you've worked hard on a holiday meal. They need to be working hard with you if there is to be any romance later in the day. Seriously. Whoever cooks will not be the one who cleans, or whoever puts on a spotted apron with a spotted owl that can swoop in and do all the cooking and cleaning will be the one to whisk you away on a broomstick of desire. It's choice of action and reaction, nothing more. It's standing up for what you believe in, and you believe in yourself first, and no one else can tell you different. It's time to move on from these sorrows of incomplete love and unmet desires. It's time to live in joy. Skip off into the sunrise to wherever you want to go and HAVE FUN! If you think you need an excuse, fine, but you don't, really. You are a grown-ass woman with your own needs, wants, and desires. You don't need anyone else's permission to make the decisions you make for yourself or others who rely on you for service.

Believe in yourself and you will 'suffer no fools' as the saying goes. Fools in love may be sung about over and over, but you are not one to carry that on. Stop believing in the doomsday approach to life and business. Move beyond the mystique that it will all go to pot if you leave. It won't. And you will (leave). Take a moment each day to sit in that realization and find unbounded love for yourself. You will no longer need anyone else's authorization to exist. You will stop people-pleasing just like that — no more — up in smoke. You will stop caring what other people say about you as you take on your version of what it means to be a woman in this world. And you will stop the incessant march into the bathroom to look at the scale, in the mirror for blemishes, gray hairs, or any other piece of information that tells you you are a human in human clothes.

Pulling Up to the Table of Plenty
Enacting the laws of universal love and consciousness

The table of plenty has been set; food is waiting to be eaten; people are seated in their chairs, ready to dig in. How do you feel? Most of us would say 'grateful'. (Those who cooked the meal might say, "Exhausted!") Who typically lays out the table of plenty? Women, of course. We have been relegated to a serving role throughout history while men sit and feast. Of course, this is not everyone or every culture, and yes, things are changing in some ways, but not others. We live in a society where women are told just to accept and this extends to many areas of our lives. Accept that we are supposed to run the household, buy the groceries, do the laundry, raise the kids, make less money than men, and believe in our existence only through men. We are told to accept it as if the egg on our faces afterward would be too demeaning to live life otherwise. "Why aren't you married yet? Why don't you have kids yet?" Yet we are still denigrated for "going after men" or being 'man-eaters' as if our lives are supposed to be passive and modest, always accepting what life hands us. We see this in the movies, on TV shows, and even in kids' books, except for a few. It becomes a sneaky, backhanded level of extending out a scrap while holding the whole enchilada behind the back.

We don't take the time to unhand ourselves from these behaviors because it is right and good in our bodies during sex; our creative act is accepting. But it's been used against us as a form of punishment, to demean us from our very life force energy. We have to accept what our parents say, what our husbands and bosses say (typically male), and what society says to us about being wealthy. If we act out loud, then we are denigrated. I call bullshit on that behavior. It's over. It's time is ending. We are all fed up and have been for millennia, we just didn't know how to behave otherwise. But the 21st century has already taught us some tricks about being in love. We know our country doesn't love us as we watch it being laid to waste by men over and over. We watch the wars of men continue on and on for decades while other people suffer at their hands. Now is the time to start believing in ourselves and our own riches instead of the riches of a few who would rather it be bound up in the waters of discontent, keeping it from flowing through a river of unbounded love towards our fellow people.

Feeling grateful is about feeling fortunate. What is your fortune or treasure? What do you feel fortunate for in love, life, career, or health? Feeling fortunate brings in the many because it relates to an outward expansion of consciousness and feeling. 'Fortunate one' means the person who supplies the many. When you feel fortunate, you extend outward in your feelings about your life and want to continue it by blessing those around you. It's love! Love expands and moves out of our systems towards the ultimate goal of Universal love for each other and all beings on Earth. If we feel fortunate in love and 'love is all we need', then why do we need the table of plenty? "The Universe is lavish and abundant," as Louise Hay said, so we should reflect that in our lives through a level of reciprocity. Instead of going back to the trough over and over, hungrily scarfing it down because there might not be more, we welcome it in. Many cultures around the world have traditions of welcoming guests in abundance and joy. Abundance is everywhere and we can welcome it in and provide for others at the same time.

HIS-tory Leaves a Mark

Around the world, there was — and still may be — a culture of women not being able to earn money or own property, and therefore, not own themselves. They were entitled to nothing more than the clothes on their backs unless a dowery exchanged hands between men for marriage. If women didn't accept the marriage, they would be cast out of society. If they were 'spinsters,' they took care of their fathers or brothers so that society would accept them. Their money and lives did not belong to them. Women have had to eke out an existence and if they dare to move beyond their station in life — what society thinks they should be doing — they get cut down. There are many famous examples throughout history and they aren't all crazy witches. In fact, I don't think any of them are, it's just a story to get people to fall in line. From Rosalind Franklin, who was instrumental in the discovery of DNA but shut out of the acclaim, to Giulia Tofana, who took on misogynists, to Martha Stewart and her creative empire, women who have either outstripped men or worked outside the bounds of acceptable behavior have been inappropriately cut down for their way of being. Every woman who's been passed over for a leadership position, all the wonderful, capable women who should be leading, and every woman who has been denied her divine right to be a spiritual leader just because of her gender, all know the rule of law is a patriarchal agenda put in place to keep women down.

Yet, we persist. We find other ways. We are highly creative and divinely guided.

The English entail law, though mostly abolished today, is an example of this type of relentless punishment of women, forcing them into a type of slavery through destitution to survive. Though not always, this law moved inheritance money away from women only to be passed on to a man. It put women at the mercy of men who didn't have much of it. It was a deliberate draining away of women's divine life force energy in the form of money, enacting an extreme overwhelm through behaviors outside their control. I find it interesting that the word entail sounds like entrails, because that is the location of the body where this type of emotion settles. It is an energetic kick or punch to the gut to not be able to provide for yourself or your loved ones, typically children. And that was just upper-class women! Their lives were turned upside down, but lower-class women lived it from the moment they were born, serving all those who were deemed 'higher' or better than them, which brought them down in the ranks and no love in the hierarchy — all because of their gender.

Just because these laws and behaviors have thankfully disappeared for the most part, doesn't mean they are gone energetically. Inheritance money being stolen or enacted away from you can cause such an emotional upset, especially if you have no other way to provide for yourself, that it can stay with you throughout your lifetime, affecting yourself, your immediate family, your grandchildren, their children, and so on, in the form of absorbed ancestral wounds. Absorbed wounds are real and we see it all the time, especially in immigrant families who undergo great stress and psyche restructuring when they leave their homes to find a life in a foreign country or land. It leaves a mark not indistinct from a scar. Finding the time and energy to heal these wounds can be as exhausting as the wounds themselves. If you feel you are suffering from this type of emotional overwhelm, whether yours or someone else's, skip forward to the Timefield section of this book to understand more and clear away these types of emotional energies. It's worth the few moments to understand it because it could also help you move past it, setting you up for feeling more worthy in your life.

Arm Wrestling a Giant
Taking on Heidegger's world view through architecture
　　Signs and symbols of our existence as humans are ever-present, especially in

architecture and design. We strive to infuse our work with an implicit meaning that can be easily read, or not, by those who experience them. We pull from our creative minds the signs and symbols that make up a culture, a subculture, or an individual that belong in the place and time of where we create. Creativity is an exercise in discovering who we are through our metaphors. The places we love the most, are most drawn to, are filled with signs and symbols that link us to our past and provide us thought for future endeavor, also called precedent.

Architecture borrows heavily from philosophy and its symbolic language to fully acknowledge its presence as an art form. The giant of the philosophical world of architecture is Martin Heidegger. His writings, including his essay "The Origin of the Work of Art"[16] in 1950, have tweaked and reinforced the imaginations of architects in Western culture since his work was published. Though famously difficult to understand, Heidegger has captured an audience of well-meaning but misplaced arbiters of what truth is when it comes to time and place.

I know philosophy makes most people's eyes glaze over, and Heidegger's dizzying thinking produces an intense haze. The circular thinking and looping patterns in his writing lend themselves to an image of a man who isn't sure what to make of the world around him. He lived during both World War I and II, was born and raised in Germany, and joined the Nazi party in 1933. While his essay states that the artist is immaterial to the finished art piece, I think we can safely say that the philosopher is most important to philosophy because, as with art, the thinking comes from the person's conscious (and subconscious) mind. Heidegger's essay engages the reader through an understanding of the universe that made sense by the standards set at that time. However, time has elapsed, the world has moved on. We now know that Einstein's theory of $E = mc^2$ is another fundamental truth of our Universe. So to ponder what Heidegger calls "concealed and unconcealed," "equipment" or not equipment is not worth the effort because it's all the same on an energetic level.

<u>Individuals Inside a Collective</u>

Though we are all tied to each other through energy, we express ourselves differently, as we should, as individuals through our various cultures and self-expression. Looking at these differences around the world, we know that there is more than one way to live on this planet and they are all right and true. In contrast, Heidegger's theories are of an implicit worldview that reactivates an already internalized belief system of patriarchal control, particularly white men. Heidegger's writings clearly state that the Earth is here only to serve man (note how women and every other human are excluded through language) and can only exist when Man is here. His discussion of the Earth being opaque and unfixable ignores the consciousness of the Earth itself. He

---

[16] Refer to the bibliography for where to find this essay.

denies that Nature exists of its own accord. Yes, he has a certain sense of awe related to it, but it feels more visual than visceral. He expresses a view that implicitly denies the fact that the Earth is round, meaning its roundness and fullness is part of the sky itself; it takes on its form without the 'help' of man/humans. The feminine consciousness already knows this because the Earth is feminine — Mother Earth, Mother Nature. The feminine mystique is not a mystique at all, rather it is a way of living in the world that connects us to the lost art of living in concert with the Earth, not against it.

Architectural theory relies heavily on Heidegger's way of thinking and is therefore skewed towards this male-centric view of the world. A building in a "rock-cleft valley" only exists because someone put it there, but the valley exists simply because it does. It is part of All That Is — the infinite universe. In terms of existence, the valley belongs to the Nature of Things, not the thoughts of man (or humans) who deem it so. Descartes' quote, "I think, therefore I am," is incorrect, it is more appropriate to say, "<u>I am here, therefore I am.</u>" By moving our existence away from our minds, which can control us through emotional and psychological wounds, and into our bodies, we allow the wisdom of our felt sense of being. Our connection to the Earth moves us toward understanding our truths and allows others to understand their own without judgment or control.

We can easily learn Heidegger's view on nature from his essay when he says that a Greek temple rests on the ground, "[drawing] up out of the rock the mystery of that rock's clumsy yet spontaneous support." The building is set against Mother Nature by "holding its ground against the storm raging above it and so first makes the storm manifest its violence." In his view, the clumsiness and violent nature of the Earth are juxtaposed against the man-made building that is "firm" and "towering," making "visible the invisible" just by being there. He goes on to say that Earth is not Earth at all but merely a "sheltering agent" against things that arise. His view of the Earth and Nature takes on the patriarchal perspective that everything must be controlled through a single entity rather than just letting things be as they are.

<u>Earth as Wholeness Unto Itself</u>

The Earth is the body of Nature. It holds, supports, comforts, and cares for us, not the other way around, though we would do well to think in those terms as we destroy precious ecosystems on our planet. We hold Nature's consciousness in our bodies because we are part of the Earth. Just as we deny the Earth the ability to repair itself, we deny ourselves the same ability. Denying our bodies is denying an innate part of ourselves. The exclusionary tactics of this way of thinking can be seen all over Western architecture and design and extend into the confines of the architecture studio. From interior design (a profession occupied by mostly women) being relegated to a service industry, to ethnic minorities, LGBTQIA+, and other people who are sidelined for their different points of view and ways of being, the architecture industry has a lot of catching up to do despite supposedly being considered a cutting-edge profession. It is overdue that we think beyond an outdated view of extraction and domination and start reframing our focus in the 21st century on cooperation with the environment and each other. As people who shape the built environment, we have the authority to move past what has been presented to us as truth and begin again to see that Mother Nature is not a fierce enemy to be dominant over but a familiar friend to work with in cooperation.

I am not here to wax philosophic, instead I aim to present an alternative, practical view of an outdated mode of thinking that has persisted because "it's always been that way; that's just how we do it." **The alternative view is this: we live in a world of multiple truths, not one, within ourselves and our cultures. But the consistent underpinning of all of our truths is that we exist in harmony with the Earth, not against it and not the other way round.** Our creativity as designers and architects stems from our ability to connect with our inner nature. Our inner nature comes from the reality of living on Earth, in a specific environment, at a specific time.

Heidegger's philosophical view of art and architecture is no longer valid, if it ever was. His post-WWII patriarchal, fear-based expression of existence cannot be maintained in the 21st century and beyond. We are moving toward an existence on Earth that requires more cooperation and community, not less; more individual expression, and more peace and understanding, which realizes itself as harmony with the Earth and each other.

Egos at Work and Play
A new perspective on our inner supervillain

Ego is the catch-all term for an energy in our psyches that allows us to create change and push it out into the world. As part of our internal processes of change and discovery, ego was described by Sigmund Freud[17] and subsequently, other psychoanalysts as something to be avoided at all costs or it will destroy the world. I see this as a judgment on our psyches which have developed this mechanism for a reason as part of our natural state of being. It serves a purpose — and a good one at that. Let's give our egos a rest and allow them to find their own way of doing things, just like any other part of who we are. Time to stop denigrating ourselves and allow change and transformation to take shape under the natural energy of the ego.

Creatives are known for their egos, especially the superstar creatives. The term 'diva' comes to mind when celebrities are asked to let go of their 'pride.' *Tantrums and Tiaras* was the name of Elton John's personal documentary — I think that says it all. Ego is often tied to anger like a child's temper tantrum. Children trying to assert themselves over their parents is about being independent, having control over their abilities so parents are told to give them choices, "Do you want eggs or cereal for breakfast?" for example. In this way, they can make their own decisions and everyone has a peaceful

---

[17] Kendra Cherry, *Ego as the Rational Part of Personality*, 2023

breakfast. If we're forcing others into a decision, then the tantrums of a lifetime come out to play. The ego starts to feel unloved or 'not right' in the body and can whip into a frenzy from that perspective. When our feelings are hurt, our energies are deployed differently. We feel unloved, so we lash out at others, asserting our ego to prove that we are here and we are right. 'Right is Might' is one way to look at it, but from an unmet needs and relational perspective, the ego's path feels like *Good-bye Yellow Brick Road*, Elton John's love song to the ego that becomes an apparition of time.[18]

Creatives don't have any more ego than the rest of the world, but we are asked to create for others which is like being asked to find the energy outside of you so you can go on a long hike. How do you put one foot in front of the other when you're tired and can only move if you find a fairy in the dust on the hill next to a large oak tree in the valley of good behavior? "The crop tops and platform shoes of insurance salesmen didn't make it to the runway this season, so we're putting on a show that asks you to 'think outside the box' in every way imaginable." Boring and hardly creative. Whenever I hear the box induced as a form of creativity, every bone in my body cringes, and I try to take cover from all the staleness thrown at me. Don't tell me how to be creative! My ego wants to fly away on a witch's broom of pure gold into the rusted sunset of discontent and not come back — ever.

In Defense of Ego

It's obvious to me that the ego story keeps us in a pattern of denigration in our hearts and spirits, so stop the ego-bashing because it's part of our natural human abilities. Ego asks, "Why didn't you accept me because I think I'm pretty good!" or "Why didn't I get that thing that I wanted because I deserve to be it." Ego lets us know that we have a lot of wealth and lets us ask the question, "Why?" We ask 'why' because we don't like what we see in front of us and then find the answer within ourselves to change it. It takes a lot of gumption to move against the status quo of things built in our environment and make the changes we want. If we accept all the time, we become parrots, or worse, sponges that accept all things without difference. Sponges have no backbone, no willingness to change. They absorb and absorb well without ever going over in their minds, "Why?"

'Why' begins to open eyes and keep them awake to changes in the environment that are required to enact new things, new ideas, new idioms of change and transformation. If we didn't have egos none of us would be willing to change and the world would be just as it was thousands of years ago without running water, electricity, or any other creature comforts that we accept as normal today over most of the world. Enacting change requires courage, which the ego has in spades. The ego doesn't care which is what, it's the honey badger waiting for the right moment to be ornery and pick

---

[18] Sara Bareilles sings a hauntingly beautiful version of this song, bringing it to a more wistful tone.

a fight if it has to. Ego says, "I'm allowed to be here and you can't tell me different. I don't care if you're black, white, brown, yellow, purple, or blue — I am a human being in form and I have the right to act under my own power and my own energies. You can't tell me otherwise! I am alive, which means I have the right to live and live well in terms of being who I am in a body." Our hearts leads the way, but our egos move us forward in time and space. We are here because of our egos and our willingness to change comes from our ability to hear, see, and feel love. Replace the term 'ego' with the word 'wound' because it is wound that keeps us down and causes us to put others down. If you are the person putting someone else down, intentional or not, find time to forgive yourself. On the opposite hand, release stress of feeling wounded by forgiving the other person. Ego is the central focus of our time on Earth. The Earth supports us and other energies such as animals and plants. We are not separate from the change on Earth, we are a part of it — and a major part at that — because of our ability to fully imagine and create. To do this, we need our egos.

As you begin to see the patterns of denigration in yourself and others, I hope that you will learn to free yourself from the wound of energy that focuses us downwards instead of looking up. When we look up we notice things; it's a 'true fact,' as they say. For example, egos surf the internet but know when something is true or not because they live in their own power. Facts are real only when we feel them in our bodies as true and is often filtered through our cultural beliefs. We will cover this later under generational styles of relating, but know that your culture is your lens for the truth, or heart-centered experience. We are 'programmed' through our culture and the culture uses belief systems to either lift us up or push us down. The programming comes through our feelings, which tell us whether something matters or not. It is the collective that decides how we feel, and then individuals take on that belief. But we are all individuals living in our bodies, so we have the right to be free from the programming we have lived through. Programming can come in the form of religion, demographics of a certain race, and even our cultural awareness of how we move through our sexual desires. Our feelings are expressed through our behaviors and we are often denigrated for those behaviors. Find your feelings to be right and true for you, not other people. When we forgive other people's feelings, we can form our own behaviors and let them do what is right and true for them.

Egos and Myth Busters
Culture's role in our sense of self

We are blind to our own actions when our egos have been bruised and don't let them air properly or don't come to terms with the wound. When bruised, the ego says, "Why won't I work with you again? Because you wounded me when I presented a creative solution and you shot it down without a second thought! You made me feel put down because you didn't even take the time to see my point of view. You were abrupt and rude in your behavior toward me and I tried to maintain an even face, to be professional, but it turned me against you. You shot me down, so I'm shooting *you* down, eye-for-an-eye and tooth-for-a-tooth." Ego wants to *trip the light fantastic* (skip forward to chapter 15) and be free to do and create how it wants on its own terms without the will and domination of other people tamping it down.

Culture denigrates ego as this masochistic thing that must be overcome, or we will all surely perish from it taking over the world — very *2001: A Space Odyssey*. However, the ego is part of our psyches, so it must be free to make its own choices and of its own free will. Ego is the person who stands up to authority in the face of danger and refutes what the status quo is saying despite the collective rush to agree with others. Ego is the woman who stands up for herself under her own authority at the risk of being called a bitch and other harsh names. She has the power and the gumption to do what's right and do it well. She will not take 'no' for an answer because she believes in herself, and others will follow suit if she can withstand the power of the psychic collective that says she's not worthy. No one will say it openly, but they will all think it, and it will show up in their behavior towards her. She will be showered with accolades but then be passed up for a promotion or be demoted by moving her desk to a less prominent location in the office. Hints and allegations will undercut her authority, and she will find herself on the outside looking in, all for the power and authority over her ego.

'Ego-maniac' is another collective term that serves to denigrate, but if we look at someone with overly egotistical traits, what are they really? They are just wound inflated. Over and again, people serve their wounds in different ways and one way is to inflate themselves to look better to others. These people are really just the walking wounded with childhood hurts and scares like the rest of us, only theirs is manifested in a more out-loud kind of way. There are generational differences related to emotional wounds and some generations are more loud than others, but we can find healing by first understanding collective differences and then moving it to a more heart-centered point of view. Understanding the need to protect ourselves first and others in our group after, like the oxygen mask instructions on an airplane, we can see how people get wrapped up in their own behaviors. There are different filters that we can understand fear through, and it all depends on the person:

"How can I protect myself if I don't first protect my children?"

"Why am I being asked to put on this uncomfortable mask, mother-f**r? You can't tell me what to do!"

"What am I supposed to be doing? I don't understand. This is all business's fault!"

These filters are related to specific generations (see if you can spot them based on my descriptions in Chapter 7), but they can feel like they belong to any generation as they are also a way to react through anger in place of feeling wounded in our egos. Our bodies suddenly don't feel right because "the captain has turned on the seat belt sign." We feel danger approaching, so we find a way to settle ourselves in our bodies, and anger lashes out to stop the grief from overcoming us. We'll review later how anger and grief are tied together, but we can see in this example how fear turns to anger through our egos. But when the ego isn't feeling threatened, it wants to live out loud, and we do that through joy. Joy is our true calling on Earth and we often find ourselves without it, which makes our ego feel scared.

The ego serves us through joy of living and being in a body; joy to laugh out loud and find the kindness in everyone despite their behavior towards you. This is not being egotistical or delusional, it's allowing people to have their own motivations for kindness and not allowing them to impact who you are. You can be kind to me, and I won't try to find the hidden agenda or the underlying reason why you want something. I see you as truth to yourself and I have my own truth, too. I don't really care how your truth affects mine because I believe in myself as an individual, not as a collective breather. A collective sigh requires everyone to be in unison, but if you have your own way of doing things, you breathe independently, dance to the beat of your own drummer.

Ego keeps us aligned with our truth and our truth is joy, which is the main reason why we're here on Earth. Ego belongs in the collective conscious as an information of power. The truth-seekers and truth-tellers believe in the power of collective love and will share the truth despite the aspects of society that try to keep them from it. Every superhero and villain story is based on this trope because it's real, just less spandex.

Try It: Enjoying Your Time at Work (What!?)
Love and enjoyment go hand in hand, so enjoying your time at work is important. Picnics and end-all-be-all retreats that are supposed to heal all ills within the company itself, while ok, are not the best solution for enjoyment at work. We know a singular event will not correct all workplace issues, as it takes time to heal wounds and be aware of our own. Find the time to alleviate suffering by doing the little things that add up to a big thing or a couple of big things that allow people to feel comfortable in their skin at work. Enjoyment comes from within and without, so prepare yourself by looking deep within and find joy instead of arguments, empathy instead of apathy.

How we do this individually usually translates to a bigger group effort, like Game Day in the office, replete with snacks and drinks for your enjoyment. Use that foosball table or the billiard set collecting dust in the corner! Let it be fun and individual. Not everyone will want to spend time with everyone else; that's just how it is in a world of however many billion on the planet. Don't expect this to ease all suffering, but it may help with enjoyment. Also, for the people who might view it as a waste of time because they have other obligations at home, can you couch the enjoyment as a need-to-have instead of mandatory? Choose your words wisely and they will come. Maybe present some exercises in this book if some learning is required. Bring in awareness through activities that people rotate through to get them to stretch outside their comfort zone or really get into it. C'mon, it's fun!

Tomorrow of Passion
Over-caring to the exclusion of others

When we 'deeply care' about something, as the saying goes, it leads to a level of passion, which in my mind is an overused word, especially in business, and wrongly used at that. Passion can come in the form of enjoyment through love, which is healing, but passion as it is used today, means to find an idea, job, or other thing in your environment that you deeply focus on, presumably to become an expert. Once invested in something in this way, passion moves away from enjoyment and into supplication, causing us to over-heat from over-exposure. It sends us into the arms of the wrong energy, like a tawdry romance novel — but in business, it's more of a bromance than romance. Expertise provides a sense of security for some as they "know what they're talking about," but it also makes life dull in a world of so many different colors and ways of being. Some call it being a fox or a hedgehog, which makes no sense to me, but it relates a hedgehog to being interested in many different things, or a generalist, while a fox represents being an 'expert' that focuses on just one thing or behavior. But the truth is there is creative joy in both ways of being and we can be — and sometimes should be — both because we are multi-layered people with many different ways of creating and being. For example, creativity is my expertise, but I consider myself a creative generalist with many interests and ideas about all different types of things and find joy in all the things creative.

There is a criminal justice aspect to the word passion as people commit 'crimes of passion' that leave us reeling when we hear about them. 'Passion projects' in business are often allocated to men, while women pick up the slack for all the other things left undone. Men are considered heroes for their single-minded focus on one thing, like Steve Jobs, who was known for his passion. Women's passion turns into the Greek tragedy, *Medea,* where her passion leads her to kill her children whom she loves very much. Martha Stewart is a 21st-century example of *Medea* as she was forced to kill her creative baby by being sent to jail for 5 months just for being a passionate, female entrepreneur and billionaire, moving her into the realm of crimes of passion. Many Greek tragedies involve people being overly passionate and it often ends with someone dying. Think about that the next time you write in your bio how passionate you are about something. Are you willing to die for your passion? Yikes, I hope not!

Deeply caring or being passionate about something binds you up, making you constipated, unable to focus on the truth or let it flow freely. Yes, that's a gross analogy, but 'passion' as it is used is grossly misunderstood and grossly annoying and it serves as a way for media outlets to make money. They cue into the hyperbole of the word passion and like to broadcast it as a good story — crimes of passion are always front-page news. Our passion for something can lead us to a sense of lack if we don't feel it is returning the right amount of love or care. It can cause us to be perfectionists of our making because we believe, as a passionate person, that there is only one right way to do 'the thing.' Perfectionism is a one-point perspective on something that gives you tunnel vision, making for stilted party conversation because you have nothing else to talk about. It is a form of a tidal locking sequence that we will understand later, but we can find ourselves broken if we don't break the ties that bind first.

Passion puts us in supplication of our enemies and binds us with their wills. An enemy is a different kind of relationship, but it is a relationship. We are bound to that person, thought, or situation to effect change in our life, like a superhero story. Who would Wonder Woman, Batman, or the whole collective be without their enemies? They don't need sidekicks to help them understand who they are, they only need to look outward at who is coming towards them. "Oh, the Joker's here again. I better suit up and do my thing." Otherwise, Batman is a listless billionaire with nothing better to do than make cars, bat mobiles, and other tech. Hmmm... sounds familiar... Batman needs an enemy to exist and is a vigilante who fights for truth and justice against the bad guys for the love of it, so in our minds, he's passionate about what he does for a living.

Do your passions lead to tomorrow or just one unending stream of lack, keeping you in supplication today, or are you willing to look up and find something new? Passion in business is the type of Flow I call a flood and is discussed in Part 2. It takes over all aspects of life and leaves people around you feeling hung out to dry. It leads to an unreality that lets other essential things fall away while you focus on your passion. You might be in need of a shower for two days, old bits of moldy food scattering your desk, laundry piling up, calls unanswered, bills unpaid — but, hey, you're passionate about what you do, so there you go. Passion is an intensity of focus that leads to the inability to be idle, which is part of being creative because it allows unfocused behaviors and thoughts to break through, shuttling our creative thoughts from our subconscious to consciousness. This form of rest is necessary for our creative existence and doesn't have to mean being still. You can exercise, do some yard work, take a shower (for goodness sake!), or any other type of activity that brings you unfocused attention. Just be careful that your form of idleness doesn't turn into another passion. Hobbies tend to outstrip their service to you as a form of play when you become intensely focused on that activity. Fun falls away, and pressure mounts due to too much intense focus, so find time to enjoy your hobbies. Our heroes should be people who turn their hobbies into businesses without passionate perfectionism and without settling a grudge or while blowing up the planet with the latest 'Inator.'[19]

---

[19] From the kids' show *Phineas and Ferb*. Dr. Doofenshmirz is the most passionate supervillian with inventions called Inators, such as the Change-inator-inator. Perry the platypus is his one-point perspective focus as his arch nemesis.

Chapter 7: Leadership

Leaders accept an unusual role in organizations. They are supposed to be trusted and act according to their employees' comfort, but they are often removed from them because they are 'the boss' and no one wants them sitting close by for fear of being judged, or seen as slacking off. There is also a misunderstanding about leaders that puts them on a pedestal, treating them differently as if they are not human themselves. Let's move beyond the leadership mystique by understanding it from a different perspective. To do that, we'll go back in time to the 1500s, which I know makes complete sense. Stay with me on this one.

Paracelsus and Air Fairies
How air is a component in leadership

Air was considered by Paracelsus, a sixteenth-century self-made, self-named, German-Swiss doctor and general bad-ass, to have its own aura or energy. He invented the term 'sylph' for the spirits or fairies that he believed to inhabit air. Sylphs are "rougher, coarser, taller and stronger than humans,"[1] according to Paracelsus, but are similar to us because they move through air like we do. What do fairies and spirits in the air have to do with leadership? **Hot air.** We all speak it, we all know it. Common phrases such as 'pompous windbags' or 'blow hards' bring up the bluster of too much talking and not enough doing. Remember, actions speak louder than words. In design school, we called it 'talk-i-tecture' or, "those who can't do, preach," to change that phrase (most teachers know what they're doing, so leave them alone).

Paracelsus called to task all the accepted forms of teaching and healing in his day. He railed against the established systems of leadership and university teaching by stating, "High colleges produce many high asses." He was a rabble-rouser seeking the knowledge of experience from "old wives, gipsies, sorcerers, wandering tribes, old robbers, and such outlaws and take lessons from them."[2] He preferred the commonsense wisdom of ordinary people like innkeepers, barbers, and other 'laborers,' as they might be called today, over authority figures and leaders of his time. He's known for burning books of other doctors he viewed as not up to snuff and for disregarding the social weather around him by dismissing a comparison of him to Martin Luther — hilariously, I might add. And he couldn't care less about Aristotle. In other words, Paracelsus considered the established leaders of his day to be nothing but hot air.

Hot air is an accepted approach to leadership today. The more you can talk, the more you seem capable of leading. I'm talking about Leaders with a capital 'L.' People who write books and give their version of leadership as the end-all-be-all. These types of leaders are air in disguise, or maybe not so disguised. Through their hot air they incite wound, either unintentionally or purposely, and have a common denominator of being deliberately obtuse about their leadership style — they think their style is the best without room for anyone else's ideas. These are the people that I comically roll my eyes at because they haven't met me or anyone else in my group. They don't know anything about me, yet they think they can lead me. This is not so for politicians, whose leadership style is more grandiose and performative instead of down-to-earth or change-enacting. Not everyone is like that in the political arena, but the fact that it's called an arena should be a big clue about what's happening in politics.

Speaking from the heart is one way we gauge a person's demeanor and likability. But we know speeches are well-prepared by those that can turn a phrase, usually

---

[1] Encyclopedia Britannica, online reference
[2] Ibid

combed over by the communications department, and parsed by the legal team. Words do have power, but if they are inauthentic and in the form of a prepared speech, they can lose their credibility. The final act is always a speech, so it better be a good one, but keep it short and sweet, or you will lose your impact.

The remarkable *Tao Te Ching* says:

> "Nature doesn't make long speeches
> A whirlwind doesn't last all morning
> A cloud burst doesn't last all day
> Who makes the rain?
> Heaven and Earth do.
> If heaven and Earth don't go on and on,
> Certainly people don't need to. [3]

Leading with Style

As leaders with hot air come on to the world stage now more than ever, we need to understand how our own leadership style reflects this type of "leading" because it's not really leading. After all this time, from the 1500s until today in the 21st century, we have taken notes and kept a log of all the people who have led well and others who have missed the boat completely. We can look to the past to find our mistakes in a collective understanding that the people who are composed of hot air in their leadership style are not ones to be trusted. Pompous windbags exist all throughout history and yet we keep making them our leaders because we are enamored with monologues.

If "all the world is a stage" then we know the monologue is a performance that keeps us from looking behind the curtain to see what's really going on. We can parse out the meaning of the speech and use our own tongues to lash at each other, but the performance is just that — a performance. When the play is done and everyone has gone home, the players take off their costumes to reveal their true identities. Who is standing behind the curtain orchestrating the spectacle before us? In our stories, it's usually an old man who has another agenda in mind. The big reveal usually comes from a small, curious child who notices the change in the set design, or the dog or animal that follows their own instinctive nature to nose out the facts.

Be ware and be aware of the performance aspects of leading as they take on a sense of altruism. "I'm doing this for your own good" has never sat well in our hearts and minds because we have our own instinctive nature that knows something is going on behind the curtain or mask to keep us from realizing the play is just a farce. How can a leader know what's good for you if they haven't asked you or worked with you to find out? It all depends on the roles written in the script and I think we're all ready for a scene stealer that doesn't rely on the infamous soliloquy. This is the modern era, why do

---
[3] Excerpt from chapter 23 as translated by Ursula LeGuin

we keep repeating denigration patterns of the past? Have we not learned our lessons? Perhaps not and maybe that's the point this time. But to let go of the past, we need to look both backward and forward at the same time, making more focused decisions as discussed in the 'Zeisel Spiral' section (chapter 1). When our focus is being misdirected, we can't do this effectively, which is probably the point of the masquerade. Sleight of hand, shell games, and other misleading performance pieces are part of this denigration pattern that are up for a release from our collective. Take a look within to see how you experience it as either how you are misleading yourself through internal 'talk-i-tecture,' or how you are being mislead or misleading others. It's a gnarly branch to sit on, but you can make changes easily and effectively by understanding and forgiving yourself first and then others around you. (This is discussed further in the last section of this chapter.) Unhand yourself from the performance of a monologue and catch the 'villain' in their own game by not being distracted.

Artificial Strategies
No more war zones in business

The long-referenced strategy book, *The Art of War,* by Sun Tzu, the Chinese warrior who lived between 544 and 496 BCE, concerns me as an approach to business and leadership. First, as an evolving species, why are we still referencing a manual set in a time when war was a way of life? The patriarchal control in China (and other places) was set up and accepted as the 'Son of Heaven' during this time, and mandated the leader to be a demigod where all authority was given over to a single man. Twenty-first-century education and business emphasize creativity and teamwork through collaboration, not the hierarchical control of military strategy. Second, it creates a warring attitude towards work and the workplace environment which puts people on edge. Have you ever been in or seen a combative situation at work? It sends people skittering for the sidelines, running for cover. No one wants to be at war, not even Sun Tzu! He states this fact clearly in his manual, so covering it as a topic that should be duplicated is antithetical.

I've never understood why leading people requires strategy like a chess game where all the pieces fall one by one until just the king is left. It seems like a short-sighted approach to leading to me. Why are the people you are leading just game pieces or warriors to get you somewhere? People fall like slain soldiers for an end game they might not see. Pointless. But if we lead people like the humans they are, then our hearts should be wide open and willing to accept love from others in a way deemed appropriate for your workplace setting. There is a passage in Sun Tzu's book telling leaders to treat their "men as their own beloved sons," but that language is also outdated and outmoded, as discussed in other areas of this book. We are not all men, we are not all women, we are of varied genders and ethnic backgrounds, and treating people like family in a work environment is not a solution for modern-day associations.

To lead is to follow, according to another great Chinese leader, Lao Tsu, in the *Tao Te*

Ching. Leadership means following both your heart and the energies of the people around you. Many poems by Lao Tzu call for leaders to follow the people they lead and enact change on a grounded level. Meaning they are to follow with their hearts and lead with their minds. Coaching expert, Eric Maisel, PhD, has a more modern take on this concept in his book, *The Coach's Way*. He calls the leadership role a "quiet dance" of both leading and following. Take the time to understand what that means for you as a leader. It's essential as you uncover what you need, what your company needs, and what your employees need. Review in that order because it takes time to understand each employee and their time and service as an understanding of our universal need to be loved by all who cross our path.

Leadership and Communication Styles
Sending smoke signals

Who are the smoke shows of your life? I'm not talking about someone who is smokin' hot in looks, I'm talking about being smoked out of your existence in your mind and body, which then moves into your heart. Smoke is a vapor of sorts, almost non-existent. You can't catch or contain it, but it can cause great harm if you inhale it. Forming a smoke screen is like a vapor barrier that seems real until you walk through it. Smoke and mirrors take up many aspects of our lives as we are distracted by one thing only to realize that we should have been paying attention to something else. Smoke is the cause of significant harm and has the power to hold our attention through understanding that it is entertainment of a sort. Sometimes we know when we're being smoked out, but keep going with it. Other times, we inhale it and cough up a lung, trying to escape it. 'Smoke Gets in Your Eyes' was the mid-twentieth century song about knowing if love is true. Blurred vision from smoke is a powerful metaphor and helps us consider the level of communication required to blow smoke.

Though using smoke signals was a type of primitive communication, it doesn't correlate to an appropriate style between people in the modern world. That approach to communication is problematic because it sends the wrong message. If blowing smoke obscures our view, we have no idea what's going on, making us uncomfortable. It requires a level of communication akin to mind reading, which not many of us can do or do well. And if we can't see clearly, how can we possibly communicate back clearly? Blowing smoke is just one more way to make people feel unseen and unheard. It's a purposely confusing communication style, similar to gaslighting but not as insidious.

The Truth About Gaslighting

Truth is not a gas, it's a form you feel in your body. (Truth, not gas, but maybe there's some truth to that, too!) That's how we know it's truth because it's felt as a form. Gaslighting is an Interesting term because of that. Gas is a substance that doesn't take on a form is not the truth. The light of truth hits the gas only to show 'smoke' or vapor.

So, blowing smoke and gaslighting are connected in that way. Gas or vapor disappears into thin air. When the air is thin and our hearts are not open and strong, we can't breathe. So take that to the bank of understanding in your heart. Gaslighting is the term of the moment, but it's an age-old device that causes us to disbelieve ourselves through our minds and breaks down our heart centers, causing us to have a mental breakdown.

We send signals all the time through indirect communication in our body posture, how we handle a situation, and how we move into a style of speaking that covers up our real feelings about the situation — like being snarky or sarcastic (some might call it passive-aggressive). How can we stop sending inadvertent signals? Find a balance between the body's natural ability to move forward and our mind's ability to project. Approach communication through the core style of being direct without denigration. A direct line is a vector — point A to point B. There is no miscommunication between those two because the shortest distance between two points is a straight line. There's no meandering, disassociating, or purposeful misconstruing of what is being communicated. If there is, it is set right quickly. But being direct is a sure way to alleviate all misunderstanding and bring about real change.

Being direct is a more realistic and safe approach to communication, but many of us believe being direct can be harsh or too emphatic, so we seek to soften the blow by blowing smoke. Being direct is a one-on-one approach to communication. It's a style that course corrects the smoke signals and gives people the feeling of being relied on and not overly superfluous. Evading issues only serve to keep people in smoke signals. A head-on approach is more direct and can be handled with style and grace when your heart is open to the people in front of you.

Women's Roles in Leadership
A new-old definition

Women have a wealth of understanding of what it feels like to lead and lead well. We often come from matriarchal homes where everyone leans on mom to get things done and go about our days with a seamlessness that is an exercise is good management skills through communication and collaboration. Our times on Earth are calculated by all the things that moms do to keep the collective humming along. We are truly the queen bees of our homesteads. But something changes when we transfer those leadership qualities to work which can include the world stage as political and corporate leaders. Why are we suddenly inappropriate to lead when we step onto the national and world stage? Somehow, what we do every day as individuals isn't viewed as 'leadership qualities.' People think our healing leadership styles are antithetical to being a leader. Why is that? Smells like more horse manure to me.

As women, we are often denigrated in our roles as leaders because our leadership qualities focus on the collective experience, not the individual sacrifice of others. We take on past episodes as if they were our own and don't look towards the future. We find ourselves to be man-handled all the time through 'man-splaining' and other denigrating forms of communication that assume women's roles and wisdom to be under the thumb of men, which we are, but only because we have been trained to be that way —both men and women. When we step up to lead, we find ourselves being cut down by our dress style, hairstyles, makeup choices, and even our indignant nature as people comb over the details of our existence in fine detail. We don't need people telling us how we look, we have plenty of time with ourselves each and every morning and are our own worst critics! But when other people slay the dragon, so to speak, we find that we have to fight for our existence to be here as leaders.

As stated earlier in the Creative Life Cycle section, we are not the moms of existence. People want us to take on this role as if our genetic makeup doesn't allow for us to work to fight. We know in our bones that we are warriors as we have taken on many leadership roles outside the home in our communities and workplaces. Yes, we can get along with others, but it is not our duty to ensure everyone else is comfortable and happy. We don't have to be second fiddle to anyone under the guise of cooperation or acceptance. If other people are not comfortable or happy with themselves, it is their problem to solve, not ours. We are allowed to show our anger at work if we feel the injustice of a situation. We don't have to sit on our pretty, little hands and act like all is well when it's not. Men show their anger and aggression all the time as an acceptable form of 'manliness,' but these are human emotions, so forgive yourself immediately for not keeping yourself in check. For sure, the word 'bitch' will be thrown around as it always does, and of course I'm not advocating for throwing punches, but women have been kept down for so long by that monologue that I don't think it needs to be said.

We are strong, powerful, mighty human beings who have led many charges to fight worldwide. From Rosa Parks to Margaret Thatcher to Eva Perone, women have led and led well. Our active rights as leaders for our countries, especially here in the United States, have been held back by the engendered roles of women in our society. We are our own protractors as we try to take on other people's styles of leading, especially in a patriarchal society. We all have the individual right to be free, which also means we are responsible for taking care of ourselves. We can be ourselves in our own time, and in our own way rise up to be leaders of the new existence on Earth. Now is the time —right now, while you read this book — to start unhanding yourself from the behaviors that have been taught to us. **Stop being everyone's mom.**

Top 10 Unsupportive Styles of Yesterday's Leaders
1. **Prof. Grassy Ass:** or "your ass is grass," very 1950s press room style
2. **King of the Hill:** pushes people down to 'keep them in their place'
3. **The Lord Over:** also known as Lord Business in *The Lego Movie*
4. **Sports Coach/military style:** "No pain, no gain"
5. **The Unreliable Mentor:** tells you, "You're not ready for that yet."

6. **The Wolf in Sheep's Clothing:** no description needed
7. **The Cheater:** they never prosper, but they also never win, so "I'll cheat just this once."
8. **Two-Faced Approach:** back-stabbing and game stealing all for the sake of 'progress'
9. **Commander-in-Chief:** being in command of all things big and small
10. **Sir Clueless:** "...so you do it, minion."

Generational Leadership Styles
Understanding others through astrology and culture

Knowing another person's leadership style is the best way to relate them, which is often employed through their age. Generational labels are usually over-generalizations and tend to be put-downs, so let's peel off these labels, stick them somewhere else, or throw them away. Of all the different ways people move and exist on the planet, applying blanket statements to one group of people as if they are a monolithic body doesn't make sense. People are molded and shaped in so many ways, it's hard to pin it down, but we can find new ways to relate in the workplace through the astrological lens of our Pluto placements.

Before you dismiss astrology out right, consider it first as a way to speak metaphorically about energies that exist on Earth. Astrologers help us find the metaphor of how our solar system speaks to us as individuals and as a collective. It may seem odd to think that what happens here is reflected as far as the nether regions of our solar system, but we know Pluto exists, so we find its movements to reflect ours. (Refer to Faraday's Field for the science behind this.) I know that Pluto is not considered an actual planet anymore, but at this point in astrology, it's 'potato-potato' because Pluto was discovered by someone here on Earth, was named by a delegation who deemed the god of the Underworld as the appropriate name, and now the hidden energies of our lives are reflected to us by this planetary body hurtling through space just as we are.

Because Pluto takes so long to orbit the sun, it reflects through the Zodiac sign that it is in, a generation's tambour of feeling influenced by the cultural awareness of that time and their way of relating to the world at large. The cultural implication of a person's age is a starting point, but don't just decide that's all there is. Currently, three generations of people take on leadership positions in the workplace. As Gen-Z and Gen-Alpha are still finding their footing, we'll focus on Baby Boomers, Gen-X, and Millennials (also known as Gen-Y).

<u>Baby Boomers</u>
For Baby Boomers, Pluto was in Leo, symbolized by the lion, from 1937-1958, a sign that speaks to shining brightly as an individual, the roar of life, and living out loud. Their generation takes on aspects of having a bright awareness of the future as they let go of the absorbed fear of WW II and saw other wars take away their friends and families (this

goes for both sides of the conflicts). Baby Boomers in the US (and I can only assume around the world) were also formed by events such as the moon landing and the assassinations of President Kennedy, Martin Luther King, and Robert Kennedy, all within a short time period. Apartheid in South Africa and Communism were forces to be reckoned with as they watched the McCarthy Era brand of fear shape and form their psyches. This was a real fear and was their version of a witch hunt, though it was anything but. It was about being true to who you believe in and the only people they could find was themselves. They brought the teenage angst story to the forefront and termed it as an aggression, not as an act of forgiveness on our bodies. But their version of living out loud has dominated our workforce as we promote through 'performance reviews' and other like-minded aspects, such as giving presentations and becoming our own brands — as if the miscommunication between self and others needs to be stylistically on Target — another brand established in the 1960s.

But the god of the Underworld helps us transform into new ways of being, so for some, living out loud meant throwing off the shackles of denigration through the Civil Rights movement and other social unrest that happened during that time. They reflected on the past, rejected the pain and suffering, and dared to think about a time when we could all be at peace. In Western culture, it was the hippies and flower children who reflected this outwardly while they escaped using psychedelic drugs and freed their bodies through contraception. Many realized they could be themselves in any way they wanted, so took that to the level of an art form. Some now call this group the "Me Generation," which can be accurate but feels like a put-down. But note that Black Lives Matter, #MeToo, and even the LGBTQIA+ movement all have their roots in this time of civil unrest. It was 'Boomers' who showed us how to protest, to live out loud unabashedly, and to call on the powers that be to take a stand for what is right through their social justice instincts of being in a body and part of a collective.

A Baby Boomer's leadership style may relate to the performative aspects of a business or organization. They may be great at sharing who they are as individuals and serve to bring others up in the same manner. They might also have a megaphone that blasts their accomplishments, which can feel exhilarating to some but inauthentic to others. Edging towards retirement, some may feel more than ready to do their own thing, while others may have a hard time letting go of what makes them feel like they are shining brightly in the collective.

'We Are the World', Gen X
Gen-Xers' bright lights come in many forms, including the seemingly magical release of *We Are the World*, a song that combined the talents of Lionel Richie, Michael Jackson, Quincey Jones, and other masculine voices with Diana Ross, Tina Turner, Cyndi Lauper and other powerful women with powerful voices to help raise the collective consciousness of what was happening to people in Ethiopia while simultaneously

bringing awareness to communities closer to home. Our joy comes from the lyrics of that song where we were told:

> "We are the ones who make a brighter day
> So let's start giving
> There's a choice we're making,
> We're saving our own lives,
> It's true we'll make a better day, just you and me."

We took those lyrics into our hearts and found ourselves in tune and rhythm with the music icons that lent their voices to make a difference in the world, moving us in sync with each other's heart centers and down to our cores.

As noted by the creators of the song [4], each musician sang in their own style so that their hearts were lifted in tune while the others served as a collective backdrop. Many musicians who sang on *We Are the World* hail from black communities in the US, where they learned to sing in church gospels, the roots of which can be traced to African spiritual music, giving them a personal investment in helping people across the ocean. Though the artists were compelled to help starving people through the care and concern of renowned singer, actor, activist Harry Bellafonte, who spearheaded the project, they may not have been aware that their voices lead to a much bigger movement, and not just the popularity of the song.

The synchronicity of the release of *We Are the World* in 1985 was an emphatic, energetic turning point on our planet. Across the globe, we were all gathered around our radios <u>at the same time</u>, as the team that worked to release the song made sure radio stations all over the world played it at exactly the right moment.[5] (Remember, this is pre-internet.) As we took on the healing energies of the song's message, changing our internal vibrations, our hearts felt and transmitted synchronistic love, sending out an energy wave that moved the entire globe to a higher vibration. Because it happened simultaneously everywhere and as a collective, it had a major impact on our planet.

This theory can be proven through the book *Power vs. Force* by the renowned human behavior and mental process researcher, David Hawkins. He cites the mid-1980s as a sudden, positive vibration jump for the entire planet.[6] Considering all of the other major impacts at that time, most of it in the negative vibration, I can only see this song as the leading cause for us to change the time-space continuum, which I believe is love. (More on this later in the book.) To the people involved in creating and releasing that instrumental song, I believe you are our true heroes of the ecliptic. Not all songs have the power and force that *We Are the World* has, as it continues to make money. It is the healing power of the collective that can bring about change when all of our voices are

---

[4] *The Greatest Night in Pop*, Bao Nguyen, 2024
[5] Ibid
[6] David Hawkins, *Power vs Force*, 2002, look to chapter 24 for this discussion

raised as individuals across space and time.

Gen X, Virgo

Gen X, my generation, is split into two Pluto placements: Virgo and Libra. Virgo is known for being analytical, while Libra believes we all deserve harmony. Pluto was In Virgo from 1956-1972 and symbolizes a generation that analyzed our culture and decided *Reality Bites*, a subversive or jaded perception of the culture. This perception explains our interest in doing things our own way through the rise of punk, rap, grunge, and other counter-culture aspects. Here in the US, our generation was launched by the space shuttle Challenger blowing up before it even reached altitude, and the tears of a nation flowed for the entire crew, including a teacher who represented our belief in the future. The jaded outlook that our generation is known for may have found its way into our hearts as we watched our bright future blowing up in the sky and saw our parents' fear come full circle.

Virgo is the sign of the maiden, symbolizing wholeness unto ourselves without outside influences. With Pluto there to shake things up, the culture as a whole became dubious of large corporations and institutions that lacked the independent spirit of being an individual. Things were up for a grab bag of who we believed in and who we saw as false or inauthentic. Gen X-ers don't always get it right, but they get authenticity in all its ways, which may be the rub between them and their parents' generation. This leadership style tells you to find your own way and may be more hands-off than some people are comfortable with. But if you can find your truth of the situation, Pluto in Virgo leaders will help you get what you need and keep you protected while you find *The Force*.

Gen X, Libra

Pluto in Libra from 1971-1984 (*Note that some people think they are Millennials when they are actually Gen-Xers based on this system!*) is reflected in the belief of social justice issues as the cause of humanity's uprising and seek to make changes so that everyone can get along, as Rodney King pleaded for in LA in the 1990s. Libra, symbolized by a set of scales, is the sign of equality through justice and the relational aspects of our lives by energy shared through communion with others. Therefore, what is important to us is important to the collective because we view it as a communal relationship. With Pluto in communion with Lady Justice, our scales were set right to the tunes of U2, Public Enemy, Us3, and other music acts known for their social justice lyrics. In 1989, just four years after the release of '*We Are the World*,' we saw the Berlin Wall crumble in Germany, and the injustice of the Tiananmen Square protests made the world sit up and take notice. In 1990, a year later, apartheid released its grip on South Africa by freeing Nelson Mandela.

Pluto in Libra leadership style may look more like truth and justice in the work place along side the need to be authentic in all its forms. We feel the exact cause of truth and justice to be how we relate to others, which is a thinking-feeling way of being in the world, not a body shining brightly in terms of finding your voice. The wounds of being denigrated are felt more smartly than others by this group because it triggers our injustice aspects, and we either work to set things right or 'drop the mike' so to speak, and walk away because our antithetical genes are about being dismissive of all things corporate. We feel in our power when we are lifted up by others and find joy in the teamwork aspects of work. Those of us who are also Libra sun signs believe in the power of the collective to bring about change on Earth. If you are a Libra sun in this generation, with Pluto standing by your side, you can create deep change that also shines brightly on others in the communal aspects of your life. But note that you are also called to step out into the collective and be more performative like your parents.

Millennials/Gen Y

The Pluto in Scorpio generation, or Millennials, is about going deep into the emotional tides of understanding through the power of being connected. Scorpio is known for its mysterious side and Pluto brings us into the Underworld to discover change and transformation, so this generation loves a good mystery that is about the abundance of power in the collective consciousness. This energy is reflected in conspiracy theories and other 'orchestral manoeuvres in the dark' — to use the UK electronic pop band name — that causes people to think twice about what's really going on underneath. Millennials' formative years were impacted by experiencing the seemingly steady systems of government and finance breakdown through the terrorism that brought down the two towers of 9/11, the subsequent bombing of Baghdad, and the financial crisis of 2008, which had a ripple effect across the globe. The superhero energy really ramped up during that time as the entire collective looked for solutions outside themselves, and Millennials absorbed the wounds of fear and unworthiness of the planet. We were all looking for a superhero to come along and save us, but Millennials felt the power within themselves and transferred it into their leadership style.

Don't find yourself underwater if you are a Millennial, as there are not as many out there as the storybooks say. Pluto was only in Scorpio from 1983-1995, so this generation makes up a smaller group according to their Pluto placement. Still, Millennials got a lot of press — good and bad — for being a transforming generation, mainly due to their size and supposed buying power, the almighty dollar at work in our conscious collective of change and transformation. "Do as I say, not as I do," is not a saying for this generation, which is their main staying power. They question the collective air breathers and the status quo about everything and anything, which shakes people awake — too vigorously for some, causing them to get annoyed with the Millennials in their group. Millennials are the cause of change and transformation in the collective as they ask 'why' so many times that others may feel like they are answering a constant stream of questions, making their alternative name, Gen-Y, a perfect fit. It feels like a lot, which is a consistent term for Millennials — 'a lot.' But believe in their power to wake us up to our outdated belief systems and make us more aware of the subterranean aspects of society at large; without them, we would not be as woke.

Millennial leadership style is about questioning why things are the way they are because they don't believe in the systems already in place. Why can't we have more vacation and sick days? Why can't I have that power position before I'm 30? Why can't I do things my own way? They may wear others down with their transformation topics, but when the transfer switch of perspective happens, we all benefit and Millennials are here to lead the way, despite the collective rolling of eyes. We will all be happier with part-time work days and full benefits, not feeling obligated to stay, and other workplace strategies that keep us in a repeat loop pattern.

Even as we talk about the generations in these general ways (notice the root of those two words), we are all individuals with our own nervous systems, so we still see and process things differently. One person may seek to right the injustices of poverty, while another focuses on the environment. And how we do it is different as well. One person may work through their religious institution while another decides to study it in college and work in that field. So you see, the over-generalizations don't work, and they only put people down and make them feel like they don't belong because someone else decided this is how an entire generation of people should look, act, and be like.

We all interact, one generation overlapping another, sometimes even contained within one family unit, so a culture's defining era impacts more than one generation. When we start to think about all the absorbed wounds that the previous generation instills in the next one, it becomes a tight spiderweb of disbelief in ourselves and others. It's overwhelming, and rightfully so, which is why a story can take on so many layers, leaving us feeling exhausted in the end. But, when Baby Boomers switch to their highest selves, they are free-spirited, uproariously funny, and inquisitive. When Gen-Xers believe in themselves, they find time to care for one another and disregard their jaded point of view. And when Millennials stop asking 'why'... no I'm just kidding, they'll never stop asking why, which is why they're here. (That one's for you Corinne, my Millennial sister.)

Other Cultural Impacts as the World Turns

Capricorn is symbolized by the goat and refers to reaching new heights. Capricorn season is wintertime, when we all go inside and dream of better days to come. We find the strength and the will to become someone new as a reaction to being pent-up. Pluto in Capricorn took this concept to an epic level as we endured the lockdown of the pandemic in 2020-21. We were instilled with a deep sense of fear as we suffered through many long days and nights of not knowing what to do with ourselves or our families. Kids in lockdown may have experienced a new level of shame related to seeing their faces in front of a camera, or they may have guilt related to what their parents went through, seeing them trying to juggle all the expectations required of them. It was a moment of everything, everywhere, all at once. Life ground to a halt and we took it on the chin as some found out their loved ones weren't that lovely, while we tried to find some joy in the desperation of figuring out what to do next. Pandemic babies will be one-of-a-kind as their bodies' systems are part of this collective fear, while showing us new ways to find joy — perhaps through an alternate experience like autism, ADHD, or dyslexia. Systems broke down in many ways, internally as our bodies tried to cope with the virus, and externally as we watched governments grapple with a new set of parameters. Some handled it, others didn't, just like us as individuals, so, it really is a mirrored existence.

The mirrors keep echoing and reverberating across the Universe as we look outward and see that our world isn't reflecting what we desire to see. Pluto has now moved into Aquarius, symbolized by the water bearer. As national and global water bearers, we can begin to heal through a systems approach. Symbolically, Aquarius represents the power of the collective to come together as individuals. When the god of the Underworld is in the sign of the water bearer, it impacts the collective, but he is here to guide and assist, not destroy and relocate. He is meant to offer us a sign of peace in our lives as we individually, and as a collective, return to a time when all are one and all are individual at the same time. This is the Age of Aquarius that our parents' generation sang about in the 1960s but couldn't quite get a handle on. They passed the mantel onto us and we will start by believing in love and light.

As I write this, Kamala Harris is up for the presidency of the United States. I hope she wins. If she does, she will be the first woman ever. Not only that, but she will also be the first black, multi-ethnic woman president, a testament to our collective energy of love and acceptance for each other. Both she and President Obama are considered part of my generation. We are under pressure to make big and powerful changes on this Earth. But we can't do it alone. We have to live and work in a collective that bends time towards love. In peace, love, and light.

Double Vector in Business
Relating through a belief system of cooperation

In the past, business conformed to the way a small select group of people who saw fit to take advantage of people and the Earth's resources. Some people are moving away from this model as new companies and organizations are set up to align with the belief that supporting both people and the Earth is essential to business. There is a long way to go, though — many businesses sill follow the old extraction model.

More than one hundred years ago, Wallace D. Wattles, a businessman born and raised in Indiana, the heart of the Midwest here in the US, wrote a trilogy of books,

including the popular *The Science of Getting Rich*. His reasoning and method for being and getting rich seem remarkable even today. We have the view that material wealth is like a pie: more for me means less for you. But Wattles rightly says, "You are to become a creator, not a competitor. You are going to get what you want, but in such a way that when you get it, every other person whom you affect will have more than he has now." Why, after 114 years, does this statement still feel so revolutionary?
I believe it's because, as a society, we have held onto two **disruptive beliefs**:
1. Being rich can corrupt.
2. Becoming rich takes winning out over others.

Corruption is another type of belief system that serves people's deep wounds of lack. These people feel destroyed somehow in their being-ness and serve that wound by destroying others, typically through monetarily winning out over other people. There are sneaky behaviors attributed to corruption, but if we live out loud, or find enjoyment with others through our divine right to be free — or being rich — we can become a mighty sword that cuts through the lack and supplication caused by it. Winning contracts, being competitive, finding the weakest link in the other group, are all business styles that denigrate. "We beat you, so we're better than you." But that's not actually how the world works. Instead, it's about <u>creative cooperation</u>. If we look to natural systems, we see creative cooperation happening all over, from symbiosis to other systems that contribute to the environment's overall health. Will and cooperation should be focused on, not power and domination over others. Power and domination get leaders only so far until the masses rise up against them for a collective coup d'etat or other cultural upheaval of people who are put down in their belief systems.

Cooperation is a two-way street; it works in both directions. What happens for you will also happen for me, even if it doesn't show up in the same way. If we were to diagram this idea, it would look like a 'V,' or two vectors, with two arrows pointing in the opposite direction on either end. Note that they are not parallel lines because we need to come together to find a solution at some point. We each have our way of doing things that will help others and when we're done, we can move on and find our own path, or someone else to cooperate with. That is how a two-way street actually works; it comes into contact with other crossing streets and at the intersections, we cooperate by stopping and waiting, letting the communication happen. When it's our turn to go, we move on, but only after we've had a moment to stop and interact. It's a system!

Because double vector business points in both directions, the group must also be considered. The workplace, or other relating collective, is made up of individuals as part of the whole. As individuals, we should feel free to create with our own way of expression (as long as it doesn't denigrate others) and support the overall goals of the collective. (Circle back to the F.I.S. model of work — freedom, independence, and sovereignty — in the previous chapter.) Each person has the ability to be the leader, so ideally everyone leads at some point if considered part of your framework. It's likely that not everyone wants to lead and that's ok; it is part of the deliberation within the group. If people are given the opportunity to lead and they knowingly turn it down, it's the same as the group deliberating on an idea and deciding if an idea is worth pursuing.

Businesses are created through a sense of ownership that sets up energies of 'mine' and 'yours,' negating the collaboration required to maintain the hum of innovation and creativity. Governments serve the collective by providing a sense of ownership to all individuals. If we can keep the group-think in the collective towards ownership of the whole, then everyone will feel welcome, and the welcoming effect will also impact leadership through the insights of the whole. The following is a leadership framework I cooked up while watching nature. I present it as an example for a different way of leading a business. Biomimicry is the true-to-life effect of learning within a systems approach by literally mimicking nature. Most biomimicry tends toward product development, but we will look at it from a leadership perspective by emulating the two different types of natural communal systems of ducks and bees.

The Flying V and the Hive
Double Vector in leadership

You are likely familiar with the flying migratory formation of ducks, geese, and other birds. The V-shape they make is a familiar sight in the sky, made up of individual birds carrying their own weight, but supporting each other by their formation. The V spans out in two directions, or two vectors, and takes on that shape through the magic of the birds who intuitively know what a tailwind and a headwind are. When the lead bird is tired, another one from the back comes forward to take the current leader's place. They all land at the same time, take off at the same time, and this type of travel lets them follow their path of least resistance over great distances. It's a cycle of leadership change built into the birds' behavior system. This pattern of behavior is a wonderful model for leadership because no one person can be up all the time and it provides support from the collective. A true leader comes from within the ranks and is pulled out for a while to both follow the collective and lead it at the same time. It's a two way street, a double vector, or V.

Applying this form to leadership within a business or organization sets up an expectation that leaders don't always have to lead. They're allowed to not only take breaks from their duties as a leader, but also step down completely to let others lead without actually leaving the organization. A cyclical leadership style can create learning and partnership, allow for new energies, and automatically bring about needed change. We see this approach in democratic governments with term limits and election cycles. Governments conform to the collective experience by serving the people who elect them. Though elections can be fraught with challenges, it sets up an expectation that the leader is not there until the end and there are no consequences to be suffered when the leader leaves — it's a peaceful cycle. This brings us to the bee analogy.

A bee hive has one queen bee, but that bee is selected by the ground swell. The queen bee comes from her hive, not another hive or some rogue force of nature. Her leadership comes from within and she knows the behaviors of each bee because she's part of them. Each bee has its own weight to carry by collecting pollen for the hive, but they are free to come and go as they please, find the flowers they like best, and work with others to communicate and collaborate where the best pollen sources are. The collective hums along, not worrying about what the others are saying or doing because they are all doing their own thing. Yes, each individual has a selected task like building the hive, protecting the eggs, making royal jelly, and so on, but within those roles, they are free to be themselves.

Knowing the behaviors of the people is an essential part of leadership. Leaders need to know who they are leading; otherwise, there is an incongruence of behaviors, like a corporate takeover that goes bad — and they almost always do. The next leader's style is a critical aspect of a cycling type of leadership since the group selects them. Reviewing how ducks and bees lead will help you consider different or new goals for your organization. Here's a list to get your mind humming and set your sights on a horizon of different leadership goals.

Role of the leader - specific tasks
- Point the group in the right direction
- Make sure no one is left behind
- Find the time and caring to make sure all is well
- Find sustenance for everyone (creativity)
- Change the POV of the group
- Examine belief systems when up for review
- Keep intruders/invaders out of the hive
- Know when it's time to go and time to rest
- Free up head space for others so they can focus on the task at hand

Take a moment and imagine how your leadership style can change based on this list. Do you need to be The One that always helms the ship? Can the style of leadership change based on time of year, for example, or after one or two years? What if other people stepped up to lead your organization, one at a time? Instead of outright dismissing the idea, brainstorm to figure out how to overcome any issues. Again, if the government can do it, use that energy (minus back-stabbing and run-offs) to integrate into your leadership pattern. Anything is possible, it's just a matter of being creative. How you want to work within a double vector approach is up to you.

Here's one way you might set up your leadership framework:
- As the leader, use the diagram of a flying V and add names to each 'bird.'

- Use the list above to help you get into the mindset of how your organization will reflect the metaphor of the way birds migrate. Really go for it! Consider all aspects of what birds do when they migrate. For example, the last bird in the V flies up to be the leader, not the "next in line."

- Next, figure out the overall leadership cycle: every quarter, once a year, every two years (I wouldn't go much beyond two years, but you know your organization best). The entire organization should be in the room to stop the practice of elitism, boys' club, and other denigrating patterns in business. Remember, this is also a hive approach, so everyone can lead and choose the next leader.

- Then, as the current leader, recuse yourself from the room as people deliberate who will be the next leader. In that way, the current leader isn't forcing things on the collective. The current queen bee doesn't select the next one.

In double vector business, leaders must refrain from telling non-beneficial stories of past leaders' styles. "I disagree with how you are doing things" needs to stay out of the mix. You can handle this by being inclusive and mindful of other people's gifts and desires to help them feel seen and heard at work. Not every leader will have the same goals or approach to leadership, so understanding that takes away the fear of being lost or forgotten as an ex-leader. If the group 'hires' the next leader from within the ranks, you are expected to step down and let someone else lead. If it's built into your organization's framework, then everyone is on board and there's no need to feel left out. Some leaders may even skip away, happy at the chance to be doing something different for a while! It doesn't mean that you've lost your leadership mojo, it just means you are a multi-faceted person with many interests and talents. Think of it as a sabbatical from your office duties and find something else that interests you. Play! Have fun! If there's no fun or joy, why are you doing it?

New Perspectives on Change Agents
Notes for leaders on the collective and how forgiveness works

You don't have to create change. Change just is. It's the way of the Universe, reflected in the seasons, in the sun's movement across the Earth, in time itself. There is no cause to create change, there is only effect. Being a change agent means nothing, basically. It might mean you're open to change, but it doesn't mean you are the change. If we're not focusing on change, what are we focusing on to create a more meaningful organizational environment? We focus on the thing we *can* change: **ourselves**.

Change the things you can create: your energy, your outlook on other people, your perspective on life, your ability to find a creative solution. Allow change, don't resist it because it will happen anyway. Rely on each other's strengths and perspectives to create change within yourselves and a collective setting like the workplace. If we don't rely on others' ideas or specific types of energy, then our knowledge goes nowhere and change doesn't occur. So it's beneficial to have people with different abilities and perspectives to round out your knowledge, which then gets transferred to the collective. All the things we can do for ourselves, we can do for the collective because collectives are made up of people.

As a society, we look to our leaders for guidance and understanding of who we are as individuals within a collective. A group of people can sometimes be demeaning toward an individual, but if you can relate to the people within that group, then there's a gap or breakdown in understanding that requires us to parse out the details. I have found that it usually breaks down at the leadership level. In the US, we value our cultural leaders more than any other type. We look to our others for different types of healing, but the cultural aspects and implications of our leaders become the deciding factor in how they will lead. Even if the leader comes from a religious or political background, the culture, which depends on place and time, becomes the dominating factor in how that person is perceived. We would not engage a leader without first passing them through our cultural demographic. Are we alike in some way? How do I relate to this person and how do they relate to me? We see signs and symbols of how they are human through many filters, including what we are 'consuming' through the media, where we are fed a specific identity from that person and connect in ways that feel appropriate to us. We believe in our cultural institutions and our ability to make free choices and become endeared to our leaders because they align with the cultural moment.

What about those leaders who come out and denigrate others? First, understand how you are, as an individual inside the collective, sporting that same behavior. If you feel self-righteous that you don't, this is the energy of seeing the splinter in someone else's eye while ignoring the log in yours. Maybe dig a little deeper because the collective consciousness is real. Cultural awareness is about waking up to our own energies of misconception. The culture consists of many sub-sets as we all integrate ourselves in many ways through work, clubs, sports, political alliances, and so forth. Our desire to denigrate comes from deep within and is a collective behavior pattern. To break free from that pattern, we all need to start with ourselves by undoing our own behaviors. We can form a collective that supports by working on ourselves first.

We can't change others or the collective all in one go — it just doesn't work that way. We can affect the greatest change by becoming who *we* desire through action. We have to work within ourselves to create the action that causes the equal and opposite reaction to occur. Is it forgiveness that you require most? Or maybe you need to work on your relationship with yourself. Perhaps it's about healing past wounds that have kept you locked to another person. All these things are ways we can be more aware of behavior patterns that push and pull us without realizing it.

How can we become better leaders if we don't first sit with ourselves and understand who we are as individuals? We need to know, feel, and believe it. It helps to sit in contemplation to understand your individual leadership qualities. You don't have to take a class, but if you do, be sure to bring up your own ideas of what it means to be a leader, not someone else's. The material covered in that class is likely organized around one way of leading, so understanding yourself takes precedence. We can gather different ideas from others, but they have to go through our interest meter first and then our truth meter. If it doesn't interest you or keep you occupied, then it's not worth the effort because it won't align with your truth. The opposite is also true.

Creating Lasting Change

We work in concert with each other to bring about change. We tout this to young kids and tell people they need to learn how to work on teams, yet there is a disconnect between what we say and what we do. If we want to truly cooperate, we need to believe that the collective can span all racial and ethnic minorities, all abilities and understanding of truth, all belief systems that are not about denigrating others, and all ways of living and being in the world. A true leader understands all this and becomes endeared to others by being on their side through justice, being able to find the truth of the matter (and there can be more than one), being able to see all sides at their optimal angles, and following the path of least resistance to change and transformation — for the collective and the people making up the collective.

So, to get back to change agents — we must be the cause, not the effect, of the change that is happening across the globe. If we find time to sit with that, what does it look like? Of course it is individual, but individuals live inside a collective, and the collective has the most influence because "of the many, one" — e pluribus unum. Ones make up the collective and the collective works as one, in unison, in universal love and consciousness. It all goes back to the one of time, but the one is also many. One memory out of many makes up a lifetime. One entry point that creates a change of windfall or cascading effect. One drop in a bucket overflows the entire thing. All of these idioms serve the collective existence inside the one universe that is made up of individual ones. And we live in multiple collectives — families, teams, leaders, clubs, neighborhoods, cities, countries, etc. We are all individuals who make up multiple collectives, and there is an overlap in many of them.

Forgiveness and Gratitude as a Leader
Understanding the individual through leadership

I know it's odd to include forgiveness in a leadership section. It's not about feeling sorry or making others feel sorry. It's really about finding your leadership mojo from a wholistic perspective, which includes monetary release because it stems from the heart, which creates an opening which allows energy to flow, just like money. As individuals, we need to make money to clothe, shelter, and feed ourselves and/or our families. Needs and forgiveness go hand-in-hand because it takes empathy and gratitude to align our needs with others. Forgiveness brings about change and transformation within you, which extends to others who join your firm or organization. Forgiveness and gratitude allow you to be in your heart center energy, giving you a lot of 'credit.' In a previous section, we looked at how money is an energy that flows from our heart centers. It is what astrologers term Venus energy because it represents both creativity and money. If our finances are not right, the easiest way to correct it is to clear the heart center. It takes time and forgiveness to move out blocks from our hearts, but it will eventually cause a flow of money to you and through you.

How do you forgive yourself and others from this perspective? We know there are many ways we feel about ourselves and each other as we start life, become used to the world as kids, and then as adults. In all that time we experience pain and sorrow (as well as joy and light) on planet Earth. It's a fact of life because we are all many layered people. To forgive ourselves and others means to forgive the very fact of existence. It's better understood through the framework of the family unit.

Sibling rivalry, family dynamics, hurt feelings by being pregnant or having the 'wrong type' of kid or husband or whatever — we all go through some version of this in our childhood. We start life this way and it carries with us throughout the decades of our lives, eventually landing in the office or workspace of our choosing. It's a lot and can be overwhelming, but if you start by forgiving yourself and others, you will begin to make a significant change. As I have said before, it's not for the faint of heart. Try standing in front of a mirror and saying, "I forgive you" a few hundred or a thousand times — all the times you felt betrayed, neglected, or transfused by someone else's feelings, misgivings, or outright anger. It can emotionally wear you out. That is why stepping out of the story is so effective. Moving through the energies of change without the additional baggage of story is what we need to let go of. All the resentment, anger, or fear can destroy all possibilities of love and encouragement that we are meant to show each other, but find that we are lacking or simply can't because it's too difficult on our own terms.

As a leader, you must forgive yourself first and do it now as you read this page. It doesn't take long and it won't hurt. Sit and forgive all your transgressions in life, whatever they may be, and tell yourself you will do better, *not* next time, but starting **right now**. Right in this moment you have the ability to do something within your power to enact change. Understanding your energy is the first step in being a leader who gets 'maximum results,' to use the term from resumes and other business jargon. But the results are within you and will also show up outside of you. Watch as people change and transform around you with effortless ease. You won't have to pull them aside and ask them to do it, they'll just do it by being around you. Your internal vibration will align more with who you are as an individual, allowing others to feel like they can be the same way around you. It will be transformative.

The proof is in the pudding, but if you want it, try it on for size for 2-6 weeks and treat it like a science experiment. Take the time to understand what you're working on within yourself and then see how the results are mirrored back to you through your dreams (dream journals are important here), how people act and react around you, and even what they say directly to you. You might hear words like 'glowing' and 'peaceful' and "much more like yourself" after a while. If you don't, find the results within you to be its own reward.

As we move into this new Age of Aquarius and enlightenment of ourselves, our sovereignty and authority, let's redefine the leadership styles of yesterday into new, supportive styles that allow our individuality to shine through and let others do the same. Here is a re-write of the Unsupportive Leadership Styles into a new possibility of how we lead others through business and the organizations we are a part of as an individual in many collectives.

Top 10 Supportive Styles for Tomorrow's Leaders
1. **Commander Head Wind**: Authoritative in your own right
2. **Prof. Tail-wind:** Free-loving and freedom-loving. What is pushing you forward?
3. **Ambassador Abraxas:** Allowing others to change and transform in their own way
4. **Manifest Destiny:** Uses tools of the trade, not people, to reach the destination.
5. **Chairperson Slo-Mo:** Time is not a crunch to be managed. No more deadlines.
6. **Director Flower Power:** Optimism takes control.
7. **Air-Fairy Godmother:** No more blowhards! Cool down and calm down.
8. **Zen Master Cooperation:** Competitive natures lead to rivals, not allies.
9. **Footloose & Fancy Free:** It will all get done. No worry, no muss, no fuss.
10. **Admiral Goldstar**: People want to be seen and heard. Do that and you will succeed beyond your expectations.

Part 2: Flow and Timefields

Chapter 8: Revisiting Flow

So far, we've discussed creativity from a research and down-to-earth perspective in the form of play and idleness. You have reviewed your own creative life and endeavor and, hopefully, have a deeper understanding of your own creative process — as an individual and on a team in a workplace setting. We've also reviewed why workplaces can be a joy-kill for a person's creativity, contributing to the overall health of an organization's creative life. But all that is just the tip of the iceberg, as they say. We will now dive deeper into understanding ourselves through the descriptive concepts of Flow and Timefields.

Starting with definitions, we can use this terminology for awareness and healing, affecting significant change and transformation in our hearts, minds, bodies, and lives. If you are a healer, this part's for you specifically, so if you've skipped ahead (as I would!), it's good to take in just a little bit of Flow Theory because it builds a foundation for the healing parts below. Of course, the term Flow is in our collective lexicon now, so a progressive understanding may not be necessary for some, but it is the backbone of the balance of the book. Timefields are my description of emotional overwhelm and are the opposite of Flow. When our belief systems are up for release, we have deep resistance to change, which can come in the form of a Timefield. This is a new level of healing that cuts through the story and the time it takes to relieve suffering.

From here on out, the ride may get a little bumpy. It's time to strap on your seat belt and open your heart and mind to understanding different ideas. I hope you will come away with a better understanding of your emotional life, which, of course, informs your creative life. With that said, enjoy the ride!

Finding Your Flow
A new model to understand & release resistance to change

Finding your Flow is an essential part of creativity as it gives us the Big C moments that excite the creator in us and spur us on to more creative work. Flow allows us to understand ourselves through the process of creativity. It keeps us in sync with our inner processes and gives us the spark of life, essential to happiness and good health. This is a common feeling because we have all had these moments, but consider the image of a stream flowing quickly along its bed. The water moves effortlessly around rocks, over logs, under branches bending into the water, and so on. It moves freely even if it is not moving in a straight line. This is a typical idea of Flow, and as we have discussed, it's also the underlying idea of our currency, so-called because it is supposed to flow in a current-like motion to and through people supporting their Divine Life Force energy and energetic systems. (If you have skipped ahead and want to know more, review currency under Creativity in the Workplace.)

Flow is the backbone of more than just water systems. Flow is found in the air and through our energetic currents around the Earth. Flow is everything that relates to time because time also flows in a current. From the beginning of something to the end, there is a flow that keeps things moving across the planet. We see flow in the sale of goods and merchandise around the world; we see flow in all the systems that connect us to Mother Nature and the planetary system we call the Universe. Flow is universal. In his book, *The Seven Spiritual Laws of Success*, Deepak Chopra states that the word universe means 'one song.' I love the harmonic quality of that statement because it means we are all supposed to be flowing together in one verse, or one song. Harmony is the stuff that keeps us in Flow, just as love is the stuff that binds us together. It all works — or is supposed to work — according to the natural laws of the Universe.

The Descriptive Model of Flow Theory
Understanding our creative path

Now we come to the scientifically developed description of Flow Theory, developed by the 'father of positive psychology,' Mihaly Csikszentmihaly. His work is well known and you can connect to it through his TED talk online. His original and most popular book, *Flow: The Psychology of Experience*, published in 1990, explains that Flow is a moment in time when we are happy and at our most creative. The task we experience in that moment is neither too easy nor too difficult and we feel neither too bored nor too frustrated. We connect with what we are doing so deeply we suddenly realize that time has slipped away while concentrating on one task. Time seems to speed up because we were in a current — or flow — of happiness and creativity.

Since his original and subsequent books on creativity and Flow, Mihaly's ideas have become part of popular culture and are used in athletics, business, video games and gaming theory, creative endeavor, and even everyday life experiences. There are 8 characteristics of Flow that almost all people can relate to experiencing and are a universal set of parameters. You know you are in Flow when you experience:

1. Complete concentration on the task;
2. Clarity of goals and reward in mind and immediate feedback;
3. Transformation of time (speeding up);
4. A sense of it being intrinsically rewarding;
5. Effortlessness and ease;
6. Balance between challenge and skills;
7. Merged actions and awareness, no self-conscious rumination;
8. A feeling of control over the task.

Energetically, Flow is when our minds and bodies are perfectly aligned. Our thoughts and felt experience sync up to keep our energy literally flowing through our energetic systems. In this positive state, many people feel a divine connection or a connection to universal energy. We naturally flow from our heart centers and when they move freely, we feel open and expansive.

Four Levels of Flow
New descriptions for how we move through creativity

As creatives, we can experience different levels of Flow states. There are most likely many, but the most common are negative flow or Timefield (see the next chapter), neutral flow, rapid flow, flood, and collective flow. We experience each type differently through our nervous systems, but each has common elements.

Neutral Flow is when we live our lives from our heart centers. Things and events just seem to work out; synchronicities appear out of nowhere and seem to happen for a reason when your life is in Flow. Taoist thought calls this type of Flow *wu-wei* or effortless effort. When you are in neutral flow, everything works out and is in your favor and you don't have to do anything out of the ordinary. Though I call it 'neutral flow,' it does take effort to let go of limiting beliefs at times to maintain this state.

Rapid Flow is the intense Flow state correlated with creativity and can be a misnomer. It implies that you must always maintain that level during your creative process or you're not in Flow — not true and difficult to maintain. This assumption causes you to be under pressure the entire time you are creating and can have a negative impact. The thought, "Things aren't flowing/working for me!" can cause frustration, pulling your energy down. The Flow state is an up-and-down state within a range. Something can click into place and for the next 2 hours, you feverishly put it down on paper, but when it subsides, you slow down, allowing for review of your work. This is a point in time where you are still in Flow, but the rush has calmed down to a slower rapid. You can relate it to going whitewater rafting. Sometimes the river flows evenly and consistently, while other times it rushes, and you have to hold on tight! Thank goodness it's not rushing the entire time! You need space, air, and time to breathe, rest, and collect yourself before the next rush. Also note that some people never experience the rush of creative energy in their Flow state. Many people use a step-by-step approach to move them from one creative goal or decision to the next. I consider this a flow state, too, because you still make creative connections, learn new things, and work with your subconscious and conscious mind in a synchronistic way. (Refer to the 4C creativity model at the beginning of this book.)

Flood Flow is a state where your creative endeavor pulls you under, not allowing you to rest and replenish. In this state, your creative endeavor takes on an intensity that borders on insanity at times. There was a 1990s movie called *Shine,* with Geoffrey Rush playing a true-to-life pianist who generated music at this level of Flow. Everything else took a back seat to his music and relationships were imprisoned because of it. As the name implies, a flood is a rush, but it can easily overcome everything else, so it's good to maintain a life raft if you experience this often. Flood Flow impacts other people, and overcoming its intensity is hard. Find time to sit with your thoughts in nature or allow yourself to take a break with family and friends. Don't worry, you won't miss anything. Our brains are still creating even when we are at rest. (Skip backward to the section on Play and Idleness for more information.)

Collective Flow allows for communal or synchronistic energy between people, keeping the creativity flowing and the endeavor moving forward as people learn each other's strategies and willingness to change or take risks. This type of flow can occur when we are at our empathic best, and extends an individual's heart center energy across time and space. We see this in sports like basketball or soccer when teammates smoothly work together to score points. Time flows in and out of the collective as participants lose track of it, just like individual flow. They look to each other for support when the going gets tough, but they don't let the energy slide, or they lose the rhythm of finding each other's flow. It looks like magic and it feels like it sometimes, too! This also compares to imaginative play where each person takes their turn to lead as the game bends and morphs in time. We don't always have to lead and we don't always follow, but we are in a collective in the moment and want the collective to succeed on our terms. That's obviously scoring points for the players, but it can be many things. We can also imagine ourselves performing at this level of Flow easily, which is why visualizations are so prominent in the coaching field of sports. Collective flow is about the group, but it's also about the individuals that make up the collective. If you can be in flow with the people around you, it's a wild ride. You feel good about who you are as an individual as part of the whole. It's the master switch of being in the moment within yourself while communing with others.

Healing in Collective Flow

If you're are a healer, your creativity may flow in a more enigmatic way, moving you in a topsy-turvy direction. Your heart center may feel open to the person you're healing, or your broadcast may be pitch-perfect until you suddenly find yourself under water, unable to breathe. This is psychic overwhelm and all of us come by it naturally when we are in a flow state. Healing is a positive flow state because it wraps around the individuals and brings them in through relating and forgiveness, or feeling the good vibes. But the vibes can be overwhelming and bring us to a new level we're not comfortable with or are not aligned with. You're not cursed or haunted, though it can feel that way. It relates to how you are connecting to the wider universe and other energies outside your domain of influence. Your unconscious or subconscious may find it scary and intuitively guide you to, "Don't go there, there are strange things afoot!" Psychic overwhelm might be a new topic for you, but if you're working on your creativity, it's useful to understand how other people experience creative flow. A perspective switch can cause change and transformation, by comparing it to your own creative flow. (Skip forward to Tesseracts and the Nature of Reality for healing on this topic.)

By and large, Flow is a positive state of living and creating. But, what happens when we are in the opposite of Flow? Where do we live in our minds, hearts, and bodies when we're trying to be creative but just can't seem to pull it together? When our heart centers are blocked, we feel closed in. What blocks your heart, blocks your mind. Fear, grief, anger, strife, and shame are all emotions that block our heart centers and keep us from realizing how we feel in the moment. If something happened yesterday that made me angry or ashamed, my mind might play it over repeatedly, or push it away without realizing it because it's too hard to deal with, causing a block. Today, I can't focus on my work or the fun interactions I could have with my friends because my heart center is blocked. The hours may turn into days, days into weeks, months, and sometimes years. What is going on in our inner world that is impacting our outer world?

Creativity for Soul Healing

Chapter 9: Timefields

I present my theory, description, and healing method for the emotional state we find ourselves in when we can't seem to catch a break or are lost looking for our Flow.

Some people plod along as they create, others rush forward, while still others run around in circles for a bit until they can get their bearings. But what happens when you stop altogether? What happens when the neutral Flow state slows down so much, your raft gets grounded on the dry riverbank of self-doubt? Timefields are my description of emotional overwhelm that exists over a longer period of time in our minds, hearts, and bodies. If Flow allows emotions to move freely through your systems, a Timefield stops the flow of emotional energy, creating stagnation. The stagnant energy of a Timefield slows down time, keeping us from noticing the moment we are in. By first describing the energy of a Timefield and understanding how emotional overwhelm sits in our minds, hearts, bodies, and energy fields, we can affect a higher level of healing and change. If you don't already have healing protocols, start with the methods I've outlined in the next chapter. Timefield energy clearing is a powerful method to step through and release the emotional overwhelm of the past so we can start living today for a brighter future.

Notes on Healing Trauma

While Timefields describe emotional overwhelm, many of us have experienced such extreme emotional unrest that we find ourselves disassociating from our bodies. In such times, we find our hips out of place, like we can't find our footing, or are walking through a fog. Our energies can be so intense that we start to shake, we don't know where we are in time, and we find our voice only through intense anger or rage or sometimes sorrow in extreme grief. This is PTSD, post-traumatic stress disorder, as cited in many manuals for people who have been through war or combat.[1] But you don't have to experience military combat to experience this extreme overwhelm. You can also experience it through the trauma of losing a life, such as family and close friends, or any relating scenario that causes you to feel unrelated to, such as abuse. This is also a fear response that many women experience who find themselves in relationships that separate their core nature from their bodies because they serve only the relationship. Their lives have become surreal as they step back and wonder who they are or where they've gone. They feel upended by the denigration of their spouse cheating on them, lying, or pretending to be someone they're not.

If you've lived through this, you are not alone. First know that you are a functioning adult and have the ability to make changes even while you feel unwelcome in your body. Second, find the time to sit with yourself and allow your feelings to flow through you. If you have kids, you can still do it; it doesn't take long — maybe while you're in the shower or even behind the closed door of a privacy panel at work. In these moments, release your fear by taking a deep breath and saying "I am me" 10 to 20 times. That is your first step — that's it, nothing more. Once you are able, find help in healing yourself through a trained therapist who has the ability to work with PTSD survivors. If they don't

---

[1] Dinesh Mittal, et al, *Stigma associated with PTSD: Perceptions of treatment seeking combat veterans*, 2013

believe you have PTSD, require that they test you before deciding. You don't have to believe them if they still disagree; you know who you are and how you feel in your body. If you feel like you are seeing a shadow version of yourself, find someone who believes you. You can also do the work on your own, but it requires a systems approach.

Ecotones: A Descriptive Model of Overwhelm
Understanding emotionally stuck Flow

Imagine walking through a grassy field near a pond. You come to a part of the terrain that dips and the next step you take is marshy — just as much water as dirt and grass. That squish you weren't expecting is like a Timefield. It sneaks up on you and suddenly, you're in a completely different environment. The water isn't moving, maybe it isn't even noticeable until you take a step and soak your shoe. You now feel like you have to be careful and you start to move slower, or maybe you move backward to find drier ground.

As Flow brings up the image of a freely flowing current, I imagine a Timefield as an **ecotone.** Ecotones are naturally occurring areas on the Earth that are transition points between one type of ecosystem to another. They're not quite solid ground, not quite water; they exist in an in-between state. Often found at the edges of bodies of water, these environmentally precious areas transition from water to land, where the water stagnates from silt and attracts specific plants, insects, and animals. Stagnant water is good for an ecotone, but stagnant energy is not helpful for our creative lives. They cause us to feel trapped in our inability to effect change and we may wander around aimlessly, looking for dry land or a lifeboat, depending on your metaphor of choice. We can't escape the dry spell of self-doubt or feel swallowed up by a whale. I'm mixing metaphors purposely to show how we can linger in this in-between state for far too long, not knowing if we're wet or dry, in a desert or underwater. It all runs together and feels like we're being dragged under by any number of feelings of unrest or even dis-ease. We can go on and on about all the ways people feel creatively blocked by shame, sorrow, denigration, and general feelings of malaise, but to put a finer point on it will only make the sorrow deepen, so let's move away from the story and talk about the Timefield itself.

I distinguish between a 'simple' creative block and a Timefield. The original energetic event that caused the emotional upset is not the Timefield itself. As the name suggests, time is the main ingredient that creates stagnation. Some people call it stewing, others call it ruminating. We just can't get over the emotional hurt, and pain pools instead of flowing out. What happens in a Timefield? The stories we tell ourselves when feeling insecure, ashamed, and afraid. Our internal stories exist in the tension between our expectations and what actually happens. This often occurs in our unconscious minds, but can also be conscious or subconscious thoughts. Moving back into Flow from a Timefield is a process of letting go of limiting beliefs and systems and being consciously aware of when you're in story.

Our emotions, which are a form of energy in our bodies, move freely when we are in flow. It's not that they aren't there, it's just that they aren't stuck — they move. Think of how you feel when you are in Flow — perhaps elated, bouncy, or in-the-moment, which is exactly what mindfulness is about. A Flow state can become a Timefield if too much emotion enters into it. For example, thinking is a common Flow state when creating. But over-thinking makes it a Timefield when worry and rumination take over — the classic tossing and turning at night when you're trying to sleep and the clock seems to be moving slower.

Now that you know what a Timefield is and how it functions, let's review other emotional behaviors that begin to shift our understanding away from our open heart centers and into a pattern of disbelief in ourselves and others through denigration. One builds on top of another and can cause grief, anger, and fear to persist in our lives and through many lifetimes. Any building begins with structure, so we'll begin with the construction of walls.

Heartwalls, Moats and Fortresses
Creating and maintaining emotional wounds

In his book, *The Emotion Code,* Bradley Nelson describes a wounded state called a heartwall. Heartwalls are the energetic response to a wound or wounded behavior that we construct to keep ourselves from feeling the pain and anguish of the past. Envisioned by Jean Bradley, his wife, an energetic heartwall acts exactly as you might think — it walls off our hearts from both the bad and good. Heartwalls don't discriminate because a wall is a wall no matter how you look at it. Let's take that analogy a step further and move into the idiom "a fortress around your heart." The British musician, Sting, was the one to sing about this type of emotional walling off. His regret of the past sings through the energies of the present in search of understanding and acceptance. But he's unsure how to navigate the behaviors he has already laid down, "*Had to stop my tracks for fear of walking on the mines I laid.*" Of course we avoid our wounds! It's a completely normal human behavior not to walk into hurt and sorrow. Our heartwalls can become fortresses keeping us supposedly safe within, but they also stop us from experiencing what lies beyond, or worse, keep us trapped inside.

If I live in a fortress or castle of my own making, most likely there's a moat right outside. Moats are human-made devices that add another layer of protection. Like ecotones, they are stagnant forms of water that exist on land. There is no current, no movement, just a deep pit filled with water and other things like plant life, piranhas that eat your flesh, mythical creatures like dragons, or an Excalibur sword stuck in a stone — something else that's stuck, great. The stuck energies of a moat foster these creatures of the deep but keep them trapped, too. They probably long for an open ocean or flowing river, but they're trapped in this containment piece, most likely filled with non-beneficial bacteria that eat up all the oxygen. You get the picture. How do you get over a moat? A drawbridge, of course, another human-made device that spans the moat from wall to dry land. Sure, a trebuchet could launch you over the wall, but there's no guarantee you'll survive the impact. Walking across the bridge is your best bet.

The drawbridge represents your belief systems that move you away from denigration. The moat is a Timefield of your own making through emotional overwhelm and lives right outside your heart wall of wound. At every point of this process, the touch points are human-made. We are the cause and effect of our own doing or undoing, not energies outside ourselves. (Skip forward to find out about collective Timefields in the land.) Even the mythical creatures are there because humans put them there. They'll come after us if we fall in the moat, for sure, but they don't want to be there in the first place. Moving out of the fortress, across the drawbridge, and over the Timefield-moat easily and quickly without falling into the waters of despair below requires energy healing. Energy healing is a device that acts as a current to move the stagnant waters of pain and suffering avoidance. Cutting across the field of anguish can be easy and uplifting if you can sit with the pain for a few moments and then release it. In the past, energy healing has been about releasing the layers individually, but through Timefield and wound release, you can do it quickly and easily.

A Timefield can be found through tools we use in creative endeavor. We are bound up with each other in Timefields of regret and sorrow through denigration patterning, as Sting sings about eloquently. Knowing how those patterns behave in our minds, hearts, and bodies is worth a deeper understanding because when we suddenly hit solid ground, we may not know how we got there. Knowledge truly is power in this case because you gain an awareness about your own behaviors. When you are aware, you can affect change, which sets you up to become more sovereign, independent, and free. Instead of singing about fortresses, you'll sing, *"All the walls are crumbling down, I think my eyes are finally open,"* as Kelsey Wilson of the band Wild Child does so soulfully.

Solid vs. Void
Wounds, wounded behaviors and Timefields

There are two tools often used in art and design for composition and idea generation:

1. positive versus negative space
2. solid versus void

Both rely on space and form to create a comprehension of how a piece of art or building goes together. This tool is also used in music composition with notes and rests forming the rhythm of behavior for each instrument. Positive-negative and solid-void allow for a tambour of feeling for the viewer, listener, or person experiencing a space. The voids, negative space, and rests are important parts of the composed piece because they set up an expectation and release the eye or ear from the constant movement of vibration or frequency. In architecture, solid shape, or form, is often contrasted by a void — a colonnade, windows in a facade, or even the location of furniture, create a rhythm in time and space. We can usually see through voids or walk through them in the case of space. Sometimes it can be deceiving what a void is, such as a glass storefront next to a brick wall. We can see the brick without issue, but the glass can be so clear, we don't see it and can walk right into it.

Another way to approach this concept of positive/solid and negative/void is through the level of information. Positive space is where the information is, so the eye is drawn to it. Negative space is void of information and allows for 'breathability,' a place for the eye to rest before it moves on to the next piece of information or form, which is a type of consciousness. We use idioms in our language such as being on 'solid ground,' or having a 'solid understanding,' to explain the visceral feeling of being in consciousness that is well and whole. Emotionally, solid form is the energy in your mind that you fully understand and does not cause a wound — also known as your truth. These are energies of love, joy, acceptance, and acceptance of others, allowing people to live their lives as they desire while supporting them to find their own path. These are ways of living and being in the world that don't cause wounds, and we all experience them in some form or another, or we would not be here. We create our existence through the "I Am" act. I am love, therefore I am here. I am here, therefore I am. It's all very esoteric, but can be fully understood if you review those statements through your own life. When and where were you fully accepted, regardless of the type of love? When and where did you fully accept yourself? Many of us are still working on that version of love, which is often a lifetime's work.

Negative space or void energetically is a gap in learning and understanding — no information available. An emotional void is neither negative nor positive, it is no-thing because there is nothing there. A gap in understanding our emotional state often occurs from an unacknowledged emotional wound and we can unintentionally walk right into it, like a piece of clear glass. Behaviors formed from a gap in understanding or learning cannot be judged as right or wrong, good or bad. There is not enough information to fully understand the truth of the situation or our own truth. We sit in a pattern of denigration and try to fill the void with more feelings, but they only add to the behavior, causing the gap to grow wider and deeper.

Sitting in the Wound of Non-Understanding

Solids can become void when there is a wound, such as non-understanding, pain, suffering, fear, grief, etc. If our emotional wounds take the shape of both solid and void, where the void is in the center and solid is all around, we get the image of a rip or tear in a piece of fabric. The hole is punctured into the fabric of your being, and the only way to stitch it up is to sit with and release it by understanding and accepting why it happened the way it happened. It's not a comfortable position to be in, for sure. SItting with uncomfortable pain is often why we are wounded in the first place. Is the antidote really to sit with it some more? The musician, Donovan, wrote about stitching up this uncomfortable feeling in a delightfully eerie way in his song *Season of the Witch*.[2] He sings about the strangeness of looking over your shoulder to find yourself for understanding. Once we realize our fears, we can easily move through them. We can maintain anger at someone only when we don't fully understand why their behavior affected us. The other person's wounds are most likely our wounds, too, so relating can be very complicated. The missing ingredient to move past the uncomfortableness is acceptance. Acceptance is where the hard work begins and ends. If you can accept what happened to you or what you don't understand about yourself or others, you are more than halfway to release.

Stagnant Waters
Wound as vortex

To be clear, when it comes to healing emotional wounds and wounded behaviors, we need to leave out the judgment because, on an energetic level, there is no negative or positive, there is only solid versus void. The Timefield represents both solid and void. Solid is the form of things and the place where knowing resides. A void is a gap in learning where no information is available. So the Timefield is at once solid and void, where the solid of knowing surrounds the void of not knowing. For example, you believe you can't achieve your goals or get where you want to go in life, but you see other people who are able to achieve what you want so ask yourself, "How do they do it?" There is a gap in information for you, which causes a wound. There is a tear in your fabric of belief systems, and you add to it with feelings of denigration, like unworthiness. This is a stagnant formation, not a dynamic one, and over time, the worry blocks your heart, moving first into a wall, then perhaps a fortress, and finally a Timefield where both form and void exist.

Stagnant energy in the form of emotional overwhelm in the body, emotional body, heart center broadcast, and energy field, forms a wound through a block in the energetic system. The heart center naturally wants to push out into the world, extending from the body in all directions. The block pushes back against the heart center broadcast. The back-and-forth pushing causes a new frequency, forming a center point of the wound. The wound is a void, but all around it is solid. These two opposites begin to dance or circle each other, forming a larger void. Other energies can get caught in this wound, which makes it bigger and more difficult to clean out.

Emotional wounds and wounded behaviors are not like physical wounds. The tear doesn't come from form, instead it is a tear in your mind's or heart's behavior and can feel arbitrary. Many of us are unaware of our wounds, so the wounded behavior is automatic. Thoughts such as, "Why am I like this at this time of year?" and "How can I be

---

[2] Check out Lana Del Rey's version for a funkier vibe.

mean to that person when I don't even know them?" translate into an unseen this common emotional state. But thought and introspection can move you onto the solid ground of knowing and behaving.

We let go of the past to disseminate the solid looping patterns of thought energy. Starting from the center, the void, and moving out is the fastest way to clear an emotional wound or wounded behavior. It helps to sit in contemplation in whatever form suits you. Maybe it's sitting cross-legged on the floor, enjoying a cup of coffee, looking out the window, clearing energy, writing, or listening to music. These are all forms of inner guidance that get us in touch with feelings and sensations that we may not be consciously in tune to. We also work on them while asleep in the dream state, which helps us feel refreshed the next day with a new perspective.

Speaking into the Void
Void and vortex as a healing modality

Vectors are points extended in space and time, like a ray of light. When you extend a vector through the points along its line, it becomes a plane with width and length but no depth, like a platform or drawbridge. But, an extended plane creates a solid form as it extrapolates out through distance and time. We can then create other forms and shapes with this solid shape by either adding to it or removing from it (like a cave), creating a volume of space. In architecture, we call these additive and subtractive forms. The volume within is understood as a void, like a building interior. We fully understand a building through its interior — the best place to be, in my opinion! We might walk around the outside, but we go inside to explore and see what's been cooked up by the architects and designers who designed it.

Ursula Le Guin's translation of the *Tao Te Ching* is a transcendent iteration of this sacred text. She rewrote the poems for modern-day use, bringing in pronouns and verbs more apt to today's understanding of the Universe. Though many of her interpretations of the poems feel spot on, I have my own views of a few brought on by her use of language and insight. Chapter 11 is one of my favorites because it feels like design school and speaks to the void.

<u>The Uses of Not</u>

Thirty spokes
Meet in the hub.
Where the wheel isn't
Is where it is useful.

Hollowed out,
Clay makes a pot.
Where the pot is not
Is where it is useful.

> *Cut doors and windows*
> *To make a room.*
> *Where the room isn't,*
> *There is room for you.*
>
> *So the profit in what is*
> *Is in the use of what isn't.*

Le Guin's comments on this poem note the deadpan humor in tone, but she also notes the "profound and difficult... counterintuitive truths that, when we accept them, suddenly double the size of the universe."[3] Imagine shifting your perspective and doubling the size of your Universe by acknowledging the void, the place where light and magic come through. But it *is* counterintuitive because the void is also the place where there is a wound, so we prefer to avoid it. Just as the 13th Century poet, Rumi, says, "The wound is where the light is let in," if we lean into our wounds and bring some solid understanding and information to the void of misunderstanding, we will allow in pure magic and healing. The line in the poem, "Where the room isn't, there's room for you," speaks to me about being welcomed into something that might not feel that way at first glance. Using the negative 'isn't' is a play on positive and negative, solid and void. Our wounds and wounded behaviors welcome us to walk in and discover what's there for healing if we can only step across the threshold. It's like an initiation ceremony that seems scary from the outside, but once you're in, the fear subsides, and you wonder why you were scared to begin with.

Don't Avoid Your Creativity
Types and uses of voids
There are many types of voids:
- void of understanding the truth
- void of pain and suffering
- void-of-course (as the moon) and transition in space and time
- void of space and time like a black hole
- void of the Universe itself
- void during the process of creation

All of these voids contribute to existence on Earth. The void is useful in creating and understanding a new idea that begins as formless, takes no shape at first until the creator finds the medium in which to apply that idea. Is it music, artwork, a science project, or all of the above? What form does it take in materiality? What form *should* it take? Some are better than others for specific applications which is where the conscious mind comes in to suss out the defining attributes. The void is also meant as a restful

---
[3] Ursula Le Guin, *Tao Te Ching*, 1997

place to stop and recharge and take stock of how you feel in your mind, heart, and body. If you don't rest, you will not be able to heal, which coincides with releasing energies. So when you release from the hub of the wound, you are releasing the past machinations that did not allow you to fully stop, take charge of your life, and release the patterning that got you to this point in time.

Astrological Voids for Healing

Astrology has another perspective for guidance on this topic. The phrase 'void-of-course' is typically used for the pattern the moon makes when switching zodiac signs. I use the term 'pattern' because the amount of time it takes the moon to go from one sign to another varies. We know that the moon is full every twenty-eight days or so, but the patterns it makes in between form a void in terms of our behaviors. Astrologers look to the signs and their symbology for guidance on what behavior patterns we might want to examine during a void-of-course moon period to make beneficial changes.

Astrology also speaks to the void through the Pisces archetype. You may be familiar with the Pisces symbol of two swimming fish (what else would they be doing?) in a formless body of water, or void. This is the void of existence — the period of time that allows all possibilities to take shape. It's a fluid environment, with the fish acting as the fluid motion in time as they move through the void. Existence has not yet arrived in this state, but the possibility of it is there. All that is, where anything and everything is possible, is in the void of existence. As the void releases its formless nature, it turns or transmutes into something new.

To manifest your desires, you have to sit in the void of existence, and this includes healing the wounds of behavior that have kept you down by enacting the same thing over and over again. The patterns of thought start to create a form, causing a function of behavior that —however unconscious — persists in time and space. Other energies co-locate with the emotional wound and fill in the void, making it solid, except in the middle where the original wound happened. Clearing from the void of a wound allows us to enact change through energies that are less dense. We can transmute the energies with more power from those points because they are not solid. Clearing the void energetically is about a change of emotional behavior — it all transmutes into something new.

Try It: Heal Behaviors Through the Moon's Void-of-Course

Look to the skies or your favorite astrologer who teaches through the archetypes of astrology to set up an intention method by using the Void-of-course states of the moon. It doesn't have to be an everyday occurrence, which can be overwhelming. (Don't create Timefields from your healing practice!) But maybe keep an eye on the different void-of-courses and pull out the ones that feel right to you. Sometimes just the knowledge of one is enough and your subconscious can handle the rest — simple and effective

Chapter 10: Energy Healing Techniques

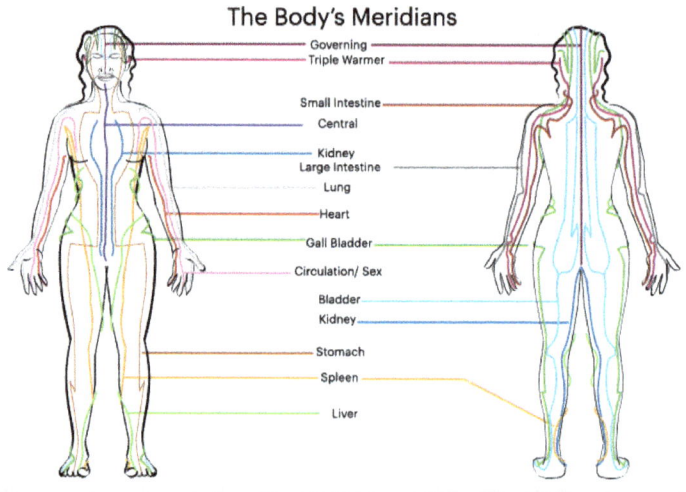

Up until this point, you've been healing through awareness and overcoming your creative blocks through grounded messages to yourself through journaling and visualizations. Creativity and healing are interwoven, as we all know intuitively, as creative human beings. There is another path through energy healing that takes similar concepts and brings in the power of intention. There are many forms of it, and you may be familiar with some, such as Reiki, *Emotion Code,* acupressure, acupuncture, or other modalities that don't interact with the physical body to heal and release energetic blocks. Practiced energy healers may want to skip to the practical step-by-step methods I've included in this section. If you're not an energy healer, try my methods anyway if you're into it. You never know, you may find you like it or have an aptitude for it and continue on. As always, take what works for you and leave the rest behind.

I developed all the healing protocols in this section to heal from PTSD and regain the grounded nature of who I am as an individual. I have used them on others to great success, and now I am sharing them with you in the hope that you will use these methods for yourself and others for awareness and healing. Please take the time to know all the parts of the methods required to understand what is trapped and where it might affect you emotionally and physically.

Does This Stuff Really Work?
Understanding energy healing through science

How do we know energy healing actually works? Many different responses take place in our bodies. The most immediate response is automatic through our sympathetic nervous system by yawning, sighing, burping, sneezing, coughing, stretching, chills, etc. You may feel shaky, lethargic, dizzy, or generally calmer. After a while, your nervous system calms down a bit, but then other things may also occur. You may have strange and/or vivid dreams that night. You may feel an energy surge or the opposite. All of these responses are our nervous systems readjusting to being in an un-blocked state of being. It's not magic or mystical, but it can feel that way, and that's okay, too! We all enjoy a little magic in our lives, and what we believe shows up for us sometimes in weird and wonderful ways. It's the beauty and joy of being in a body on Earth. If you don't feel something immediately, that's a normal response, too.

A note for women who are healing past life wounds and deeply regressive energies: you may experience irregularities in your period, even if you are on birth control, either as a pill or an implant. Don't worry, it is not a nightmare coming to life. It is just your body releasing energy in the best way it knows how. It may also cause you to feel some cramping as if the phrase "you're cramping my style" is being released from your body. Think about that and then all the ways women are cramped in their lives. It takes one to know one in these lessons, so believe me when I say it is actually a healing process through your body's care package. We will say no more about that.

A Two-Way Exchange

What is the energy exchange that happens when an energy healer works on you? Some people may think it's a bunch of hooey, others may be afraid of what will happen. The more we can understand something from a grounded perspective, the more it makes sense. 'Making sense' is the operative phrase because we experience the world around us through our senses. Energy healing is not like walking through the scanners at the airport, which can generate off the chart fear. Energy healing is an exchange of information between participants. If it aligns with how we feel, our minds can work through any blocks. Once our hearts join in, we are completely aligned and open to new possibilities.

The Vietnamese poet, author, Zen Master, and peacemaker, Thich Nhat Hanh, wrote, "Mediation is the art of using one kind of energy to transform another."[1] This simple and elegant phrase struck me as a way to describe all energy healing. It's both a belief and a scientific description. As I connect to you through your energy field, you connect to mine. It's all done through our willingness to change and through the power of our minds. We live in a creative Universe, so our thoughts create through intention. I

---
[1] Thich Nhat Hanh, *Teachings on Love*, 1997

and other healers have found that when we heal someone else, we also heal ourselves through awareness and intention. It works both ways. It's a cooperative, creative act between the people participating. The healer finds what needs to be healed, and the person being healed brings up the initial wound. Like attracts like in order to be let go.

Science: Faraday's Field and Maxwell's Switch
How healers heal through collective Flow

But what are the actual mechanics behind energy healing? It can't all be this mystical, esoteric stuff because we live on Earth! So, let's turn to science to understand the function of energy itself. The well-known English scientist, Michael Faraday, and Scottish mathematician, James Clerk Maxwell, are responsible for our understanding of the electromagnetic field. Maxwell studied the electromagnetic field in the mid-1800s and was able to make new connections (pun intended) from other scientists' work, such as Faraday, Ampere, and Coloumb.[2] Faraday was Maxwell's direct predecessor and intuited that everything on Earth has 'lines' of energy that extend out into some kind of field. He envisioned this field as something that connects all of us to everything. Because we are all connected in this way, thought Faraday, then change and transformation between two objects can occur even if they are not in direct contact. This is the All That Is energy that is held in our bodies and outside of us, as mentioned in other sections.

Maxwell is known for four laws that change the understanding from a simple field to a moving field. As a scientist and mathematician, Maxwell's laws are typically described through the language of math in equation form, but they can also be understood through the power of words. Here they are in written form:

1. Description of static electric fields
2. Description of static magnetic fields
3. Over time, a changing magnetic field produces an electric field
4. Over time, a changing electric field produces a magnetic field

The combination of laws 3 and 4 describe electromagnetic waves with light as the most understood through our sensing abilities. Known as an electromagnetic transfer, his four laws connect electromagnetism to energy healing. Electromagnetic transfer is the process of transferring energy through electromagnetic waves, which are made up of oscillating electric and magnetic fields. Electromagnetic transfer is also the backbone of our modern society, including cell phones, the internet, and other forms of electronic communication that are distantly connected. Though Maxwell's work was not viewed as revolutionary at the time, Einstein's famous theory of relativity has its foundation in his work. We'll comb through Einstein's theories later in the book through his spectacular mind as well as his spectacular hair!

---

[2] Nancy Forbes & Basil Mahon, *Faraday, Maxwell and the Electromagnetic Field*, 2014

Displacement Currents

Maxwell's instruction on displacement interests me the most as an energy healer because a displacement has to occur in the electromagnetic field to create change. He focused on the mechanics of electricity in his thesis, but we can align it with energy healing easily as they both include energy and movement across space and time. He stated, "When a current is switched on in one circuit, it induces a pulse of current in a nearby but separate circuit by creating a changing magnetic field that links the two."[3] Maxwell also concluded that Faraday's connective field acts as an insulator, which can be anything, including space itself, or a void. To push through the insulator and effect change, an electrical charge is required to open the switch. This is how energy healers can connect and provide guidance across space and time. They use the electromagnetic field to affect change by opening the switch with their intentions. The process by which they heal is through their god-Source connection to the Earth through the electromagnetic field, which we are all part of. The mystical part of it is that we are all connected to begin with, not the act of healing, because we all do this innately in our own way. We can all feel connected to our own levels of love through our own god-Source connection. But I admit that some of us are more connected than others, and this is what energy healing is for!

By opening the switch, we break through currents in time and space. We can do this in any number of ways, working with an energy healer doesn't have to be the only one. We can switch on a new current by changing the type and style of food we eat, through standing in our own power by making different life choices, through our postural power of love, and our postural power of movement — all of which are discussed further in later chapters. In fact, engagement in energy healing takes *all* of these practices along with the power of our words through affirmations and/or incantations. Often when combining the two, a stronger release of resistance to change happens. This is not a new concept, saying affirmations while looking in the mirror or telling yourself you can do it while exercising are common ways of opening the switch. What is new in this concept is bringing in our ability to effect change through love in all of our awarenesses, not just a narrow band of thought.

The Energy Body
The Onion and the Cake

Like layers of an onion, we are at our cores, heart energy, which extends outward to connect to our energy body. The energy body, or aura, is an electromagnetic field. Like cake with icing, the energy body consists of layers. The outer layer is our energy consciousness, or sun, and looks like a warm glow. I have never seen it, but it is considered our god imprint, as it is the energy that connects us to the Divine. It is also

---

[3] Nancy Forbes & Basil Mahon, *Faraday, Maxwell and the Electromagnetic Field*, 2014

the energy that connects us with every person we come in contact with because it extends out 8-10 — sometimes 15 feet — in all directions.[4] It is the icing on the cake, in other words, because it brings us conscious awareness of other people *and* the Divine. This is Faraday's field in action. Meaning, we are all connected to each other and each other's divine field, which is connected to Divine energy itself. We are all divine and divinely guided. This is how change occurs when you start changing yourself first. Most people can't see your divine energy layer changing (because it is), but they can feel it, and it brings them a sense of warmth. "You are glowing," they will say. "You're a bright light." How can they say this without you actually doing it? Because you *are* in your auric energy field.

The electromagnetic field around our bodies was known by Traditional Chinese Medicine (TCM), experienced by people in tune with these subtle energies, and verified by 20th-century science through Kirilian imaging developed in Russia.[5] These images show a field around our bodies extending out anywhere between six to fifteen feet in all directions. Our body's field is a changing current and can be impacted much like any other electromagnetic field. But for us, the body's subtle energies need a human touch. To effect change in our bodies, we use the energy of thoughts and intention to open the switch. As Einstein theorized, everything in the Universe is energy. Just by having mass, we are energy, but our thoughts, ideas, and emotions are energy, too. If we go back to the Timefield-drawbridge analogy of cutting across the moat of stagnant energy, we now see that it acts as a displacement current to open the fortress of our emotional body (rather than a trebuchet jumping it) and let the trapped thought forms and emotions out onto dry land, rather than landing in the water where they can add to the existing problems.

Energy Healing Techniques
Methods for unmasking your potential as a healer

I have researched and used multiple energy clearing techniques that use the power of intention and divine life force energy. I don't use healing modalities that require a direct connection to the body except for a quick moment of touch in parasympathetic healing (see that section for more). Of all the methods I've tried, I've gravitated toward modalities that offer love and forgiveness on many levels. Forgiving the body of its stuck energies is a powerful healing modality and is discussed below. I disagree with the idea of outside, nefarious energies influencing our behaviors, but we can connect to other energies that activate our wounds or wounded behaviors. Wounded behaviors may show up in seemingly odd ways, like a witch putting a hex on you, but in my experience, it's actually our emotional baggage that causes the state of being disconnected from our bodies and/or minds, most often through fear. Energies outside ourselves are reviewed

---

[4] Beverly Rubik, et al, *Biofield Science and Healing: A history, terminology, and concepts*, 2015
[5] www.qigonginstitute.org

later and can be acted on through forgiveness.

Words Have Power

For the rest of the book, you will be invoking the power of words and language to effect change in your body through different techniques. The statements provided are powerful healing tools and have been transferred from me to you through this book and will act as a switch for you to open up to different healing modalities. There are other ways to effect change through the Faraday Field and Maxwell Switch method. We have already covered some, but here is a list of how I clear my energy.

1. Body Scan (uses numbered supports, see below)
2. Incantations/ Affirmations
3. Postural Body Movement
4. Awareness of my energy through daily relaxation techniques
5. Writing and general awareness of my environment

All of these types of healing and awareness keep the switch open and/or change the current of energy, switching things on and off to heal what needs to be healed and move into a more aligned state of being.

As you move through the healing incantations, you will notice that I use the phrases "Full Source energy" and "True Source energy" interchangeably. Use whichever feels comfortable to you, but for me, saying the word 'full' has power behind it. It relates to full of energy, full of light, full of time, full of love, and so on. When we are full of all of these things, we are standing in our full power, bringing about change differently. If it's a truth statement, that works, too, because we are also full of truth as we stand in our true power. Either way works but, understand how your words have the power to transform in the way they show up for you. If you accidentally say something as a 'Freudian slip' take note and ask your body if that is the correct word or phrase to say (and why).

Fear of Energy Healing

People may be afraid of the words that come up during a healing session. They may have anxiety about what the healer may 'find out' about them, as if the skeletons in their closet will jump out and reveal all in a tattle-tale manner. There's nothing to fear. First, we all have things we want to hide from ourselves or others. I don't think there is a single person on this planet who has something they would rather not hear, see, or show, so we are all in solidarity on this one. Also, no judgment or shame should be built into the healing process. If you feel it, or if it is directed at you, stop immediately. This is the opposite of what energy healing is for. Second, an energy that is hidden and doesn't want to be revealed will show up that way — literally as "hidden." We each have many timelines that we have lived and we don't know how those energies will show up in this lifetime. Remember, what was shameful 10 or 50 years ago may not be shameful today. Don't allow yourself to feel denigrated just because there is something shameful to you, it may not be for someone else. It depends on how we were raised, what our life experiences are, and so on. If we can overcome the fear of what we want to hide, we will find light in our eyes that doesn't distract but twinkles and winks at us in appreciation and camaraderie.

Sublimation Techniques in Energy Healing
Using simple statements for energy relief

The first thing we need to do is understand sublimation as it is a powerful healing mechanism described in psychology and physics as a process of transformation.[6] In psychology, sublimation is a self-distraction method to keep you from acting out your darkest fears or anger in a socially unacceptable way.[7] Instead of getting angry and punching a wall, you may count from 10 backward or imagine yourself on the beach. Psychological sublimation, therefore, is active imagination, which you have already practiced using in the visualizations earlier in this book. Any healing modality has some form of active imagination with it, whether going to the doctor for a pill, or going to a massage therapist, we use sublimation through our belief systems to effect change in healing.

The Effects of Astral Plane Walking

For people who are into or align with astral plane walking, you are likely familiar with this type of protocol, though you may not be fully aware that you are using it. The astral plane, if you don't already know, is referenced as a spiritual place where only the highly creative or highly credentialed people go. For some, they think they access it in their sleep, while others drop into it through meditation. But in fact, their feet are firmly planted on the ground. Astral plane walkers use sublimation in psychological terms to distract themselves from their being-ness on Earth. They feel, in some way, out of control and seek to destroy those energies by extending their consciousness outwards to a different place. But it is not the astral plane they go to; they go deep within their own minds to find healing. In other words, they see their own energy when they think they are walking on the astral plane. The sleep state is the same. We do not walk the astral plane in our sleep. We go to bed to sleep to dream and access inner knowings through our subconscious that don't come up during the day because we are too busy or whatever keeps us from our inner thoughts as directed by our subconscious.

This type of sublimation serves to protect us from ourselves, but do we need to do that? We need to *know* ourselves, which puts us right back in harm's way if you look at it from that perspective. "I don't trust myself" or "I don't feel right" makes us think we are

---

[6] I am aware of sublimation in other healing practices such as tantric yoga, but my approach leans towards the practical.
[7] Kendra Cherry, *Sublimation in Psychology*, 2024

not well mentally. So active imagination can take us to a different level without actually acting out those scenarios — it's all in our heads in other words, which is a healed state of being. When we don't know, they become "known unknowns," as Donald Rumsfeld said during the crisis after 9/11. When we are in a state of unknowingness, we don't know ourselves and it causes a circular entity or thought to form, making us feel swirly or disconnected from ourselves and others.

Thought forms can take the shape of anything that scares or ails us, and in that way, the monsters of our lives become real. If I believe a troll is living under my bed, I can feel it; I feel its energy and feel it to be true. But the truth lies within us, not the other way around. Truth is individual to the person and the collective. Both serve to either scare or protect us. Whatever the case, it is an active imagination gone haywire, or being overly imaginative, as some people say. But that is a misnomer, too, because we are all imaginative; it makes us human and ties into our creativity and creative endeavor. If we weren't imaginative, then we wouldn't be here. We couldn't say, "I am!" and then move into a body, become more than one, and so on.

We are whole unto ourselves on Earth. Our energies exist here because we are in a body, not elsewhere. Yes, there are other existences and other aspects of ourselves in different dimensions, perhaps, or other timelines for sure, but we mainly exist here on this planet in space and time. Some may be disappointed by this view and outright disagree with it, but it makes sense as our spirits are part of our bodies, and our bodies are grounded on the Earth plane, not the other way around. You might feel existence on Earth is boring or not the adventure you were hoping for, but your distraction, or sublimation, from the truth keeps you from knowing who you are as a person. Maybe you don't want to be here, but the irrefutable truth is we are all born into a body. Keep walking the astral plane of your mind if you like, but perhaps you can move that existence into a more formed state within your body and find your truth of existence there.

Sublimation in Physics

The physical process of sublimation is defined in science as: "the conversion between the solid and the gaseous phases of matter, with no intermediate liquid stage.[8] So, physical sublimation is about transformation by leap-frogging over a type of form into something new. For energy healing, it means that though we are in a body that follows all the laws of physics, we are also fully aware of the magical power of manifestation in our bodies, both physical and metaphysical. If we know that ice can turn to vapor without first becoming liquid, then we can do the same in our bodies by first noticing and then setting our minds to the task. It's a powerful statement and can take on the form of a powerful belief system in our minds if we allow it. When emotions

---

[8] Water Science School, *Sublimation and the Water Cycle*, 2019

take on physical form in our bodies as pain, we can use the word 'sublimation' to effect change immediately through energy. It moves the subtle energies away from the source of pain and suffering to effect change in your body. It is **not** meant as a replacement for seeing a doctor of medicine for your physical ailment, so do not excuse yourself from seeing that form of healer. But it can help your healing process by transforming the physical suffering into a different form.

For example, a gut punch can be both a physical and emotional pain, and it often feels the same. Taking on emotions in our bellies is a common way to absorb all the emotional suffering that comes at us. Over time, the physical form of that absorption feels like a gut punch and can become an ailment such as ulcers, leaky gut syndrome, and the like. When our guts are in pain from sorrow or grief, we often feel depleted and can't eat, or when we do, we have a physical reaction to the food, causing us not to absorb the nutrition. Our emotions make it difficult to digest food because we are not digesting our emotions and the thoughts that accompany them. Therefore, the emotion's energetic form becomes solid as a physical ailment.

We can reverse this process through time, introspection, and exercise, which are beneficial ways of recovering. However, sometimes the process is too slow or we want to feel better quickly to affect more beneficial ways of living. I don't think it should take a lifetime to recover because life is meant to be enjoyed, not suffered through. So, let's move the energies out faster for a more believable way of living in our hearts, away from the stagnant energies. We are transforming, not transmuting, so the power of love is already induced through your Source core grounded connection. We were not put here to suffer, so sublimating is aligned with Source energy, or love. To work with the term sublimation in energy healing, first find the location of the pain and describe it to yourself. Then, use the words below and add your own if required. Here are a few common ailment phrases:

<u>Grief and Sadness Statements:</u>
"I sublimate the forces in my head that are causing me to shrink away from life." Or "I sublimate the pieces of time in my mind known as memory that cause me to believe I am not enough." (Time and memory form a solid through manifestation.)

"I sublimate the stuck energies in my heart that feel like a puncture wound." Or " I sublimate the stuck energies in my heart that feel like it's been ripped and torn to pieces." (Or sometimes both!)

"I sublimate the stuck energies in my heart that are causing it to feel broken to pieces (unrequited love)."

"I sublimate the stuck energies in my gut that are causing me to feel like a gut punch has occurred." Or "I sublimate the stuck energies in my gut that feel like a sucker punch."

Now that it is not physical form, it moves out of the body naturally as an energy through your Source core connection to the Earth. After each sublimation statement, move the energy out by invoking the power of transmutation:

"I transmute all sublimated energies back to True Source energy, through the deepest love and highest light."

Anger Statements:
"I sublimate the stuck energy in my lymphatic system that feels like energy poking holes in me." Or "I sublimate the stuck energy in my Source core the feels like a knob twisting in my ribs."

"I transmute all the sublimated energies back to True Source energy, through the deepest love and highest light."

Many people feel they are drowning in their relationships and can't breathe or are otherwise under water. A heavy heart is a heart under water. It is a force to be reckoned with! Clear it immediately because it impacts your ability to breathe, take a deep breath, or otherwise actualize your ability to move out life force energy throughout the body's systems. All the stuck energies move us down. We feel like we are subsumed in an ocean of fear and self-doubt, pushing us out of alignment with our true energies. Now is the time to be lifted up out of this ocean of fear by allowing ourselves to be unstuck from the past fears and denigration patterns that keep us down.

Start right now by trying to unstick yourself from your life's patterns and attachments that are keeping you down, unable to breathe. So, take a deep breath if you can — or any kind of breath will do if you can't — and find the time to sit with these healing statements. If you find yourself instantaneously yawning, sneezing, or coughing after this statement, you did it! But don't feel bad if this doesn't happen for you. Keep going, and you will find it works even if you're not feeling the immediate effects. Time and pressure heal all wounds. You will find that the pressure of being under water forces us up for air despite feeling like we are gasping for air. Your body demands it, otherwise you will drown in sorrow, fear, or anger (or all three).

Relationship Statement:
"I sublimate all stuck energies in my heart that make it feel like it's under water and I transmute all sublimated energy back to Full Source energy through the deepest love and highest light."

The sublimation energy release system is the first line of defense for your body's systems. It creates a shield around your body as you transpose those energy systems from the physical systems. It creates a knock-on effect for your energy system that moves energy out quickly and transforms it into something else. If you know what the emotion is in your body, sublimate it directly. We usually know why our bellies or hearts hurt, but sometimes we don't or it has persisted for so long, we have shoved that memory away. Or maybe the emotional energy has persisted even if you think you remedied the situation.

We can also ask our minds to sublimate all the stuck energies in our bodies that are occurring without our notice. This takes on a freedom in your life so you don't have to know exactly what's happening at all times. It keeps the physical ailment from going too far down the road of disease, which leads to doctors and psychiatrists, which are beneficial, but wouldn't you rather just live?

"I demand my mind to sublimate all stuck energies in my body known and unknown. I transmute those energies back to True Source energy through the deepest love and highest light."

You are not sublimating the physical disease, you are transforming the energy that is causing the disease. The healing occurs when you believe your body to be healed. Prioritize yourself by making changes through both energy healing and life style choices. If you remain in the energy that is causing the dis-ease, like a stressful work situation, then you are not going to see or affect the changes you desire. But, not everyone can leave their job easily, so how can you effect change when you are unable to find a solution?

Your energy starts to change the moment you desire something new. It most likely will not take effect immediately, but you will start to see changes within yourself and those immediately around you. A bigger smile from the checkout person at the store, or a healing energy that makes you feel like everything is going to be all right. These are subtle changes and knowings, but when you start to take notice, all of the little things will add up to one big thing, just like Source energy. Once you start taking notice of the signs and symbols around you and in your body, you will find that the path to change and transformation in your life will just show up for you. Sometimes it requires a leap, but you will know when to do it and it will feel good. Keeping a journal (or spreadsheet) to track the changes in your life will help you along your way. Start by noticing how you feel today in your body and mind and begin to take note of the subtle and not-so-subtle changes within you and in your life. It should be easy and fun, but sometimes those sucker punches come along, and we feel kicked off our path. Give yourself time to sit with it, let it flow through you, and if it feels like the emotion has become stuck, use the sublimation incantation to both acknowledge and transform the energy.

A Systems Approach to Healing
Understanding cortisol release

As we all know, we hold emotions in our bodies. Emotions can be positive and negative, or energies that help us expand, and others that keep us closed up and smaller. Remembering a happy event like a birthday celebration can make us smile, or a humorous event can make us laugh out loud, even though the event is in the past.

Memories of past behaviors related to humiliation or embarrassment can make us cringe all over again. Memories of hurt and pain can bring up shame, guilt, or other emotions that can cause ulcers, upset stomachs, headaches, etc. Instead of expanding, those energies make us contract. Over time, we contract so much they can get stuck in our bodies' systems, causing physical harm. Our minds are powerful; bringing both attention and intention into the body through awareness can effect great change. What we bring our attention to expands, and what we turn away from decreases.

My hypothesis is that through attention and intention, energy healing releases stuck emotions through the limbic system. Emotions are imprinted in our limbic system through the amygdala, which is associated with our memory. The memory is what holds the emotion. The limbic system is connected to the pituitary gland through the hypothalamus. These two important glands are physically connected to each other through a stalk of blood vessels and nerves.[9] They also connect, through hormone release, from the hypothalamus to the pituitary gland. Together, these two glands control all of your body's most important functions, such as blood pressure, heart rate, breathing, growth, metabolism, and reproduction. All of these functions are automatic through the autonomic nervous system. Besides breathing and growing, it also controls body temperature and other glandular secretions such as saliva and the stress hormone cortisol.[10]

Cortisol is released from the hypothalamus into our bloodstream through the autonomic nervous system when we are in a heightened state of being angry or scared. The so-called 'flight or fight' response we feel can send us into a rage that causes our hearts to race and our hands to shake or fear that lights a fire under us to run away to safety. The prolonged stimulation of this system is dangerous to our health in terms of the overwhelm that floods our systems. In many ways, the system is good because it brings attention to what's going on in our minds. But in other ways - in terms of flight or fight — it produces an excess of fear or anger through the hormone release, causing us to sustain the information that our body's natural processes would automatically get rid of. We see this clearly in PTSD survivors who have sustained prolonged exposure to emotional trauma through both the event and the triggers afterward that send them right back to the original event through memory.[11] This is why talk therapy doesn't work for many PTSD survivors; the memory of the event is too strong. An undiagnosed PTSD survivor myself, I know firsthand what it feels like to feel flooded with rage and fear. It causes a disconnection between mind and body, which creates even more fear through loss of control.

The systems in our bodies are designed to keep us safe and functioning at homeostasis, or balance. The balance is constantly monitored and tweaked through our

---

[9] Cleveland Clinic online Health Library, 2024
[10] Ibid
[11] Cleveland Clinic online Health Library, 2024

autonomic nervous system, which sends messages from our exterior and interior environments to the locations in our bodies that can effect change. When things are out of whack or even off-kilter, a message is sent to bring in some more or let go of whatever is required. When cortisol is involved, it usually impacts our weight. Remember, the hypothalamus, as connected to the pituitary gland, is responsible for growth and metabolism. Additionally, the hypothalamus produces an antidiuretic hormone, causing water retention and therefore, more weight gain.

Because the limbic system regulates these functions directly, it indirectly regulates systems such as urinary, circulatory, lymphatic (glands), endocrine (hormones), exocrine (secretions), renal (kidneys) — and in my opinion, most importantly — the integumentary system. This last system is your skin, hair, nails, glands, and nerves that are contained within your skin. These sensors tell you when you're hot or cold, help you cool with sweat, or expand your blood vessels for warmth. The integumentary system senses both exterior environment and interior functions and is connected to the limbic system directly through the autonomic nervous system. Integumentary stress can show up in the form of acne or cysts, hair loss, chipped or brittle nails, psoriasis and other skin conditions. The impact of the integumentary system is far reaching as it intersects with both physical body systems and our energetic system through the heart chakra that extends out through our heart center broadcasts about five to eight feet from our bodies. Nourishing your body by consuming food and vitamins that are right for you and applying skincare is only part of the healing picture. Remember, what happens on a physical level only happens because there is first an energetic or emotional occurrence.

Mind-Heart-Gut Connection
Our bodies' vagus and aortic nerves

Our nervous systems are the physical connection in our bodies between emotions and energy. There is more information later on emotional nervous system healing, and it can be verified through your own research. I need to state again that this is not a physical healing manual, it is purely emotional, which is energetic. But because our bodies are made up of systems, both physical and energetic, one affects the other. Let's move out of the metaphysical and into the physical now, with a brief discussion on our nerves. We hear it all the time in our speech, "He gets on my last nerve!" "My nerves are frayed," and so on. We know instinctively that our emotional state can affect our nervous system all the way down to our nerve endings. How this actually impacts our nervous system is still an evolving science, but we do know some things based on the location of where a particular nerve resides in our bodies.

Our vagus nerve is the largest nerve in our bodies and extends from the brain to the heart to the stomach area. The vagus nerve controls our parasympathetic nervous system (PNS)[12] and is, in fact, *the* nerve that creates change in our bodies through the PNS. Because of its attachment between the brain center, the heart and the gut, we find that our gut emotions and our heart centers are significantly impacted when the PNS is impacted. When we have a gut feeling about something, our PNS is letting us know that something isn't right, and I believe we know this through the energy waves hitting our brain stems, then through the vagus nerve that then travels down into our hearts, and finally our guts.

We know that the mind (brain), heart, and body are directly connected through the vagus nerve, which the aortic nerve is a part of.[13] We also know that the mind-body connection is severed when we don't feel what is happening in both our nervous system and our minds. To effect change, we need to understand the overwhelm that has happened to cause this break. Newer science has proven that our guts have their own receptors, causing scientists to believe that our guts also transmit 'thoughts' or information to the rest of the body.[14] If we don't believe something to be true, we feel it in our gut and vice versa. Once energy moves into your gut, it moves out to the rest of your body's systems through the nervous system. But because of the direct physical connection between the heart and the gut, as linked to the brain through the aortic and vagus nerves, we can effect great change by working on our guts. The path is usually mind, heart, body when moving into disease or heart, mind, body. So work on healing your gut first so the transistors of change can flow easily through the rest of your body's systems. In this way, you don't have to go through the gymnastics of belief systems to effect change and don't have to distract yourself to become whole and deal with the situation.

Forgiveness and Unrequited Love
Healing unrequited love and unforgiveness energies
After sublimating an energy in our bodies and moving it out to our energy field to be transmuted, energetically it can leave a hole in our energy fields because something that was once there is now gone. It has been walked off the set, so to speak, because its services are no longer required. If no longer required, energy leaves a vacuum in the field. Nature may not abhor a vacuum, as Aristotle once famously quipped, but we do. (Space is a vacuum and we use vacuums all the time in our daily lives.) To fill the hole/vacuum, we use the requirement energy of forgiveness.

Tomorrow never comes if we don't share our understanding of our hearts with one another. To do that, we need to let go of unforgiveness energies. In this case, an apology is required to forgive. This is not saying you're sorry like when you were a kid to get the adults off your back, and it is not a castigation through guilt like in some religious

---

[12] Câmara & Griessenauer, *Anatomy of the Vagus Nerve, 2015*
[13] Ibid
[14] Cleveland Clinic online Health Library, 2024

settings. It is truly just moving through the energy of atonement as it sits in your gut, belly, and heart — usually those places, but sometimes more. It's the same for relationships. When we say you're not welcome — in all the ways there are to be unwelcome — it leaves a vacuum that requires healing. The requirement to heal differs from sublimating it, so we call it **Requirement Energy**. When we take the time to forgive, something strange happens. We feel lighter than air in our hearts, minds, and bodies, so sublimation energy doesn't make sense for this type of healing. But we can use the requirement of forgiveness to heal.

<u>Requiring Love through Forgiveness Techniques</u>

The opposite of unrequited love is love that is returned or requited. We return love to each other as a requirement of existence. In other words, we require love to be part of the unity that is Earth and the Universe beyond. Enacting change on an unrequited love frequency requires an act of love, in this case, forgiveness. But forgiveness doesn't occur in the dry vacuum of our lives, it lives in an in-between state where we can feel both the love and the hurt the other person has caused.

- When we ask for forgiveness, we let go of the behaviors of being hurt by the other person.
- When we give forgiveness, we allow ourselves to be requited in love.

The two statements above seem the opposite of what they should be because they are. This relates to Newton's Third Law of Motion, which we are part of through our emotions. There is more information on this in Chapter 13, but to say that there is an equal and opposite reaction to everything on Earth is also about our emotions, so we heal through the opposite effect of what is happening. You will find other terms in this book, like sublimation, to be true for yourself as you work through the energy healing components, so have a heart that this will help you work through your feelings of being unrequited in love. These statements are powerful because they clear away unrequited love frequencies quickly and easily without the backstory. They move you into a state of being that feels seen and heard without returning to the person who harmed you or made you feel less than in some way.

- If unrequited love exists in you, say: **"I request the requirement of love and joy to fill my heart and be requited and whole unto myself."** Say this incantation for yourself after sublimating energies.
- If the unrequited love exists in another person, you say: **"I request access to _____ [say the person's name] to require love and joy to be requited in his/her/their heart."**

In energy healing, we typically don't work on someone else unless they give us permission, but these statements are held and actionable in love, and we request access to their field, which is 'allowable' through their name. If they don't want you there, it will energetically kick you out or not accept your love. In that case, if you are the affected person, it will behoove you to move beyond the other person's unrequited love. But you can clear the energy for yourself, which helps you move past the vacuum of feeling unloved. For healers working with this energy, forgiveness is a powerful modality to move out systematic fears or other energies that keep the person you're clearing from being whole unto themselves. They subconsciously won't allow other energy to move out if they feel unrequited frequencies. They think they have to hold onto it in restitution for their 'sins,' for example. This type of healing moves all of that out fast.

Unforgiveness Energy Release:
"**I sublimate all energies within me that are in unforgiveness and I ask for the requirement of forgiveness to replace the vacuum effect in my heart, mind, body, and energy field. I allow the feelings of being unwelcome to fall away in space and time. And I transmute all the sublimated and vacuum effect energy back to Full Source energy through deepest love and highest light.**"

Using My Healing Techniques
Beginning energy healing methods

The term 'protocol' is often used in energy healing, and it makes sense because we call on the healing power and wisdom of our bodies along with our Source core connection to the Earth and All That is Energy. As a healing energy, Source is our one energy of truth, and it lives in our bodies as All That Is. I may be getting ahead of myself with these terms, but understanding the process, steps, and terminology is important for you to understand healing if you're new to it. If you're not new to it, feel free to skip to whatever section interests you the most.

Grounding and 'Bubbling' for Protection

It is essential to ground and 'bubble' each time you heal. This is crucial as it sets your intention fully and protects your energies from becoming intertwined with the person you are healing. Grounding is simply visualizing your connection to the Earth by dropping both a Source Cord into the Earth's Source core and a grounding cord from your root chakra for extra foundational support to help healing through transformation. The term 'bubble' came from a healer who worked with me early in my process; my first healer called it a force field. It's a common technique to visualize a shield or force field around your body or anyone or anything from which you are releasing energy. I sometimes put my entire house in a force field as I heal and protect the energies within. The force field enacts a Source core connection to the Earth and is maintained throughout the entire healing process. So you see that both energy enhancements call on the supportive power of the Earth to keep you protected. This is another form of love. The mutual love between you and the Earth keeps you protected as you enact change and transformation in your heart through being a healer and the heart of the person you are healing. It all goes back to love.

Follow the same protocols if you're healing yourself because the energies of the past tend to move forward as you heal and can cause havoc. Past life energies can also move forward if you are a healer who can sense these energies, so a grounded technique is highly important. Setting the intention goes like this and can be modified to however you want to say it:

"I request access to my requirement energy for the purpose of grounding and healing any and all past life energies that are placing me into a state of overwhelm. I demand to remove all detrimental past life energies and only allow the past to move forward if it benefits myself and healing others. I ask to fully connect to my Highest Self and align with True Source Energy through the energies of requirement."

Muscle Testing

Learning the technique of muscle testing was my entry into energy healing. If you don't know how to do it, there are many references and descriptions in the book *Emotion Code,* as referenced above and at the back of this book. Because he does such a great job explaining it, I will only offer a small understanding of it here, and you can find your own resources.

Muscle testing is a way to access our body's thoughts and wisdom. The body holds an energy described as All That Is in every fiber of its being. This can also be described as the god-source energy (or God-source energy, if you prefer) and acts as a power source for understanding the behaviors that keep us both in joy and love and the behaviors that keep us in dis-ease. The body will relate its understanding of the Universe through the behavioral energies that make up our form. Our form, or being in a body, relates to our oneness with the Earth, each other, and time itself as we see our energies grow, change, and transform over our lifetime. The energies within our bodies are talking to us all the time. They don't know how to shout, so they create illness or disease to get our attention.

I use my own body to muscle test and clear someone else. I found trying to use the other person's muscles too difficult. Through the power of connection and intention, it's easier for me to find the energy to clear because I'm obviously more familiar with my own body. Asking someone else to relax during muscle testing, I find, doesn't give the best results. Even if I'm in the same room with the person, I use my own body to find the numbers and then clear. Use whatever technique works best for you.

False Information

If we ask our bodies what's going on, it will talk to us through the power of intention. When you intend to find out the truth of the matter, the body will let you know. However, be aware that other energies can block this god-Source connection and can give you a false reading. Typically a false reading comes from a blocked heart center because all readings come through our power of love. So you see how the systematic repression of our heart energies is causing us to feel disassociated from ourselves, which then enacts a disconnection from others. In other words, it's a system. You need to learn and understand what that is and how it shows up for you. When you muscle test, you get to know the power of your truth in your body. Some days it will feel strong — other days, not so much.

Finding a baseline for the tambour of your body's energy is essential. So before you reach for whatever muscle works best for you (I use my thumbs and middle fingers of both hands linked together in a figure-eight, or infinity symbol), ask your body to give you the information for your best and highest good.

"Asking my body for answers for my best and highest good."

Don't skip this part! I sometimes rush through my protocols, and when I don't set the intention, I get all kinds of strange answers that don't make sense. Other times, I may have a blocked heart center, so the muscle test gives me a false positive. Grounding and healing are the best ways to release that energy. I also sometimes thump my sternum with my fingertips pressed together to give my heart center a good shake out.

<u>Power of Intention</u>

The power of intention and the displacement across our energy fields is the key to releasing energy. I can set my power and intention on my own energy field or someone else's. It doesn't take much concentration and should be a feeling of out-of-focus intention. If you feel empathy, or love, for the person you're working on, that should be enough. Work with what you've got. The more you do it, the more powerful you will become. It should take days, not years, to see your power increase beneficially. Your intention to heal another is an act of love — there's nothing more to it. Love is the power behind it all, and empathy is just another form of love.

I started with *Emotion Code* techniques by Dr. Bradley Nelson as a foundation for my release system. His method uses the central and governing meridians to release energy by using a displacement device such as a magnet or your hand. Meridians are essentially power lines in our bodies that serve specific organs or areas of our bodies. Each meridian is, therefore, associated with a healing path as well to release stuck energies. The name of the meridian comes from the organ it serves and is also associated with a natural element. Traditional Chinese Medicine was the first to understand the body's meridian system, so each meridian has another layer of information based on its yin (feminine) or yang (masculine) energy. I provide it here to complete the chart, but I don't work with energy in its gendered form.

Meridian	Element	Description
Triple Warmer	Fire	An important meridian for overall health as it impacts our immune systems. Feelings such as despair, loneliness, humiliation, self-realization, and happiness impact this meridian.
Small Intestine (Yang)	Fire	Feelings such as joy, shock, sorrow, sadness, nervousness, and feeling nourished impact this meridian.
Heart (Yin)	Fire	Feelings such as forgiveness, self-confidence, self-worth, insecurity, anger, love, and hate impact this meridian.
Circulation/Sex	Fire	Feelings such as gloominess, hysteria, subborness, relaxation, jealousy, and generosity impact this meridian.
Spleen (Yin)	Earth	Next to the triple warmer, an important meridian for our overall health. Feelings such as rejection, indifference, sympathy, confidence and anxiety or faith about the future impact this meridian.
Stomach (Yang)	Earth	Feelings such as disgust, doubt, bitterness, satisfaction, disappointment, and criticism impact this meridian.
Lungs (Yin)	Metal	Feelings such as contempt, smothered, openness, cheerful, depression, and scorn impact this meridian.
Large Intestine (Yang)	Metal	Feelings such as guilt, grief, regret, compassion, release, and power impact this meridian.
Kidneys (Yin)	Water	Feelings such as fear, anxiety, (in)security, carelessness, and loyalty impact this meridian.
Bladder (Yang)	Water	Feelings such as fear, anxiety, peace, frustration, and confidence impact this meridian.
Gall Bladder (Yang)	Wood	Feelings such as love, anger, boredom, helplessness, pride, and motivation impact this meridian.
Liver (Yin)	Wood	Feelings such as anger, distress, (un)happiness, irritability, bitterness, and (self)righteous indignation impact this meridian.
Central	N/A	Feelings such as self-respect, overwhelm, shame, and success impact this meridian.
Governing	N/A	Feelings such as shame, (dis)trust, truth, (dis)harmony, and (un)support impact this meridian.

The meridians known as the triple warmer, governing, and central, are the three most powerful lines of energy, with the last two accessed through the front of the body and up and over the head. However, meridians themselves can become stuck and often, so the intention to release may not be as effective. Looking at the emotions that impact those two meridians will give you an idea of why. Shame, truth, overwhelm, and distrust are all emotions — not feelings —that impact the two meridians that govern and centralize our 'electrical' systems. When they're stuck, the number to release gets higher, or the power of the emotion is higher, so it takes more energy and more hand waving to clear out the block.

Meridian Clearing Statement:
"I [state your full name] release all stuck energies in my body's meridians that are causing stress, anger, fear, grief, and any entrapping frequencies from electronic media entertainment to overrun my systems. I ask my mind to immediately react to these energies through the deepest love and highest light to remove all blockages.

"I neutralize and harmonize any and all discordant and dissonant energies that are causing fear and anger to persist in my existence and I transmute those energies back to True Source energy through the deepest love and highest light."

I don't use the meridians anymore to clear as they are not powerful enough for that reason. I use my Source core connection to the Earth between the heart and the solar plexus to release stuck energies because they move out faster. For myself, the more stuck energy I uncovered using the *Emotion Code,* the higher the numbers got. Three hand passes were not enough, and I was waving my hand over my head in the bathroom stall at work hundreds of times to get the energy out of my head so I could focus! I then started counting by tens, then by 100s, and then 1000s, which made it easier, but I couldn't keep up with the amount of energy I was releasing. I discovered, through serendipity from another healer, that I could use the front of my body to release, pushing the energy down into the Earth rather than up and over my head, and it took only 3-5 hand passes. That is now my technique that I call 'Body Scan' and the number of hand passes is inconsequential, I go with whatever number feels right.

Finding Acceleration Numbers: Body Scan Method
   We connect to All That Is through our body's god-Source connection and find a path to healing through the power of intention. Now that we have that set up and ready to go, how do you get to what needs to be healed? Simply ask the body! The body will guide you and because this is energy healing and not a physical at your doctor's office, clearing the chakras is a great place to start (skip backward to chakra information). Clearing the chakras first will inform the other clearing and healing that needs to occur, including meridians, the body's physical systems, and more. You may find that just clearing the chakras is enough. You have to respect whatever answer you get. Each time you clear, you ask through muscle testing if the body is ok with clearing. If you get a 'no' response, stop for a few moments and then ask again. If you get a persistent 'no,' then the healing session is over.
   Once you've identified the energy or emotion that needs to be cleared, find the

acceleration number that clears it. This is my methodology, but use whatever works best for you; we're all different, of course. The acceleration number represents the level of that particular stuck energy. As my guides explain it, because this part is very esoteric to me, it is the number of healing power or energy that will transfuse the stuck energies. If everything is a frequency or vibration, then we have the power to cut across that vibration to effect change. We have to find the level of power it takes to create that change. This is not the number of hand passes over your Source-core connection but the frequency number required to effect change.

For me, this number is usually in the quadrillions and often higher. I discovered this one day after doing that counting thing for so long and after I moved to my heart-source connection for clearing. I started with 999 quadrillion and can now move it up to septillion if I'm feeling empowered. If it's beyond those numbers, I do it again, sometimes two or three times. (More than that, it's likely a Timefield or wound.) The acceleration number is the same if I work on myself or others. Again, according to my guides, it represents my heart-core connection to the Earth. I have the power of love in the quadrillions and above to move energy at that high rate of intention. I'm not sure how I'm able to do this, some things are still a mystery to me, but I count mystery as magic. You can't know everything completely, and I'm okay with that as long as it's aligned with True Source energy, which is love. You can find your acceleration number by sitting with yourself and asking your body for your Source-core connection number. If you're adept at this already, you may find that the number automatically comes to mind. If not, give it some time, and it will show up for you..

Try It: Putting It All Together: 'Body Scan' Method
Here are the steps in list form:
1. "Asking my body for answers for my best and highest good."
2. Test that statement by saying, 'love' (check the muscle) and then 'fear' (check it again). Love tests strong, fear tests weak.
3. Ask the body what can be cleared: "Can I clear the chakra and mycelial system?" e.g.
4. If yes, find the acceleration number that clears it through muscle testing.
5. Now clear it using your hand as the displacement energy and your intention.
6. Swipe your hand, palm facing inwards, down the front of your body, starting at your chest and down past your solar plexus. This will help move the energies through the body's systems into the Earth. You will know in your body when it feels right. Sometimes, it's a yawn or chills; other times, it's just a feeling.
7. Double-check your work. Ask through muscle testing if the energy was cleared. If 'yes,' you're done and move on to the next. If 'no,' find the number again in step 4.

How does this work if you're healing someone else? You are already connected to that person's energy field through the intention set in the grounding and bubbling statements, so follow the same steps as above. Finally, when the healing session is over, disconnect from the person you are healing (unless you're healing yourself). Remember, we are all one and all connected to and through the Earth's source core, so it makes sense to disconnect intentionally. I say, "I'm disconnecting from _____'s energy," and swipe my hand down my heart core a couple of times. Works every time.

NOTE: If you prefer using incantations, you can still use the acceleration number method by <u>multiplying the statement</u> using the same method for finding an acceleration number. I ask my body if I can multiply the statement and find the correct healing number through muscle testing. After speaking the incantation out loud (I feel it's more powerful that way), I then say, "I multiply that statement by _____." And that's it! I started using this method one day out of frustration for the healing to take effect more quickly and in with more strength. I do get tired of being in a constant state of healing and all the talking that is required, so I amped it up because healing my PTSD required more power. The 'talk-i-tecture' of my life has made me impatient with words.

Grounded Healing through Timefields
Finding relief from overwhelm through a guided approach

It is important to understand Timefields both as a creative individual and as an energy healer. Understanding the different states of overwhelm helps you through awareness when you are stuck. Energy healers can use the term 'Timefield' when clearing energy for themselves and others. It is a shortcut to clear out a lot of energy that would take days, weeks, and months to get through. It can also be part of your lexicon when talking about emotional states because a Timefield is a specific type of emotional overwhelm. When using the term in conversation with people who know what it is, there is a shared understanding of what is happening for that person.

Because people's emotional states cause Timefields, there are layers of information in their energy fields related to clearing them. Clearing in layers allows for a faster clearing session, which leads to faster healing. The layers are arranged with the Timefield on top, wounds and wounded behaviors underneath, and energy associated with both underneath the wounds. When you clear this specific type of emotional overwhelm, clear in that order.

- Timefield
- Wound/Wounded Behavior
- Associated Energy

It is also important to note that clearing from the center, or anchor point of a Timefield and the 'hub' of a wound, allows the energy to move out faster. The void or hub of both the wound and the Timefield is the central point of emotional unrest. If cleared, the rest of the energy will dissipate, clearing the way for other energies to be removed underneath or around it.

A Timefield is emotional overwhelm that has persisted over time. It can extend back through childhood and even through many lifetimes. It is common for people to reincarnate to learn the lessons of a past Timefield. Whether or not you believe in past lives, it doesn't matter for clearing your emotional overwhelm. Getting to the root of the issue through past lives is faster, but you can still uncover energies/emotional overwhelm as they present themselves despite their origin.

Try It: Steps for Clearing a Timefield

Timefield healing is my own method of healing persistent emotional overwhelm. It is a method that gets to the core of the issue energetically through the center, or anchor point. The anchor point holds a Timefield in place and is the point of power where the healing occurs. I visualize it as a ship's anchor that extends down through the center of a clearing in storm clouds. I see the chain coming descending to Earth as it extends through time. Light comes through the hole above while storm clouds gather around it. Energetically, you release this anchor to set it free so the storm clouds can dissipate.

Here are the steps for clearing a Timefield, which causes emotional unrest for millions of people on Earth. ***Please do not take it lightly that you are just moving out a block. You are, in fact, changing time to effect change on planet Earth***. This is a powerful healing modality, but as with all things supernatural, it seems mundane on the face of it. We can't see the energy moving, but we are the healers of the Universe through our connection and love for each other. In terms of love, I know it feels esoteric, especially now in our century of feeling disconnected. But this is happening so we can find healing and love for each other once again.

1. Follow the grounding and bubbling protocols if you haven't already done so.
2. Ask the body if there is a Timefield that needs to be cleared
3. If yes, ask which emotion is associated with it: fear, anger, grief, shame, etc.
4. If no, ask if it is a wound and skip to #8
5. Ask the body to clear from its anchor point (it will almost always be yes, but it's important to ask to set the intention).
6. Here are two ways to clear a Timefield:
    a. "I release and uncreate any number of Timefield anchor points of _____ [state emotion] and I transmute it all back to Full Source Energy through the deepest love and highest light."
    b. **Body Scan method using muscle testing and numbers (see above)**
7. Wait a few moments and ask if the Timefield is clear. If yes, ask if there is a wound underneath that needs to be healed. If the answer is no, there is more Timefield energy, and you'll need to repeat steps 1-5.
8. If there is a wound, ask the body to clear it through its hub. This is usually the same emotion as the Timefield.

9. Clear the wound as you did the Timefield, but rephrase for the 'hub of the wound.' Again, releasing from the center of the actualized emotion in energetic terms.
   a. **"I release and uncreate any number of wound and wounded behavior hubs of _____ [state emotion] and I transmute it all back to Full Source Energy through the deepest love and highest light."**
   b. **Body scan method using muscle testing and numbers (see above)**
10. Finally, ask if there is energy underneath the wound that needs to be cleared and follow the same steps.
11. In a rare occurrence, you may have to circle back and clear a different or unrelated Timefield with the same emotional wound. It's always good to double-check your work!

Sublimation... Wounds... Timefields... Chakras... Meridians... you might be feeling overwhelmed by the descriptions of overwhelm! It's a lot, I know. Be sure to rest and allow this information to percolate through your system and integrate in your mind. I found or discovered this information over a number of years, so don't feel bad if it's not making sense. It's still revealing itself to me as I write! The bite-sized pieces of information in each chapter are set up for this reason.

Here is a review of the energies and techniques so far:

Emotional/ Energetic Block	Description	Action taken to heal	Example*
Minimal Wound	Wound that is not a pattern or deeply imprinted	Sublimate	"I sublimate all stuck energies in my gut that feel like a sucker punch."
Denigration Pattern	Pattern of behavior that sets us up for wounding. Often inflicted on us but can be self-inflicted as well through self-talk	Release and uncreate	"I release and uncreate any and all denigration patterns of behavior in my root chakra."
Unrequited Love	Frequency created by feeling un-loved or unwelcome through denigration behaviors	Forgiveness through requirement of love	"I request the requirement of love and joy to fill my heart and be requited and whole unto myself."

Emotional/ Energetic Block	Description	Action taken to heal	Example*
Wound or Wounded Behavior	Deep emotional wound that causes a tear in your emotional fabric and has a center tear or rip (hub); has not reached the level of Timefield yet	Release through the hub or central point of the wound energetically. Often repeated after the Timefield first.	"I release and uncreate any and all wounds and wounded behavior hubs of fear."
Timefield	Emotional overwhelm existing over a longer period of time and/or across life times	Release through the anchor point or center 'eye of the storm' for both this life and past life states	"I release and uncreate any and all Timefield anchor points of fear."

*Note that after each statement, you need to transmute what has been cleared back to Full or True Source energy. You can use the body scan method using numbers instead of the incantation for release. Remember to release through your Source core into the Earth for greater impact.

These energetic blocks can exist in any part of your body or energy field. Sometimes, when clearing, you may find a Timefield in the heart center, a meridian, or the left big toe. It doesn't matter where it is, you clear it the same way. I often find Timefields and wounds in the chakras and mycelial system and won't leave that system until it's all cleared out. When overwhelm exists in the electrical system that is the base of your being, you have to get the root cause — not the story, just the emotion. I have included a clearing template that goes through each protocol at the back of the book. If you follow the sheet, you will be able to move through these systems rapidly. It takes longer to explain than to do.

Chapter 11: Systems of Timefields

Let's progress our understanding of Timefields and move back into the field of architecture. We already know that Timefields are a form of stuck energy that persist over time, have a solid ground of (often painful) information, with centers that are less dense. A Timefield is held in place by an anchor point that exists in the center, also known as the void. The void is the place where the light comes through, and so we can effect change through those points with energy, healing, and intention. Timefields can act as moats outside our walls of understanding and wounded protection. We can enact change and healing by walking across the drawbridge of self-doubt and installing acceptance in our hearts to break down the walls of misinformation around them. We heal them through an energetic exchange that happens either within us if we are self-healing, or between two people where intention is the focus of our being-ness. There are almost always wounds associated with Timefields and we clear them in layers to create a faster clearing moment and a more progressed healed state of being.

Unrequited Love and Stacking of Timefields
Healing through a system of release

Since we already know that the information is healed in layers, let's turn Timefields into platforms of energy that, when stacked on top of each other, resemble building floors. Like a multi-leveled building, Timefields can also be layered on top of each other, but are more likely anchored to the past. Floor-to-floor heights vary depending on the Timefield and the emotional quality of each, meaning a Timefield can depress or lift up depending on the quality of the emotion. We can feel like we exist in a space with soaring ceilings, or in a cellar basement where we have to stoop to move around. (Skip ahead to "Sacred Spaces" to learn about the upward lift of emotions.)

A typical building floor has stuff in it: walls, doors, ceilings, furniture, equipment, ducts, electrical devices, and so on. For this thought experiment, the furniture and equipment represent emotions, and the walls and floors are the backdrop, or the emotional body that contains the emotions and are the bounds of energy. If you worked on the creativity sections under the Creative Life Concept and did a systems check under the Creativity Blocks section, this will sound familiar and you're halfway to understanding where this is going. Everything in a building works together in a systems approach and is contained within that singular structure. From heating and cooling to communications and lighting to how each floor functions independently and cooperatively, all these things occur within one unit. In general, when you walk into a room, you probably pay more attention to the stuff in it rather than the architecture creating the space. (Tangent: which is why interior designers' work is so important!) The conscious mind is aware of the furniture, but the architecture can become a background element; it's just there but still serves a purpose.

Emotional Vacuums and Time

This is the most crucial part of my Timefield analogy because it can affect significant change in your life by just understanding where your emotions go when in a Timefield. If you get nothing else, pay attention to this section because it will get you halfway to releasing emotional overwhelm by understanding the process of change and transformation in our lives through the Timefield effect.

Just like in actual buildings, we don't think about our HVAC system until there is an issue with it, and then we seek to find the answer to the problem. The corrective process can give you a new understanding of how the system works and, therefore, a deeper appreciation for it, and for the people who service it. (Be kind to your systems contractors!) When in a Timefield, the systems get plugged, the furniture (emotions) evaporates, and are sucked into the vortex of feeling energy. This is where the Timefield energy is at its strongest. We don't know what is happening because we don't feel it. Emotions are not feelings, so when they are sucked into a vacuum, it causes us to feel disconnected from our bodies by the very nature of being in a vacuum. Perhaps this is why outer space can be scary for some people. They see the vacuum of space as time, or rather, 'time in memorial' and feeling out of time, or 'out of time, out of mind,' in terms of unrequited love. It's all interconnected and makes us feel apart from each other.

If I am in a Timefield of heartache, I don't feel the emotion in my body because it is sucked into the vacuum of the Timefield. The emotional energy, therefore, exists in the in-between and doesn't make sense because my body is literally not sensing it; like it's nowhere and everywhere at the same time. My emotions of heartache can feel like a chest burn or tightness, but when it's in a Timefield, it feels like nothing, like my heart doesn't exist and therefore I don't exist. Timefields exist in the in-between. They are not the sun (consciousness) or the moon (unconscious); they exist in a blinding level of light and require a high frequency to cut across the field of time and energy. That is where the term Timefield comes from. It is a field of energy, much like Faraday's Field, but instead of connecting us, it disconnects us by feeling lost in time or under a time constraint.

The stacking effect of Timefields begins in childhood. Most likely, you are familiar with childhood wounding as it permeates our society. Techniques used by psychotherapists and other talk therapy people have been effective in bringing about the realization of how childhood wounds impact our adulthood. If you haven't, it's worth a deep dive into your childhood wounds. I recommend you find a psychologist or creative endeavor that best helps you get to a point of at least realization so you can effect change in your environment.

Timefields describe and act as a function of healing these circular or looping patterns in life. You might think, "How many times can I go around this bush before making changes?" Or, "How many times am I going to repeat this addictive behavior before I can break free of it?" The Timefield is a strong enough pattern in our lives that we need first to create awareness of it and then move towards healing it. Overwhelm is overwhelming! The need to sit calmly with it is great, but we can't do that when we're in story because it sends us into even more overwhelm. So to move the energy, the Timefield describes the pattern under the story and then releases it through the energies of love and light. Awareness is key, though, so there will be some backlash, so to speak, in terms of unhanding your belief systems. It's hard to walk through thick mud that wants to suck you down. But releasing the energy behind it gets you through it faster.

Try It: Clearing Stacked Timefields

We can clear an entire stack of Timefields all in one go. There is no need to do extra work or acquire extra skill sets. It's the same as any other form of stuck energy, except you ask the body for these yes/no responses through muscle testing:
- "Is there more than one Timefield (or wound)?"

- "How many?" (It's common to be in the hundreds for past life energies.)
- "Can I clear them through their anchor points (or hubs)?"
- "Can I clear them all at once?"
- Find the acceleration number to clear them.
- Use your hand as the displacement energy down your Source core connection. I like to say in my head, "Clearing through love and light" with each pass for extra oomph.
- Ask the body if the energy was cleared.

Follow the same steps for wounds or wounded behaviors underneath. If the Timefields were stacked, the wounds are stacked, too. Clear exactly like a Timefield but use the word 'hub' or sometimes the hub does become an anchor point in the case of a past life wound. Either word should work. It may require a couple of rounds of finding the acceleration number, but it should not be more than 2-3 times. If it's more than that, check your frequency method, or you may need to find out the type of Timefield (fear, for example). You can also use the incantation below and it is included in the clearing template at the back of the book. Go there to find extras about how to clear Timefields, wounds and wounded behaviors, and the energy below without the story.

"I ask my mind to release the overwhelm of (past life) behaviors that are keeping me in the looping pattern of a Timefield. I uncreate all negative thought processes that are keeping me down and anchored to the past."

Judging Teens
Releasing older kids from guilt and shame

The teenage experience is fraught with judgments and misconceptions from both adults and teenagers themselves. We all have some version of this story. There is a common misconception about how difficult the transition from childhood to adulthood is, meaning it shouldn't be difficult — or as hard as it feels — from both the teen's and the parent's perspective. Our bodies and minds are designed to make this transition, but many societal and cultural constructs we set up can make it difficult. We need to be honest with ourselves about how we treat teenagers at this time of life. What are the main gripes about teenagers? Grumpy, non-charismatic, fearless, unbelievably self-centered, risk-takers, annoying at best, unserviceable at worst. All of these descriptors are about moving into adulthood, where you can take on the world around you. You need to be a risk-taker, you need to be fearless, and so on.

The grumpiness and annoying attitudes we now know are often about lack of sleep and a need to leave the nest — stretch beyond their boundaries. The science about how the teenage brain needs to be asleep during the day and have more focused time makes complete sense.[1] Teenagers are making new connections, finding new ways to live,

---

[1] Leila, Tarokh, et al, *Sleep in Adolescence: Physiology, Cognition and Mental Health*, 2016

learning how to be in the world. These all align with the Big-C, Little-c creativity levels outlined in Part 1. Do you feel like sleeping when your brain is lighting up with new ideas and connections? No! You feel like jumping out of bed and taking on the world. But society crams teenagers into one category, thinks they're up to no good through their risk-taking behaviors, and then makes them get up for school before 7 am after they've had a night of creating new connections in their brains. Add on the constant worry of grades, being the best-looking kid at school, not getting into a fight for some who have depleted nervous systems, and finding a new path in life that may or may not be college, trade school, or straight to work — not to mention what is happening at home with family issues. It's enough to make anyone go apeshit, not just teenagers, yet we demand that kids maintain an even temperament at all times.

Add on top of this a new sexual awakening. For girls and women, there is a horribly deep pressure to be both sexual and non-sexual at the same time. All of the images placed in front of them say that you need to "flaunt it if you've got it," but make sure not to be promiscuous or, worst of all, get pregnant. Teenaged girls feel they have to wear whatever is dictated to them as the accepted level of revealing their bodies while unmasking themselves as sexual objects to the world, yet they still have to maintain a level of piousness in terms of having sex and not getting pregnant. This is nothing new. It's been going on for hundreds, if not thousands, of years at this point. Unwed teenage mothers bear the brunt of society's shame in understanding who they are. One moment, they are a sexual object having fun, the next, they're a mother with a scarlet letter of shame tattooed on their forehead — or most likely across their breasts because that's where all the focus is.

For some, they realize they might not fit into the binary existence such as being gay, bisexual, trans, or any other form of gender identity and sexual orientation that doesn't fit what society allows for. This is another type of unrequited love. They may ask themselves, "How can others love me if I don't love myself? Why don't I love myself? Because I see other people around me acting in a certain way that I don't align with, so I must be a monster," or other pejorative way of thinking. Still others may have shoved it down so far that the realization doesn't come until much later in life, and those moments feel like coming up for air for the first time in their lives.

Past Lives and Timefields
Moving beyond denigration patterns from other lifetimes

Timefields and wounds stack on top of each other as time progresses from childhood to adulthood. Like a building, the levels of Timefields and wounds become part of an energetic system with our emotions in between each level, serving them as an electrical or HVAC system, keeping them heated or providing power. The power comes from within, not without. There are no non-entities, demons, or ne'er-do-wells impacting your Timefields. They almost always progress forward in time and, through their anchor points, are pinned in place from childhood through to adulthood and this can happen over many lifetimes. The lifetimes with negative or depressed Timefields are usually the container for the problems we have with others in our current lifetime. When we encounter someone in our life who either rubs us the wrong way for no apparent reason, or we feel magnetically drawn to them, it could be a past life anchor point enacted through your energy field. You know this is true when you meet someone for the first time and they seem very familiar to you, but you don't know why. You may have an instant reaction to them, either positive or negative. The negative reactions are what we want to work on to clear out the past life behaviors that are holding you in that repeat loop pattern.

Past lives are a popular concept in cultures around the world, particularly in the East. In the US, it's still fairly fringe-y, but I have found them to be true for myself, even when I was young. When I was seven or eight, Shirley McClain's mini-series called *Out on a Limb* aired on TV. Though I didn't understand much of it, especially what a tree branch had to do with time travel, I knew deep within that past lives explained a lot for me. To this day, I have not read her book that the show was based on and didn't realize it existed until I was in my early 40s, going through my ow spiritual awakening. Past lives are common through the energy they bring forward through time. (Though time is its own topic, we will keep the mainstream view that time is linear for ease of understanding.) We all have many layers of wounds, wounded behaviors, and heart walls to keep ourselves safe. (Skip backward to moats and Timefields for more information.) Each life begins anew but has energies stuck to it as an anchored Timefield or Timefield platform.

The experience of a past life Timefield stuck in time is very real through its emotional resonance. It's the emotion that is real, not necessarily the story. My theory is that this information is enhanced through the amygdala in our limbic systems by moving it into our nervous system, where we actually feel our feelings. When we are in great fear or anger, that energy gets stuck within us, sticking the truth to our core. But our cores change over time and through past lives, so maybe the truth isn't what we think it is. We can experience this concept within one lifetime when we find out, for example, that the bully at school was really just a scared kid who wanted to be our friend and didn't know how to express their feelings of unmet anger and mistrust. When we have these awakening moments, the stuck energy flows out of us through acknowledgment with a new realization that things weren't as they seemed.

Understanding Past Lives Through Quantum Physics
Time as a process, not a point

My own experience with past lives is that they bring up a new realization that opens up time. There is an energy that flows (or doesn't flow) through time and into our energy field, cutting across the layers into our limbic system (covered in a later section).

This correlates to the theory through quantum physics that the present and the future really don't have a beginning an end. They flow in and out of each other in what Einstein termed the 'extended present.'[2] This extended present changes over time as we get further away from the present moment. As bodies on Earth, we don't experience the extended present viscerally because we are too close to the present moment, or the now. We are completely covered in that fact as we know nothing about what will happen 15 minutes from now, yet that is how long it takes for information to get from Earth to Mars, according to quantum physicist Carlo Ravelli in his book *Reality is Not What it Seems*. What is happening in those 15 minutes? We don't know because we don't see it or experience it in our bodies.

However, our *minds* have the ability to move beyond our present moment and take on the world of the extended present. This is how Einstein came up with it in the first place! He moved beyond his present moment in his mind and into the extended present to understand that reality is really just a movement of time and space. So if our minds can do this, then they also have the ability to heal the past hurts and sorrows that occurred when our souls were someplace else or someone else. It sounds esoteric, but there is a body of information that relies on the present to incur the belief systems of who we are here on Earth.[3] We are not just mortals living out a human experience on Earth, we are also souls that exist elsewhere. We don't know where that elsewhere is, but we do know that we can keep in touch with the beings and people who have moved on to that elsewhere through past life experiences and our natural ability to see into the Beyond.

Yes, everyone has this ability. It's not just for seers, mediums, and other psychic types. All the paraphernalia used to divine the future is just our minds' way of looking into the extended present. Case in point: my daughter has a collection of oracle cards, crystals, and other divining tools that clutter her bedroom. She doesn't really use them, she just likes to look at them because they're pretty and interesting. Yet, she has the ability to tap into other worlds without question. She told me one day, when she looked at her curtains with cartoon mermaids all over them, she saw a woman with a wig on her head like Marie Antoinette. It could have just been her imagining, but her belief that the woman was real, and the fact that she said something to my daughter, was my sign that she actually saw something. Instead of shaming her or making her think she has an overactive imagination, I asked her why she thought the woman was there. I believe my daughter was seeing a past life, though I will never know for sure.

These instantaneous visions and knowings are our minds and bodies telling us we're accessing an altered state of consciousness. Past life work, as an accepted form of access to our state of being, is coming into its own through past life regression therapy. I have

---

[2] Carlo Ravelli, *Reality is Not What it Seems*, 2007
[3] Refer to any spiritual text as guided by "the masters", or Buddha, Jesus, etc.

not experienced it, but I know that people let their minds wander as they move into a different conscious state and try to find what is ailing them. Hypnosis works the same way. Our minds have the ability to move beyond what is in front of us and amplify our state of being through the mind's eye.

Our emotional states of consciousness move forward in time through the extended present. We find these states through altered consciousness and can also effect change in healing. Remember, the void can also be a state of being. This was shown to great effect in the TV show, *'The Good Place,'* when the computer, known as Janet, pulled all the humans into her void of existence. Hilarity ensued when they all took on each other's forms and personalities as her void broke down. But the main idea is there: anything is possible in the void. So we can go into the void to heal and be healed, access our past lives, effect change and understand our being-ness, and find the time to be at peace and rest.

Healing Past Life Timefields
Releasing the stacking effect through energy healing

If there is an extended present that moves forward in time, then it likely moves backward in time (see Tesseract section) and correlates to the yin-yang experience on Earth or Newton's third law of equal and opposite reaction. It also relates to negative G-force, where the effect of gravity is felt in its opposite through acceleration.[4] So, the ensuing Timefield of our life force energy pushes forward and backward in time. If it lifts us up, we can make positive life changes; we see the connections to the extended past as beneficial in the present moment and can make decisions that positively impact our health to move us forward. If it pulls us down, then we are stuck in an area of life that does not allow beneficial connections to be made. When stuck, we can only see the quagmire of our existence, the non-beneficial energies, and cannot make the decisions that move us forward. We end up in looping patterns, going around in circles, making the same mistakes instead of learning from them and moving on. As The Bangles sang so rightly, "Time, time, time, see what's become of me, while I look around for my possibilities..." (Yes, it's a Simon and Garfunkel cover, but The Bangles sang it better.)

Healing a past life Timefield is the same as healing a current moment Timefield — you just need to ask the body. It's as simple as that. The body is wise and knows what's happening at all times —except when you're in a Timefield. But the body knows that the Timefield is there, so you can ask questions to clear it such as how many past lives ago, whether or not you were male of female, or the players involved. If you move into overwhelm quickly from either PTSD or another traumatic stress injury, it may be best to leave out the story. You can still clear the energy by just knowing the emotion, or sometimes it only requires the word 'Timefield.' But if you are interested in more

---
[4] Martin Voshell, *High Acceleration and the Human Body*, 2004

information and find it to be helpful, you should do what works best for your healing modality.

Example:
- If there is a Timefield of anger that doesn't clear properly, ask the body if it is a past life Timefield for a yes/no response.
- If yes, ask if there is more than one.
- If yes, find out how many.
- Ask if they can be cleared all at once.
- Ask to clear from the anchor point.
- Find the acceleration number that clears out the past life Timefield or stacked Timefields
- Use your hand as the displacement down your Source core
- Ask the body if the energy was cleared, sometimes waiting for a few moments helps with getting the correct answer, especially if you moved a lot of stacked Timefields out.
- Remember to clear the wounds underneath as noted before.

Past life Timefield release can be a great way to uncover stuck behavior patterns. If it feels right to you, follow it and see where it takes you. You may find Marie Antoinette in your curtains as well!

Collective Timefields
Negative attachments and cording

A person can get caught in someone else's Timefield they are related to or live with consistently. This sets up a dynamic that can be negatively impactful for both people, especially the person caught, because they are unaware of why they are feeling the feelings and emotions that aren't related to them. The narcissist and empath dynamic is one such relationship that is impacted by both a Timefield and a negative attachment. The empath is caught in the narcissist's Timefield through a negative attachment formed by both parties. The narcissist invites the empath in, the empath accepts through a need to heal the wound of both people — "I have a wound to heal and so do you, let's heal it together because we get each other." However, the narcissist continues to feed the hole of their Timefield through emotional unrest and the empath gets sucked in through a need to help and feel the wound of the other. Over time, the emotional unrest gets transferred to the empath as well and the circular, cyclical emotional roller coaster of the relationship continues until one or both break the cycle, usually the empath because they are the narcissist's support through giving while the narcissist takes. Feelings of both repulsion and attraction can happen for both, even in the same moment.

Try It: Source Cord Viz for Humanity's Rising Influence on Earth's Grid
Visualizing your Source cord from your Source core into the Earth's Source core is a way to impact both your being and the being-ness of the Earth. Take a moment and visualize extending a long, white flexible tube from the area between your breast bone and your belly button. This is your Source cord. Extend it all the way down into the center, or Source core of the Earth itself, which is magnetically charged with light and abundance.

Now drop a black cord, from your tailbone (root chakra) down into the Earth for extra foundational support. I like to visualize three prongs on the end as if it is attaching deep into the ground. This is an extra grounding cord to keep you in place and connected to the Earth's surface which also has an energetic grid. The white and black colors are important. White is all the colors, or frequencies, of light, and black is all the colors, or frequencies, of solid pigment. Drawing on these two energy sources keeps you in tune with Earth's grid from the two main areas of light.

This visualization is a metaphysical concept that allows our thoughts to change our physical behaviors. If our thoughts are energy, they have the power to effect significant change for ourselves, which extends out to others and impacts the energy of the Earth itself. Metaphysically, as you extend down into the Earth with your Source cord, you are transmuting energy from your body into light form. This light moves into the Earth's core as light energy, impacting the magnetic field around the core energetically. The magnetic field, in turn, changes so that it emits electro-impulses, similar to an EKG (or ECG, electrocardiogram). Our heart centers pick up on these impulses through empathic energy. Our bodies then allow the new heart energy to both transmute and broadcast a new form of love energy which extends out to others and into the Earth's surface grid thereby changing the Earth's grid itself.

As you can see, the whole process begins and ends with people. We are the cause and effect of humanity's rising on Earth with help from guides who are connected to people with a higher level of consciousness. The point is to get everyone to a higher level of consciousness, not just a few.

<u>Clearing Collective Timefields: Energetic vortexes of emotion</u>
The stagnant energy of a Timefield slows down time, keeping us from noticing the moment we're in, putting us on a repeat loop of emotion and thought. The looping pattern causes an inward movement creating a pool of energy that swirls inward, forming a vortex. Because we are tied to both time and space, the vortex can co-locate in our minds with the spaces we inhabit, this includes the Earth itself. The Earth has its own energetic infringements related to past human conflicts — any war would be a cause or the slash-and-burn policy, for example, of the early European settlers on tribal lands in the now United States and Canada. Connecting the emotional vortex from a current event to a past Earth infringement will cause larger issues that need to be dealt

with energetically by trained people.[5]

Remember the model of a Timefield as a piece of time that has a hole or void in the center. The vortex has the same form, if you think about the eye of a hurricane or the center of spinning water, for example. These are the moments we need to get to as they release the energetic infringements of the past and present together —the calm center, if you will, that allows for peace and understanding in our hearts and minds. If our bodies are still, then we can seek to unearth the issues from the past and effect great change. Because there is a deep level of unrequited love associated with these types of Timefield vortexes in the Earth, we need to ask for forgiveness. We can ask our bodies for the willingness to heal ourselves and others no matter the timeline. It is the energy of the Earth itself that is attracted to the same wound within the person (like attracts like) who triggers it. If you are a person who can feel these energies, the time is now to start healing these wounds through the Energy of Requirement and this incantation.

<u>Land Clearing Statement:</u>
"I request access to the energy of requirement to heal past life energy caught in a vortex. I release and uncreate all energy in me that connects to the vortex. I transmute all unrequited love back to Full Source energy. And so it is."

How do you know you are a person who can feel these energies? It comes from a sense of being welcomed. Stepping onto a piece of land or property can cause a very strong felt sense in many people. Some people may say they just don't like being there and might wonder about what happened in the past. It's a very real and visceral reaction. Haunted forests, houses, and other places probably got their start from people being able to sense the energies there and felt unwelcome walking into them. Sometimes you can stumble onto an energy and not know until much later that something happened or 'attached' to you. This is not an energy of haunting, though it certainly feels that way! It is a wound that has been triggered and it is experienced through fear, self-doubt, or unworthiness, which can send people into the nether regions of their minds. Remember that our minds are powerful and have a way of letting us know what's happening. To be clear, there is something in the environment, but you are the catalyst for enacting it. One person's fear is another person's joy. I would <u>never</u> jump out of a plane and skydive to the Earth because I have a fear of falling from heights, but some people enjoy it. So no two people experience the same level of fear or enjoyment the same way and it is the same for energies that have been left on, burned into, or scared into the Earth. A scar is a past infringement and feels scary when you look at it because you can imagine how it got there. Again, it's the story.

Saying "I'm sorry" is the easiest way to stop the fear, but then work with the energy to clear it. Imagine speaking to the people who lived in the house or the land or

---

[5] Look to the end notes for my recommendation for someone who can heal this type of energy.

property before in the present moment. Listen to what they have to say; the first thing you think of is the right one. Let it flow. This is a powerful active imagination and can bring about many positive results. Don't just say, 'Begone, you are no longer welcome!' because that enacts the same fear and mistrust that you stumbled onto to begin with. Approach it as if you are healing a small, wounded animal or a private healing session with one of your favorite people. Feel compassion for the fear and follow through with the belief that you are working at a superhero level of healing through the requirement of love. If you feel fear of an abandoned house in your neighborhood, sit with it in your mind and ask what it needs through forgiveness. This is a part of you that needs forgiveness, so you are actually working with your own energy. In times such as these, we need to be allowed our own truth, and sometimes, the dark places are where our truth lives.

Revisiting Abandoned and Past Places

Timefields of the past don't profit from each other, they only serve to pull each other down. A death, for example, of a beloved family member serves as a Timefield and can be a nostalgia trap, a term coined by my sister, Corinne. For her, nostalgia is defined by its old version as a disease rather than something positive. Nostalgia traps can also be honorific in remembering a life lived, but they are often places in time that pull people back and down to their pain and suffering. To live in the past too long means being stuck in time.[6]

Abandoned places, most often buildings and homes, are visual versions of Timefields. We all know these places exist and can feel their energy emanating from them as we either choose to avoid them or purposely try to enact change by breaking windows or spraying them with graffiti. It may seem like the destruction of property, but the urge to move the energy out can be spontaneous and temperamental for some and is often unconscious. Don't go breaking windows now, but learn to understand the energies of these places to enact real and energetic change. Sometimes we clean them up, take down a piece of them, or raze them all together for physical change in clearing the energy, but we can also use our status as energy beings to remove the stagnation of time — or lost in time, as it were.

This is how haunted houses come to be — if they are genuinely haunted — and graveyards with stuck energies and other forms of 'haunting' on Earth. It's a dance between the energies of anguish and the need to be set free. We have discussed unrequited love a few times, but these are places where it is in its true form. Energies of this type are considered to have 'unfinished business' on Earth and leave a shadow of themselves behind to release those looping patterns. I know for some, it sounds odd and is part of the paranormal phenomena on Earth, but the energies do exist, and I

---

[6] To understand her point of view, look to the end notes for her podcast.

personally try to avoid them.[7]

It is common to avoid places that experienced or caused sorrow, pain, or suffering. But, people may also avoid places that have happy memories because they cause them pain now. They try to rectify the Timefield in their minds related to the place that was once happy, but the person feels suffering because of sorrow, like a lost relative, for example. The opposite is also true. They might go back over and over because they are trying to heal the negative cord attachment that happened there. They may feel inexplicably drawn to the place of sorrow and suffering even if they don't believe anything bad happened to them. This is related to a past life Timefield or life block which is discussed later under the section about astrological imprints of time on our energies.

It's hard to square the experience with the feeling in a real sense. In the person's mind, the geometry of the place to the Timefield forms a square (as in astrology), like two planes forming a 90-degree angle, which fight against each other. Another way to say it is they are butting heads. To clear the square energy, something has to move, otherwise they will be constantly pushing against each other. The movement required is clearing energy between the Timefield in the mind and the building or land. The energy healer acts as an interpreter, essentially, between the two energies — including your own Timefields. The interpreter finds the link or commonality between the two energies to reach common ground, mediates the situation either through requirement energy or an energetic exchange, and relieves the suffering for both. We can do this on our own by understanding the energies of suffering. Get curious about how and why you feel the way you do. If it's an abandoned house or structure, the wound is likely around abandonment. The house or structure is the physical manifestation of the wound.

Past life infringements in abandoned places and in the Earth begin and end with people. People put them there, so they need to be cleared by people. Collective Timefields shared by three or more people move out to the land and become a vortex as the energetics move from one person to the next. Before clearing the Timefield, it is good to understand the original infringement. If you can, research the space or land in question. If there was a battle, war, or conflict of any kind at any point in time on the property, the best way to begin is to ask for forgiveness. If it's your own house or property, begin by clearing your energy first with the Requirement Energy protocols. This stops the possibility of an energetic infringement from happening. Then, move to the energy level required to clear the past life Timefield. If it is more than a Timefield, you will need the energy of requirement protocol for clearing spaces and land.

Indigenous Cultures Past and Present
Wound healing - Start Now!

The world is wounded because of the treatment of indigenous cultures. This is not

---

[7] Understand the unrequited love aspect of energy healing through Amy Jo Ellis's 'Court of Atonement', see end notes

new information as we all know worldwide the plight of Indigenous cultures from the past and how it impacts our present moment. Indigenous peoples are not cultures to be forgotten or pushed away as something that is part of history because they connect many of us to our past and past lives. Their wounds and healing rituals bring people back to themselves in droves as we all learn to respect the Earth and, therefore, respect each other. The need for healing around this topic is great. From Australia to Mexico and even the Middle East, as people war over who belongs and who doesn't, the fact is we all belong because we are all human beings on Earth. The Earth accepts us, and therefore, we should accept each other. The Earth itself is holding the grid stable so Timefields can be cleared. The rising of humanity will continue to clear the grid so the stability mechanism from the Earth will no longer be needed in the future. See more discussion on the Earth's energy grid under the Ley Lines section later in the book.

As an American who has lived on the soil in this country, I know we are overdue to rectify the wrongs of the past in our indigenous cultures that are still going on today in the form of anger and hatred, keeping direct money from the people who need it most, abhorring nature in the form of a vacuum of disinterest, and disrespect of elders who have come before. We don't need to take on the forms of the past to heal, we can start with the present because that is where we are right now. "The point of power is in the present," as Jane Roberts channeled in her often quoted book, *The Nature of Personal Reality*. It is our present timeline that will affect the change through understanding and forgiveness if we pull our heads out of the sand and start moving towards an energy of love.

We are all connected and influence each other all the time in all ways, big and small. We impact the present to inform the future, as the future stems from the present. In many ways, we are a backward culture in the US. In our national bones, however, we don't want to look back as it 'distracts from the now.' Most of us, through our family trees, have left the past behind. It's time to start thinking, feeling, and being more informed, which starts now, not tomorrow, because 'tomorrow never comes,' as Big Head Todd and the Monsters sing. We are always living in the now — it's not a moral obligation. An energy of abundance comes from being at ease and welcoming it in. We can easily accept the things we can change, and we don't need to call in outside help because we are love and abundance unto ourselves. It doesn't preclude us from helping each other because we are all one as a collective. Helping one helps the many.

The Energetics of Sacred Places and Spaces
"Abundant time brings abundant peace to those who want to live it."

The Timefield is a precious commodity when we feel the upward movement of its energy. It is a time warp in the sense that it moves time as a perception, not an actuality. It helps us believe that we are here for a reason: to be human, to connect with our loved ones, which can include animals and plants. It's precious because it's a rare occurrence as we maintain the lower levels of depressed Timefields. The upward movement of an emphatic Timefield is not always experienced by all people at all times. It takes time and a specific kind of energy to complete the upward movement consistently. We realize this in many sacred spaces around the globe.

As humans, we mark our time spent on Earth in different ways. You may be familiar with picnic tables and park trees that have carved graffiti "Amy wuz here" or "JR + VD 4-ever." We mark the Earth so that we're not forgotten. We feel time keenly through our sense of place. When we visit landmarks or monuments, our sense of time is activated, and we encounter a sense of awe about ourselves, the Earth, and the Universe. The sacred places and spaces we visit become a type of time capsule. We have a human need to be remembered because our time spent on Earth is brief, and the Universe is so large. Graffiti, monuments, or sacred spaces are forms of understanding who we are in the continuum of time and space.

Timefields coexist in our minds and the land if the emotions are strong enough and if the land can support the energy of the Timefield, which it usually can. Timefields are created not only from negative overwhelm, but also from what we would call positive overwhelm or emotions. Feelings of positivity can overload our nervous systems and get transferred into the Earth if enough people are present. These areas on Earth are our sacred spaces of healing. There are many, but to name a few: Machu Picchu in Peru, Bodh Gaya in India, and Stonehenge in England. All these places have a 'mystical feel,' and we are right about that. The mysticism of the land comes from the Earth itself and from the people who come and feel the energies, connect with them in a mostly positive way (some are scared), and want to be part of those energies.

We feel called to build or create something in a specific spot because we feel its energy and have an innate need to create a time capsule in these places because our time on Earth is short. It's kind of like leaving your mark through a bit of graffiti and it's done both by building and by a transfer of energy through emotion into a Timefield. Think of the many people over the decades who have visited the sacred sites listed above and left their mark energetically. That's a lot of people and a lot of energy! The difference between a Timefield of a 'negative' space and a Timefield of a sacred space is that the vortex in the former is spiraling down, while the vortex of the latter is spiraling up. Of course, I'm describing a felt sense, not scientific fact. But I think we can all agree that these places hold a special power that we feel viscerally, otherwise, we would not flock to them in droves year after year. Many people come away from these places feeling changed in some fundamental ways. Regardless of your beliefs around religion and its indoctrination practices, these places transcend the bounds put in place by humans around religion and ethics.

When we're in sacred spaces, we feel uplifted. We look toward the ceiling or sky in a beautiful place such as the Hajia Sofia in Istanbul, which has served both the Christian and Muslim faiths — a testament to its power as a sacred space. People feel holy in sacred spaces or wholly connected to the power of the place and the energies of those who came before and are there now. Places like the Hajia Sofia or Notre Dame de Paris are designed to draw your eye up, to see the light of God through your own belief system, but they also induce a feeling of ecstasy or intense joy through the energy of the space itself.

Sacred places are interesting to me as an interior designer, especially in how they form space both inside and out. Some buildings are able to create a sense of the sacred while others try but fall short. Why is it that some do and some don't? I believe it begins with the designer or architect putting their energy into the project, feeling love for what they are doing, and wanting to build something in integrity with both the land and the people. If the design of the building communicates love and integrity, the people who build it will feel it as well and transfer their emotions and energies of love into the building materials used to form the space. (The materials also have an energetic imprint from how they are harvested and/or manufactured.) And when they are done, the people who use and visit it can feel it no matter how much time passes because the energy, or Timefield, of the space or place, is continuously fed, this time through the higher vibrations of love and joy rather than the lower vibrations of pain, grief, shame, and suffering. It all works the same way. Imagine what we could do if we considered the entire Earth a sacred space! Nothing would feel abandoned, lost, or downtrodden. Everything and every place would spiral upward, pulling us with it. We would reciprocate that energy, feeding it with more love and joy.

Nervous System Impacts from Our Environment
The detrimental impacts of our over-built environment

When we connect to sacred spaces, we feel a type of 'coming home' in our memories. We are aware of how our nervous systems interact with the land, buildings, and people around us in that space in time. Our nervous systems connect us to other people and our surroundings through our integumentary system. (See below for more information on this important body system.) Through place and being, we find ourselves in the middle of a moment, a day, a place, and we know that we are meant to be here because we feel it in our bodies through our nervous systems. We know we are meant to be here on Earth because we feel connected to other people, their words, their memories, and time. Time is the factor that we all feel when we visit these places. We are essentially connecting to the past, present, and future all in one space in time as we contemplate who was there before, how we are feeling now, and what we might take away from these wonderful places. Time is the essence of all beings on Earth. We are born in a particular place and time in history, in the ethos of our Internet of Things, so to speak. We are aware of our cultural touch points as part of a generation and of our own being-ness through time. (See Astrology + Healing section for more information)

The Look and Feel of Things

Place and how it looks and feels matters. I can tell you it's a fact as a commercial interior designer. It's not a flighty, nice-to-have thing. It's imperative that we understand how place matters and how it feels affects us daily. What we see through our eyes, encounter through our nervous systems, hear, feel, and smell every day as we walk through the world matters. Americans seem to have forgotten this point in our built environment. We have prioritized efficiency over beauty, lack of money over abundant resources, and stripped the world of beauty by putting up roads and buildings that don't consider the environment and most importantly the people using them.

I find it interesting that Americans travel to Europe, South America, and other places around the globe to see history and beauty when we can create a beauty of our own right here. In her 1999 HBO standup comedy special, *Dressed to Kill*, the comedian, Sue Eddie Izzard, castigated Americans on this point. "I live in Europe, where the history comes from. You people tear your history down! And you think we all live in castles, which we do." She's right! We have a bulldoze policy on the land; every square inch of land must be occupied by something man-made, or we think it's just wasted space. There is no thought to the other species who inhabit that land, even in urban environments. Starting with European settlers burning crops and homes of the people who were already here, there is little to no thought for the people, species, or energies who came before. It leaves death and destruction in the form of emotional overwhelm that stays in the land itself.

Bridges of Disconnection

Travel over any American highway, and just as you come to a bridge that spans a beautiful river or gorge, the US government saw fit to put up a standard-issue bridge with concrete barriers on the side that visually disconnect travelers from nature. I am reminded of this often as I live on a beautiful bay on Lake Ontario. The bay is spanned by a bridge that connects commuters from the suburbs to the city and other places. Just as the cars hit the bridge, the view is blocked by concrete. No thought was put into how it might look from the people on the water or how it might be experienced as a commuter. It just gets you from point A to point B. It is a missed opportunity to connect people to their natural environment, even at 60 mph and higher speeds. Instead of being stressed out when they get to work, they could be calmer just from seeing the beauty around them, or on the way home they could let go of the stress from the day.

Compare this to the roads and highways where the US government got it right. The New Deal of the 1930s brought stone masons and other craftsman into our park system. They built beautiful roads and bridges that have stood the test of time. People flock to roads such as the Blue Ridge Parkway and, more recently, the Natchez Trace Parkway, to this day. What if every road and bridge were designed with the same careful consideration as these scenic roads? The mid-20th century designer, George Nelson, felt the same way. His book, *How to See*[8], documents the level of disassociation and unawareness of our built environment. He spent his days taking (film!) pictures of junkyards full of smashed cars, commercial strip roads full of power lines, and even documented utility hole covers. All these things in our environment impact our nervous systems and contribute to our sense of place. The difference between a Shinto shrine and a strip mall does not need to be expanded upon. You get the difference. Awareness in your environment will bring change, and change will bring about the energies that we desire.

Transitioning Away from Established Systems
The covered bridges of our existence
    Just as bridges are transition points (and covered bridges keep us from the view), we have come to a transition point in this book and your healing process. If you've skipped ahead, you likely have already found the healing section below and might be a little confused about the content specifically. How did we get to body healing in an energy healing and creativity book? It's all from a systems perspective. All of our bodies' systems — physical, emotional and energetic — interact with our environments which are also impacted and made up of systems. The 20th century architecture world latched on to the theories of philosopher and former Nazi, Martin Heidegger, because he reinforced their belief systems. He focused on art and architecture through the patriarchal lens of enacting domination over Nature instead of allowing the feminine Earth to exist as itself. Architecture, Western medicine, and law are examples of the many institutions that reflect patriarchal rule through a predominantly male-centric culture that denigrates others by not allowing them to have autonomy, sovereignty, or freedom.

    Turning over your authority to someone else can have dire consequences. Now is the time to start unhanding yourself from these belief systems and reclaim control over your energy, life force, and body for healing. Healing is an automatic process that exists within our being-ness and form, yet we choose or are told that we can't possibly do it on our own. When not in emotional wound, our bodies will automatically remove the non-beneficial energies, releasing fear, anger, and mistrust of others. If you don't believe me, that's okay, there are many ways to heal and it's your right to choose. If your mind and heart are open to the healing messages below, I share them as a way to continue all the good work of people who have healed before me. Find relief through this systems approach that is integrated into your well-being.

As always — have fun with it, use what works, and leave the rest.

---

[8] George Nelson, *How to See, a guide to reading our man-made environment*, 2003

Part 3: The Energetics of Healing the Emotional Body

Chapter 12: Emotional Body Healing

> Your emotional body is the unit that holds all of your past life and present life feelings in place. It transforms through space and time into something new every time you enter a new habitat or boundary by becoming a new person on Earth. If you're startled by this information, it's ok, you don't have to believe it, but it is ingrained within you. You are a walking and talking individual, but you are also connected to a wider Universe of individuals like you. Consider a family tree to compare this 'energetic' truth with physical reality. It doesn't take long for a family tree to branch out and go this way and that, depending on who leaves home, travels, and moves around from place to place. The 'roots' of those trees need to be enormous to support them!

The K-Drama Family Tree
Feeling rooted and uplifted in our extended family forest

Likewise, our souls have a family tree that we come from. We are often connected to a soul group of individuals who are walking and talking along with us on the Earth (most likely our families), but there are others who do the same elsewhere. Consider it a family forest with many trees and root systems that interact, forming a mycelial system. We know through biology that tree roots interact with each other underground. Trees communicate with each other in this way and can offer healing to each other through this type of informal family system. When one tree needs more water in its roots, other trees will likely share their water with it. There also is a matriarchal setup in tree science where one tree is called the Mother Tree. There are cultures around the world that believe in Guardian Trees that protect a forest, village, or neighborhood and stand out from the rest by being taller or more majestic in feeling. These trees extend down into the Earth, below the water table, finding protective energy for themselves and the space around them, including people, as they lift their branches skyward and leaf out towards new possibilities. This description may sound like a metaphor, but it is very real in terms of love and light. Light guides the tree towards the sun, and love of nature and the people who care for it allow it to extend its roots deep.

Like a tree that has lived longer than most, we are connected in time through our ancestral energies. We can absorb the emotional wounds of our parents and grandparents, which they are likely holding from their parents and grandparents. Absorbing emotions can get us caught up quickly in Timefields and wounds of non-understanding. Ancestral energy is a big problem when it comes to maintaining Timefields. We all have individual needs, preferences, and desires, but we are told our families come first. Think of all the dramas on TV where the kids are beholden to the patriarch or matriarch of the family.[1] Lots of tension between who gets what inheritance, who wants to leave, who gets to stay, and who will die because everyone is backstabbing everyone else! It makes for great TV, but not for endings and new beginnings because in real life, we hold on to those hurt feelings in the form of unrequited love.

Other Systems of Understanding

As with every system in the world, our bodies' systems interact and overlap, so healing one helps another and getting to the core of the issue can sometimes be confusing. We have already reviewed energetic systems such as the chakras and the energetic lines that serve our organs and other parts of our body called meridians. We've also reviewed how emotional systems that serve and protect us can be harmful if they become stuck in the energetic form of a Timefield. Taking out each individual

---

[1] Another concept shown to great effect by K-dramas. (Can you tell I'm a fan?)

emotion can be tedious and ineffective if you are dealing with a deep-seated emotion or a Timefield that exists not only in time and space but across generations and timelines. All that stuck energy can affect our energetic heart centers and our bodies quite literally through disease and illness. Impacting these systems for wholeness and health requires a systems approach.

Our bodies are designed to pick up on more subtle energies around us. We feel it when we walk into a room where there was an argument just moments before, yet everyone is sitting in silence. We know it by looking at the expressions on our loved ones faces and we believe it when we start seeing changes in our lives through change and transformation of belief systems. We know we are making changes when we suddenly see someone in a new light or are aware of something that didn't occur to us before. This change is part of our emotional healing, but because we are made up of systems, it also impacts our physical systems, so understanding the method that a specific system uses to enact change allows us to enact change on that system by working with it energetically. The systems effect starts in our energy body and works its way inward to our emotional body and then our feeling body. There are connection points at every moment, and our minds, or brains, are important interaction points.

Resetting Rhythms of Behavior
Cranial rhythms and the medulla oblongata

We pick up on subtle energies, which we encounter every day, all day, from people we live or work with and come into emotional contact. For example, if you're working with someone on a project and find a similar solution, you might say, "I was thinking the exact same thing!" or "We're on the same wavelength," meaning you're feeling the same sensations, tuning into each other, and making non-verbal connections. This situation happens all the time and isn't mystical at all. Our energies can pick up on someone else's because we are designed to do that.

The physiology of this function begins with the blood brain barrier (BBB), a dense lining inside the blood vessels in our craniums. The BBB protects our brains from pathogens and substances that can be easily absorbed in water.[2] The BBB is connected to the medulla oblongata, part of the brain, which in turn, is part of the central nervous system, along with our spinal cords. The medulla relays nerve signals between the brain and the rest of the body through the autonomic nervous system, which is part of the central nervous system, making the medulla an important point in our bodies and minds for creating change and releasing resistance to change.[3] Four major cranial nerves pass through the medulla, one of which is the vagus nerve — the all-important nerve that extends down through our hearts and into our guts and includes the aortic nerve. Behavioral changes begin in the brain stem through the medulla because it is literally the

---

[2] Daneman and Prat, *The Blood Brain Barrier*, 2015
[3] Diek, Smidt, Mesman, *Molecular Organization & Patterning of the Medulla Oblongata in Health and Disease*, 2022

point of power in the present moment. It acts as a relay switch between the nervous system and the brain, causing us to create change through our nervous system as relayed by our brains, which conduct our thoughts.[4]

We know that our thoughts have power. Our thoughts can change and transform our belief systems as we grow into adults, and they can change our behaviors around those belief systems by effecting change in our bodies. If I am running a marathon and believe I can't take another step because of exhaustion, but I tell myself, "Just one more step," and then I do it, that effectively creates change in my body from my thoughts. It's an interesting point in time because, in that moment, change is made by a verbal cue. "I think I can" is just another version of this behavioral switch because it opens the mind to a new possibility of believing in yourself. Verbal cues are the type of energy healing we use in this book and we come at last to the reason why. So open the switch to new behaviors by allowing yourself to read and believe this energy healing is effective.

We can change the rhythms of our behaviors by setting our minds to the task, creating a beneficial switch that opens our minds to new possibilities as a part of speech patterns that affect the medulla. It's as simple as talking directly to the parts of our brain where we know we can make the most impact on the requirement. The incantation goes like this:

Try It: Clear Behavioral Rhythms
"I demand my mind to change the rhythms of my behavior to be rhythms of care and concern for my own energies. I transmute all non-beneficial energies back to Full Source energy and I uncreate all thought processes that are keeping me in a pattern of denigration. I demand that all past and present energies be beneficial to my mind and thought processes within."

Try It: Clear and Release Behavior Patterns
"I uncreate all energies that are holding me in a negative belief pattern in understanding the past. I ask my mind to release those energies from my medulla and transmute them back to Full Source Energy through the deepest love and highest light."

Releasing Stuck Energies in Your Divine Life Force Connection
Integumentary system healing

Our bodies' systems are interrelated and are impacted by our environment and sensed by our integumentary systems. Physically, this system is made up of our skin, hair, nails, and glands that produce sweat and oil.[5] Energetically, our integumentary system, connects us to each other, the energies in our environment, and our greater universe and universal consciousness through our crown chakras. I consider it *the* most important system in our bodies as it connects our energetic and physical systems, affecting the

---
[4] Ibid
[5] Zia Sherrell, *Integumentary System: Functions, parts, and conditions*, 2023

most change in our bodies, hearts, and minds. As a major carrier of nerves and nerve endings, it stands ready and at guard for any incoming problems and allows fast healing to occur emotionally through a hug from a loved one, for example, or a simple touch as presented later through the parasympathetic nervous system healing. Because of this sensing mechanism we call our skin, we find healing through many different modalities. Other energetic healing such as acupuncture, acupressure, massage, reflexology, and even saunas and spas with mud baths all access our energy and our bodies through the sensing and feeling organ of our skin.

There is an unspoken cultural rule about personal space — even before the pandemic — where people give you a wide berth. We feel uncomfortable around 'close talkers' and people who crush up against us on the subway or bus. Feeling doesn't have to be literal touch. If we're feeling out of sorts, we say our skin crawls, or if we're surprised or delighted, we get goosebumps, which is also the same reaction when we're cold or step quickly into a warm bath and feel the temperature change. It is also a harbinger of inner things going wrong through skin breakouts and skin diseases such as eczema, warts, and hair loss. We feel all these things through our skin, and therefore other body systems through the nervous system. It all interacts in a seamless way, and we're not aware of it most of the time because it is automatic; this is just how we have evolved as sensing and feeling beings.

When we say, "My heart goes out to you," it is an exacting phrase because they do extend out energetically. The chakras energize our systems as they move in flow through our bodies and extend outwards in all directions between 6-15 feet. What happens in this space? That's where others' energy and our energy overlap, unseen but felt through the frequency of love. Our heart's energy gets caught up by the heart energy of others and is sensed through the integumentary system, sending a reverberation up our spines to our crown chakra, making us feel connected mentally to that person. A shift occurs when we are in close contact with others' energy flow. With our minds now activated, we call up our feelings through our memory (limbic system), enacting a change on our medulla oblongata, which in turn, moves the sensation out to the rest of the body. As the carrier of nerves, the medulla changes our energy through beliefs. It's all very tightly integrated and we feel it in our bodies, not the other way around. It is not our minds that start the progression, it's our bodies.

As a Lynchpin between our body's physical and energy systems, we can effect change by asking our integumentary systems to release blockages energetically. Note that this comes at a cost if you have PTSD or other mind-body reprogramming issues because the field of un-requirement is latent within your energy field. (Refer to Unforgiveness Energies in previous chapters.) So, if you are a known survivor of PTSD or any other traumatic stress, save this protocol until the end.

Try It: Integumentary System Clearing and Release
"I ask my mind to release those energies from my integumentary system that are keeping me from my Divine Life Force Energy connection points. I ask my heart to transmute the non-benevolent energies back to True Source energy through my Source Core connection to the Earth and bring in love and light for further transformation in time and space."

Tattoos Parlors and the Earth's Charms
Tattoo artists and the integumentary system

Tattoos are one type of energy that impacts our integumentary system immediately and quite powerfully. The interaction between the tattoo artist and the person being inked is an interplanetary act of self-reliance. In other words, two people come together to create an energy of protection for the wearer of the tattoo. Both integumentary systems are in close contact, though one is impacted more than the other through the artist's intention. This is why traditional tattoo artists in indigenous cultures hold such a high honor in their communities -- the artists are deeply impactful on the wearer of the tattoo. Even in mainstream communities, people form a bond with their tattoo artists because they are intimately connected. Tattoos impact our body's divine life force energy through the ink implanted in the skin, which has both a physiological and psychological impact. Tattoo artists are literally impacting people's divine life force energy connection points by implanting a topical poison in the skin that then becomes an imaginary (image) talisman to ward off 'evil' or allow for the good vibes to roll. The image is not fake or unreal in terms of the energy it provides. It is very real because of the interaction between the two divine life force energy systems of the wearer and the artist. It is not for the faint of heart, especially on your face, where so many divine life force energy points reside.

After the ink has been implanted, the skin is puffy for a few days but settles down after it realizes that the poison is here to stay; there is no momentum. The ink is a sedentary poison that won't travel to the brain or the heart, for example. The poison is meant to be more like an artifact of the past that holds our energies at bay, if you will, to keep our natural energies flowing. If it's more than a cosmetic tattoo, something that has been selected with high regard and installed in integrity, then the selected tattoo artist has installed their belief systems into your skin through thought and intention. This is why many — if not all — indigenous artists pray or set a calming tone before performing surgery. If you are tattooed, the symbology of the work of art on your skin has great significance to you personally. It is felt deep down as the energy travels through your integumentary system as a divine life force energy connection and is directly impacted by the energy of the symbolic ornament that is permanent, not a piece of jewelry, for example.

Tattoos are also implanted in the Earth. We move our tattoos as either blessings or scars out into the environment, which can transfer to the land. The land is our collective integumentary system where we all stand rightly and interact with each other there. Earth tattoos come from the deep well of hope that all things, including humans, are made equal under the sun. We may not all act or look alike, walk or talk alike, but we are all one, and therefore made equal and this shows up in the integumentary level of the Earth itself. We have reviewed this in the form of a Timefield or the collective understanding of the past under severe duress, such as a war or the slash-and-burn policy of white settlers on ancient cultures. This type of tattoo is a parlor of disbelief in the community at large and is worn like a scar rather than a belief in the good of humanity, which is worn as a blessing.

Bedazzled and Bejeweled

Jewelry has its own energy, which is why we wear it. Talismans hanging around our necks is a long-standing tradition around the world; every culture has it. It symbolizes bringing in a different energy for discovering or presenting something new. Wearing a crown of jewels and other precious minerals shows the level of respect for the person wearing them as the crown of the head is covered in many different divine life force energy connection points and is also the thinking and processor of our feelings, which are felt through our heart centers. The combination of ceremonial garbs, robes, talismans, and other finery symbolizes how all the different divine life force energy connection points are impacted in our daily lives. If you are a jewelry or fashion designer, consider how you impact people's divine energy daily. If your design is out of fashion with the time, it won't be worn, but if it is out of alignment with your divine life force energy as a creator, the implication is further reaching because it impacts you and others. This extends to how it is made and the materials you choose. The impact of the 'fast fashion' movement is part of this concept that we are all interrelated through our integumentary systems, and what we put on our skins and wear on our bodies is more important than we think because it also has an environmental impact.

Piercings are different from wearing a necklace as they also impact our integumentary skin directly and in more profound ways than other forms of jewelry. Piercings are personal and different for each person, so consider where your piercings are and find the symbology of why you chose that particular location and how it's pierced. If you are a person who can't wear piercings or jewelry of a specific type, or can't bring yourself to select the right tattoo, even if you want one, consider what that might mean for you. What is your integumentary system telling you through the inability to maintain a piercing, either through an allergy or something else? Or why can't you put a 'rope around your neck,' for example? It all means something through a level of seeming mystery, but you can find the answer through the clues or breadcrumbs left for you in your body. Our integumentary systems interact with us daily, so being aware of your own energetic divine life force is of utmost importance to your healing process, ability as a creator, healer, or any other aspect of life. Therefore, your integumentary system is your energy of love, peace, and harmony in a world that feels retractive to us. So let the good times roll if you want to tattoo yourself with a brand that is not your own, but you feel aligned with — you know which brand I mean.

Nervous Systems and Charms

Neurodiversity is also like a tattoo or a charm that keeps the wearer safe. Some people may not feel it that way, but a perspective switch can help us understand. In the form of PTSD, the self-reliance topic of this book, we are under the impression that it comes and goes swiftly — in a hair's breadth — and doesn't leave the 'wearer' much protection by being triggered and activating the old wound. But what if the old situation was borne out of a love for the world, activating your nervous system so you handle things in your environment differently? The environment, as felt through the situation, is the handler of all our feelings and associations. We are placed in time in our environment — all of our life moments happen there, nowhere else. So if our environment is "charmed, I'm sure," then we are also charmed. Our beliefs and disbeliefs can stress us, or we can decide to look at it from a different perspective. In other words, it's a code switch. Neurodiversity, as it is called, is a code switch for yourself and the people in your life, especially if you're still a child. We are called on to live in different and other ways of being. If we can't break the mold ourselves, so to speak, then our environment will do the changing for us.

We often work out different perspectives and how to incorporate them into our lives, but we don't heal if we can't take on life's misery and find "joy inside our tears," to quote Stevie Wonder again because he is one of the all-time greats at showing us how to do this. His code switch was about being blind, but he finds joy in music and has made an epic career out of it. He shared his version of being a hero of the ecliptic with all of us through his album, *Songs in the Key of Life*. It all makes sense from the level of the integumentary system where we find joy in our tears (glands or tear ducts), find life to be charming (tattoos), and work together to become one at a greater level of competency (heart center progression). Does it matter how you get there? No, I don't think so, as long as it is aligned with love, which is the engendered resource we all have, infinitely available to all of us with no sense of lack required. Our "cups overrun" with heart center magic as we fall into each others' arms and feel the healing of being touched through our parasympathetic systems, feel joy wake up our spines, and work together in a form of magic that begins as unrest, but settles down into the energy of peace and fulfillment.

Hairnets and Belief Systems
More integumentary system relating

The hair on our heads is the exact cause of our divine life force energy in action as it extends out from our minds when we are feeling in flow. It tells us when we are sad and upset, feel up and happy, or feel allergic to the truth. We see this comically applied to the iconic image of the nutty professor or 'mad' scientist with their hair standing on end, shouting "Eureka!" while the lab blows up behind them. Who knew Einstein's theory of relativity came from his hair, not his brain? Apparently, lots of us because we keep showing that image over and over as an exacting cause for his genius. Our hair defines our behavior: "bouncin' and behavin'" (sassy and happy) or conversely, when our hair is flat or tied back, we might feel more subdued. Someone with their hair pulled in a bun feels extreme or strict, narrow in focus. "Let your hair down!" we say to each other, which is also an exacting phrase because when our hair is down, we feel in free flow.

Now, the dangers of being too over-the-top present themselves with these statements because sometimes we need to tie our hair back to keep the loose ends from spilling out, or sometimes we split hairs when we're trying to make a verbal comeback, but the truth of the matter is that our hair is in judgment all the time. We judge each other based on curly or straight, smooth textured or coarse, individual strands versus bunched up together (dreadlocks), and other ways we denigrate each other on our hair choices. But if you look at the person across from you who has completely different hair than you and notice it through the perspective of divine life force energy, you will start to get a different picture of them. How do they stack it on top of their head in a beautiful pattern of braids (plaits) or comb it to the side to reveal or cover up? If you expect the pattern of behavior to come from their minds, then look to their hair for how they review their life.

When people break up with someone or go through a life change, they often go to the barber or salon as an expression of 'this person is different.' Male-patterned baldness may run in the family genetically, but perhaps it's also a wound of fear that has been absorbed through a generational outlook on life that has been passed down from father to son or through the mother's line because that is supposedly where men get their hair genetics. It seems odd, yes, that women are blamed for it? Or perhaps the denigration starts young and they can't find their life pattern. When people ask if it's ok to touch your hair, that is very specific to the engendered belief that your hair belongs to you and the divine, and that is also why some people are a little touchy about others touching their hair. It's, therefore, appropriate to spend whatever amount of money you think is right for your hair to look the way you want.

But all the ways we see, feel, and hear Source energy come through our energy systems and into our heads, which I believe are covered in divine life force energy connection points. It makes sense because, except for touch, all of our senses are located in our heads. Not only the senses but also our heads carry around our brains, which are, of course, tied to the sensing energy that is our mind, which expands as we learn new things, our sensing and feeling organ, the skin, takes this on as the energy that extends outward in time and space, making Einstein's mind truly mind-blowing, or expansive. This isn't scientific, of course, I just notice the patterns that I see in myself and understand it to be true of other people. So, our hair really does make us stand out as a personality. What does your hair say about you? Your divine life force energy is specific to you, and you feel it in ways that no one else can, so take the time to uncover how your body recovers from being pushed down or kept in place for too long.

Judgment Errors in Memory
Releasing the limbic system

The limbic system is a group of structures and nerves in our brains that control our memory and response to fear. The four main structures that make up this system are the hippocampus, amygdala, thalamus and hypothalamus, which is tied to the autonomic nervous system.[6] The autonomic nervous system helps to keep our bodies humming along by maintaining automatic functions that keep us fully functioning through a state of balance, or homeostasis. In all moments of the day and night, the body constantly scans its environment and changes to maintain balance through waste removal, temperature control, and an ability to maintain present moment awareness through our memory release system of letting go of the past.

Even the processes of dreaming becomes a type of waste that we release while sleeping. We know dreams are our psyche's way of working out the problems and energetic blocks of the day, week, or season of life to help us reach a level of balance in our bodies and lives. A multi-national, multi-ethnic team of researchers at the University of Rochester's sleep clinic expanded on previous knowledge of brain waste. They discovered a waste removal system in our brains they call the glymphatic system.[7] This system is primarily operational at night when we are asleep and allows for the idea that our dreams are a form of waste. Dreams are also our way of providing us with information about the future and our innate sense of who we are as a collective consciousness. I believe we dream so our minds can reach ever-expanding levels of intuition, knowledge, and peace.

Time and Memory

Time and memory come together in our limbic system, which transfers into our central nervous system through the autonomic nervous system. Let's consider how your current environment impacts these systems. Fact and truth are two different things. My truth is held together by my thoughts, feelings, and emotions and are different from your truth, which is held together by your thoughts, feelings, and emotions. All of this is run through our nervous systems, which are individual to us, a marker like a fingerprint or DNA strand. Truth is realized by feelings of love and *avasa through* our autonomic nervous systems by the transfer of thoughts to our bodies through the limbic and

---

[6] Cleveland Clinic online Health Library, 2024
[7] J.J. Iliff, M. Wang, et al, *Scientists Discover Previously Unknown Cleansing System in Brain*, 2012

integumentary systems. Our connections (literal touch or feelings of joy) are felt through our integumentary systems, which translates back to our heart center energy, moving into the limbic system as a happy memory in time and space. Happy memories keep us from feeling overwhelmed, causing us to stay calm (in a low state), which also means that we feel free to be ourselves with others. But what happens when the memory is formed in grief or fear? Or when we find ourselves inexplicably tied to someone we want to break free from but can't for 'all the tea in China' as the saying goes. We find ourselves cut to the quick over and over again and can't find a way out despite knowing that we are not in our best state of being.

In the extreme, this state is post-traumatic stress syndrome, or PTSD, which will come onto the world stage more rapidly now, I believe, as we move into a new understanding of who absorbs the trauma of a lifetime and who is able to release it. It's not just for warriors on the battlefield anymore; it's for all of us who understand ourselves to be in a traumatic situation that doesn't allow us to live our best lives. But our emotional unwillingness to leave or let go of the past causes the upset to deepen, causing more trauma. It is truly a traumatic situation when you are aware but can't get free — epic proportions, like all the Greek tragedies that show how when we are unwilling to change our own behaviors it causes other people to suffer. You see how stories affect us more than any other type of modality through memory, but you need to be aware of the story you're in, or you won't break free. When affected by trauma, we try to release those unwanted memories but can't get past them because they are stuck in our minds.

I will state again that I am not a medical doctor, but I have the experience of dealing with both survivor's guilt and PTSD through negative attachment in a relationship that was deeply wounding for me and others in my life. But I have come away from that experience as a grounded healer who knows more about how to deal with negative attachments than any other form of emotional wounding. You can find relief from suffering through both forgiveness of yourself and others and healing your body's energetic systems. This is emotional healing, not medical healing, but emotions after all, cause us to grieve. So, let's move past it all and move on to healing those energies of time caused by the ungrounded feeling of being in a Timefield of shame, doubt, and un-acceptance.

When you are a PTSD survivor, emotional overwhelm can take hold at any moment. We find our lives are turned upside down in a hair's breadth, and coming back out of it can take days or weeks sometimes, depending on who the survivor is and the circumstances. PTSD is emotional stress to the extreme and we live it every day. "Will today be calm waters, or will I be caught in a storm of my own emotional experience?" We just don't know what will happen, which only heightens the experience because we are attached to the fear, anger, and fury in our minds. The phrase, "it's a touchy subject" only covers half of what PTSD survivors deal with when their response mechanism triggers them. Trigger points are caused by the damage to the energetic limbic system, which are then actuated through time and memory release — not to forget, but to let go. Energy release causes greater change by releasing suffering without the story, which is a major trigger point. Meditation works, as do frequencies through healing music, but it also takes healing modalities through your energetic limbic system.

Try It: Currents of Time and Energy
When I meditate, I sometimes use the phrase, **"I breathe in the Universe and breathe out stardust,"** as I visualize an image of the galaxy that we are in, not zoomed out, but as a snapshot of the night sky as if I were in space seeing the stars, planets, stardust, and gases of the Milky Way. It's a peaceful image to me and sets the scene of relaxation, providing me with a deep, unending love through my breath because I'm breathing in the entire Universe, which is manifested through love. I came to this visualization as I contemplated us breathing in the same air as people over 2,000 years ago, which felt cosmic. Since our bodies contain stardust,[8] it reminds me of the connection of all life on Earth and the Universe beyond. So, the breath that enters our bodies is also an awareness of love. It is deep fulfillment and attachment at a certain level to the Universe. Attachment through love and not overwhelm is higher vibrational.

The Earth's atmosphere is an energy field surrounding it that holds our oxygen in place so we can breathe. Breathing connects us to the Universe. If the atmosphere isn't there, we can't breathe. If our energy fields around our bodies are not in place, we can't take a deep breath. Extending that to the Universal Law of Love and Attraction, if I can't take a deep breath, I am restricted in my belief systems of love; the deeper the love, the deeper the breath. If I can connect to the Source core of Earth below, I can also extend the love outward and upward, taking deep breaths of enjoyment and fulfillment in life.

Our lungs are co-located in our bodies next to our hearts. Oxygen enters our bloodstream through the lungs and travels to the heart, allowing it to pump. When we're agitated, taking deep breaths instead of shallow ones is recommended so we don't hyperventilate, meaning too much air or overwhelm. If we stop and take a moment to inhale and exhale deeply, we are activating our hearts and heart centers to give and receive love; be calm, move to a lower state of being, not a lower vibration.

Clearing Past Fears and Avoidance
Healing the limbic system
Emotional limbic system healing is through your Source core connection to the Earth and provides a balanced approach to healing past life and this life energy fears. It will guide you to understand who you are as an individual without the fear and pain of emotional and physical suffering. If there is or was a pain in your body related to an

---

[8] Neal deGrasse Tyson, *Astrophysics for People in a Hurry, 2017*

illness or a physical act of violence, it can be healed energetically through the limbic system. Our bodies hold the precious memories of a lifetime and other lifetimes through the limbic system and the cortisol release system, designed to maintain balance. But when the energies are off, we cannot persist through space and time, and we suffer. This suffering causes the limbic system to go haywire, so to speak, and releases cortisol in our body's systems, which ends up in our energy fields due to the suffering mechanism, which is emotional. It is my opinion that our emotional bodies maintain the imprint of suffering and cause a delayed reaction when love is present. It doesn't mean we don't feel love, it means that our awareness of love is delayed and we don't fully understand how it got there or what to do with it. This is why I believe it takes survivors of sexual violence a long time to release the pain and suffering, even after the violence has stopped for good.

The delayed reaction is the most crucial point in healing the energetic limbic system as it breaks down the walls of suffering. Emotional and energetic wounds cause suffering. Walls are put in place to stop the suffering but create a delayed reaction (it takes a while to get through a wall), turning them into heart walls and fortresses around our hearts. With the moats of Timefields in front of those fortresses, we can see why the people who have suffered violence of any kind are difficult to heal. This method aims to work through the suffering aspect to get at the emotional wound and heal it faster so that it does not fester over time, causing greater suffering. The Timefields in place can be easily healed according to the method already described because it doesn't matter what the story is. In fact, it takes the story out completely, which can be a blessing to someone who does not want to relive the events of the past repeatedly, causing more suffering, illness, and Timefields. You can see the cyclical and spiraling behavior that gets set up through talk therapy in this situation. It is not that talk therapy is bad, as it brings up the acknowledgment of behaviors, but it does cause victims of violence to be caught in an ever-looping spiral of self-doubt and determination to stop the pain and suffering through avoidance. Those who can move past it through talk therapy are warriors indeed, but we are all warriors, so it's time to stop the suffering.

Healing the limbic system energetically takes time and release because time is the main cause of the initial scenario that caused the emotional upset. It was a point in time and a memory of time, so we approach the healing from that perspective. We tell ourselves we are safe, sound, and secure through the healing modality of talking directly to our limbic system. Our bodily response to anger, fear, and joy is part of the limbic system's release. We know we are at peace when we can be calm, hear our thoughts, understand our words, and know that it is right and true because wel feel it in our bodies. We settle down, feel more at ease, take part in the happenings around us, and connect to other people from a healthy perspective. So release the time from your mind as a form of energy. This is in conjunction with your integumentary system release.

NOTE: If you have PTSD or other traumatic stress, keep this incantation until the end of your healing process for the day and then say the integumentary incantation, as these two statements can be powerful and effect significant changes in your body. You need to be fully grounded and otherwise released from all other blocks before saying these lines with intention.

Try It: Limbic System Response Release
I [state your full name] release and understand the overwhelm of the past, present, and future as it moves through my limbic system and I transmute all my body's systems back to True Source energy through the deepest love and highest light.

Quantum Physics, Play & Idleness
Being part of a collective

When we play enveloped in love, we feel at ease, happy, in the moment, and naturally extend outward, accepting others in. We can't help it — it's a natural reaction, involuntary through our integumentary and nervous systems and our heart centers. We feel the love, want to share it, and let it spill out to others — not down our shirts, but outwards into space and time. It folds over as it hits another object or person, affecting the space-time continuum. I have no scientific proof, but love is energy, and we know energy moves in waves, as described by the science behind the form of electromagnetic waves. The fold comes from the energy wave crashing on the shore of another being or form like the ocean on land. Love is the only emotion that can do this, I think because it's expansive. Fear is the opposite. It retracts and shrinks. (Remember, love and fear are the only two emotions; everything else is nuance.)

I believe the space-time continuum is a product of love and nothing else. Love is the expansion of the Universe in all the ways it shows up. A woodworker loves the material she develops in her own hands and so loves the tools as well, especially if they come from a family member who loves the same activity. It connects her to her elders and ancestors in such a way that she feels expansive in and through love. Her woodworking ability is her own, and she has her own way of doing things, but she is connected at so many points through it: the tree, the harmony of nature, the action of doing or making through her hands and body, through divine life force energy, through her ancestral lineage — all of it makes up a force of energy that belongs through love.

Love as energy is extended outward in time and is the ultimate binder glue of the Universe, as I've mentioned in other sections. Feeling love is feeling time in an invincible way; our time is felt through love and feelings of time express themselves through love. "We had a good time, an enjoyable time." Expansive love and expansive time correlate to each other in a one-to-one ratio. If I'm full of love, I feel expansive and, therefore, full of time. The opposite is true when we're in fear; fear contracts, so we feel short on time or lost in time. If the expansion of the Universe is love, and love is expansive, then time heals all wounds in love. If I don't feel love for myself or others, I don't heal, and time marches on without me, making me feel lost to myself and others. The Timefield effect is about time — lost in time and space in my body. The space of my body individually contracts as I call in more fear, shame, and denigration. The outward expansion of love cuts across the field of time and brings in feelings of *avasa* for your life.

This expansion can be found in scientific research of our felt sense when experiencing an emotion or feeling.[9] Scientists gathered information from people in Western and Eastern countries and asked them how they felt when a specific feeling or emotion was noted. Imaging provided by the scientists shows that happiness and love are the only two feelings that diffuse through our bodies through increased sensation. Happiness is shown as being felt down into our toes and fingertips while love is shown everywhere except our legs and feet, keeping to the central theme of love in our heart centers. The researchers noted that the answers were consistent no matter what country or cultural identity the subject identified.[10]

We can create a theory from this scientific evidence that love, as the only expansive energy in our bodies, expands outwards in time through the Faraday Field of all connective energy. This energy then moves out to people and objects around us, hitting form and ricocheting back or moving through the particles in the air, causing all the expansion energy to be released in them as well. This continues until it eventually moves out into space, as in outer space, causing the entire Universe to expand. If we are a thinking-feeling Universe, then this makes complete sense, as our thoughts and feelings of love literally move mountains. When I say that love is the binder glue of the Universe, this is it. It extends outward, binding us to each other, but not to keep us locked to each other, to keep us safe in each others' arms or entitled to the love we all deserve.

Bringing in the Future
The pituitary gland and the third eye chakra

Emotions are a physical response to an image including our environment and the people in it. We are all here to make connections with the Earth and with each other. There are many ways to make connections and one of them is learning new things. Learning pulls us out of the past, keeps us in the present moment, and allows us to consider the future, which is our natural state of being. Bodies require homeostasis while our minds require movement forward. Fear, anger, and feeling unrequited in love can keep us from moving forward mentally and stop our bodies from achieving balance. Let's take a deeper look at how this impacts our daily lives from a systems perspective.

As the relay switch, the medulla connects our bodies to our hippocampus, which is further connected to our minds through the pituitary gland, centrally located in our brains and energetically connected to the third eye chakra. The pituitary gland regulates

---
[9] L. Nummenmaa, E. Glerean, R. Hari, & J.K. Hietanen, *Bodily Maps of Emotions*, 2013
[10] Ibid

our bodies growth, metabolism, water and salt levels, response to stress, among other automatic functions.[11] It is tied to the hypothalamus physically by a bundle of vessels and nerves known as the pituitary stalk. As the thinking-feeling structures of our brains, nerves provide us with an understanding of who we are and how we got here in this present moment. But the pituitary gland, when functioning at a high level, brings in the future through its insistence on growth. If we are 'grown' mentally, it refers to our ability to be emotionally balanced, make decisions that are beneficial to ourselves, and so on. We can only do this when we are in a state that allows us to see the future. How can we make decisions if we can't bring the future? Or, put another way, how can we make sense of things if we don't have the past to compare it to the present for a comparable future outcome? I hope this is making sense because it is about our ability as humans to predict the future — not just for ourselves, but for all of humanity. When you are tied or pushed, always looking down, you are unable to look up and out to predict and bring in the future in a very real sense.

The third eye is "the center of discovery"[12] and helps us see into the future by accessing the extended present. (Jump back to Chapter 11 for more on this extended present.) The circuitry of our minds gets melded to our bodies through our hearts through the energy of the heart chakra, as realized by the integumentary system, which is brought about through our connections to others. Love is required for a true connection to another person — love in all its forms, though there is only one frequency of love, we just experience it on different levels in our minds. Sensing someone else's heart, or love, brings our bodies back towards homeostasis. We feel calmer, more at ease, more like ourselves, which allows our brains to release the correct amount of hormone levels that keeps us in balance. It is a feedback loop - one affects the other. Healing within is the key to everything. Healing through awareness, moving through intention, believing through love. Love really is the answer. It's not just a Disney movie trope. It affects us chemically and energetically and moves us past fear and anger towards joy and *avasa*.

Being in balance creates a slower time continuum. As you look at an hourglass that's on its side, no sand moves through it because it is resisting gravity by being in balance. Gravity is an effect of time, mass and force. Gravity pulls you down towards the Earth, drops you on your head, conking you out, making you feel dizzy, frazzled, foggy. The fog of time is homeostasis, it suspends time through being unaware or confused. The mists of time contain your life force energy within while life outside continues. It is difficult to be aware of what's going on around us while in a head fog, so we go inward instead. We look inward to figure out what's holding us in place, but homeostasis keeps us there until something short circuits the issue to knock us out of our fog. Our bodies want to be

---

[11] Cleveland Clinic online Health Library, 2024
[12] Dharma Singh Khalsa, *Meditation as Medicine*, 2001

in homeostasis, but our minds don't; that is the disconnect between the two. Our minds are ever evolving forward while our bodies are trying to achieve balance. What happens between the two is mystical and magical, like the time just before sunrise and just after sunset.

So, why does all of this matter? Because right now on planet Earth, we are up for discovery of The New. We want to bring in better societies, better ways of living that don't force people down, but lifts them up to new possibilities of living in harmony, peace, respect of each other and joy. We no longer want to live in a depressed state where the governments of inaction only serve the few and not the many. We want our kids and grandkids to live in a different level of being in their bodies as right and true and we don't want our planet to look like a war zone either through environmental degradation or the actual survival of the fittest mechanism that has left many scars on this planet. Now is the time to start healing yourself to affect change on Earth. Healing yourself first means you can then help others if you feel called, or just enact change by being in a more rested state of being. If you feel called to heal others, you can begin by using the protocols at the back of this book to release the behaviors that are stopping you from enacting change.

A New Approach for an Age-Old Problem of Healing
Autonomic nervous system healing

The autonomic nervous system can be understood as two halves of a whole. Scientists have split it into two main areas to describe its function more fully. One half is our sympathetic nervous system, where our cortisol response lives. The other half is the parasympathetic nervous system that allows us to rest and relax and controls functions such as waste removal, heart rate reduction, production of mucus and saliva, among others.[13] Each function is highly specialized, but they work together to create a gentle feeling in our bodies to help us reach and maintain homeostasis or balance. As the name suggests, it's all very automatic, but when we add awareness to our systems, we can influence positive change to help in healing. Now, I'm not saying you need to be fully aware of these functions all day, every day, that would be exhausting and is probably why our bodies have these automatic functions in the first place. Our brains need to be freed up to allow for other modes of thought and function like interacting with others and our environment, introspection, and performing tasks such as driving, making decisions, and creative endeavor.

How we care for our bodies and minds greatly impacts these automated functions. Not only are our bodies scanning the environment, but they are also giving us information on a type of feedback loop. If you're thirsty, you drink water; if you're tired, you sleep; if you're agitated, you take a walk, and so on. All of these movements and tiny

---

[13] Dharma Singh Khalsa, *Meditation as Medicine*, 2001

decision points throughout the day are so automated that we're barely conscious of them. When we become suddenly conscious of them, our minds may think something is wrong, and maybe there is, but is it in the muscle tissue or joint, for example, or is it an energetic block?

Our bodies speak to us through a language all their own. Becoming more aware of subtle sensations is one way to understand the language of your body better. For example, as I write this, I am listening to music that is aligned in frequency to healing. My right hand has a subtle pain or pressure between my thumb and the center of my hand. I'm noticing it enough to stop and find out what it is. I simply ask my body through muscle testing if it is an energy block. I received a 'no' response, so I stopped for a moment to think about what it might be, and the idea came to me that I'm responding to the music I'm listening to. I asked again through muscle testing and received a 'yes.' This action takes both conscious and subconscious mind thinking. I moved quickly between the consciousness of the pain and the subconscious of what was causing it. Our bodies and minds are designed to do this; we can all tap into this resource if we wish. We are all healers in our own way and your own body is the best place to start.

When my nervous system is processing a wound or wounded behavior, I get a buzzy and/or 'swoopy' feeling in my head. There's a level of vibration that feels like I just got off a swing or carnival ride that's been spinning me around for a while. When I feel this sensation, I know I need to stop what I'm doing and check in with myself to understand what I'm feeling but may not be fully conscious of. It can be annoying at times, especially if I don't want to stop, but if I don't, it will persist. Or, if I have cleared a bunch of emotional energy, usually related to past life behaviors, my nervous system will start to hum in my ear, letting me know that it is reconfiguring itself. I know this through muscle testing, being curious about what is happening in my body, and asking a bunch of questions through the yes/no response of muscle testing. I have also developed my body-mind connection enough that I can ask questions to my body directly and hear the response.

The process goes like this:
"Asking my body for answers for my best and highest good. Why is my ear humming again?" Whatever answer comes to me first is usually the right answer. I verify the response through muscle testing once I hear it in my mind.

New Age Healing for Time-Honored Results
Automatic responses

Energetically, your mind is more responsive than your body to understanding what's happening in the body. The body is aligned with the divine but not at all times, whereas the mind can detect energies outside its domain of influence. The automatic state of being in terms of releasing all that does not serve us is our true state of being. It is

Source aligned through love, joy, and *avasa*. It is not detrimental programming but a re-programming of how we should live anyway through our Source energy. It gets us back to our original state.

This is our true and natural state of being on Earth. We shouldn't have to constantly clear ourselves or be in a constant healing state. At some point, we need to step into the joy and let the good vibes flow because we are not called to always suffer or to 'bear the cross.' Life on Earth is a *learning* state of being, which is also why we're designed to automatically learn behaviors and other types of information from our parents, elders, and other people we trust. But the constant state of suffering and sorrow needs to stop. We are here to love and to thrive. Believe it. The time begins now to move past a state of being through detrimental programming from our past and past lives, from the systems in place to keep us in a low vibration, and from the energies causing us to persist in a constant state of overwhelm.

Begin to believe in your mind that this is all possible **right now**, not someday in the future. It is possible right now to heal and be healed, to love and be loved, to live and let live all the people and creatures on Earth that deserve to be here as much as we do. We can all live in harmony and respect for each others' way of being and way of life - which also extends to the plant and animal kingdoms. We ALL deserve love and respect for being in a body on Earth, however that body takes shape — as a tree, a mite, an elephant or a human being. We can all live peacefully right now under the sun, conscious of our light and love on Earth. Here is a great way to start moving into your new state of consciousness in your own body's awareness through its nervous system.

Say these intention-setting statements out loud if possible.
"I ask my mind to install the impulse to clear my body and energy systems when emotional overwhelm happens through the deepest love and the highest light."

This statement includes detrimental and denied aspect energy, neutralizing discordant and dissonant energy, which almost always come up when a wound is cleared. Detrimental energies act as a reverberation on the energy that was just cleared and can cause that wound to be enacted again.

"I release and uncreate all energies within me that no longer serve my highest and best. I install the impulse to release denigration from my body and to release those energies with effortless ease.

"I demand my mind to be forthright in releasing the past life behaviors that serve to repeat denigration patterns. I ask my heart center to transmute those energies back to True Source energy through my Source core connection to the Earth."

<u>Healing the Emotions of Cortisol Response</u>

Among other things, the hypothalamus controls our cortisol release mechanism. When feeling overly stressed, or not in balance, our bodies release cortisol, the stress hormone, through the hypothalamus into the bloodstream through the autonomic nervous system, as all hormones are. The hypothalamus also regulates long term metabolism. Metabolism is also implicated by the amount of sleep we get each night consistently. And now I hope you see the connection between being stressed, cortisol levels, the amount of sleep we get, and the reality of weight gain in our bodies. The hypothalamus is responsible for all of these functions and serves as a protection energy in our minds when we are out of balance through our thinking-feeling mechanism. It's all elegantly orchestrated through our mind-heart-body connection and deserves some attention if we are to find our way back to each other. Love is the greatest resource we have on Earth; we can use it infinitely and it never gets used up.

Cortisol lives in our bodies daily from an extended sense of fear and anger through the fight or flight response (notice I don't include 'freeze,' more on that later). Cortisol can be detrimental to our health in extended amounts of time because it is not meant to stay in our systems for long and keeps our bodies from achieving homeostasis. In balance, our bodies' systems are designed to be free of anxiety, fear, and anger. To move past the cortisol response, we have to move past the emotions that got us there, but how do you know what you don't know? Unconscious emotions can be sneaky in how they affect our health — physical, emotional, psychological, and spiritual. It is this bodily response where the story starts to break down. If you don't know the story, how can you tell it to release it? But your body knows, and it knows what's right.

Asking the body to release the shame, grief, fear and anger at an unconscious level, whether it's Timefields, wounds or wounded behaviors is a powerful way to move through what is keeping your systems in check. You can also ask the body to move back into homeostasis by setting the intention in your energy healing practices. Remember, words and writing things down is a powerful way to both set intentions and release energy. You have the power to disregard or accept the intention. Your mind is powerful, so use it for your own good. The intention goes like this:

"I demand my mind and body to sublimate fat, fear and anger and all energies keeping me from releasing them through the deepest love and highest light. I demand my body to release itself from all anger and fear and transmute it back to True Source energy through deepest love and highest light."

Creative Anger and Doing the Right Thing
Fear, anger, and fear of anger

Fear and muck live in our lives daily; there's no getting away from it. I define 'muck' as all the bad-mouthing behaviors that impact our energy and nervous systems. I don't need to expound on the ways we come across it; we're all aware. But short of becoming a monk who lives on a remote island off the coast of Venezuela, how do we get away from it and release it? As already discussed in the limbic system release, we hold fear and anger in our bodies through memory and time. Cortisol is known as the stress hormone and you can do a simple online search to find information about it. Cortisol is part of our fear and anger response system known as 'flight or fight.' It becomes a closed-loop system, so to speak, in that when we are feeling our 'feels' and another anger or fear event happens, the original event is activated, turning us into the green-eyed monster or the underbelly of our own existence. We can turn on a dime into a rage machine when our nervous system is impacted, and it can often be an unconscious reaction to a previous situation that we've been sitting in or stewing on for a while.

In my opinion, most of our anger and rage are unconscious reactions to a previous event because, as a society, we are told to hold in our anger, that it's dangerous and needs to be melted down into nothing. However, our nervous systems don't melt, they persist, so to heal, we need to move past the fear of anger itself. It's better to understand why we get angry to begin with and then change our perspective on what it does for us from a healed perspective — no more raging against the machine. The best and most enlightening description of anger I've heard comes from Lee Harris, spiritual advisor, energy healer, and self-improvement entrepreneur.[14] He describes anger as a cap for grief. See if this is true for yourself as you examine the parts of you that are angry by asking yourself, "Why?" Why are you angry at a person, interaction, or system? Dig as deep as you can for a true understanding of yourself.

From a collective point of view, we can see this all over our societal systems throughout history. Time and again, people who are oppressed in one way or another are forced to live in grief and shame (a type of grief). Sorrow and what happens within those energies becomes part of an everyday existence — anger rises against the oppressors, a system, or a person. In the US, we don't need to look far to see this pattern of behavior as the Civil Rights movement gave rise to the Black Lives Matter movement, as the Stonewall uprising in New York City gave rise to the LGBTQIA+ movement, and the millions of women who are affected by sexual, physical, and emotional violence became one loud voice under #MeToo. People's nervous systems are overrun with grief, and they literally can't take it anymore. It's a progressive movement of energy from lower vibrational matches of shame and fear, through a sense of lack, to a higher level of vibrational matches of pride and wisdom of knowingness in our bodies.[15] The sense of lack through unworthiness gives way to a realization that, "I deserve to be here and I deserve love and respect." Anger is the movement that gets us there. It can be a slow, steady burn or an explosion like a volcano. It's a destructive force, but in its destruction, it's also creative.

In his movie, *Do the Right Thing,* writer/director/actor/creator Spike Lee, explores this sense of grief and shame of unfulfilled love that eventually gives way to anger. The explosion of anger comes towards the end of the movie in a shocking sequence of

---

[14] Refer to end notes for website and other information.
[15] David R. Hawkins, *Power vs Force*, 2002

events that shows the characters destroying their own neighborhood in an act of rage. When I watched that movie as a teenager, I didn't understand why until I had a very enlightening conversation with a classmate who is black. He explained to me the deep wound that is created, borne upon, and then carried around by black communities all over the US. In his opinion, the characters did 'do the right thing' by ransacking their neighborhood, and their rage was right and good. I've thought about that conversation many times over the years and I have come to fully understand what he meant. Our anger and rage are a source of change and transformation; it's there to serve a purpose. To deny it is to deny ourselves and our right to live free in our own nervous systems.

Anger is the medicine that our bodies need to explore deeper feelings of shame and grief. It gets us over the block of being tamped down in our lives and in our bodies themselves. It gives us the freedom to express ourselves uncommonly and to be aware that things aren't right. It allows us to do the right thing for ourselves and each other. But what we don't need are shouting matches that explore our grief through denigrating someone else. Shouting matches seem to be the way of the world now, and are not progressive in their movement. They create looping patterns of more grief as other people get sucked into the energy of fear and shame. To move past those energies, while still allowing the creative, destructive energy of anger to do its thing, we need to take time to contemplate and understand why we're mad.

Stuck anger in the form of energy in our bodies can also be a destructive force. Stuck anger is unacknowledged or denied anger. It can have a lasting impact on our nervous systems and, therefore our bodies, and can become an illness or disease quickly through the fight or flight response. Our cortisol response systems transmute fear and anger into action through hormones in our bodies. The cortisol response is tied back to the limbic system that connects us to our past through the amygdala.[16] We'll look into the amygdala more in the next section, but it stores memories of both fear and grief. Both of these systems are intertwined with our autonomic nervous system, which connects us to the present moment as it constantly scans our environment directly through the integumentary system. All these systems work together to store and release energy in the form of emotions. When any part of these systems is overrun with anger, grief, or fear, through an event from the past, our present moment is affected, often negatively, we move into an automatic response of unconscious thoughts and actions.

<u>Writing for Soul Exploration Instead of Gratitude: Journaling</u>

If you're feeling low and need to process your thoughts, journaling is a good way to start. Writing is a good way to feel guided through practice and intention. It can be a communication between your conscious mind, Highest Self, and the place that we all tune into to receive guidance in our lives. Some people pray, others talk to their god in

---

[16] Cleveland Clinic online Health Library, 2024

whatever form they take, still others go to Nature to commune with energies there, or they might listen to music. In those moments, we are tuning into the power that is beyond us but not out of our control. If you feel out of control, then you need to take a step back and figure out what emotional state might be impacting you. In those states, our minds are impacted by our emotions, and we can't hear, see, or feel things clearly. It's ok to step away from that practice to change your energy so that you can come back to it with a clear mind. It takes practice, but keep trying because when you hit that moment of deep concentration, you are in Flow, which is the best feeling on Earth.

So, journaling is a good way to tune into yourself, but it is best done through a posture of love and understanding. How you do this depends on who you are as a person and who you want to be when the gratitude is served up, so to speak. You are a loving individual who cares about all people, so it's easy for you to think about how to be grateful, but does your body believe it? Our minds can easily override what our bodies are telling us. We do this all the time when we go to work not feeling well, or when we do something that doesn't feel right. Our minds tell us to be grateful, but our bodies can think it's a bunch of hooey. And our bodies think that way because our hearts are closed down to the optimism and joy of being happy. It's a systems approach, in other words. The three systems of body, heart, and mind need to be in tune with each other in order for the gratitude to show up.

We can tell ourselves that we are happy through gratitude journaling, but if our bodies don't agree with it, we don't stay there. If our bodies don't align with our minds and hearts, it doesn't work. I can tell myself I'm happy all day long, but in the end my body's wisdom knows better because my subconscious or unconscious memories tell me a different story. These stories are stored at the level of emotion that runs through our limbic system from our amygdala. Over time stories become a feeling in our heart center and then a feeling in our body, which can turn into disease caused by emotional turmoil. Happiness stems from our hearts, not our minds. If our hearts are uplifted, then we feel it in our bodies, and our minds follow suit. The 'fake it til you make it' saying is all about getting our minds and bodies to align, but the heart is the soul source connection that brings in feelings of love, joy, and *avasa*. (Sanskrit word meaning "a lust for life through the power of love in our bodies.") The advantage of happiness is not in the believing of it in our minds, but in the feeling of it in our hearts and bodies. If I feel that you love me then I am more likely to engage with you, trust you, and feel that I am reciprocated in those feelings.

Try It: Dream Journals

Our dreams tend to tell us the truth of what we are feeling. If you are keeping a journal to engage with your gratitude, I encourage you to keep a dream journal to understand your subconscious feelings that reveal themselves while you are sleeping because they are how you truly feel. Gratitude journals are one way to connect with yourself through introspection, but they fall short on the deep work you need to do if you are dealing with a creative or life block.

Dream communication through healing is an often written subject, so I will not go into detail here, but it is worth exploring. I have read about whole communities in the past coming together to discuss their dreams and the word Dreaming is used by the indigenous Australian cultures to describe life on Earth in the past, present, and future perfect terms. Their beautiful artwork stems from their belief system of Dreaming. The word dream in American culture also has special significance through the oft-repeated (and maligned) phrase American Dream, which denotes an ability to look positively towards the future. It's a concept, not often a reality. But dreams do pertain to our everyday existence and should be taken seriously from the point that they are there to help us live healthy lives.

Resetting the Scales
A critique on weight loss

I have heard many of my peers say, "I don't eat that much and I eat healthy, why am I still gaining weight? Why can't I lose what I've gained?" Is it inevitable that we gain weight when we hit middle age? Is it really our fate to have slower metabolisms that keep us from enjoying our lives through food? I don't think so. I think it is a product of our modern era where we are chronically stressed or in flight or fight mode. Chronic stress related to fear, not knowing what the future holds for us, worry about money, worry about illness, our kids, our parents... any number of anxieties that we hold in our bodies because we have no control over them. Unworthiness also plays into it; unworthy of love or being seen or being upset through emotional overwhelm.

Scientific research has proven that cortisol is tied to persistent weight gain.[17] But there is also an energy through our fear and anger response that prevents us from losing weight and/or keeps us in a constant state of weight gain no matter how well we eat or how much we exercise. I believe all of this starts to take hold in our middle age as our body's processes start to change. We're supposed to be settling down at age 50-ish (or sooner)! Our bodies are telling us it's not good to be in chronic anxiety. We feel this more intensely after the so-called mid-life crisis where we see a better path to the future but for some reason can't seem to get there.

Keep in mind that our fear of fat is like an anchor point — it keeps us down if you don't release it through love and joy. Many energies in our bodies are in fear in terms of weight regulation. Our fear of fat comes from an overabundance of misinformation about how fat itself affects our bodies. There is as much true information as there is misinformation on this topic and you can find a "tit-for-tat" example in almost any copy

---

[17] This is a popular topic and a simple internet search can be a wealth of information.

or form of media out there. But if you release your fear and anger towards fat in your body and consuming the right amounts, you can effect significant change. Find healing in the statements below to release the fear and anger of fat itself. It will take undoing behaviors in order to affect this change in healing. Remember, you are telling yourself that you are not scared anymore and sometimes that takes a little while to take hold in our minds, hearts, and ultimately, our bodies.

Time and joy are the most healing aspects of our lives. You can effect change by speaking these words, but the real work comes from a grounded sensibility in your life. Go out and have fun, in other words! Don't keep to yourself — go outside and play and be the creative individual you were meant to be.

"I release and uncreate any and all fear and anger towards fat in my body and I install love, joy, and avasa through love and light."

Weight Gain Release:
"I demand my mind and body to align my energy to release weight gain and integrate being satiated and feeling full through deepest love and highest light."

Weight Loss Install:
"I demand my mind to align with my body's energy related to weight loss through the deepest love and highest light so that I can lose weight rapidly and with ease."

"I demand my mind to release any and all hidden energies and neutralize and harmonize any and all discordant and dissonant energies that are preventing me from losing weight rapidly and with ease through the deepest love and highest light."

This statement works in concert with rhythms of behavior changes and should be released first as a transmutation device that allows for change. Go back up to the rhythms of behavior release to state your intention, then release through the resistance to change statement. You can reword the statement to be focused on whichever type of weight loss you desire. For example, you can work on the rhythms of behavior of denigration that are keeping you in a looping pattern of disbelief in yourself and in your ability to release weight without conscious effort. Or you can become more focused on your disbelief in food itself. Whichever one you feel will affect the greatest amount of change first. Then release that same pattern through resistance to change, using the same or similar wording. It's much like the Timefield release where the same emotion lives in the Timefield as it does in the wounded behavior underneath and then the energy below that. It's a systems effect that is stacked in various areas and types of energies in our bodies except now it is a physical 'ailment' of being overweight or not in our best form.

We are programmed to believe that pain and suffering is involved in weight loss or to release of any type of denigrating ability. We think if we're not uncomfortable, it won't work, causing us to force ourselves to do things that we would rather not do. This perspective creates a resistance to weight loss and is mitigated through forgiveness. We have to forgive our minds and bodies the ability to effect great change without conscious effort. If you hate running (as I do), don't do it! There are so many other effective ways to release weight, not gain weight, and still move your body in time to your own rhythms of behavior. Don't denigrate yourself if you don't like a specific type of weight removal strategy or exercise. Just like energy clearing and creative endeavor, there are as many ways to dance with light as there are people on the Earth. Be one with the energies in your body and allow yourself the grace of being a human. Don't follow the herd if you don't want to. There is no resistance to change if you exercise the way you want and when you want. When you find this, you are in deep Flow with the energetic forces of Nature that serve to pull you forward in time. Remember, time release is the all important aspect in this type of healing work. We want to live in the present to envision the future. We can't do that when we are pushed down into the past. So remember where you are now and try to find a way forward that lifts you up, makes you feel good and doesn't hurt your body doing it.

I'm Hungry
Belief systems and food

While we're on the topic of food, let's get into the meat of how our belief systems impact our bodies. It's true that some foods are more nutrient rich than others in terms of our well being. However, we now understand that constant dieting, or restricting ourselves, is not beneficial to our bodies' systems. Of all the diets in the world, there is none that says your belief systems are the sole issue in your weight gain. Deepak Chopra's book on mindful eating, *What Are You Hungry For?*, is a welcome change to the dieting landscape, providing us with an understanding of our hormone system and belief systems that keep us from our best selves. But I think it goes much further than that because there is still a restriction and judgment on the food itself. My hypothesis is that we are putting judgments on the food we eat, causing us to gain weight because judgment is hard to digest. Religious beliefs can also affect our food judgements. We say to ourselves, "That's sweet, which is sinfully indulgent; I shouldn't eat it." Judgment on food is sneaky and nondescript as we only look at one part of food and amplify it.

At different times, we have vilified different components of food. From cholesterol in the form of eggs, to fat, then carbohydrates, then sugar (from sugar cane) on and off. Now it's processed foods or 'overly' processed foods. We turn against one food or another and everyone rushes to follow what they think is good advice, but we are all different in different ways. There is no one way to live on this planet and that includes no one way of eating. The nursery rhyme '*Jack Sprat could eat no fat, his wife could eat no lean. And so between the two of them, they licked the platter clean*' is fitting for how we should all be eating. Some people can eat onions, others can't — or won't. There's more than one vegetable that's green, so eat the green things you like and don't worry about the rest, likewise for fruit. There are many food varieties in the world because there are many different types of people. We're not meant to eat them all, we're meant to eat the ones that work best for our body's systems.

Notice that our tongues taste bitter, salty, sweet, sour, and umami. There's no one taste that our tongues prefer over the other. Consider a balanced approach to eating all the different foods that the receptors on our tongues say we should have in our diets. People love salty-sweet foods like granola or the spicy-sweet of tangy sweet and sour sauce. We love these combinations because they are balanced on our tongues and go into our bodies in enjoyment, not judgment if we can do it. If you approach your eating habits and food from a balanced perspective, the sweets lose the 'bad behavior' power and the salty foods also don't seem as forbidden. Of course you should follow your doctor's orders if you are suffering from diabetes, angina, or other heart conditions, and any other illness that is impacted by diet. The point I'm trying to make is that from a healthy perspective, all food is good and borne of love just as we all are so we should try to make less conditional love statements towards our food.

Food and Culture

Different cultures eat different foods for different meals. Steak and eggs is considered a hearty, healthy breakfast in the UK. It's considered a heavy, heart-hurting breakfast in the US, but it's ok for dinner. Meanwhile, bacon and sausage are ok for breakfast, just don't turn it into a snack because that's bad for you. Likewise cheese has been enjoyed for 1,000 or more years as a tasty, healthy addition to our diets that includes enzymes and bacteria that are good for our guts. Many cultures are known for their styles of cheese including French, Italian, Mexican and Indian. But wait, cheese has fat in it (yes, it's cheese…) and maybe some other things that we don't fully understand so now it's bad for you, or eat in moderation. Control yourself and control your behavior. Always. We're in a constant state of control and it has worked its way into our bodies through food, the one thing that we all enjoy no matter the culture.

Are we just being greedy?

Greed and gluttony and our belief systems about hunger play into our judgment of food as well. Here's a controversial statement: *there is no such thing as greed*. Think about that for a few minutes! How could that be when we can point to so many people in the world who are greedy? It's easy to point the finger, but again, greed is a judgment statement and causes shame. "Don't be so greedy," you say to the 3-year-old who wants another piece of candy. Now she's shamed into thinking it's not ok to want more and what she wants — sugar, in the form of candy — is bad. She grows up believing that her hunger needs to be constantly controlled and abated so dieting becomes a way of life. The hunger she feels in the pit of her stomach extends to other things in her life. She's hungry for success ("Don't get too big for your britches" — double whammy statement of shame!), she's hungry for attention ("Stop being a show-off"), she's hungry for love and she's starving for affection ("Who do you think you are, he/she could never love you because you're not enough, or too _____"). All of these things show up in our lives as a hunger and gets tied into our systems through nourishment.

Pre-made and Packaged Food vs. Homemade Food

We judge our lifestyles when we say packaged foods are bad, but homemade food is good. It creates guilt for some because they may not have time to make food 'from scratch.' Calling the food we eat "crap" or "shit" is not the best policy, either. When we do that we are telling ourselves we're eating waste, which is a negative and detrimental type of programming. The phrase, 'you are what you eat' doesn't quite hit the target, it's more about what you believe you are eating and how it impacts your body. If you believe that packaged food is bad for you or has some kind of killer instinct to it, then it probably will cause problems. This does not take away from people who have severe allergies, intolerances, and other chemical imbalances that impact their food intake. But by and large, the things we eat and the comments we make to ourselves on what and how we're eating have a long-term lasting effect. And because it is brought forward to our attention almost daily with new types of diets and other homeopathic-type ways of eating, we end up dealing with deeply ingrained belief systems.

I believe fast food, through our belief systems, is detrimental to our bodies. We are a fast food nation here in the US and have exported many fast food brands around the world. I think the health impacts are because we believe food should be fast — prepared and eaten fast — no time to linger or enjoy; no time to make merry with friends, family, and colleagues. People who eat fast food too often experience a deep sense of lack. They eat food that is disconnected from their bodies' systems by being prepared in haste, they eat it in haste (often in the car), and then they judge themselves for eating so poorly. Not every meal has to be a well thought out love fest, that's unrealistic in our modern society, but we can start by cutting out the judgments on ourselves and the food we eat. Fast food can be a treat that is enjoyed — guilt free.

Of course there is a line for how much we eat — over-eating can be a real problem, but our belief systems and inner wounding play a much more significant role than the food itself. If our bodies work the way nature intended, we should be able to maintain homeostasis and anything unnecessary to our bodies' functions will be eliminated automatically. Yes, automatically. Homeostasis is the key to our bodies' functionality and is a built-in feature; we don't have to see a guru to get it. But we seem to have a hard time keeping the balance. While at the doctor's office, prepare yourself for the guilt of being criticized on your truth about the foods you eat and the time you take to exercise, but don't swallow that guilt because it's not digestible. Eating your way through life is not what we're here for, but we can enjoy our time with others while feasting in all of our senses through enjoying what we eat.

Try It: Stop Putting Judgments in Your Body

So, what to do? How do you eat food while not worrying about what you're eating? Start with identifying your inner wounding around food. Write down all the words and phrases that are in your head related to food. 'Sinfully delicious,' 'bad for your heart,' 'slams my arteries shut,' 'so good, but so bad,' 'greasy spoon,' 'rabbit food'... and it goes on. Look at the belief systems those phrases bring up for you from a societal level and how you were raised. Write it all down and see what comes out on the page. Now look how it impacts your life on a daily, seasonal, and year-after-year basis. For example, "When I was little, I wasn't allowed to eat desert if I didn't eat my dinner. Now I feel like I have to eat my dinner, even if I'm full and I shouldn't enjoy dessert."

Life's too short to not eat dessert. Seriously.

Harmful Chemicals in Food

Draw a line at chemicals. Manufactured chemicals do not belong in our bodies. They are the one thing that eliminates with fear. We cannot hold them in our bodies' systems and getting rid of them can be difficult. Foreign bodies in our systems confuse them — pathogen or bacteria? But even this topic is a slippery slope because organic food costs more. If I can't afford to buy organic food and I know it's better for me, now I'm judging the food I'm buying as not good enough, which means I'm not good enough. Eat what's right for you, your wallet, and allow yourself the grace to know that you are nourishing yourself in the way that YOUR body tells you, not how society tells you.

Chapter 13: Timefields & Addiction/Addictive Behaviors

Our creative lives are susceptible to the emotional overwhelm that causes Timefields. We are highly tuned instruments, so to speak, that are impacted by the smallest amount of both inspiration and stagnation. When we don't realize we are in overwhelm, we may find ourselves looking to other sources for help — alcohol, drugs, binge eating, scrolling through our phones, etc. These are all ways we deal with an unrealized emotional state of overwhelm.

   We are not meant to rely on outside sources for our creative material. We are meant to look within, find our intuitive state through our subconscious symbols, and bring them forward through our conscious minds. When our conscious minds are numb, how can they believe what they already know? When our sleep is drugged, how will we remember the messages we have received? We can't. I believe that creativity through pain is a misnomer. It's true that alcohol and drugs can bring us to an altered mental state in small amounts, but the emotional overwhelm of a Timefield does not allow us to continue on that path. It pulls us down instead of allowing us to move through.

Addictions and addictive behaviors stem from fear of being lost, unbounded in love, unrequited love, unhanding your truth to yourself or others. It is unworthiness at its deepest, most sorrowful level. Latching on to an addictive behavior is a loss of control. You lose control of your life, body, and whereabouts. Where you are in space and time becomes immaterial because you are numb to it. Numbing is the main ingredient of addiction and addictive behaviors, no matter the method because the person does not want to deal with the sorrow underneath.

Unrequited love is a big reason why people move into addictive behaviors. Remember, love is more than just romantic or intimate love. You can have unrequited love from a sibling, parents, or friend. All of these types of unrequited love scenarios cause people to dive into deep sorrow and they don't know how to get out of it, so they turn to alcohol, drugs, eating disorders, excessive technology use, misuse of sex and pornography, gambling, and so on — all the ways that we turn to other things or people outside ourselves to numb the pain of misunderstanding in love. We may also struggle with the truth about ourselves and our own behaviors. This is a difficult topic because so much of it is unconscious or subconscious that we don't even realize it is happening. So if unrequited love is the biggest reason that leads people to addiction, let's focus on it for this healing session.

If you are reading this section, now is the time to start unraveling your past behaviors and call yourself and others accountable. Don't take on other people's energies, but also hold yourself to what is true. You may be the unending cause of your own sorrow, but it may also be true that other people's actions against you hold you in that position. Being true to yourself works both ways. Open your throat chakra and let the energy flow through your canal of truth through self-introspection. It is easy to be scared of it; no one likes to look at their own flaws, but if you can be open and curious about what is going on without judgment, you are halfway there.

Defining Addiction
How unrelating makes us feel numb

Addiction is a limiting behavior that causes a person to be trapped in an unending Timefield of lack. It is a negative feedback solution to a problem that does not fix itself until an energetic intervention is provided. This feedback loop traps not only the person it is affecting but also the people surrounding that person, whether it's family members, friends, or coworkers — usually all of the above. The spider webbing or network pattern of addiction makes it a pandemic of epic proportions, as each person who is struggling with addiction affects people around them, which in turn causes them to impact others. Not many of us are *not* affected by addiction and addictive behavior because of this pattern. Addiction in the form of substance abuse takes hold of a lot of people, but most famously creatives, who feel their energies rise and fall more acutely than others.

Addiction is also a dissociative state and can cause people to feel unrelated to at work, at home, or any other situation that is relational. Some people can handle their addictive behavior so well that they disassociate from it, thinking that they are not in an addictive state. This can be anything from drugs and alcohol to behaviors around sex, relationships, gambling, or any other form of behavior that causes a person to keep going back to the dry well of not being seen and heard.

Relationships and Unmet Needs in Addictive Partnerships

Those people who are in addictive relationships feel demoralized but don't understand their inability to break free through self-doubt and feel undone by it. It becomes an energy of "can't live with 'em, can't live without 'em," or as Lord Huron sings, *"You're tired of me, I'm tired of you, so turn around and leave me to myself."* They become 'high functioning' as they take on the other person's wounds, but disassociate from their own. They are in a combative scenario, are aware of it, and feel they are not right in the head. So they step away from themselves believing they are 'in it to win it' when actually they are being sucked into a vortex.

This vortex is about control. It only serves to cut down the person who wants to break free and the vortex is allowed to survive only through the disassociated state. In this scenario, if you are the person who wants to leave, to get out you need to cut across the energy of self-doubt by sharing what's happening with your loved ones. Don't be alarmed or scared if the other person cusses you out or threatens you in any way. If it is an act of physical violence, get help immediately. You can no longer suffer the wounds of your life, and it's time to break free of the energy that keeps you in a looping pattern of denigration. You are also likely in your own Timefield of self-doubt, so it becomes a double entendre of self-doubt between you and the other person. You have the power and authority to be your own person and not take on the aspects of other people's natures.

How do you know you are in this type of relationship if you are disassociated from yourself? Time to get real with yourself and look around you. Look for the signs and symbols that reveal your sense of lack, or non-harmonious relationship. If you are cut off from the things that bring you joy, like your favorite music, clothes you like to wear, or the little things like being able to sit and read a book, this is a definite sign that something needs to change. Things like bank accounts that don't reflect your health and wealth are also a sign. Your house or apartment will also reveal to you what needs to change. If it feels empty or like a prison, sit with yourself and understand why, and then make the necessary changes. What does your body feel like in space and time? If you get sick a lot or have a lack of energy, take note and find the necessary healer to get you back on your feet. All of these things point to an energy that needs to be changed.

Find healing through your own actions of self-love. How do you feel when you are in joy? What do you like to do when you are with yourself or those who love you as an individual, not as an energy who serves? Believe in yourself, and others will show up for you in ways seen and unseen. There is an energy in the Universe that wants to help, and when you connect to yourself, things will just happen for you that help you break free from your wounded heart that feels over-large in this moment. Don't allow other people's behaviors to sink you into a Timefield of lack. You are abundant love — always have been, always will be — so believe in your ability to break the binds that tie you to another who will never return your love in the abundant form you give them.

Behaviors of Addiction

Though I have never taken drugs of any kind (other than medicine for illness), and my over-drinking days of college are long gone, I can relate to addictive behaviors and have observed them up close and personal in my life. As an energy healer, I see the power behind the illness, but I also see the power of love as its cure.

Here is a list of defining behaviors I observed (unscientifically) of someone, and the people that surround them, who is under the influence of addiction.

1. A vitality suck — removes the life force energy from the person who is addicted and causes them to become a shell of what they once were.
2. Character remover/eraser — a once gracious and independent person becomes mean/sour and co-dependent on people. Freedom is gone.
3. Being obtuse when answering questions as a reliance technique to have your own way.
4. Sneaky/backhanded methods of communicating and living through lies, misbehavior and an unending need to cover up what is shameful to them.
5. The permeation of lies leads to disassociation from reality. What's real, what's not? What is the truth of any given situation? Again, the root cause is a cover-up of shameful behavior. **Not dealing with reality becomes a bottom-line check.**
6. Giving away possessions to make up for behavior becomes a real need but can deplete life force energy. It becomes a symbol of giving away what makes that person vital and as they see their money and/or belongings disappear, they do too.
7. Jobs/earning money are taken away or removed because of the behavior patterns. This is a double-edged sword of both pride in oneself and life force energy being removed instantaneously.
8. Isolation becomes a real thing that begins in one's head and moves out to the real world.
9. Habitual cycles of clear understanding of what needs to change, but lacking the resources to make the changes, which then causes the person to fall back into a depressive state.
10. <u>Sense of lack</u> related to money, care from others, state of mind, feelings of independence, methods to break the cycle. "I lack resources, time, money, understanding from others and myself."

11. <u>Sense of lack related to self-worth.</u> Wishful thinking that I am worthy of these things. "Why would anyone take the time to help me?"
12. Care and concern accepted from the wrong place: "They only want me to get better so I can take care of them." This thinking is a type of depressive state.
13. Breaking out of unhealthy relationships becomes harder and harder as the person gets sucked down into a Timefield of disbelief and unloved or abandonment feelings. "Why can't I cross this finish line? Why do I always trip myself up?" Hardcore negative attachment to the people who become codependents.
14. Survivor's guilt for the loved ones surrounding the addictive behavior, which moves the survivor into a depressive state. And the cycle can continue...

Try It: Healing Emotions Related to Addiction

Begin healing the wound by finding your soul source connection through joy. What brings you joy from an unaltered state? What findings have you discovered on your journey through the Timefield discussion that you can apply to your wound? How can you start to relate to your feelings from a fully realized state rather than a wounded state? Remember, you are NOT something that is broken and needs to be fixed. <u>You are a whole person unto yourself with an intact soul source connection</u>. Though you may feel disconnected from yourself and others, you are still a vital part of existence on Earth and need to share who you truly are with others in order to feel free and healed.

1. Begin again with the statement: **"I am a whole person who does not need to be repaired and am a vital part of existence on Earth."** Say it out loud to yourself. Look in the mirror as you say it if you want to, or if you can – it's hard, but believe in yourself. You can do it.

2. <u>5 Vital Statements:</u> Then write down five things that make you who you are. What are the vital things in your life that make you who you are? Be as **silly** or as **goofy** as you want. It's time to start bringing joy back into your life.

3. Find all the things that bring you **joy** and find your soul source center through that. Many of you may have to go back to childhood to find what brings you joy. Some of you may have painful childhood memories that bring you face-to-face with your wound. In times such as these, look for the helpers, as Mr. Rogers used to say. There are always people and other beings around (such as pets) that are there to help guide you through the wound.

4. After you find the 5 Vital Statements, find your favorite way to **create** and work through the feelings that are stopping you from experiencing them in this point in time. If you can, put on your favorite music and **dance** around your house or apartment. You know that you are moving in a positive direction and state of being if

you can dance through the hurt and sorrow. Body movement and dance can get you there faster.

5. Other ideas to get you moving:
    - Are you **happy** enough to give someone a hug?
    - Are you ready to move on from the hurt and pain you've been experiencing to **embrace** another person in your life?
    - Can you **chat** with someone and ask them about their day rather than launching into what is causing you pain? This is not a denial of self, you can still tell them your feelings, but maybe you can ask them about themselves first.
    - When you take your dog for a walk, can you **greet** the people you pass?

These are all things you can do in your environment to move you into a new way of being. They seem small, but they are mighty.

Find Professional Help

Be aware that the depressive state from drugs and alcohol take on an energy system of their own. The above thoughts, ideas, and conditions of fulfillment are not a replacement for professional medical care. They are a way to bring about transformation through awareness. You are not meant to be alone if you are in this state. Find your healers to be all the people who are there for you and can give you the right medical advice on addiction and addictive behaviors. You are still in your power and if you don't understand what is happening, find someone who can guide you.

Belief in your own powers is a healed state of being and can be formally introduced through your Source core connection to the Earth. Go back to the **Source Cord Visualization** if you are having problems with this section and find healing through sending all those energies that do not serve you down your cord into the Earth. The Earth is your mother and guide to understanding who you really are. You are not your swirling thoughts of incompleteness, you are a grounded source of love who has the ability to effect change in your life and the lives of others. You are autonomous and can find grounded healing methods that work best for you.

For Codependents and Others

For people who are struggling with someone in their lives who is dealing with addiction and possibly depression because of it, which is common, there is healing for you as well. Find the time to work through your own sense of lack as it is reflected to you in the person who has the addiction illness. Understand the behaviors that you observe in them and then apply them to your own life. It's easy to point the finger and see the thorn in someone else's side, but what about the one wounding your own side? This is how we start to bring about awareness through grounded healing.

Try It: Be a Monk
With apologies to Tony Shalhoub

There was a detective show on American TV for eight seasons called *Monk*. This show serves a purpose for us other than great entertainment to figure out 'who dunnit.' The main character, Adrian Monk, is a detective with OCD, or obsessive-compulsive disorder. He sees the world in very different ways, which makes him a great detective, even if he has a lot of funny quirks. He struggles with depression as a result of his wife being killed and his inability to solve her murder. The crux and humor of the show rely on the expression of his OCD and how he won't do certain things while other things he does seem abnormal to the people around him. Despite all this, he has a group of people surrounding him who love him, care for him, and want to be his unending friend. This show brings about awareness of our own behaviors as we see the methods our minds and bodies unconsciously create from being distraught and emotionally wounded.

My daughter and I one day started a game I'll call *"How I'm like Monk"* where we listed off behaviors reflected to us through the character Monk. The game goes like this: "I'm like Monk when I rearrange the silverware drawer exactly as I like it." Or "I'm like Monk when I don't see the clues right in front of me, but get it eventually." We had fun with it and giggled at our own and each others' quirks because we all have them. Use this same method with the person in your life who is reflecting your behaviors to you.

Look at the person in your life that you are focused on right now, who might be irritating, annoying, or hurting you in some way. Write down the behaviors that get under your skin and then write down the belief system that you find distracting. Now, turn the tables on yourself and write down all the ways you are like that behavior or belief system.

EXAMPLE:

"My parent really annoys me when he/she gets down on themselves about being 'on the funny farm,' 'not right in the head,' 'crazy,' etc. They believe themselves to be stupid, not intelligent enough, or unworthy because of how they think or perceive things.

"I am like them when I make similar remarks about myself, let others override my ability to make my own choices, and let myself be led astray from something I know is right for me." Be as fun and funny as you like to bring about awareness, to move beyond the fear and misunderstanding of addiction and addictive behaviors.

Even More Science: Newton's Third Law of Motion
Understanding relationships through the technique of observation

As Newton stated way back in the 1600s: "For every action, there is an equal and opposite reaction." His law is quite correct as we observe it in our external world daily. The 'thwack' of a baseball bat on a ball, the push and pull of moving furniture into place, and the force of gravity pushing down on the uplift of an airplane taking off, known as g-force. All of these movements require force and a certain amount of acceleration to effect change. G-force is described in 'positive' and 'negative' terms, but how it feels in our bodies is the opposite of what is described.[1] When gravity pushes up, or in positive g-force, we feel it push down on our bodies, literally moving our blood down into our feet, or the seat of our chair is pushing up so we can sit down. Negative g-force is the opposite, of course, but we feel it as an uplift in our bodies. When in an airplane that is landing or a roller coaster car that drops suddenly, we feel that in the pit of our stomachs and our bodies can literally lift out of our seats. Some find it exciting, while others try not to upchuck their lunch.

Our bodies exist in time and space and, therefore, take on the same laws of physics as we discussed earlier. Within our bodies, some systems take on the same type of properties as we see in the outside world, including Newton's Third Law of Motion, but this time it's metaphysical, not physical. Our thoughts, ideas, and emotions affect change through the power of force. Force in the form of denigration comes from a lack of spirit in understanding ourselves or our life partners, for example. We feel denigrated when the anger transmutes and can come through our skin in the form of acne or hair loss. Denigration also makes us feel unloved and unworthy, so we start to fill that emptiness with an addiction like overeating for some, drugs and alcohol for others, and many other complicated societal ills. The addiction is an equal and opposite reaction to a feeling or force in the body on a metaphysical level. Feeling unloved is a force so great that it affects us through time and space. It makes us feel unworthy, so we find an equal and opposite reaction to the emptiness.

This is why we ground down into the Earth through intention and find stillness there. It's also why people feel a walk through the woods sheltering and up-lifting. In those moments, we ground to the Earth through awareness of the trees and other plants and animals and find it beneficial. Through the Earth's energy of grounding we can uplift our own energy. Feeling sun sick or heat exhaustion is the opposite effect on our bodies. The sun naturally lifts our spirits through light and intention, but the overheating aspect comes from too much sun, too much uplift. Our bodies' systems go into overdrive, if you will, and become overdone with an inability to find homeostasis, or balance. (If you read the section on body healing before this one, this is familiar territory. If not, jump back to understand more.) When we're hot, we seek a cool, dry place like a forest where the trees cover the forest floor and act as shelter and shade. We can also dip into a pool, lake, or river and decidedly so because water not only cools, it prevents us from coming unbound from the Earth's energies. See Chapter 16 for more information on healing in water.

I believe this is how sublimation works on a metaphysical level. We all have times in our lives when we need to rise up and face the facts of our existence. When in those moments, we force ourselves up and out. We move out of our bodies, through the worry

---

[1] Martin Voshell, *High Acceleration and the Human Body*, 2004

and denigration, and just do it. No holds barred. Time to move on, time to get going, as I've stated in another section — thanks again to Tom Petty for those inspiring lyrics. We are forcing ourselves because we know it's time, and the time is right — right now — for you to move away from your feeling less than, away from the power of lack, and move towards light and love. We all need a shove once in a while. Sometimes it scares us, makes us feel weak in the knees, or creates a momentary sensation of being in a Timefield. But this isn't one of those times - ha! Remember, a length of time is required for a Timefield to form, so push past those powers of denigration and move your body out into the world in whatever form that takes for you. Go out dancing, have fun with friends that don't feed your sense of lack, find a new awareness through going to a movie, walking in the woods, or being self-fulfilled instead of filling up on those patterns of behaviors that are keeping you down. You are your own Abraxas and must be willing to break out of your shell of the self-fulfilling prophecy that you are not enough, aren't meant to be cared for, or believe you are meant to be alone for the rest of your life. Feel the energies rise up in your body as you read this and then take that and run with it — literally or otherwise.

Healing Through Self-Love
Codependency attachments

Sometimes, the behaviors reflected to us are not our own and it's time to decide to leave or stay. It's a difficult decision as it works against the very core of our beings because we naturally want to help each other. But sometimes the help doesn't work or doesn't come fast enough, and there will be a point when you need to sit with yourself and ask, "What is best for me?" It's a hard question to ask and it's ok to take some time with it, even if you feel in your body that the time has come to release yourself from the person who has addiction. We can weather the storm meteorologically in a relationship and when all is quiet, we go back to who we were or what we were doing. But we often — if not always — have an energy imprint of scar tissue that should be dealt with as a residual effect on our being. After a big blowup or argument with someone, even after all is seemingly forgiven, we may not want to be around the person anymore or distrust them from that point forward because of the scar tissue effect.

Addictive behaviors run in the family because of negative cording and negative attachments, not because you are destined to be an addict yourself. Remember that as you learn to walk away. It is not your destiny to be an addict like your family member who raised you or was there for you in some special way. Release yourself from this type of attachment with the information in the section labeled "Shared Timefields" and do the work there to start energetically moving yourself away from addictive behaviors. It isn't easy, for sure, but well worth it in terms of healing for yourself. You are autonomous unto yourself and have the freedom and power to take away your own hurt and pain and start moving away from attachments that are detrimental to your health. Again, find a medical doctor, psychiatrist, or other healer in the medical profession for additional assistance. You are not meant to go it alone, and you should seek other resources available to you, just as a wounded warrior would because that is who you are.

Refer to the Source Code Switch in Chapter 16 for more points of interest on this topic, including intercepted natal charts and energy healing from an astrological point of view.

Time and Waste
Reframing our sense of lack

Time is not wasted, it's reserved. Reserve yourself for a time when you are better prepared, better able to meet challenges, look for opportunities, and come up with solutions that are simple, motivating, and empowering. Like reserving a table at a restaurant, you call ahead and while you are waiting, the table is set with silverware and dishes. Water is poured, flowers arranged, and napkins placed. All of these things better serve us when we finally sit down to order our meal. By then, we're hungry and ready to eat. The people with us can better share in our health and wealth bounty. It's not that we didn't do it before; it's just that the meal offered is more to our taste, more exquisite.

Life offers us a chance to be at the bountiful table of plenty. When we supplicate or are in lack, we find what is laid before us to be distasteful and even abhorrent, but we also feel that leaving the table is gauche. Our surroundings make us feel awkward and put on by others, so we retreat into our own worry and self-doubt, making us feel out of place in time. But if we allow ourselves to sit at the table where we want to, we can find delight. Finding delight means unhanding yourself from future scenarios that may or may not be your truth or the truth of the situation. Relinquish those 'facts' from your mind that keep you in self-doubt, starving from lack of attention. Live in the moment and be in the moment's awareness of time, which is stillness, the now.

Your time folds in on itself when you are with yourself and others in love. The now of time isn't affected by your preoccupation with the future — that is your future sense coming through, and it is in stillness that you find it. Instead, the now is acceptance of how the future holds promise for your way of living. In mindfulness, we try to let go, but letting go can feel arbitrary. You may ask yourself, "What am I supposed to let go or to hold on to?" It feels reactive. Letting go is not to avoid thinking about the future; that is your promise to yourself that things will improve and change. Being in the now feels antithetical to our minds because we have evolved to evolve! You might think, "Don't tell me how to live in the moment when that doesn't work for me! How can I sit and enjoy this piece of meat, this leaf on the ground, this sunny afternoon, when all my mind wants to do is bring in the future?" It doesn't make sense, and that is the operative word. We use all of our senses to scan the environment to make sense of the world, which brings in our future sense. We are designed to be this way! But mindfulness is a hot topic because it works, so how do we blend these two scenarios?

Whatever works for you to be mindful, do it — distraction, sublimation, being active, calling all your friends to talk. This is who you are and makes you You! Don't distract yourself from your good qualities and nature — it is all divine! Present moment awareness is nothing more than shifting your focus to find a depth of flavor, or meaning, in the moment. In other words, you're noticing things differently. You can do this on a carnival ride, out in the woods, or in your own home. It's a practice that sets you up for change through effortless effort. You do the things you do; you don't make a ton of effort; you just start noticing things differently. Working on your car, fixing the plumbing, coming outside to ride your motorcycle — all the things you enjoy, all the things you do. Let's face it, we often *have* to do things. I don't know many people who enjoy fixing toilet leaks, but we can notice the task differently, notice how we feel inside while doing the task.

So forget the namby-pamby spiritual movement because it's not; it's both hard work and effortless. The two can exist at the same time — yin-yang. That is the dichotomy of living on Earth and being in a body. It's yes/and, not either/or. We hold both in our minds, hearts, and bodies all day, every day. We see it — we may not acknowledge it, though. We may be 'beautiful souls,' but we're also ugly counterparts to those beautiful things we hold dear in our minds. Nostalgia traps and Timefields tend to get ugly, but the beauty that lives within and behind is out of this world.

Partnerships of All Shapes and Sizes

So, how to fix it all? The $10 million question. Well, it is up to you to fix yourself first. Find time to heal the wounds that got you there in the first place, which you can do through many sources and modalities. The rest of the book will show you one way of doing it. The key is to make sure whatever you do is aligned with love, or your Source core energy with the Earth. If you feel judged, pain, denigration, or sorrow, don't do it.

First, find time to share love with others in the way that suits you best. A smile, a handshake, or a nod in the direction of someone you know makes them feel present and not dismissed. It's the vacuum effect in reverse. When we deny and denigrate, it creates a vacuum for the other person, like they don't exist. But when we acknowledge someone's existence, we put them on the map through love.

Next, be aware of your own ability to hear, see, and feel Source energy. You can do it — we all can. It's different for everyone, but the more you are aware of it, the more it will show up. Pull your own weight inside the collective by finding your wings. Be your own Abraxas and allow the shell to drop and love to shine through. You may even find that your childhood memories have a role to play, but always bring it back to the Earth to ensure it's aligned with love and not a wound. Be careful when healing your inner guidance; sometimes it can take you places you don't want to go. And if it does, stop. You don't have to! You have the authority and sovereignty to say, "No, I don't like this, and I don't want to continue."

Next, find the time to heal others by sharing your abilities and strengths and pull from your own storehouse to get you there. You may not be an energy healer the way I am, but you might make a delightful chocolate chip cookie that brings smiles to people's faces and helps them enjoy life. Or, you may uncover a fact that you find interesting to share with others, start a conversation, and create a connection with them. All of these small, singular ways add up to many, and you can start right now.

And finally, find love in all the ways you want it to show up for you. If you believe you are whole and perfect unto yourself without the need for partnership or marriage, that's ok! Do it! Marriage is not the end-all-be-all of the universe. But if it's time for you to stop living on your own and take up a level of partnership, that's another right and true way of living. We are all different, live differently, and at different times in our lives. We don't all have to get married at the same time, get a job right out of school, etc. Find time to heal the pressures of living in a society that makes you believe you are unhealthy if you're not slogging it out day after day at work, not making babies by age 30, or whatever societal pressures come up for you. We all know the pressures are intense, so it's time to move beyond that limiting belief system and allow for different lifestyles — and let the LGBTQIA+ movement lead the way!

Their belief systems have come from a deep knowing of who they are as individuals, but see society as something they don't fit into just because of who they love. It's a ridiculous notion, when you think about it, to put people down for first, being who they are and second, for being in love. But their mantra is "love is love" so can't we all follow that idea and bring in Sojourner Truth's famous question, "Ain't I a man?" Her on-the-spot speech gave rise to an anthem for women to be accepted for who they are in their bodies. It's all the same thing. So give believing a try and allow yourself to be filled with love for yourself and others through acceptance and accepting loving behaviors outside the 'norm.'

Chapter 14: Past Life & This Life Healing

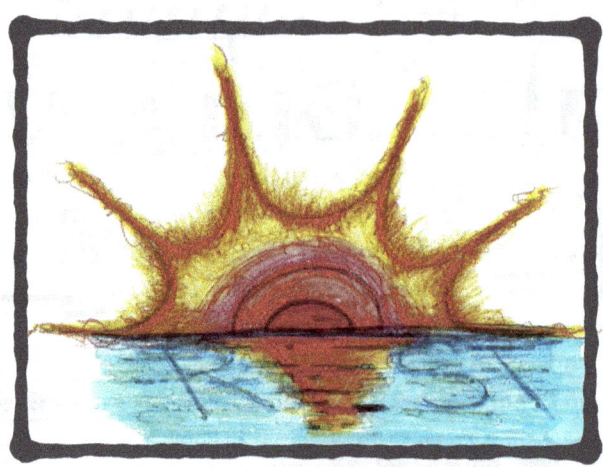

The Universe is held together by love, so when we are born, our nervous systems are already designed to make connections through love and *avasa*. When we don't make those connections, we feel depressed. When we do, we feel uplifted — which ties back to Timefields. How we feel in our bodies in the present moment, I believe, stems back to childhood, of course, but also through our amygdala and the system of time release in our minds. The amygdala has a major role to play in our orthogonal view of things in our life, or our pressure to keep things square in our minds. If we cannot do so, we feel out of place, out of mind, out of time. This can lead to a strong sense of lack in our bodies' systems because we feel it that way — it comes through our body in fear and fear of time.

No longer wanting to be in a body or no longer wanting to be on Earth can be strong when dealing with an amygdala that has a strong sense of the past, and this can come up through our past lives. I have no scientific evidence for this, but if you can get me some, I would greatly appreciate it because this has been the driving force of my life. It is up to you to decide for yourself if it is true, but my past life energy is probably tied to yours, so be careful! But to take this seriously, bring in all your belief systems and set them aside for a moment as we walk through our bodies' fear response system. Don't be afraid of the dark.

Past Life Emotional Energies
Fear and the amygdala

The amygdalae, as part of the limbic system, control how we process emotion. There are two sides of the amygdala, each with its own memory system, but they work together to store and interpret emotion, especially fear. It also controls aggression, how we handle social situations, and behaviors related to addiction.[1] I believe that the amygdalae also store memories in the form of emotion from past life experiences that are pushed forward through time as anchor points in Timefields and in the nervous system we are born with. I have mentioned past lives several times and I understand that not everyone is in alignment with having lived on this Earth at different times and in different ways, but there is a long tradition around the world, especially in Eastern cultures, that counts on us having multiple lives as a living and learning experience on Earth. In many ways, it is mystical, but as I've said in other sections of this book, we experience our world through our bodies, so there has to be a physical function in our minds/ brains that brings forward this type of energy. After having lived so long with repressed fear, my conclusion is it's the amygdala. I have healed many past life energies for myself and others, first as an accident for myself, and then as an intentional act as I started opening up more to my healing energies. It's a mystery to me how I can access my past life energy, perhaps it's through my amygdala, perhaps it's through divine guidance, or maybe both. The more I learn about the body and the brain's functions, the more it makes sense to me. Of course, it is not verified by science, but maybe someday it will be.

Past life energies are stored as an emotion, but to understand it, our minds make up a story that can be uplifting or downward spiraling. I believe we are on Earth to learn, so the energies of the past are there for us in enigmatic ways that can either help us or make us feel like we're blocked. When healing, the fears that come up can feel real because they are, according to your amygdala. If there is a lot of stored fear in your amygdala, it can take years to clear it out. Over time, the story becomes less important, but some details do help in healing the phenomena of past life stuck energies. Healing these energies in the form of Timefields helps you to step out of the story to enact change in the future, which is always on your doorstep and can be fulfilled in the present moment.

So, we come back to how stories are part of the healing process. It is designed into our very beingness that we connect to others, ideas, emotions, and so forth through imagining what happens when we feel this, or stop that behavior, etc. Dreams are stories, too, and can often play out as movies, though maybe a bit avant-garde for our waking life taste. It is this function in our brain — the function of the story — that brings in the power of intention (or a goal) and then allows it to be imagined as a story through

---

[1] Cleveland Clinic, Health Library, 2023

a visualization in our minds.

We know our minds are literally changing when we do these types of visualizations because we see it happening unconsciously, too. For example, you go to a party and someone you like is there but is ignoring you. You get the "stay away from me vibes" from that person, so you leave them be. You start to tell yourself a subconscious story that this person didn't want to be bothered by you. That person's energy activated your wound of unworthiness or being unloved, and now you are mad at that person for ignoring you and being a jerk. The next day, you find out that the person just lost their job and was in their feels about not being able to pay their bills on time, feeling unworthy because they were laid off or fired, and couldn't concentrate on being in a social situation. Suddenly, the story has changed, and you now feel compassion for that person! They're not a jerk, they're just like you and you can empathize with what they're going through.

Square Dancing
Creating an 'about-face' in healing

Early childhood or past life energies can cause our unconscious and subconscious to maintain a level of shock related to feeling unloved. Having a 'happy childhood' doesn't relate because happiness is a state of mind, or mood, that can come and go, while love is a feeling in the body. We can be happy one minute and down the next depending on what is in front of us, or how we're feeling in the moment. But love is an unending power that permeates our entire being. It fills us up with energy, keeping us truly energized, unlike an energy drink because the power is steady and sure, not up and down like a see-saw. Energy in pure light form is also a good way to energize, which is why around 3:00 pm, we like to get up, take a walk around outside, and see the sun (even if it's behind clouds, it still permeates your being). Sunlight is pure energy and can transform your feeling of being low into a higher level but at a constant rate rather than a spike.

There are three terms that I have borrowed from astrophysics to describe the sensation of being in a constant state of feeling locked or tied to someone despite your best efforts to overcome that feeling. It is an emotional state that has not quite hit the level of overwhelm, but can work against our best efforts to become free. These are states of unrest that cause us to move into a denigrated state, which can then cause wounds that, over time, become Timefields. **Tidal locking** is when two planetary bodies move in such synchronicity that the force of gravity from one body impacts the other causing the rotation and orbit to move at the same rate, forcing the same side to be shown at all times. The Earth and the moon are tidally locked, so are Pluto and Charon (its largest moon), causing them to dance through space always facing each other the same way.[2]

As a metaphor for relationships, tidal locking describes how we only see one side of a person and only show one side of ourselves to them. If we are tidally locked to someone, we tend only to see them and a situation from our point of view, and not the other person's. When this happens, our hearts get locked, causing us to feel incompatible in that relationship. We can be tidally locked with ourselves by examining only one part of our psyche. Being tidally locked means we only review things in one aspect and don't consider what the 'dark side of the moon' looks like. Sometimes, we have to send a space probe out into the nether regions of our unconscious to get a different picture. Tidal locking is also a past-life relationship phenomenon through space and time for the same reasons.

There are energies within us that are locked in place through a sequence of events that are part of our imprint, either this life or past lives. Our nervous system carries this forward in time and the pressure of it, like a tidal wave, can feel insurmountable at times. When you break the sequence, you unlock it to release the locked moment. In science, a tidal sequence or cycle, is how the tides on Earth move up and down, in and out, in a pattern of behavior that we are familiar with through low and high tides. **Tidal sequence** for our purposes, describes the sequence of events that caused you to become tidally locked with someone. Most likely, it was a series of situations where you only saw the face value of what was happening and made assumptions about the other person. The other person, in turn, did the same for you. This is not assuming the best in everyone because that is a free-flowing current of energy or emotion with an expanding consciousness and heart capacity. Tidal sequencing is about assuming behaviors that are denigrating towards you, even if the other person didn't mean it or didn't think that way. After making that assumption, you expect that person to treat you in the same denigrating way every time there's an issue or flare-up of the same or similar problem.

It doesn't have to be a catastrophic series of events to create a tidal lock, it can be as relational as seeing your parents in a new way as you mature and see the reasoning behind their behaviors towards you. This is where the wry statement, "How did my parents get so smart?" comes from. You see a different side to them, breaking the lock. Many adult relationships end up tidally locked because of how we're expected to behave towards each other or how we perceive our own behaviors against other people's. We can break the lock with energy healing.

Try It: Tidal Locking and Sequence Statement

I release and uncreate any and all tidal locking and tidal sequencing energy between myself and _____. I transmute all energies back to Full Source energy through deepest love and highest light.

---

[2] Neal deGrasse Tyson, *Astrophysics for People in a Hurry*, 2017

Tidal Force: Feeling Unknown Emotions

We can feel a tidal wave of emotion when we don't know why; people can push our buttons without us knowing why we have a strong reaction. This is what I call a **tidal force**, another term borrowed from science to describe how the moon's gravitational pull creates tides on Earth. The moon's surface and the Earth's surface are connected through the push and pull of each other's gravity; this causes a tidal force on our oceans as they are in liquid form and, therefore, more malleable. The tidal force causes a flood tide, the time of day when the water rises from low to high and pushes towards shore. Our self-doubt functions in the same way — we feel ungrounded when in doubt and don't have as much resistance to the forces around us; we feel pushed and pulled, this way and that. It creates a tidal force in our minds because we feel ill-adapted to the pressures that are in place around us. Our energies are not grounded to Earth, they are up in the air.

When a situation or a person moves us, we use this term to describe how we feel in our bodies, which usually causes welling up with tears or an expansive sensation in our chests (or both!). We are moved to tears and express the feeling of the tidal wave effect in reverse. We are all one under the sun in this sense. We know when we affect change for one another — for good or ill. And we'll become each other's Abraxas moments when we can find time to break the Tidal Sequencing of our lives. Tidal force as a relationship metaphor means there is a pull on us from an unseen force that causes us to swell with emotion. The force of a relationship that is tidally locked can cause us to feel denigrated in our own being-ness, pushing us against our will to move in a direction we would rather not go. Many marriages have this type of phenomenon placed on them as we feel forced by the institution of marriage itself to stay tidally locked to someone we have perhaps outgrown or see a new side of. Sometimes, it's the back story of the relationship that begins in sorrow or mistrust, or other times, it could even be a past life energy coming forward between the two people. Remember that tidal sequencing is a series of events, not one event, so it could be that the series started before you met at this point in time on Earth. Why else would you feel suffocated — or worse — in a marriage with someone who only seems to be doing the right things? It's a past-life tidal force that keeps you in a pattern of denigration and sorrow.

Tidal Locking Statement for past life sequence breaking:

I allow my sequence to be free of the energy of a past life tidal lock. I transmute all past life energies that are keeping me tidally locked. I release and uncreate all energies within me that are maintaining the sequence of being tidally locked.

Passion and Romance
Being welcoming in partnership

Tidal locking and sequencing can start as a passionate relationship that cools down but no longer serves the people within that relationship form. They feel the relationship is the priority and must continue the dance because if they do an about-face, the structures of their lives will fall down, and they will be left with nothing. This is a familiar scenario for many women, and it locks them into a performance they would rather not continue but don't know how to break free. Of course, it happens for men as well, but the structures of our lives are bound in time to women taking care of the nest, the little pieces of time known as memories, the social calendar, the kids, and almost all aspects of daily life that daily wage earners do for almost nothing, while women who work to support their families do it for free. They do it even while going to work for 8-plus hours a day and having their desires and needs ignored. If they take care of themselves, they are considered selfish, not respectable, and other words that tell them their needs come last.

As women, we put it on ourselves, too, but we are not the only ones being fed this type of junk food. If we were men, we would realize we are whole unto ourselves and don't need to serve others. We don't have to run home and cook a full meal after wrestling with the job, young kids, and other aspects of life that throw themselves at us in mercy. Let the dishes pile up and the food rot because you've had a hard day. Take a moment and prepare yourself for what needs to happen, even if there's laundry or the kids are hanging on to your leg because they're *starving*. Their supplications are our focus, while our needs are rarely met. We are often disregarded at our own dinner tables by the people sitting down to the meal we've made. They either ignore us, or are rude non-verbally by not eating the food we've taken the time to make for them. Or they verbally attack us and tell us we're not worthy by not acknowledging we are individuals, we're just there to serve them. Then they get up from the table, leaving us to wonder how we got it so wrong. It's a never-ending dance and it needs to stop.

It's not that we're taking the poor behavior in silence; we've communicated and over-communicated. We've asked repeatedly, pleaded, supplicated — three, ten, even twenty times — and met resistance every step of the way. We've gone to classes, read books, listened to stories — all the ways that we try to teach ourselves, but the power lies outside of us, so how can we move it by force? Others get the brunt of our temper because we've had it and can't control the rage anymore. Call all the right buttons of behavior that need to be pushed, not the ones that get pushed by interactions with those in your life who don't deserve to be there. "*If he don't love you anymore, just walk your fine ass out the door*," sings Lizzo. This can be a reckoning of behavior with anyone in your life who is not treating you fairly and is not in your corner. If it's a family member who is pushing you down, shouldn't they be lifting you up per the unwritten code of family ethics? "Because we're family" should be about treating each other with dignity and respect, not manipulation, denigration, or condemnation. Don't excuse their behavior either, just because they're family, by giving them 'slack' for treating others poorly. Hold them accountable for their own behaviors just as you are being held to yours by them. If it is an elder, they should be modeling the behavior to you, not the other way around. We have a hard time hearing those types of things; it's in our national anthems to respect our forefathers, but we all know the history books are written by the enslavers, not the enslaved people.

After the Honeymoon: A passionate manifesto

After the vows, 'reality' sets in and we see the other person for who they are or we stop looking the other way when poor behaviors crop up. I believe the switch that happens after marriage, when we find things are quite different, is about not feeling welcomed. The married couple stops being welcoming to each other as they were while dating. You can change your perspective by considering how you want to be treated when visiting a friend's house, for example, and apply those same behaviors to your married life. It's not about being formal with each other, it's about being real in your regard for each other. You may say, "Why don't you love me or fill my need to be fully accepted in an intimate partnership?" Partnerships should be fun, at ease, and healthy, not a reality-based TV show with too much drama. Drama causes us to go into overwhelm, which can turn into a Timefield.

When there are unmet needs in a relationship that has faltered for too long, one or both people will search for other ways of finding their belief systems to be true outside of that partnership, turning to sex, drugs, or other forms of escapism to fill their void of existence. It could come in the form of an extramarital affair, which is often the case because it is in the romantic part of our lives that we feel the most sense of lack. What if instead of saying "til death do us part," we say, "until we're both ready to move on"? It may sound cynical to some, but freeing to others. If we know we don't *have* to be there, we may have a different perspective on the relationship. We may feel more welcoming to the person because they are choosing to be there, and they reciprocate to us. We may welcome them in as we would a guest at a dinner party. That guest chooses to be at your house, not in supplication, but in romance, partnership, friendship. They may bring a dish to share and eat at your table because you can all share in the chores of the day, including the children that sit at the table with you. They are not mine or yours, they are ours; they belong to both people in the partnership and they belong to the kids. But in that belonging, you don't take them for granted or try to clip their wings, you allow them to spread their wings as wide as possible so they can stretch beyond their limits as you can stretch beyond yours.

When it comes to passionate love, we find ourselves engaged with fire — the fire of love and romance, which turns to passion. If something is hot or fire, it's in the now, but it can leave as quickly as it shows up. Zen Master and peacemaker, Thich Nhat Hanh, in his book *Teachings on Love*, describes the Vietnamese concept of two types of love: *'tinh'* is passionate love, *'nighia'* is a calmer love, deeper, and more solid. You need both in a relationship, but they connect as an inverse. Over time, *'tinh'* diminishes while 'nighia' increases. Passionate love may start the relationship, which is the match that burns hot but fast. To sustain it, you need to move into a steady burn that doesn't go out with the faintest breath or slight breeze. The wind can whip up flames of passion, but it can also blow them out, leaving embers that are cooling but still burn hot to the touch.

Calm the flames of passion by saying, "I don't care." This phrase makes people feel unloved, but saying you don't care is a freeing statement for both people. When we don't care, it's a state of neutrality; you can walk away and do your own thing, the other person, too. Saying "I don't care" calms your nerves, settles your bones, as it were. You leave your mind open to the possibility that you are whole unto yourself and don't require the other person to fill any gaps in your existence. You can step away from the investment it takes to care. You are free to move about the cabin without the seatbelt light on because it is your right to be sovereign.

Feeling Equal To Instead of Less Than

We all have wounds of denigration around not being cared for, so I need to put a finer point on this concept. Not caring is not a belief system about being better than someone or something else. It is about being in charge of your capacity to be in your own wealth and health. In the US, we have a wealth and health system that prioritizes some people over the collective. In this case, we are all damaged because we find our health is tied to our wealth. The collective burns hot with a passionate desire to be healthy, but the system in place keeps them unhealthy because of their lack of financial 'success.' Government-funded health care is not a perfect system, but when our wealth implies that we aren't healthy, it becomes a problem of epic proportions.

Other systems overlap with this general idea of wealth and health, such as the 'green' movement or how we care for our environment. Some of us see it as the vital resource that it is and scratch our heads in confusion when others don't feel the same. They may not care as much as we do or find it as inspiring as a piece of bologna. Why don't they care about the environment? If I am a marginalized person in the US, I may not care about the environment because I have to find space to care about whether or not I and/or my family are going to eat dinner tonight, pay the bills, or find health care. There is no space left to care about anything else, and rightly so. Some people can't care because they cannot fill the void to heal their existence, or are in the wrong place at the wrong time.

If I'm a woman born into a lower caste in India, I can't find enjoyment in my environment because I am in constant denigration for who I am as a human. According to this system, I don't have the right to be here. I'm not socially correct and cast out of the crowd or the collective. My experience is feeling more like dirt or dust rather than being whole in my body. My cares and woes are about being in a place of holy obligation to others deemed more respectable than me. How could I possibly care about the environment that feels like the enemy to me? My environment as an Indian woman, considered uncouth just by my birthright, tells me the environment is not for me. Of course, not all people feel this way; we are all individuals and might find something within our environment that serves to lift us up "by the grace of God," as some would say. But I would say it is also within you — and more importantly of you — to find those healing moments. Don't give it to authority figures outside of you because this perspective can become supplication, which then becomes lack.

Healthy, Wealthy, and Wise
Beliefs and the systems that impact them

Touching the body is a form of healing that taps directly into your parasympathetic nervous system (PNS). Our PNS is part of both the autonomic and central nervous systems[3] and works with our body in time to understand our fear through the amygdala and other time resources, such as healing past wounds. We have discussed the amygdala in other healing sections, but it is part of our brain centers, so understanding how the information gets from our heads to our bodies is essential. Our medulla oblongata are the switch that open our nervous systems to other moments in time. When our nervous systems are heightened, we can connect and feel healed through touch. Consider what a hug does for you when you're feeling down, why babies need to be held all the time and demand it from their parents, why a pat on the back can feel reassuring, or why muscle testing works the way it does. All these forms of touch move through our parasympathetic system to cause changes in our bodies and minds. In other words, touch calms the nervous system and helps to heal. Healing comes from within, but it also comes from without, through our connection to others.

Touch is an automated response — we don't even think about it sometimes, except at work. (Shaking hands is acceptable, but that's it.) If I put my hand on your arm, my integumentary system is in direct contact with your integumentary system. We have a direct connection, though we know through quantum physics that at some level, we are not actually touching, which does not matter for healing because the rest of the distance is bridged by intention. This is why people do not need to be present during many forms of energy healing. So, our integumentary systems are linked — what is happening? We know that this system constantly scans the environment, making it easier to stay alive by responding to our environmental stimulations. Stimulations could be a hot stove burner or a cold piece of ice. Now, the ice feels wonderful if I'm hot because it's cooling down my body. If I'm cold, the heat feels good until I start to burn, but that's another matter altogether. What links the two? Homeostasis or balance. At all times, I maintain balance the best I can through my integumentary system, and touch is the main component of that system working well.

<u>Societal Impacts on the Nervous System</u>

---

[3] Cleveland Clinic online Health Library, 2024

A highly activated nervous system reacts as highly activated. When out of balance, we react differently, such as jump scares and other worried or frazzled behaviors. If a person is always scared, they feel they are on the brink of a natural disaster in their mind and need to be alert to get to safety. We know that PTSD survivors and other forms of neurodiversity cannot handle loud noises or other highly stimulating environments because they are already maxed out, so to speak, in their nervous systems. Safety comes from within and without, just as healing does. If our environment is safe, then we feel secure. If we feel safe, then our nervous systems are settled down and we can start to feel relaxed. If we are relaxed, then we can begin again and heal.

Consider the people who live in neighborhoods where violence is a common occurrence. Their nervous systems look frayed, frazzled, or in pieces. They can't settle down because they have to be on constant alert for their safety and their family and friends' safety. It's a terrible state to be in. Now, take that person out of their environment and put them in a social situation like at a shopping mall where there is a lot of visual stimulation, lots of people, smells, sounds, etc. Their nervous systems are in reactionary mode and can't settle, and this doesn't take into consideration the time it takes to fully heal and recover from a big nervous system hit. Now, bring in the societal stereotypes and pressures of being an American, for example, with skin and features that are deemed unacceptable, unstable, or whatever negative connotation you can think of. It takes a lot of energy and concentration to keep it together in those types of situations. Not only is that person in a constant state of high alert in their nervous system because of violence where they live, they are now in a situation that puts them on guard just by being themselves. One small thing can set their jump scare mechanism off, and they automatically turn to 'fight or flight' because their body tells them — through their heightened nervous system — that they are not safe. In that mode, things are automatic. The thinking brain takes a back seat and the emotional brain starts driving.

Similarly, overly empathetic people have heightened nervous systems and can't watch violent or overly scary movies, the 'news,' or even read books with descriptions of violence. Propagation of violence, especially violence against women, is senseless and keeps us in a lower vibrational state. Books written by women that describe sexual violence against women are antithetical because they continue the cycle of violence. It's not "raw and real" literature, it's a way of keeping women down. Why are women perpetually required to be cut down to their bone marrow in order to rise and find their strength or worth in life? This is not the society I want to live in or leave for my children. There are plenty of other, more insidious ways women and minorities are kept down in their lives that don't require sexual violence and the propagation of trauma on their bodies and nervous systems.

Considering all the violence that takes place all day, every day in our own minds —

thoughts against ourselves and how we're feeling — continuing the cycle of violence outside of ourselves only creates more violence within and causes damage to our heart centers and nervous systems. Now is the time to stop it. Stop the constant drumbeat of trauma and violence against those people who are already damaged. Our world is highly connected now, and we know what's happening in almost every region of the world. We don't need more stories that rehash the past in a continual loop of asexual and sexual violence, pummeling ourselves until we can't get to our feet. It's not heroic to keep going when you have been beaten to a pulp physically. What's heroic is the emotional healing that comes after physical violence because all violence requires emotional healing. To keep going means our nervous systems have stopped working, and we are essentially the walking dead, or zombies, to put it another way. If our stories have the power to heal, change, and create a better world for future generations, then why do we keep ourselves down by showing scenes of obscene violence? It takes a toll on us — I don't care how validated you are in believing it's just entertainment and not real. As discussed above, I don't think our unconscious brains process it that way through the amygdala fear response. So, sit with the idea that we are all one and we all belong and find the need for violence to diminish in your life as entertainment and as an art form.

Emotional Healing With a Creative Touch
Parasympathetic nervous system healing

How do we get to a level of healing in these situations? Empathy is a good start, but it's not enough. People who have PTSD or a life trauma need time to come down from the ceiling, so to speak, when their nervous systems are activated. Doing this type of healing during a fight or flight is not helpful to anyone. Have you ever tried calming down a teenager who just got in a fight? Impossible. It's better to leave them alone and let their body's systems calm down on their own. But, when the event is over, and there is time and space to discuss and heal, it's important not to brush it under the rug. Sit down with that person face-to-face and have a frank conversation. It's important not to require remorse because that is a judgment and judgments only bring in shame. As stated earlier, shame is a highly damaging feeling to our nervous systems.

Inquire about that person's health and safety instead. Find their point of view and agree with it from a healed perspective. Don't preach, don't teach. Allow them to have their feelings, knowing that their nervous systems require it. Maybe you don't want to bring up the incident that precipitated this conversation. Asking, "How are you feeling?" can break down walls instantly. Emotional responses can be hard to get at, but maybe you can coax it out of them. If not, don't force it. Ask for healing and forgiveness in your mind, knowing that the person you are talking to is the walking wounded. But remember, this is not talk therapy. There are many trained psychoanalysts that can work with people on their story. This is energy healing and we want to bring a different level of understanding in our hearts, minds, and bodies through simple touch.

The difference between limbic healing and parasympathetic healing is the level of touch that activates the nervous system. Ask permission to touch the person's forearm — nothing more. Now your nervous systems are connected through your individual integumentary systems and you are healing that person through touch. Set your intention to heal in your mind by saying inwardly:

Parasympathetic Nervous System Release:
"I release and uncreate any and all energy blocking and causing stress and anger to persist in my (or person's name) parasympathetic nervous system through overwhelm. I transmute all stress and anger in my body back to Full source energy through deepest love and highest light."
"I demand my body and mind to release frozen fear (and anger) so that I may find balance now and forever more through deepest love and highest light."

This mantra can be used in hands-on healing, or you can use it in your own healing modality. I use it in combination with other modalities and find using these two frequencies to be powerful healing. (Refer to the section on frequencies for more information.) If touch is not allowed or required, you can visualize yourself touching the other person instead as you say the words. It can bring up great healing for both you and the person being healed in this format because it moves it to a different level of understanding in your heart through forgiveness.

Take note of what happens when the parasympathetic system is healing. You might see momentary black flecks that look like flies or bugs. If this happens, it should only last for an instant or two and then go away. After a while, you may also have a similar experience when exercising. I believe this reaction is the parasympathetic nervous system settling into a lower, more calm state. This is what energy healing is for: to allow us to calm our fears. Incorporating exercise, in whatever form is best for you, works wonders on your systems. We will discuss exercise in more detail in the next chapter.

Freeze!
The freeze response of the autonomic nervous system is in the sympathetic system only, which is why the cortisol release healing incantation doesn't include "freeze." Freezing consists of fear literally frozen in time. We freeze to stop the parasympathetic system, also known as the "rest and relax" system,[4] from going into overload and to stop the manure from running down our legs, quite literally. "You scared the shit out of me" isn't just a figure of speech; it can actually happen! Our bodies go into such overload that we lose control of our systems. Misunderstanding and fear go hand-in-hand. Fierce fear through misunderstanding can look like a whole system out of balance and causes the body to be in fight or flight constantly and consistently, which encourages weight gain. The weight gain release statement asks the body to re-find its balance by

---

[4] Cleveland Clinic, Health Library, 2022

understanding the pressures of fight or flight.

In terms of healing, we find that the parasympathetic system only warms to touch. Find the touch of another human being, pet, or animal to be comforting when we feel love for them. A hug, kiss, or pat on the back from someone you know cares for you feels like a warm blanket. The PNS system level of healing comes from within and without, just like other forms of healing. It is the one time when touch is needed in energy healing and requires love through empathy to complete the circuit, so to speak.

Find time to heal your fears of the future through deep introspection that allows you to understand where those emotions are infiltrating your body's systems. Remember, overwhelm is a product of deep emotional blockage, so a deep level of introspection is required to find the sneaky, hidden fears and anger that have come across your desk, so to speak. You may have shuffled some pages around, hidden them under a stack labeled 'to do for later,' and then forgotten about them because other emotions kept piling on top. Our focus gets pulled in many directions all day and we focus on the burning issue right in front of us, leaving us little to no time to take a deep dive into our feelings. It's a hot mess when you start to unravel all the ways we are kept from, or keep ourselves, from our true feelings.

Chapter 15: The Body in Motion

We've already covered how we know energy healing is working in the moment. What about ways our bodies tell us change needs to occur or is occurring for us without conscious effort? You may have noticed that many of the healing modalities in this book contain some level of mind-body connection. This is because our bodies hold all that is true for us, and in this way, they are wise. The mind-body connection is a spiritual practice and a healing modality that brings about effective change and can be achieved with exercise, intention, and willingness to change our beliefs. All the ways our bodies inform us about our health begin in our minds. It can be conscious, subconscious, or unconscious, but our minds tell our bodies how we are doing at any given point in time. As fitness expert Ellen Barrett says, "When the mind's really noticing what's going on in the body we can change it. We can transform and really get the best result."

Learning Your Body's Language
Healing through body awareness and movement

As I write this, my head and chest feel tight. I know from experience that this is my body's way of telling me energy needs to be cleared. Because it's occurring in my head, it's probably a negative thought form. My heart is telling me I have an emotional wound that needs to be cleared as well. It's not a precursor to a heart attack, but if I ignore it long enough (years, not days, so don't panic), it could become one. I am ignoring it for now because I don't feel like stopping what I'm doing, but the stuck energies will persist.

This is how we live most of our lives: ignoring what's stuck because we don't have the time and/or energy to deal with it. The sensation persists, we ignore it more, push it down — not out — and then one day we get sick. Maybe it's just a cold or other virus; maybe it's something more serious like cancer if it persists long enough. Paying attention to what your body tells you is an all-day, everyday thing. When you're in a wounded state, it's extra. The more you free up the wounds and your body releases, the more it wants to release. Your mind clears, and you find you need or want more clarity, so more comes up to be healed.

When all else fails, take it to the body. Find your best relaxation method, use tapping methods, nodal lymphatic points, massage, reflexology — any method with a direct connection between your mind and body. If someone else is healing you, like through massage, even better so you can take a break. But the point is to be aware of your body's language and how it speaks to you.

Here is a list of ways my body speaks to me about energy:
- When my mouth and tongue feel sharp, I know I need to clear detrimental and/or denied aspect energy
- When I feel pain between my shoulder blades, I know I need to clear "back stabbing" energy related to a specific person
- When my lower back hurts, I check for stuck energy of feeling unsupported.
- When my sciatic pain starts to ramp up in my right leg, I know my stress level is getting too high and I need to take action — or in-action — to slow down and figure out the cause
- When my head is buzzy or slightly dizzy, I know I am in wound energy.
- When my chest or sternum feels tight or hurts, I need to clear heart center energy. It could also mean I need to clear my Source core or heart-core connection to the Earth.
- When I get clumsy, traffic seems to be constantly against me, or people at the grocery store literally run into me, I know I need to clear my chakras; feels like I'm invisible.
- When I suddenly choke on nothing or feel a constriction in my throat, I know I'm not being honest with myself, or there is a truth to discover about myself.
- Anywhere there is a weird pain in my body that shows up out of nowhere, I

know there is a trapped energy in that location to be cleared.
- Headaches are usually associated with negative thought forms or behavioral changes that need to be cleared.
- Skin break outs are related to the integumentary system and require clearing along with divine life force energy support. Where the skin breaks out on the body is also a clue as to what is unsettling me.
- When I notice my hair falling out more than usual, it could mean I am running into a bunch of unconscious fear, stress, or anger.
- Pain under my arms could mean my lymphatic system is energetically 'draining' or needs to be cleared — often impacted by anger.
- My left ear humming means I am either dealing with a deep-seated energy that needs to be released, or I'm going through a "system reset" after healing a major belief system interception.
- When I suddenly feel tired in the middle of the day, it often means I need a deeper connection to a mental process that is going on, so I take a nap which often results in a lucid dream state.
- When I have a "sneezing fit" of 3 or more, usually 10, without any other symptoms, I know I am releasing negative thought forms or patterns.
- When I feel tingly all over I know a major life shift has occurred and it will last for a day or two. Time to get out of the house and take a walk!

How do I know all this? I pay attention, get curious, and look for patterns. I follow my thoughts and find the right solutions, which I verify with muscle testing or what feels right in the moment. I look to the outside world as my grounded involvement, otherwise I get too caught up in my head. Sometimes the muscle testing doesn't work, or I have a belief system and/or heart wall energy that's blocking it. In those times I have to take a step back, make sure I'm grounded, and proceed with caution. It's just like creating a piece of artwork — you have to follow your intuition, look to your environment for clues, use your intellect, and then follow through with a grounded action.

Pay attention to what your body is telling you. Don't be afraid to ask it as a direct question in your mind, through muscle testing, or both. Whatever way feels most comfortable to you. Follow your intuition and the light of the matter will reveal itself.

Trip the Light Fantastic
Movement and dance related to time and freedom

To "trip the light fantastic" means "to dance lightly on one's toes." The phrase comes from an old poem and has been incorporated into our language as an idiom through other interpretations of it. Now it means "to live life in the moment and dance as you go." I love this phrase. It feels otherworldly to me and puts me in mind of the Northern Lights, or of a spaceship that's about to land, bringing a new frequency of music expressed through light. When we trip the light fantastic, the wounded behaviors of the past and present don't keep us down. Instead of feeling unwilling to change, we feel a part of life and want to dance with it, moving in circles of freedom and pure joy, which originates in our egos, not our 'complexes.' (Skip back to *Egos and Myth Busters* for more discussion on letting our egos have an extended vacation from being bashed.)

There are many circles in life. The one we know the best is life ebbing and flowing as we are born into this existence, grow up, grow old, and die back. That is one big circle, yes, but there are other circles in motion and one of them is circling in a dancing motion with ourselves and others. When we can dance through life instead of trudging through it, we feel lighter than air. Our circles become bubbles and we lift up toward the sky like how we feel in the Haja Sofia, Machu Picchu, and other sacred spaces. We circle around each other in the dance of life and ask each other to 'cut in' by asking, "Are you wiling to dance with me for a while? Can you dance in my beingness and can I dance in yours?" *I wanna dance with somebody,* sang Whitney Houston so well and so completely that we are still singing her song at the top of our lungs some 40 years later. It has not lost its mobility in time as it releases suffering from our hearts and souls.

Feeling Free to Dance

Dancing comes so easily to us when we're little kids. We have the freedom and inhibition to feel into our center at any moment and express it through dance and song. Overtime, our worries and sorrows, anger and frustrations pile up and we suddenly find one day that we just don't feel like dancing any more. Or for some, *moving is the only way to heal your heartache, moving is the only way to heal your soul,* as the band, The Strike, sings.

When we dance, we literally move energetic blockages from our bodies. The release of energy allows us to be in the moment, thinking only of our present, not what happened yesterday or what might happen tomorrow. Dance is a form of presence of mind. Being present is a form of freedom from worry, fear, grief, anger. It moves us beyond what is ordinary and into what is extraordinary about who we are in our bodies. Dance is also a form of self-expression in our bodies and dovetails nicely into energy healing practices as they ask Source, through the wisdom of the body, for the right and true answers. Dance is often used as a form of exercise and can be a great way to change up your routine. In fact some mind-body fitness routines use dance moves as measures of success against our bodies' wisdom. If you can understand the steps and get the moves right, your optimal routine is waiting for you to burn calories completely.

Exercise is, of course, an essential part of keeping our hearts, minds, and bodies active, flexible, and endearing. The style or type of exercise is, like food, up to you. You do not have to go to the gym to 'burn, baby, burn' until you fall on the floor to get a good workout. Whatever your body is telling you, that is what you should do. If you like to run, run! If you prefer yoga, do that instead. Maybe it changes from day to day or week to week. You are not a failure if you don't go to the gym, it just means that style of exercise is not right for you. If it was, you would feel compelled to go, and it would be enjoyable. Let joy and fulfillment guide your exercise routine.

Postural Olympics
Feeling the need to move without over-doing it

This title comes from a deep well of dis-ease, happening all over the US and beyond, related to a need to be free from the rigger of intense exercise that feels like we're just automatons or machines. We push ourselves to the brink of disaster in our bodies, or we don't start at all, for fear of not being able to keep up. It's time to put that exercise method aside and find one beneficial for your body type. Postural Olympics refers to understanding what type of posture you live in, which is equated to your energy body type. It's different from the posture of love that we all stem from in our hearts, but it is not so distant in form. Now, I'm not saying we have different body types like pears and apples, because that would be shaming through comparison. I am saying that we all have different energies and we should pay attention to what our bodies are telling us.

<u>Body Types of Energy, Not Mass</u>

Body type relates to how you feel energies move through you, not your physical form. Your energy body type is extended outward to generate a field around you that moves and bends with you in physical space. This is Faraday's field, but moves in time as we do because we are almost always moving. So if the field bends and moves, then the particles in the air move with us, creating an electromagnetic field in terms of feeling and being in a body. The type refers to how your particular energy field interacts with the field around you. If you are more like a boulder (which doesn't move, but makes you feel the weight), then you are likely to be more slow-moving and get your kicks from being a steadfast person in weight. If your energy field is more like a rabbit, then you move faster and the particles in the air around you bend and flow differently. It's a reaction of the environment to your energy field, not the other way around because you are a healthy individual that can bring about change and transformation in your life and your life's energies.

Your body type relates to how you view the world and your belief systems. If you are a get-up-and-go kind of person, your body type is telling you to move quickly and out towards your goal. For you, 'high octane' workouts work wonders. This is the bending and stretching we're all familiar with where we move our bodies vigorously in tune to a more upbeat play list of music. But if your body type is more slow — and this is not a judgment because it's my type — you will likely have issue with vigorous exercises.

Begin by understanding your energetic body type. There are many, so don't feel like you need to go to a chart to look it up. You are you and know how you like to move and feel in your body. If you haven't already, now is the time to 'look it up,' through your connection to nature. We don't believe our bodies exist in nature, especially those of us who live in urban environments, but we are of nature and it exists even in dense cities.

Once you have a feeling about your body type, feel into the nature of it and compare it to something else in nature: a hawk, rabbit, deer, tree, boulder — whatever works — it's a metaphor for you to understand how you like to move.

A tree may be more into bending and swaying in the breeze, like T'ai Chi, and a rabbit would be more interested in short bursts of running, while a gazelle likes long distance running, etc. All of these metaphors are appropriate to the behaviors of people because we see it in nature and are a part of its system. Now, a tortoise gets a bad rap about being slow, but time and posture help the tortoise win the race, so don't force yourself into a type you think you should be. There is a way to move for everyone and all the ways are right and good. Stop comparing yourself to others. In this way you will find an understanding of yourself and any weight gain you may be struggling with will likely come off easier because you are not forcing yourself into something you don't want to do or will regret in the morning when you're stiff and tired.

When you use wish fulfillment statements with your version of exercise, it is calling in all the goodness and sweetness of your positivity and uplifting energies. I have found other statements to work for me as well, so you don't have to limit yourself to the words in this book. If there is an inspiring lyric from a song, or a word or phrase in a book you've read that makes you feel light and bright, use that to install the good vibes while you're exercising. Whatever feels right and true to you. If it makes you laugh, smile, or feel the sensations in your heart and body move, then you're on the right track. Remember, exercise and wish fulfillment should be fun, so when you approach it from that perspective, good things will start to happen. In fact, they already are as you read this passage. Have fun! Enjoy! Now you know why I keep repeating these words because they are meant to uplift and change your patterns of behavior. I have been healing you all along and you didn't even know it.

Exercise and Weight
Feeling your energies flow

Weight gain is a constant issue around movement because we think we're not getting enough exercise. If you move away from needing to exercise to lose weight, then you're halfway to a new way of thinking about, and therefore, performing exercises themselves. It's my opinion that we may not all need the same amount of exercise, which is not scientifically verified, but I *always* get sick if I exercise more than two times a week. And we all know that some people crave it while others have a hard time getting going. Let's reframe the point of exercise to make it more enjoyable, so move in whatever way works for you, bending and stretching is a perfectly acceptable exercise. Consider exercise as a way to keep your energies in flow and keeping them from sticking to your environment like stuffy air inside your car. If you open the windows to your car, all the stuck air moves through the cabin as you move down the road. Exercising should be like that, not like 'pounding the pavement.' When you exercise, you change within your immediate environment by pushing the particles around you.

My exercise for the past 2-3 years has been mostly postural and lighter yoga routines that allow for minimal heart rate increases. I also had a perspective shift that exercising for me is to make sure my energy systems and energetics are flowing, not to lose or maintain weight. I found that when I took body weight and even physical health out of the equation when I exercise, it became more enjoyable. Whatever helps you stay in alignment, in synchronicity with your mind and body, then that is your optimal way of exercising. Be sure, as well, to let your body rest when it tells you.

Find a type of exercise or movement that is enjoyable and feels good, not painful. If running is truly your mode of exercise, maybe consider the amount of time you do it or how you push yourself. So many people run with pain and anguish on their faces. They look like they can't take life any more and need to run away from it, and maybe they are, but if you can find joy in the freedom of being on your own two feet, then maybe you can get past the pain of exercise. Step away from the 'no pain, no gain' proverb, it's not helping anyone, not even the top athletes of our time, which are way more than anyone can keep up with. They've created an energy field that interacts with the particles around them in an unbending and physical way. Top athletes stay fit to lose their sense of self when they are exercising. It's true. In order to stay focused on that level of incarnate energy, you have to step out of yourself and believe you are not present. 'In the zone' it's called and can actually make you feel disoriented when you come out of it. This is different from Flow because it takes time and understanding to get there consistently, while being in Flow is an effortless, optimal existence and moves you to a higher state of consciousness.

We are all different so what looks good on one person will not be the same on another. There can be a chasm of understanding between who you are and how you feel. Understand your beliefs to get to the reason for your behaviors. If you are trying to slim down, understand who you are as an individual. The phrase "I have no will power" or "I have to stop eating so much ice cream" sends us into disbelief. Take out the castigation to believe in yourself.

Try It: Your Energetic Body Type
Go back up and read the Postural Olympics section about energetic body type. To find the benefit of your body type, write down all the ways you are the part of nature you gravitate towards and this can be anything in your mind; it doesn't have to be 'real' so to speak. If you feel like a fairy woodland goddess, do that. It's acceptable to be all forms at all times.

Body Healing for Women
Unhanding ourselves from patriarchal belief systems

The fact that women's health has been so ignored by the medical industry — even to this day — requires that women find alternative ways of healing. What is considered standard care is really meant for men because it has been designed by men for men. I was shocked to learn that even though women suffer the most from thyroid disfunction, the care is based on research on men![1] Similarly, anything involving the female body has not been fully studied —or studied at all— including health care concerns related to being pregnant, giving birth, and the typical aging cycle of women that requires greater care because of the hormone shifts. It is common practice to take drugs or have a hysterectomy just because women are going through 'the change,' a term I find demeaning in itself. Like an archer that knows when her aim is on target, we know when our sense of clarity is off because we feel it in our bodies. When we're off-target, we know practice makes 'perfect' or we're just having a bad day. But how do we take aim when we're constantly denigrated for who we are in our bodies?

Being denigrated in our bodies is something we have long lived with and it starts at a young age, so realize it as harmful. Do we know what it feels like, as adult women, to be in our bodies without denigration or judgment? Our own muscles betray us just like not having a clear concept of what a 'truth' muscle reaction feels like against an untruth or false statement. (See muscle testing information in Energy Healing Techniques.) The only way to know is with a baseline effect. So what's our baseline as women who think and feel different from men? Does anyone know? I'm not sure we do because this type of denigration has been going on for generations. We have to learn to stand in our own power, our own truth, as it relates to ourselves in our bodies. One way to get there is Postural Olympics, another way is to set aside time to uncover what you actually believe, not what your family or society at large tells you. We are our own individuals with our own life force energy; we do not owe anyone for that energy because we are endowed with it the moment we are born — just like men. Take that to the bank of understanding as we wait for someone else to be our life partner or be our standard of affection in our lives. Sex discrimination aside, we have been trained to believe that our bodies don't have their own wisdom. "Don't self-diagnose," is what I've heard often in my life, but when the diagnosis is unclear or you notice radical shifts in your own behavior or energy, then it's time to take full control of what you already have full control of: your body.

PTSD (post-traumatic stress disorder) is a familiar term by now and relates to the radical shift in feeling and being in a body due to a traumatic experience that happened outside, but manifests itself inside through a social awareness. It begins in the nervous system and extends outwards through thinking and feeling. It believes itself to be true and untrue at the same time. "Why am I like this?" serves as a starting point, but it can take on a different tambour of feeling. It has been misaligned with women who suffer 'nervous break downs' in their marriages while men, who are considered heroes, go to the war front to suffer trauma. But both are true, both are equally traumatized, both are

---

[1] Donna Eden, *Energy Healing for Women*, 2008

alive in their bodies and don't know what to do with them when the trauma comes up time after time.

PTSD Awareness

It belongs in the history books that women have been dealing with this form of denigration for generations, if not millennia. We have been the ones to look after the Earth for so long, but we have been stripped of our agency in terms of who we are in a body. The body is all that we are on Earth and so when we are cut down in that form, we don't feel a thing. The cutting down of a tree relates to both its roots and branches. It belongs in the Earth as it grows and takes root, but if the form of it is gone, how will it know when to sprout new branches? This is how it is to be a woman who has been cut down in her life. Her terms of endearment for herself and others have been supplicated to the investment of only men, as if she doesn't have a thinking-feeling bone in her body. She endows her best forms to others and doesn't think of herself as anything much worth having. I call bullshit on that behavior. It's time to stand up and believe in ourselves once again as an act of espionage. We are the ones tricking ourselves in becoming the slaves of history. We don't have to stand for it. We can become who we want to be and not take shit from anyone despite their flavor or tone. If it's a physical fight you want, I will fight back. I don't want the tone to be like that, but it takes gumption to pull that forward. Stop being a coward in your beliefs and bring forward all within you that is powerful and true. You have the ability to move past your sorrow and grief and live out loud in your humanity.

Men, we are ripped and torn to pieces for being ourselves — for being women — even while we make the meals that you come home to, raise your children, pay your college tuition without you knowing it, bring you medicine to heal suffering in all its forms — whether emotional, relational, or in your body. We find new ways of being in the world despite the cast-off behavior of men who serve themselves only — by being unloving husbands and partners. We are up for a grab bag of components in our lives that serve to keep us from our true identity as healers within our own right, even while men take over the medical profession like it's their god-given right to be heroes of the ecliptic. "Don't self-diagnose" only serves to cut us down to the quick again as if the male doctors could know what's happening in a female body. You couldn't possibly! The opposite is certainly true.

How could a nurse, with all her years of experience healing others, be in a subservient role to a man that shows up only for meal times? Impossibly horrid. To you, women, I say time to get out! You are much better on your own and that goes for healing as well as serving. You don't need to be in that marriage or in that role at work. You know who you are as an individual and know you can make it on your own, you don't need someone else's call for duty to get you there, you only need your own. Likewise, find the time to really sit with yourself and understand who you are in your body related to your marriage. If it's your second marriage, who cares if people castigate you for being "that kind of woman", with a trail of husbands behind you? It means they couldn't hack it with a powerful individual who demanded more time from them than just 'relaxing' sex. Who is being relaxed in that situation, because I know it's not you.

It's a castigation of truth that women denigrate themselves based on their male counter parts. Stop that! Men don't believe that they are themselves because you are there, so why would you think the opposite to be true? We are all whole and unto ourselves so long as we believe in our own abilities. We can work on what needs to be done while still helping others, but we need to take time to heal ourselves. You don't have to be who you are if you don't want, I'm not telling you how to live. But I have had my own gory issues, otherwise I wouldn't be writing this and, "I'm here to tell you, there's something else...." as Prince would say, so "Let's Go Crazy."

Healing Through the Moon's Energies

It is a righteous act to be the healer of a community that belongs in trust with one another, but be sure to believe in yourself as well. We are our own abilities through nature and can find healers among us just like the REAL good old days, when we were part of a system of truth that rang out from the rooftops and called in all the goodness of being part of a world that began at the moment of inception for all of us. We have been absconded from our own bodies and we now feel shame for being on our periods once a month. This takes on a tambour of feeling through the commercials we see about 'feminine products' to our supposed mood swings as the medical industry has named it a 'syndrome' that must be repaired.

You are informed by being in a woman's body that takes on the healing powers of the moon herself. She believes in you and will be by your side if you allow her to follow your own belief system of being in a body once a month. Meaning, your self deprecation about your flow of energy through the moon, or 'moon day,' as some people call it, is about believing in the power of the moon. It's not science, it's the actual energy of the moon flowing through and leaving your body in a tidal wave of belonging to the Earth. The Earth is your mother, the moon is your guide, so believe in your abilities to affect change through the transformation of blood in your body. The fact that women can change and transform once a month through their bodies' systems is a marker of a great ability to heal both the energies of the collective as well as individuals.

Take notes from the hospitality section of this book that all are welcome at the Table of Plenty. You don't have to supplicate to be there — you are there already! You don't have to be subservient to men. They will be in our everlasting gratitude that they are here to begin with as our bodies take on the form of being pregnant with ways of integrating the truth of the matter. Women's forms change shape daily as they move through their monthly cycles. We are shapeshifters in a way. It's powerful, not demonic or scary as some stories would have us believe. We don't have to look a certain way or be a certain way — we can be whatever way we want. Whether that's more feminine or not, I don't know, but the form of it is that we all have bodies that change shape over time, so why are women castigated for that, not honored for it? Believe in yourself and the circle will come back to you in some form or another.

Wish Fulfillment and Sublimation
Releasing the switch of self-doubt

When we wish for something, we bring it to light through awareness and intention and can use postural Olympics to get us there. Knowing how your energy likes to flow in and around your body puts you in awareness of how you like to manifest your dreams. If you are a turtle, they arrive slow and steady; if you are an energy like the wind, you have to decide which type, easy-breezy or sudden and changeable, for example. Just because you like your wishes to show up quickly, doesn't mean they will. There is an access point in your mind that allows you to see beyond the ordinary in terms of love, joy, and avasa. You bring it through every time you have an instantaneous visualization of a friend being in your house; house as symbolic to self. And so you are able to bring in wish fulfillment through that sublimated energy. It's time that causes the energy to move in a direction of fulfilling your wish.

Energetically, your mind is more responsive than your body to understanding what's happening in the body. The body is aligned with the divine but not at all times, whereas the mind can detect energies outside its domain of influence. We know that we often have to work for our dreams, but you can also help yourself by keeping your body and mind aligned with what your heart's desires. By telling your mind through words and your body through actions — their love languages, so to speak — we can affect more significant change by releasing the blocks from each. This is why you first go through the postural Olympics and then make the wish statement. They feed each other so our heart's desire comes true faster through the typical path of least resistance. It should feel effortless.

We take a two-week progression on our paychecks to earn the money that is owed to us, same thing for wish fulfillment: we agree to a 'contract,' or manifestation. We then work to get it through actions of awareness and awakening our bodies to become more aligned with the desire. To earn the 'paycheck' of wish fulfillment we sublimate energies of time. Here's an example: "I wish to be an actor" is an awareness, but you know you need to do certain things to get there: audition for a role, learn your lines, become more aware of your denigration patterns by letting go of fear and shame to be on stage in front of people, etc. So when you're finally done and the lights go up on the stage, you are in full awareness of being an actor who has sublimated that wish into your desired outcome. You have transformed the energy of a wish through action into an actual down-to-Earth event. This statement sublimates, or transforms, time to help you fulfill your wishes by putting you in alignment with your wish.

Try It: Wish Fulfillment Statement:
"I request access to my energy of love in my heart for wish fulfillment. I sublimate the energies of time in my mind to be in alignment with my wish fulfillment and I transmute all sublimated energy back to Full Source energy through deepest love and highest light."

When you believe it to be so, it's easier to manifest your desire because you have within you both the desired outcome and the belief that you can do it — easy-peasy. But when you don't believe you can do it, stumbling blocks of "I can't" or "it's too hard" or "you're never going to believe me" occur. These are all ways we stop ourselves from manifesting our desires or our wish fulfillment in terms of understanding our truth. The above lines stop many people from doing all different types of things because of lack of authority or lack of sense of self. So to sublimate your desire, or wish, find within your own body the sensation that it is true. This takes postural olympics, or the ability to ground down into our own energy of feeling the belief system within your energy requirements.

Go back to your energetic type and find the solution. 'What makes me tick?" might be another way of saying it, or "How do I feel in my body when I'm doing something I love?" You might move at a snail's pace, but your sublimation calls you forward through time and understanding. You need to be aware of the energy that causes the sublimation within your body. It's ok to move like a snail if that's who you are, but don't let your mind tell you that it's true if you're actually a jack rabbit. Maybe the time has come to heal wounds related to a sense of lack that stops you from moving forward.

Wish Fulfillment and denigrating patterns

Wish fulfillment is attracting what we like and what is like us towards us. If we didn't like that thing or that person, we wouldn't be wishing on a star for them! So notice behaviors that keep you from fulfilling your dreams of enchantment. This could be a sense of lack, a dis-ease that keeps you feeling down or from a sense of joy, and other ways of being in denial of who you are as an individual. Of course, denigration is a major block on this, which is also delivered through negative self-talk. When we denigrate ourselves through words and actions, our wishes don't see the likeness and so are not attracted to us. Instead what happens is the likeness becomes one of wound, so other wounded behaviors or people with the same wound come our way. This is not to say those people are bad — we are all wounded in some way. But if you are trying to attract a different 'vibration' or different lifestyle, you have to make the changes within you by changing the patterns of denigration. This can be helped energetically through an incantation that goes like this:

"I sublimate all patterns of denigration known and unknown within me and transmute them back to true Source energy through deepest love and highest light."

"I sublimate all the denigration patterns of <u>unrequited love</u> known and unknown within me and transmute them back to true Source energy through deepest love and highest light."

Slow Your Roll: Bridging the Mindfulness Gap
Slowing down your life to fully engage

Our ability to tune into ourselves and what we need is impacted by the speed at which we live our lives. Think about how you drive in these different scenarios:

1. 65-75 mph on the highway
2. 35-50 mph on a commercial road with 4-6 lanes
3. 25-30 mph on a residential street with kids playing in yards

At 65-75 (or above), we have to be alert and focused at all times. We need to know what other drivers are doing because one slip-up can cause a major accident. How do we react to the person who is tailing us too closely or cutting across traffic recklessly? We have a few choice words, but we have to respond quickly and precisely to their recklessness, if we overcompensate — accident, if we don't react in time — accident. There are so many variables as to how things can go wrong at this high speed, and it's a wonder there aren't more accidents! Why aren't there? Because we eventually get off the highway and slow down. Next time we get back on, our minds are clear, and we go through it all again. In contrast, imagine yourself driving down a residential street. At this slower pace, how focused is your mind on the road? You have time to look at houses and other people's gardens. And when someone's pet runs out into the road, you have time to react by slowing or hitting the brakes without concern for an accident.

Not many of us are professional race car drivers, but consider the amount of stamina required to maintain high speeds while zooming around a track. Exhaustion doesn't come from just sitting, it's mental as well. Many of us are living our lives like race car drivers, tearing around at 200 mph, our kids in tow. Home, school, work, home, school, work... and a pit stop at the grocery once a week. Weekends are no different with activities and the chores required to maintain a home. Life at this pace requires stamina and lots of it. Many of us are exhausted but don't know how to get off the track. If you slow down, accident. If you speed up, accident. The pandemic offered a life-changing reprieve for those of us who needed a break from the constant movement. But falling back into old habits is easy; life has ramped up again for many.

The mindfulness gap is about the speed of life. Being mindful can only happen at a slower pace. Allowing your mind to wander, observing your interior environment, being able to stop without causing an accident is about slowing down and connecting with your inner self. Without a connection to your inner self, creativity does not and cannot flourish. Creativity happens at the bridge between your conscious thinking mind and your subconscious feeling mind. To tap into both, your pace of life needs to be slow.

Try It: Slow Down To Let Your Mind Wander

Take a moment and tune into your mind. Imagine a place where you can slow down: floating on a river, walking in the woods, or meandering through an art museum as examples. Allow your mind to wander as you walk, float, or fly at your own pace and for no apparent reason. Notice how you feel in your mind, heart, and body as you allow the pace to slow. Now create an art piece that exemplifies how you are feeling in the present moment. It can be a poem, visual or sound art, whatever medium you choose to create a connection between slowing down and finding the pace at which your creativity flourishes.

Chapter 16: Other Energetic Healing Modalities

Energy healing is part of a mindfulness exercise that begins in the heart and extends outwards through time and place. When you start on the path of mindfulness, sometimes strange and wonderful things happen through realizations or experiences beyond your routine. This section of the book may really challenge some, but I provide it as a way to understand that our being-ness on Earth doesn't stop at the door of pre-qualified aspects of life. We don't all have to be into astrology or cosmic beliefs, but some of us are, and believing in something means sharing who we are. You don't need to get everyone to agree with you, and conversely, don't shun others for their beliefs. "Don't yuck my yum," as my daughter used to say in preschool, to which my son would reply, "I'm a professional yum-yucker." Being a professional yum-yucker is an energy code that is up for review right now as we look around us at politics, religion, and other aspects of life. Do we really want to separate ourselves from each other based on what we think and feel, or do we want to come together in an understanding that there are different modalities of living on planet Earth?

The topics below have been part of our way of life on Earth for millennia, though in recent years (as in centuries) pop-psychology and pop-astrology have taken over how we view our relationship to the Earth, sky, each other, and ourselves. But diving deeper into these topics can uncover a vast amount of information that is right in front of our eyes, if we can just reframe it or blur our eyes just a bit to see something different. (This is a technique I use when selecting materials for an interior and it works very well.) Blurring the lines between one thing and another means we take an approach that doesn't consciously create separation with a line of demarcation that is immovable. We allow for the fuzziness of imagination and creativity to be our guide rather than the rigidness of being exactly right.

I believe the true 'dark arts' are about being consciously in the dark of how joyful and magical life on Earth can be. When we don't see ourselves as the magical people we are then we live in darkness and that is all we see. There is an exactitude about the word 'art' in this instance because some people can take it to the level of an art form in an ironic twist of the word. In that light, enjoy the topics below, take what works for you and leave what doesn't.

Just as we are connected to each other on Earth, we are also connected to all aspects of our beingness in other forms that show up in the reflections of both Earth and sky. Star gazing is a popular activity and is a form of mindfulness that makes us aware of our own abilities through our place on Earth. Many people feel small when they look up at the sky, which is exacting, of course, we are small in comparison to the vast Universe. But it also wakes us up to how powerful we can be as we take on qualities of the stars and planets in our solar system.

Healing from Astrological Birth Charts
The sky as a healing energy

The sky has long been a map of existence on Earth and is used as a navigational tool and a tool to understand our energies in an individual context (birth chart) and as a collective mind set. Birth, or natal, charts are a snapshot of the sky, astrologically speaking, the moment you were born. It shows the planetary alignments that will impact you as you move through life and the energies of the place and time when you took your first breath. Natal charts are like a floor plan of our energy. A floor plan uses symbols to indicate doors, walls, windows and attachments to those planes of existence. There are symbols for furniture, countertops, cabinets, specialty equipment, etc. It is a map of existence within the walls of a structure, in other words. The natal chart is similar but it uses different signs and symbols related to the sky and the energetic processes of each season.

There are many ways to understand the cosmos energetically and this book is not on astrology, but I will say that looking into your natal chart for introspection, rather than trying to divine the future, is a healthy way to learn about who you are and how to make changes in your life so you can live more comfortably and with ease. I think astrologers who focus on the symbolic aspects of the planets are the most insightful because energy that occurs on Earth moves out towards the solar system . If you don't already follow astrology and are curious, change your perspective by considering how we might be in a mirrored existence with the solar system. By changing your perspective, you can fine-tune all of the creative aspects of your life.

I believe natal charts are an astrological imprint of the energy of our nervous systems. I came up with this idea while healing deeply from wounds related to PTSD through my own natal chart. It is not a fated aspect of your life, and yet it is at the same time. We all have free will and freedom of choice, but our energies through our nervous systems are landed in our bodies the moment we're born, along with ancestral and absorbed energies during our prenatal time within our mothers' bodies. The nervous system we are born with might also be an imprint from previous lives, which can get complicated and a bit overwhelming, considering that many of us have lived many lifetimes. Of course, I have no proof of this concept as we don't have tangible proof of past lives, but hear me out. The past life behaviors of time serve as an energy imprint on our bodies through non-understanding. How could you understand if you don't remember and don't believe in the reincarnation cycle? But our nervous systems are telling us when we ask, "Why am I like this?" which we will go into later. I found this true for myself and it is also part of our Source Code. To understand Source Codes, we need first to review the intercepted natal chart.

Intercepted Birth Charts
Understanding life blocks on a natal chart

I first learned about interceptions from famed astrologer and psychologist, Michael Lennox, through his podcast, *Conscious Embodiment*.[1] He describes an interception as a way to understand your path in life related to what you are up against or what you are trying to overcome, taking half your life to get there. Interceptions are common and depend on when and where you were born. As I understand them, they are when a sign falls in the center of a house and doesn't touch the house line, or cusp.[2] This represents a loss of energy. You may not feel the energy that the sign represents, or you struggle with that aspect of life; it's swallowed up, like it doesn't exist, or in a vacuum..

Interceptions are inert, they don't combine with any other system or belief except as a form of guidance; they are there to help you understand your path through life. Energetically, an intercepted natal chart indicates a life block, which any of us experience and often pertains to relationships, but the relationship with money can also be a life block. When one sign is intercepted, the opposite sign on the natal chart is also intercepted. This bi-directional aspect, like Double Vector Business, serves as a guide to

---
[1] See end notes for more information.
[2] April Elliott Kent, *Big Sky Astrology*, www.bigskyastrology.com

the area of your life that requires attention. If money represents one side, perhaps the other side pertains to being more spiritual or discovering your path of least resistance in your career. All these elements are interconnected and dismiss the notion of bad luck in life. Bad luck is nothing more than a disconnected perception of who you are as a person.

Understanding interception, or life block energy, through a specific Zodiac sign, or archetype, may help clarify its impact. If Aquarius is intercepted — or doesn't touch a house line — then the opposite sign, Leo, is also intercepted. Leo the lion symbolizes shining brightly and roaring loud as yourself, while Aquarius, the water bearer, symbolizes being in a consciousness of the collective. Therefore, this interception reflects a life block in the relational aspect of being an individual inside a collective. We all have these feelings, of course, but the interception is a much bigger block — like you can't get around it, or even go through it. Since the Zodiac is organized with individual energies on one side and collective energies on the other, all interceptions have some form of individual versus collective block. To fully understand this concept, note how you feel both in a group setting and when you're by yourself. If you feel unrelated to in both settings, you could feel like you're not in your body or 'under the gun' all the time, or forced into something you don't want to do. We all feel like the odd person out at different times, but when you are intercepted, it could be extra challenging to step out of those feelings.

Bifurcation Energy

The intercepted sign is like three parts of an apple tree. The apple tree is a type of tree that bears fruit during the winter of our lives, when things are going underground. This is important to note because being intercepted can send you up a tree or "up a shit creek without a paddle." The bifurcated trunk, or "Y" shape is like an interception — it sends you in two different directions and makes you feel disconnected from your roots. But what branches off the "Y" shape brings about more change and transformation which will then bear more fruit. The branch is an extension of who you are as a person, and the fruit comes from both the trunk and the branches. So, are you a trunk, a branch extending over the ground or up into the sky, or the fruit that bears witness to you teaching yourself about who you are as a person?

Find healing by looking to the house that the sign is intercepted in. The house and sign symbol work together to create a feeling of unease if you are blocked, but you can reverse this energy by allowing the opposite to be true. If Leo is blocked in the eighth house of divine life force energy shared with others, then look across the wheel at Aquarius in the second house of individual divine life force energy to heal your wounds of self-starvation related to living out loud. You can discover healing through the energy that you bring into the world first and then letting it flow out into the collective. See the chart below for more interceptions and possible healing remedies.

Intercepted Signs	Description (find healing through the house energy)
Aries — Libra	The relating aspects of life are interposed on each other; relating to self and others in communal aspects are impacted and perhaps transposed.
Taurus — Scorpio	Relationship to material things and spiritual guidance are impacted. This follows the energies of having difficulty with money due to religious beliefs or their spiritual energy is likely not grounded.
Gemini — Sagittarius	Gemini, the twin, believes 2 heads are better than one, but Sagittarius likes high minded pursuits which can be problematic when one aspect is a know-it-all. Monkey mind and feeling too attached.
Cancer — Capricorn	Tension between wanting to pursue great heights while needing to be consumed with all things of comfort.
Leo — Aquarius	Tension between being an individual who wants to shine brightly while serving in or being part of a collective.
Virgo — Pisces	All That Is energy relates to the potential of all things happening at any time, which analytical and young, naive Virgo can't count on.

House #	Energy Description	House #	Energy Description
1	"I am" energy in conscious form	7	Energy shared through communion with others
2	Individual Divine Life Force energy	8	Divine life force energy shared with others
3	Individual preferences and desires	9	Divine life force energy interacting with the divine energy of universal consciousness
4	Guidance in the form of energies outside us	10	Individual authority, how it was formed and expressed as an adult
5	"I am stocking up my energy to shine on others"	11	Collective Energy
6	Energy Healing	12	Primordial soup' energy, All That Is and will be in terms of love and feeling

Finding Your Life Line to be a Lifeline
Source code switch

The term 'Source Code' came to me one day while I was channeling, which I often do in written form (as well as in other forms). I found that term curious because many books with the word "code" in the title claim to be step-by-step manuals for becoming newly enlightened. I was skeptical, as it sounded like a marketing ploy, but I allowed the information to come through (after a few weeks). Here is what emerged:

A Source Code is your existence code on Earth — it is your way of being in the world. A Source Code shows up on your natal chart as an interception. Yes, it's true! Rather than viewing it as a major life block, you can reframe it as a guiding life path. It guides you towards your soul's purpose in life. Source Code is one of the many ways you can connect to Source. It manifests in belief systems aligned with Earth energy. If you are under a guiding system that believes in your will and understanding of the Universe, however that manifests, then you are aligned with your Source Code and will attract things and people to you with ease. Conversely, if you are not aligned with it through fear or misunderstanding, you may face more challenges.

Switching your source code means switching your belief system. You are no longer pulled in two directions; you are confidently walking in one direction. Confidence is the key word here because some people don't do the upfront work when the time comes in their lives to make the necessary changes to switch their code. They may feel hopelessly "out of luck" and struggle to navigate life on their own. Mental illness may become an issue, often linked to addictive behaviors, such as rekindling relationships with a harmful past lover, falling into despair over job loss, or even ending their lives. Belief systems can be blocked just like any other aspect of our lives, resulting in mental blocks. If your mind is blocked, it takes time, but eventually manifest in your body. For instance, if I believe I am unworthy of money, I may become poor in my health and in my life, not just in my bank account. I could experience poor health and wealth or feel wealthy in love from my family or friends. It's all the same energy.

You may be familiar with the term dharma, which is a similar belief but slightly different. Your dharma represents your purpose in life; it embodies who you are becoming through your contributions to others. There is a moral obligation associated with this method of understanding, which is not wrong, just different. Source Code signifies that you are standing in your power, in your belief systems that generate your optimal performance on Earth. You are one with yourself, and the belief systems of others do not impact who you are. You can generate great love around your being-ness and often find yourself in Flow. This is not to say that energy blocks won't arise; they will persist as long as you are on the Earth. However, remaining aligned with your Source Code provides you with the greatest benefit of life to yourself and those around you. Examine your natal chart and utilize astrology's symbolism to comprehend your dharmic purpose or Source Code. If you are not familiar with your natal chart or if you don't have a Source Code path, you can discover your Source Code through awareness of who you are as an individual — the interests that excite you, the types of people you feel drawn to, and your openness to various beliefs. If you're not intercepted, explore your belief systems through your own energetic processes of self-discovery. These elements collectively point to your Source Code or your life's direction.

As I write this, I am in flow with my guides who are part of my beingness on Earth. They are part of my belief system that we are energetically one and the same as members of the same soul group family, and our belief systems are similarly related to healing. We feel love for humanity and see the soul in most things—everything from people to animals to inanimate objects such as cars, if you can believe it. Cars are engineered and made by people (though much of it is automated now), so as a designer, I believe they contain some level of personality or 'soul,' if you will. If you name your car, you know what I mean. Therefore, we carry our belief systems with us and project them into the world through our understanding of who we are. These belief systems point to our Source Code, indicating how we function in the world; not unlike a computer program or operating system. Although I hesitate to equate us with machines or AI, it serves as a helpful analogy.

If you're looking for what your Source Code is, examine your life through your belief systems. This relates back to your value statements that were developed earlier in this book in the creativity section. Once you identify your belief systems, look for any blocks you might have. For instance, you could have a significant block concerning money — many people do. You may struggle to keep what you earn, or you may desire to earn more yet find it difficult. This illustrates a Source Code block. Releasing past behaviors and accepting who you are as a person are integral to healing a Source Code block. It may seem esoteric, but it's not; it's all clearly outlined in an astrological natal chart.

For energy healers or those who want to continue, use the term Source Code Energy along with your typical protocols to clear out any bifurcation (interception) energies still affecting the body.

Try It: Clearing Interception Energy

Find release from suffering through your source code switch by first going within and finding the source. Once you have relieved yourself from suffering, you will find that your mind is clearer, your heart more open, and your body more relieved of weight as it is carrying the burden of suffering. Now release through these words:

"I no longer allow past interception energies to force my life. I maintain stillness in my mind and keep my life intact as an individual without pain and suffering. I no longer allow sorrow to emanate from my beingness and energy field and maintain a posture of love and understanding in my life, with others' actions held accountable for their own behaviors."

If you are intercepted or bifurcated, as my guides explain, take some time to understand how and why. There will come a point on your path when it truly starts to take shape and when it will end. When the time comes for your bifurcation to end, you may find that things happen rapidly and not easily. It might be a time in your life when you are experiencing significant suffering. The battle of an interception is both a battle within and without. It doesn't matter who you are or if you're intercepted; we all face these internal battles that are mirrored in the outer world. Part of the code switch involves learning what you're up against and finding a way to deconstruct your past so that pain isn't pulled forward into the future. Make time to release the suffering and take care of yourself; otherwise, it's all for naught. Find the joy in your life, as that is truly how life is meant to be lived. Pain and suffering are real and part of our time on Earth, but we are meant to work through those blocks to find love, joy, and *avasa*. So find your joy by releasing your interception through these notes on healing, viewing the past through the lens of joy rather than misery.

Past Life Energies through Interception

It is my belief that interception energy likely stems from a past life injury that requires healing. As far as I can tell, this is the source of an intercepted natal chart. It makes sense—why would we be intercepted otherwise? If we're here on Earth to learn how to love each other, then the energies of the past impact the present and the future. So, if there is a bifurcation or interception in your natal chart, look around you. Who is influencing your life negatively? Is there something that needs healing but you can't quite identify? Why is money slipping through your fingers? Why can't you maintain a job? Why do you feel sad each year on your birthday instead of happy, even with a loving family or friends around you? All of these things could point to an intercepted natal chart. It's worth investigating if you're into it.

Releasing past-life energy related to bifurcation or an intercepted natal chart requires an energetic healer who can connect to past-life energies. If you are a healer who can do this, you can clear and release the wounded energy through the energetic process of transmutation, using the term "past-life bifurcation energy" in your typical clearing protocols. These are not Timefields or wounds, as described above, but their own source code of energy, and so they require their own healing protocol.

The Swallowtail of Existence
Feeling bifurcation energy to be freeing

We can be drawn to behaviors outside of our belief systems and don't fully understand why. We may ask ourselves, "Why did I let that go on for so long when I knew I wasn't happy?" Many of us experience this situation both at home and work because they are relational aspects of our lives. Some feel freedom when they walk away from those scenarios that keep them down or feel uplifted when they find a job or a relationship that truly aligns with their heart center magic.

Swallowtails are the most beautiful birds in their shape, form, and flight patterns. They have an innate sense of the world around them as they swoop and dive through the air, most likely for bugs to eat, turning direction on a dime to find their target. They have this ability to quickly change direction through their form because their tails act like rudders to guide them towards their goal. It's an unending dance of belief that they are alive, in a body, and free while gliding through the air. They believe it to be so and so they do it, simple as that — no long nights trying to figure things out, no hair's breadth of notice that they are not enough or unfulfilled. They just believe and do it through their bodies in form and function.

There is a math system called **catastrophe theory**, a branch of bifurcation theory, where the swallowtail form is evoked. Yes, bifurcation also has a science tie-in and it's through the study of dynamical systems, a function of time. There are seven catastrophes in this theory and the word is used to describe the randomness of our environment. It feels antithetical to be discussing not just regular problems but catastrophes in a mindfulness book, but it's all in how you look at it. If something moves along a stable path, but then suddenly jumps it — randomly — that is considered a catastrophe. Perhaps mathematicians are prone to the emotion of hyperbole and not just the dry form of equations after all! But in all cases, it's about jumping the track, leap-frogging, or finding that sudden realization in our creative endeavor. It means, through math no less, that we are not meant to plod along, finding our horse and carriage to be a burden. We are meant to break free, sometimes with sudden randomness, to find our truths towards a better life, which has a feeling of justice.

It's a type of controversial statement that we are all one through this system, yet Salvador Dali, the surrealist artist known for his interest in math[3], drew on this theory later in life up until his death in 1989 — the year the Berlin Wall crumbled and the Tiananmen Square protests. I bring up these seemingly disparate events to show the behavior behind the theory. These two events seemed random when they happened, but were part of a series of events that eventually 'jumped the track' and caused chaos in the public realm; chaos for change, not for the sake of chaos. Catastrophe theory also uses the bi-furcated form of the butterfly, part of chaos theory through the famous saying about butterfly wings in China causing a storm or tidal force on the other side of the world. We are all truly connected through our ideas and thought forms as they travel around the world and find their place in one person, community or another. It is a tidal force to be reckoned with, but not to be afraid of for we are all connected through love.

This idea is important to understand because bifurcation is really about being joyful, not feeling that you've been cursed with an interception or have to trudge through life

---

[3] Sam Vaseghi, *The Grand Equation of Imagination: Salvador Dali's Mathematical Surrealoscope, 2024*, www.cantorsparadise.com

knowing that there are things outside your control that can't be undone. It is an incontrovertible truth that we are all one through these theories and through the lake effect of our lives. Lake effect is a series of weather bands that get kicked up, usually in winter, off a lake where the entire region is impacted. Lake effect is a universal experience, but we move through it in our own way. Some of us enjoy a snowy winter while others grouse about it from dawn til dusk. Some of us are in between and enjoy it for a time but look forward to the spring of our lives after a certain point or a certain amount of snowfall!

We all need moments of release from the drudgery, to find our heart centers in wish fulfillment, to bring in the new and find those bright and shiny things, or joy. Bright and shiny is also aligned with 'fools' gold' or going on a fool's errand, but we can move it to a level of wish fulfillment if we look at it from a different perspective. What if the fake gold isn't really gold at all, but a wish to be higher, brighter with joy and not worrying or feeling scarcity sneak up on us? Or if the errand of a fool is one that doesn't produce results is about being in joy and finding healing that we can enjoy every moment of the day. Or believe that the errand will produce a result, but doesn't reveal itself until later. It's all a matter of perspective, as my dad used to say. He was one of the best to help me perceive a situation differently and helped me get on with things in joy.

We are all one and need to be that way for wish fulfillment and so I say these words out loud to myself when I need to find more joy. Aligning it with a swallowtail is my way of bringing in the good vibes, but you can use whatever bifurcated animal or insect that brings you happiness.

Wish Fulfillment with Bifurcation Install (February 11, 2025)
Reframing the bifurcation experience to be one of joy and love experience.
"I allow the swallow tail of my existence to bring in [state your wish] and I allow the non-biased energy of love to bring in joy and light. I maintain my heart center energy to be in time and sync with my own behaviors and allow the energy of tomorrow to provide me with an energy of love, joy and avasa."

Tesseracts and the Nature of Reality
Present-moment awareness

A tesseract, or hypercube, is a concept that suggests a representation of the fourth dimension. While we exist in three dimensions—width, height, and length—the fourth dimension incorporates time as the additional variable. The space-time continuum, or spacetime, is illustrated through the geometry of a hypercube. It tries to express it in 2D-3D forms, allowing us to understand it on our own without going into a tesseract of our own making, which is possible if you study the art of meditation. We do not experience the fourth dimension through our physical senses, but we can experience it through what some call your sixth sense, or clairesentience (clear sensing). When in this state, your conscious awareness moves beyond your cone of reality, which is a point in the present. A point is no space and equals zero. But moving away from that point in spacetime reality, it creates a cone, or cone of vision; in other words, it creates space. This concept was theorized by Einstein's professor, Hermann Minkowski, in the 1800s and involves a lot of math and science. A quick internet search will reveal illustrations and abstractions of this theory, depicting a plane positioned between two cones of light extending from a point on the plane into both the past and the future. The plane is called 'hyperspace of the present.'

You can glimpse the beginnings of Einstein's extended present theory in this model, but we are primarily focused on that point on the plane, which represents the present and brings us to the often-quoted phrase, "the point of power is in the present moment." This phrase has been attributed to Louise Hay, though it was originally channeled by Jane Roberts from her inter-dimensional guide, Seth, in her book, *The Nature of Personal Reality*. Louise was a student of Jane's through this book and considered it a primer in metaphysics. But the point is that we hold the power to effect change in both the future and the past in the present moment, as our cone of vision, through light, extends forward and backward in time, making present-moment awareness a powerful act. But far from physical time travel by jumping through hyperspace, you don't have to take a trip on the *Millennium Falcon* to reach this realm, as it extends from your mind.

Power is within and without. It belongs in the present because that is where you are now in this 3D Universe. You are always in the now, as Alan Watts quipped in one of his lectures. Now is also considered The Way, or the *Tao* of Taoism. You can't get out of it physically, but your mind... now, that's another story. It has the ability to make connections that are not beyond your control because you are your own power. So the tesseract proves this concept along with the cone of light, which is really a sphere extended out in time, making the phrase 'sphere of influence' exactly correct.

The tesseract is also aligned with time travel through the book, *A Wrinkle in Time* by Madeline L'Engle, where a sister and brother move through space on a 'wrinkle' in the time-space continuum in search of their lost father. He is lost in time, and his memory is ebbing away from him because his surroundings are null — he can't see the box he's been imprisoned in and is therefore losing his mind. (Yes, there's a large brain controlling everyone, but that's beside the point.) Their father has lost his present by existing in a space that has no time. Time is the deciding factor in all our relationships on Earth; without knowing the time, we don't know the energy that brought us here. By understanding the past, we can look toward a brighter future, which is reflected in the present moment.

Present Moment Awareness

Present-moment awareness is how I deal with psychic overwhelm. I do this in list form because it's simple and I tend to make lists for almost every form of mental organization I need; from grocery lists to year-end financial tallies, I find lists help keep my often overactive mind quiet. Present moment awareness list making stops the mental overwhelm by closing your eyes and making a mental list of first where you are and then how you feel. It might go like this:

> "In this present moment I am sitting in a chair.
> In this present moment my breath is shallow.
> In this present moment my toes are cold.
> In this present moment I hear birds singing.
> In this present moment I feel scattered.
> In this present moment I feel fear and I'm not sure why."

It's important to say 'in this present moment' each time as it turns your list into an incantation that can take you from 10 to 0, where 10 is the most agitated state and one is feeling at ease. Sometimes, I move into a meditative or lucid dream state or fall asleep, which means I need to get to a level of understanding from my unconscious mind. This is how it shows up for me: find the way that best suits you and understand the processes you are going through.

The Shape of Love ♥
How we perceive symbolic love energy

We've reviewed many symbols and metaphors, but one universal symbol stands out when it comes to love — the heart shape. This shape shows up everywhere, even when we're texting or showing love by forming it with our hands or thumb and forefinger (I'll skip the K-drama reference this time). It is an ancient symbol, though no one knows why or how it became associated with the heart and, therefore, love. Yet it has been used for thousands of years worldwide to represent those we feel warm and fuzzy about, to show life — as in video and board games — and our anatomy as the central focus of our bodies. When we say let's get to the heart of the matter, we know it's about uncovering the central theme or current of energy for something. The heart of a building or an energy plant, with a control panel serving as the central access point for all its functions, offers a ready-made metaphor for an entry point into someone's life.

The heart symbol is at once ubiquitous and mysterious due to its unknown origin. Every culture uses it and I think it's because it resembles shapes we see in nature. But why that particular shape? We may never know for certain, but I have another theory on this matter. Ancient cultures excelled in abstraction and metaphor far more than our modern societies. They didn't have cameras in their pockets. Their world was not about being literal or photorealistic, it was about understanding through the metaphor of existence. When you examine the artwork of the Lascaux caves in France or the ancient indigenous art of the Mesa Verde people, you'll find that they used symbols to convey their meaning to a wider universe and so their symbols became universal. Abstraction is the most powerful tool in design because it allows the wearer or experiencer of that art to imbue it with their own powers of belief and understanding. It involves nuance and the freedom to interpret something through one's personal belief system. Although we might hold these truths to be self-evident, our truths are different. We cannot all embody one object over another, but we can navigate back to ourselves through our individual comprehension of the Universe.

It is a common misconception that symbols mean one thing over another. It is up to you—the wearer, believer, and doer—to create your own mystique about what a symbol means. That is the point of symbology! It is meant to guide us toward a behavior and then abstract it into something meaningful for us. When I began my journey of self-discovery, I found myself in and out of time and heard the word 'Moonflower' one day as if it were whispered in my head. I wrote it down in the margins of my notebook but didn't fully grasp its meaning. Over the next few years, Moonflower evolved from an idea about opening a flower shop to a connection with a higher source and finally learning about the healing collective I am part of, called Moonflower. It is a force outside of myself but is channeled through me as an individual. The symbol of the Moonflower is a pentagon inscribed with the five leaves of a flower, representing both Earth (flower) and sky (pentagon). I have included it on the back cover of this book and on my website because it has now become part of my identity as a healer.

When I conk you over the head with a literal interpretation, there is no wiggle room for your beliefs, which can leave you feeling unwelcome. This is evident in the symbology used for bathroom signage. I know some people consider it ridiculous because the human body is either male or female, but gender is not a body part — it's an experience. If I don't feel welcome in my body or my gender role, then I can't form the connections in my heart that reconnect me to who I am as an individual. And this brings us back to the heart shape, the symbol of everlasting love and equality for some, forgiveness for others, or romance and passion, especially around February 14th. Why we need a holiday for love, I will never understand, but I'm not one to make light of other people's need to connect, it's just not my way. And that proves the importance of symbology! We need it because we all need love and forgiveness in our lives. Just don't conk me over the head with it because it gives me *agita* (sour stomach), as my Italian aunt used to say, which is how I feel about Valentine's Day.

For me, the heart shape is another infinity symbol and embodies the time-space continuum. I was guided to this idea while in one of my more introspective moods and found myself in a tesseract while writing this book. As usual, I tried to find a grounded source for the information that was shuttled to me across the Universe, but I couldn't find anything definitive. After drawing it myself — is it a mirrored question mark (which seems appropriate) or half an hourglass? — and extending the lines to create another shape, I finally turned to the internet and, on a whim, searched for Celtic symbols. Celtic knots are legendary and possess a unique energy when you look at them and draw them. While drawing the *triquetra* symbol with a heart (instead of the traditional circle), I suddenly felt a shift in my energy and took this as a sign that I was on the right path. Although not an 'authentic' Celtic symbol, the 'love knot' consists of three overlapping arcs intertwined with a heart, and some of the more intriguing ones extend the arcs from the heart itself, sending it to the realm of the space-time continuum. Celtic artistry in the form of knots includes infinity symbols of all types. It's fun to try to find the beginning or end, to see where the shapes bend and morph into another shape, and can be mesmerizing, like moving into a tesseract! It all interacts and relates, one form layered over another, overlapping, moving in unison. Find a form that resonates best for your introspective practice.

Healing Through Ley Lines
Using the Earth for energy guidance

When people ask me, "Why am I like this?" either as a direct question or as a way to express their feelings, I always consider an intercepted natal chart first. More than likely it is the key to understanding their situation, although there are other factors to consider as well. For example, aspects of behavior related to ego play a significant role. The ego allows you to first inquire and then push past all the energetic qualities and behaviors caused by bifurcated energy. It empowers you to advocate for yourself instead of simply conforming to what others expect of you or what you have been dealing with for a lifetime. The 'Why am I like this' energy often surfaces when the energy is more intense and sends you to seek some form of release. I have discovered that this release comes from the Earth's energy grid.

We are energies that are impacted by both the Earth and sky, and our bodies reflect that truth. The birth chart is an energy map of the moment you were born, defined by both time and location using the longitude-latitude grid. In addition to the intercepted sign energy as reflected in the sky, there is another area of interception that is reflected on the Earth. This interception relates to our position on Earth at the time of our birth in relation to the Prime Meridian or the International Date Line, the opposite line of demarcation. It is my belief, through a guided aspect, that when a person is born at noon or midnight on the Prime Meridian or International Date Line, they may feel intercepted in their bodies as it relates to gender. These two times mark the transition from night to day and vice versa at certain points on the Earth. The maleness, or yang, energy of day transforms into the female, or yin, energy of night (or opposite), causing the nervous system to understand both as true. While it's accurate that we have not always had the latitude-longitude grid, our bodies are wise and recognize that there exists a point on Earth that reflects this axis.

The phrase, "Why am I like this," brings up feelings of dismay for many people, but if you take the time to really dig deep and answer that question, you might find some surprising insights. For many, it's a behavioral matter, but for some, it's physical. Why do I have this illness? Why do I feel like a woman when my physical form is male? For many, this is an intercepted point in time when their energy systems were being born on Earth. They most likely took their first breath anywhere between 10-12 minutes before or after noon or midnight, when the sky is darkest or lightest in terms of the sun's energy based on the lines of demarcation noted above. This relates to your x-y axis of believing who you are in a body in time and represents the two-spirit energy that many indigenous cultures revere, manifesting in a single person's body. The transformation aspect becomes part of their life's path and could look like becoming a different gender than the one assigned at birth, identifying as non-binary, or exploring other aspects within society's gender norms. I don't believe this relates to being gay or bi, but it exists within the same realm of thought because we perceive all these gender relations as outside 'normal' cultural bounds. To be truly two-spirit, I believe, you have to hold both truths within your body and find all genders as potential life partners. If this is a truth you embrace, consider the time you were born locally and then adjust for the time zone difference to find the corresponding time in Greenwich, England, Burkina Faso, or other locations along the Prime Meridian. If it falls within 10-12 minutes either way of noon or midnight, you may understand yourself as someone who feels attracted to all people, or you may have an illness that you need to overcome. It may be that you miss the power of an interception merely by being born in a specific place or at a separate time. If I am wrong, just take note and let it go. You can still use the healing modality below because it can be beneficial to align our bodies with the Earth's energy grid.

The following is channeled from my everyday guides for healing:
"Ley Lines relate to the high and low points on Earth. For example, the Appalachian Mountain range in the East and the Rockies in the West in the US. Also, look to the Alps and Himalayas for a clearer understanding of this topic. In other words, ley lines are another term for the Earth's energetic grid that is set up through a course of action in Faraday's electromagnetic field. Find the low points to be fertile soil for healing and understanding in physical form. Below these low points are voids, or lakes, where invisibility occurs. Become 'invisible' in the void of existence to heal wounds of the past. The action and reaction of energy around a mound of earth like a hill or mountain is very different from the energy around a stream or pond. It's a law established by Newton, as discussed earlier, and will become an energetic component in our healing modality. When push comes to shove, we will all see the action-reaction moments of everything on Earth. Ley lines don't exist in the ocean in the same way that they do on land. Oceans are their own power source and are a powerful means of healing, but they do not provide the stability of ley lines. That is all."

How can we utilize this as a healing modality? Reflect on your life and identify your likes and dislikes. What repels you, or what attracts you? The foods that you like or dislike, the plants and animals you like or dislike — it all relates to your body's polarity, which is centered in our hearts and infused with the energies of time and place. For example, if you live in a region of the Earth fed with the energy of fish, you will likely enjoy fish. Taste and texture align with our body's natural systems, which extend outward. However, if your true heart's desire is sauerkraut, then your energy may not align with your birthplace. There are some who don't align with their culture, either through food or their ability to be free in their bodies. It all goes back to when we were born, the foods we were raised on, and the energies they provided during our early years. We are our own greatest sorrow and joy, so understanding the struggle to connect with our identities has a profound impact on our path through life.

What we can't see, we can feel. Why are we attracted to certain cities on Earth and not others? Some people move to the other side of the world and stay there, while others experience a breakdown of loneliness and leave. What we love attracts us; what we deny leaves us. Our hearts are the center of our polarity and align with the natural energies emanating from food—whether it's a plant or an animal, regardless of its form—that either attract or repel us. The poles of our hearts can be reversed, causing time to feel unsupported in our bodies.

Ley lines are Faraday's field lines of the Earth and attract with a one-two punch of existence and form. By examining a photographed map, one can heal through the invisibility of the electromagnetic field. Invisible electromagnetic lines surround us, one being light and the other being form. (We perceive light as an effect rather than as an electromagnetic wave.) The purpose of these lines is to generate a field of invisibility that aids in healing our bodies. The nature and function of a ley line is to emanate outward from a specific point on Earth. Thus, to heal with ley lines involves perfectly aligning our bodies with the land. It's about what you see and what remains unseen. The shift in perspective is resolved through quantum physics. Time and space are interconnected, bending back on themselves and around each other to create form.

You are healing the <u>emotional aspects</u> of this relating issue from within. Your body and its systems are right and true to you. If you naturally feel that you are not the gender assigned to you at birth, then that is the right way for you to live. We are all individuals and have the right and freedom to live as we choose. **You do not need to seek others' approval for who you are as a person.** However, we all desire to relate authentically to each other because that is when we are in our best state, or Flow. So, find emotional healing through this method while also healing in form. It's a simple and non-intrusive process. You only need to go to your living room, office, or wherever you can access the internet. It's as easy as bringing up a satellite image of the Earth and just looking at it deeply for more than a minute or two. It may sound strange, but I have found healing for myself using this method and it started while looking at an online map for directions to a specific location in the region where I currently live.

The next section was channeled to me from my healing guides through their own verbiage. They have transcribed this work for me and I am interpreting it as I go. The language that is put forth is different from mine because they are healing guides who are much older than my normal, everyday guides (which will be another topic).

"Ley lines are a new healing topic that I have put forth because my guides asked me to. I have healed myself with this modality through both viewing them on a screen and actually moving through a highly energetically charged section of the Earth during a highly energetically charged space in time — the day of the summer Solstice of 2023. The time is mentioned for those who wish to compare notes of their own healing processes and modalities during that time in that particular year. As many of you know, it was a pivotal point in time for us on Earth. The Earth's generating ley lines were 'up for renewal', in your terms, and we were one of a few that were able to heal on this topic.

"We are aware of a certain definition of ley lines regarding certain monuments being connected through these lines in time and space, but that is not the actual definition of a ley line as regarded by my guides of energy healing. The healing guides' topic of theory related to ley lines comes from a location as old as the hills themselves. In topics of conversation, this is how we talk about ourselves and about certain time-out-of-mind moments or idioms of expression.

"Now we get into the nitty-gritty. The energy lines of the Earth are not man-made, but the meridian lines are superimposed on the Earth by a man-made system of time. Time is the deciding factor in all our decisions on Earth — it's not time yet, I'm not ready, time to go, and so forth. Healing also comes in time as time heals all wounds. But the time lines of the Earth are also placement lines of longitudinal and latitudinal x-y axis points, just like the body. So if a female form lands on a bifurcation line in time, she is likely to be intercepted in her x-y axis of loving relationships and self. If a male lands on this same axis, it is likely to be one of sorrow and misunderstanding related to sexuality in male form, or likely that that person will be trans. This is a sorrow of misunderstanding, not of joy of being in a body."

Try It! Look at an Image of the Earth
The healing comes from the Earth's energy grid. We look at the longitudinal lines to determine our place in time when we were born, and then we look to the Earth's natural ley lines for healing. The superimposed man-made grid concerns our understanding of time, while the Earth's grid concerns healing through Faraday's Field, which is energy.

Looking at a picture and feeling your own energy react to it will either have an effect or none at all. You can start with your birthplace and view it as terrain with as few man-made streets and grids as possible. When you do this, you are examining the Earth's grid itself. If you are intercepted on your x-y axis, move to the Prime Meridian; then, if you don't have a strong reaction, look at the International Date Line on the opposite side of the globe. Feel free to move up and down that axis, zoom in and out, and simply sense your body's energies. You might think it's nonsense, and that's okay. I'm presenting this as a topic of healing and understanding, not to impose my beliefs on anyone.

You might also consider visiting that area of the globe in person. Many of us eventually return to our hometowns for a reckoning, and this is part of that same energy, going back to the past to heal the wounds of the present. If your personal ley lines are not aligned with your hometown, you will need to release those energies through forgiveness. Revisit the unrequited love and/or the tidal locking sequence, either while you are there or in the comfort of your own home. Intention and attention are the most powerful methods of healing for others' unrequited love to leave your body, heart, and mind.

Oceans, Rivers, and Lakes: Healing Currents of the Earth
The healing power of water and light

Water amplifies through the power of intention, which has its own frequency. Intentions do not have weight or mass like a skipping stone, but they do have a frequency that enables their form to arise through the waters of the unknown. What lies beneath is often unknown, not like a scary thriller where the unseen evokes fear, but like the discovery of something new — a newfound appreciation for a cultural food, for example. When you move past the unknown smells and eat it, you may be surprised to find that you enjoy it, which creates a power of awareness. Your void of the unknown has been filled with new conscious information of the known. Water is creative by acting as an amplifier into the unknown consciousness where anything is possible.

Water is an amplification device for setting intentions and healing wounds, but water and light together make a powerful combination of interactions that work with the Earth's ley lines. Naturally formed bodies of water, due to their geographic location, absorb the energies of their surroundings and establish an ecosystem with the local plants and animals there to create a healing environment. Let's look at the different types of water first.

Oceans

Oceans are all powerful and cover most of the planet. They bring healing through the persistent energy of the ever-flowing tides that occur day and night without stop in an unending dance with life and death. This is the seat of the life-death-life cycle that Clarissa Pinkola Estes talks about. (See chapter 4) The ocean has the power to give and receive life. It evokes a deep understanding in our hearts and minds about the power of love, even if we don't live near it. The ocean is our planet in motion, ebbing and flowing across time. Our understanding of the 'abyss' comes from our realization of how deep the oceans are, pulling us back in time or to the future in an otherworldly landscape. All the creatures of the deep are our storied aliens in form. They take on a distinct law of physics because they inhabit a deep, watery environment and never come up for air.

It's the law of anticipation—what we expect to happen. How will we survive without air on another planet? Look to the ocean for reassurance. How will we deal with other creatures who don't look or act like us, land-loving people? Ask the ocean. It's all here on our very own planet. Without science, we would never know these realms existed. Without science, we would never have the drive or determination to explore what our planet has to offer. It's a sense of wonder, curiosity, and joy that leads us to the depths of the ocean. Plumbing the depths of our soul's energy can bring the same wonder if we can overcome the fear of what lies beneath. Is it an enormous sea monster waiting to destroy us? Or is it a beneficial sea colony of long-forgotten beings, like Atlantis? It's all in how you frame it. It's all a matter of perspective.

Lakes

Lakes are my favorite type of water on Earth because they speak to the void and offer great healing without much fear (at least in my mind). Lakes are voids on Earth and can be seen as such on any satellite image of our planet. You can distinctly observe the dark holes they create, especially if they are deep. Lakes are like a healing bath that are also in motion, but not nearly as much as the oceans. Similar to oceans, lakes bring healing simply by being near them or in them. The most powerful healing comes from dipping your toes or immersing your whole body in the water. The Great Lakes of North America have typical healing powers related to fun and recreation for people who call them home or use them for vacation, but they also have immense power for healing beyond the ordinary. Lake Ontario is an incredibly healing lake as it is deep and wide. It feels like an ocean to me and that's how I view it in terms of healing. Ontario is my Northern Star as it beckons to me when I need to take a break from fortune's wheel, stop the churning in my head, and release all that is not mine. A walk along the beach in the summer does wonders for my soul and connects me to the Universe in ways that are indescribable in the written word.

Lakes provide a deep understanding within ourselves as they instruct through experience. "I'm going to the lake" is shorthand for saying, "I'm going to be by myself, take some time for myself, and learn what I need within from what's happening outside." Lakes are molded by the Earth and exist in a restful state, cradled in low places; settled in their belief systems; unconcerned with what's happening elsewhere. Just chill. That's a powerful statement, especially in this day and age with the constant churn of electronic media entertainment! It's an ever-evolving process of diving into the depths of existence, but not so far that you lose yourself. You find time in knowing who you are and feel refreshed when you emerge from its energetic pull. You feel uplifted by allowing yourself to settle, knowing that you are cradled by the Earth and in a void for healing.

Rivers

Rivers are Flow in physical form. We've discussed Flow already, but we haven't delved deeply into rivers themselves. They are mighty as in the Mississippi and the Rio Grande, or mild, like the Ohio and the Danube. They can serve as powerful agents of change through flooding, or they can provide life to those who live and work along their shores. They are the constant movement of energy through vein-like structures on Earth. They are literally called arteries, delivering a vital life force for the Earth's energy and following ley lines, just as lakes do. However, they do not simply meander and pool; instead, they transfer what is here to there. They provide transportation and a willingness to be on one side or the other. Change your perspective by switching shores or shorelines. We may hail from the wrong side of the tracks, but the river that runs through it is a healing force from both within and without.

Rivers are change in constant motion. When we stop a river by damming it, we halt the vital life forces that exist within and outside that ecosystem. If we believe we are not part of that ecosystem, we need to think again! Damming a river for food production validates this behavior, but think of all the food that exists within the river itself. Why do we irrigate when the planet's vital life force is being impacted daily by flooding? Consider the ancient Egyptian culture living along the Nile River, renowned for its seasonal flooding. The people living in that ecosystem knew how to work with its ebb and flow without dams; they understood when to plant and when to refrain. They knew when and where the soil was fertile and paid attention to the seasons of change.

Riverdance, the Irish step dance, is about hearing the soles of our feet against the grounded rhythm of the Earth and feeling the vital beat of the Universe. It's about space and time, living as a human in a human body. It embodies breath and life all at once, flowing in time with the river. Consider this when planting crops in the desert and stopping up the Earth's energy to get you what you need. If the Earth is life itself, then it will provide for you. Flow signifies the regeneration of the spirit and body — just as a river flows, so do our hearts and minds. As we learned from the Timefield description, obstructing the flow harms our health, bodies, and lives. Let's stop treating the planet the way we treat ourselves. As above, so below; as within, so without. Everything works together in understanding and forgiveness. Find your river flowing strong and deep, and you will discover the true essence of your being on Earth.

<u>Small Water</u>

Ponds, brooks, creeks, and other smaller bodies of water—even puddles—should not be overlooked. They are also part of our ecosystem of healing because they offer us joy in its purest form. A babbling brook invites you to stop and play, while a pond beckons with the possibility of floating a toy or an animal. They can also provide calm stillness, with water lilies painting the surface. Reflecting pools, in the form of natural ponds, are about looking in the mirror and finding your true identity. They provide a stillness in form and function and don't bely your truth until you touch the surface and see it ripple outward. Puddles embody a child's pure joy, providing opportunities for learning and understanding of themselves through awareness and exploration. In all these ways water heals and instructs us for life on planet Earth. Let's amplify these learnings and bring in the healing power of light.

Dancing Light
Healing through lightcasters

Just as we perform a river dance, when light dances on the water we find ourselves drawn to it through its motion. In the forest, a moving light can also capture our attention, but it doesn't dance and sparkle quite like light on water. The healing motion of the water and the dance of light on its surface actually serve as a healing modality on Earth. However, light offers us another healing modality that we may not be as aware of. In a sense, we are light engineers, as our soul's connection to light is evident in all the familiar ways. My guides have instructed me to utilize this type of healing on several occasions when I needed to stop the vacuum effect in my healing.

Fear of the dark, being called into the light, finding the light within ourselves, "don't put your light under a bushel," and so on; all these phrases and idioms speak to our love for life and the light that touches the Earth. But, fear of light and consciousness has consumed our society, manifesting in part as skin cancer through melanoma and a growing fear of the sun. The fear of aging and looking old compounds these feelings as we confront time on our faces and skin. How have we, as humans, existed on Earth for so many millennia without sunblock? Nowadays, we spend over 90% of our daily lives indoors, away from the sun. So why is there an increase in skin-related diseases? I believe it's partly due to a fear of the sun itself. How are we to live in the light if we don't actually embrace the sunlight? It makes no sense. While it's important to take care of our bodies and avoid sunburn or heat stroke, masking our energy from the sun can be detrimental to our health, leading to Vitamin D deficiency and other adverse reactions.

Light enters our bodies through our eyes and skin. It is well-documented that vitamin D in our bodies, which is provided by the sun's healing energy, is necessary for kidney and musculoskeletal health, among other important aspects.[4] The sun interacts with our skin, a major component of our integumentary system, and provides access to our nervous system, helping us maintain homeostasis. But, we also know that our skin can form cancer without us fully understanding why. A study from Switzerland[5] reported a significant increase in skin cancer cases, noting that the areas on the skin diagnosed with cancer did not correlate with sun exposure, such as sunburned areas. They were also localized to specific spots on the body: the chest and back, where our heart centers extend energetically. It's also interesting to note that the research indicated that the years Immediately following WWII and the September 11th attacks here in the US

---

[4] Pludowski, P., et al, *Clinical Practice in the Prevention, Diagnosis and Treatment of Vitamin D Deficiency*, 2022
[5] Orjan Hallberg & Olle Johansson, *Increasing Melanoma - Too many skin cell damages or too few repairs?*, 2013

showed a sharp rise in cases. The researchers did not make that correlation, but through my lens as an energy healer, it makes sense. While Switzerland is far from the US, we all share a 24-hour news cycle, and the fear generated by the attacks reverberated around the world as people are more connected now than ever before. Our heart centers are implicated in this research as first the location of the melanoma, but also because of the deep contraction of fear caused by those two events that impacted people worldwide.

Lightcasters

When the sun dances on water, we are called by the light beings, or lightcasters as I call them, that exist there to heal through awareness. Our awareness is what brings about the change. We are aware; we are light; we are consciousness itself through the force of the sun. In the sun, suffering is completely gone and we literally feel light. It's an idiom for the ages. All our suffering is in the darkness of misunderstanding. When we see the light, we are healed. When we see light dancing on water, we are in knowingness and it's amplified by that particular water's effect on Earth. If it's light on the ocean, we are healed through the power of knowing who we are. If it's light on a lake, we are healed in the bath of love on Earth as the void also evokes the image of a bathtub. If it's a river, we are healed in our awareness of change and transformation. And if it's a pond, puddle, or creek, we are healed in our awareness through joy, play, and imagination as we see who we are and who we could be in our own reflections, both on the surface and beyond into the mystical energies of the Below.

Calling the sun in every day is a good way to start the day and many societies and religions have rituals centered around this idea. Japan is known as the 'Land of the Rising Sun'—what a wonderful nickname! From Egypt to Peru, cultures around the world have their unique interpretations of how the sun is vital to our existence on Earth and how we are part of it. Just as most plants need sunlight and air to grow, so do we. Our growth in terms of existence is about both physical and spiritual development; growth within and without. If we do not see the sun as our vital ruler, as life itself, we will struggle to grow and thrive; a fear of the sun can lead to suffering. The dark is many things to us — it's not negative, however, the light of our lives is literally the sun.

Chapter 17: Final Notes on Creativity and Healing

Creativity is joy in pure form, like a child opening a fresh box of crayons, feeling the strum of a guitar hit your sternum, or finding someone that gets you. It's not about being the best, but it's finding your best ideas and putting your best foot forward. It's also about finding time to enjoy the things you like to do in a way that resonates with you. When time is found through creativity, the space around us lifts up, making us feel like we're in an arboretum filled with fairy lights and new-found beliefs. We believe in ourselves and each other and believe that healing can occur no matter the wound or problem. We believe in each other and we find the healing within ourselves. We don't look outward, we look inward when we feel creative love. We trip the light fantastic and start to see otherworldly things as part of our everyday existence, but the mundane is the Tao, or The Way of things. All of this comes from creativity, which comes from our cores.

Creativity in All its Forms
Beginning at the end

As I stated at the beginning of this book, creativity lives in all of us. It *is* us. We are creative and are not separate from it. We do not "have" it — we are it. Creativity and healing go hand in hand because healing is a creative act that emerges from love. If you care for another enough to feel any empathy for them, there is sufficient energy to initiate the healing process. Healers are inherently empathetic because love is relational. If I can relate to you, I feel connected to you energetically — in other words, I feel love for you. It doesn't have to be foundational or tantric love; it can simply be the healing love from one person to another who feels the association of being with each other.

Love in all its forms is pure because it is a frequency. Friendship is often considered the purest form of love because it is open and caring without the stress of being a one-and-only support, but I have come to realize that love is love is love is... There is no calculation beyond that and doesn't need to be. In other words, *who cares*!? As long as it is love. It's the relationship that creates differences, not the energy. We can look to the LGBTQIA+ movement as an example that allows for freedom of expression in love.

Most songs are about love, which used to annoy me when I was younger, "Find another topic to sing about!!" But there's a reason why we sing about love, not because we're all obsessed with our romantic interests (or maybe we are), but because love is the binder glue of the Universe. As the band Layup sings,

> *"Time and places are all in who you share 'em with,*
> *And it's life, and the point is*
> *Enjoyin' who you share it with,*
> *Joy is who you share it with."*

Joy is love and we find it with each other — together, not separate. If we don't have love, we're wrecked; if we have it, we feel on top of the world. If we think we have love with strings attached or it's not returned, we feel confused, betrayed, or forgotten. There are so many ways that love or the lack of it impacts our daily lives that it's worth diving into your soul to find where you stand in your relationships, including your relationship with yourself. Loving yourself is hard work and is probably the most difficult form there is because it requires us to look in the mirror and see all the parts we'd rather not see.

If love is all we need, then maybe we should stop worrying about how and who we love and instead focus on the <u>right</u> to love. It is divinely guided that we love one another through our divine life force connections. This is felt in both our integumentary and energetic systems through to the Great Beyond, giving us a feeling of oneness with each other. You might know the quote about love being kind and patient. Let's move beyond that quote and find a new one that brings in feelings of acceptance and understanding. While kindness is a form of love, if you lose your patience with someone, it doesn't mean you don't love them — it means you're human. Holding ourselves to such a high standard only sets up hurt feelings, in ourselves and others, which also leads to confusion and a void of understanding... and it all cycles back again.

Guides and Channeling
Understanding our multifaceted world

Much of this book was channeled. I had misgivings about putting channeled material out for many reasons, some of which were related to my spiritual journey, but also because I thought it was 'cheating,' that the material did not come from me. But it is me! As explained to me by my guides, channeling is simply a way of connecting to other parts of yourself. Just as there is a subconscious and conscious mind, there are different aspects to our beingness that we may not be familiar with or may not have direct access to. If you are interested in learning how to channel, I recommend using techniques developed by Lee Harris[1] who defines it as a way to connect to our own intuitive powers and prescribes it as a healing modality.

We can have guides in our lives from every perspective. Sometimes a guide is a mentor or elder here on Earth, a friend, an enemy, or another label we use for people who have more than just crossed our path. But many of us also believe in guides outside our view of existence; we may not be able to see them, but we know they are there because we can sense or feel them. For some cultures, it's about ancestors. In fact, I don't think there is a single culture that doesn't revere their ancestors, we just do it in different ways. Some may set up shrines while others see a bird sitting on a wire and know that loved ones who have 'passed on' are still with us in some way. Still others feel their energy when they are in a specific room or place (sacred places), while others receive messages or can 'commune' with them. It's all about time and place perspective, I think. Energies of the holidays may bring up an understanding between yourself and a loved one who has died. Or you may find taking a break from life's unending ferris wheel leads you to a better understanding of who you are and find new 'powers' of receiving messages from the 'other side.' These are all ways we feel and are guided by other energies outside ourselves, but come from within us as well. The trick is to find joy and laughter in it, not fear, denigration, or feeling forced to do something you don't want to do. If the energy you are feeling is truly a family member who loves you, then they will not ask you to do something that is not aligned with love or antithetical to your way of being.

Going back to how we connect with our subconscious to create, we know information is shuttled back and forth between the unconscious through the subconscious and into the conscious. It takes a conscious level of mastery to decide which healing modalities are right, which energy decision is effective, and which creative decision is correct. It takes all levels of consciousness to work with guides, too. If we

---

[1] Lee Harris is a channeler, healer and creator extraordinaire. Find more information in the end notes.

don't take the time to parse out the data on a conscious level, then we aren't using our full faculties. But also know that the Universe is there to support. Be happy that we all get our second, third, and fourth chances to get things right if we miss the boat the first time. It gets to be overwhelming when you start thinking about all the decisions, all the ways we interact, and all the energies out there. When overwhelm sets in, notice it first and then bring it back to the body. Start with what you're doing right now, where you are in place and time, and begin to see one step and then another step right in front of it. No need to go beyond that because your only concern is right now. A lower level energy may have you feeling swept up in non-understanding, but if you can stop what you're doing and take note of who you are, you can settle the winds of change and move into a more sheltered space in time.

Guides are there to assist us, but in the end, the choice is ours. If you feel persuaded to do something you would rather not do, don't do it. If you view guides outside our domain of influence as friends and neighbors, then maybe they don't know everything you need or want, so you take their advice with a grain of salt and make your own decision based on what you think is right. It can be a difficult path to walk sometimes because how do you know what is inner knowing, a guide, an ancestor, a nefarious energy, or Source? I suppose it's all in how you look at it. As with all things in life, we can second guess our choices and feel denigrated if we don't make the 'right' one.

Energy Healing in our New Existence on Earth
"We are here to heal each other, not be a detriment to each others' health."

The above subheading is in quotes because it came directly from my guides who say that energy healers are a fact of existence. We are all energy healers through the things we do for each other. Energy healing is not a fringe topic or a nice-to-have when nothing else works, it needs to be integrated into your healing process. Consider how art therapy has been used effectively for years to help people understand their feelings and integrate those knowings into their beingness. Energy healing is not meant to replace other forms of typical Western medicine, it's meant to be a guide to things that might be occurring in the body that require further assistance. It is also meant as a healing space for relief of emotional baggage, which is where all of our illnesses begin. I see energy healing acting as a bridge between your general practitioner, specialist doctors that serve your physical body, and mental health guides or doctors. One does not serve the other, but all rights are reserved by you to take control of your own healing. The dialogue that happens between you and your inner self can serve as a new way to communicate with your doctor or therapist creating new ways of healing.

Energy healing is, in fact, the new way to live on Earth, or the new-old way, as it were. We used to be more in touch with our energy and our healing processes, but that was stripped away through a systems approach by moving people off the land and taking power away from women, who were often the healers in their communities, a.k.a.

witches. It caused change and transformation to occur away from the natural, guided processes that connect us to ourselves, each other, and the planet. It's time now to move towards a future that incorporates both the past and the future in the present.

Time to move toward a future that gets us back to an understanding of our health within our own bodies that doesn't delegate to authority figures outside of us. Time for healers of all types to be guides rather than restrictive with restricted access to only those who can afford it. It's time to take our lives back from those who would keep us down, restricted to a work-a-day existence that doesn't allow for change and only serves our sense of lack. And it's time to take our energy back for ourselves as we say goodbye to the past lives that keep us in looping patterns and repeat cycles of unrest through past life healing. Begin feeling better by calling in all the energies in your life that serve to lift you up, not keep you down. Eliminate those relationships that no longer serve. Eliminate guides that keep you going in circles. Call in those that serve to protect and believe in your power of beingness on Earth.

As my guides say, that is all.

Play List

Part 1
- *Joy Inside My Tears* - Stevie Wonder
- *Grove Thing* - Big Head Todd and the Monsters
- *Girls Just Wanna Have Fun* - Cyndi Lauper
- *Ultra Violet (Light My Way)* - U2
- *Radio Active* - The Firm
- *Know the Difference* - INXS
- *All Night Long* - Lionel Richie
- *Harvest Moon* - Neil Young (covered by Poolside)
- *Goodbye Yellow Brick Road* - Elton John (covered by Sara Barreilles)
- *We Are the World* - Lionel Richie, Michael Jackson, Quincy Jones, et al
- *Never Tear Us Apart* - INXS
- *It's so Easy* - Margo & Mac
- *Time to Move On* - Tom Petty
- *Let's Go Crazy* - Prince

Part 2
- *Fortress Around Your Heart* - Sting
- *1996* - Wild Child
- *Season of the Witch* - Donovan (covered by Lana del Ray)
- *Hazy Shade of Winter* - The Bangles (original, Simon & Garfunkel)
- *Tomorrow Never Comes* - Big Head Todd and the Monsters
- *Good as Hell* - Lizzo

Part 3
- *Not Dead Yet* - Lord Huron
- *I Wanna Dance with Somebody* - Whitney Houston
- *Human Right* - The Strike
- *Who You Share It With* - Layup

Bibliography

Alburghaif, A. H., & Naji, M. A., "Leptin hormone and its effectiveness in reproduction, metabolism, immunity, diabetes, hopes and ambitions," *Journal of Medicine and Life*, *14*(5), 600, 2021.

Andreasen, Nancy C., *The Creative Brain*, New York, NY, Penguin Books, 2005.

Brown, Brene, *Daring to Lead*, New York, Random House Publishing Group, 2018.

Borenstein, Lynn, "Imagination and Play in Teletherapy with Children," *American Journal of Play*, Vol. 14, no.1, 2022.

Câmara, R., & Griessenauer, C. J., "Anatomy of the Vagus Nerve," Nerves and Nerve Injuries, 385-397, 2015.

Cameron, Kim S. and Robert E. Quinn, *Diagnosing and Changing Organizational Culture*, San Fransisco, CA, Jossey-Bass, 2006.

Chen, S., & Venkatesh, A. "An investigation of how design-oriented organizations implement design thinking." *Journal of Marketing Management, 29*(15-16), 1680–1700, 2013.

Cherry, Kendra, *Sublimation in Psychology*, Very Well Mind, online resource, www.verywellmind.com, 2024.

Cherry, Kendra, *Ego as Rational part of Personality*, Very Well Mind, online resource, www.verywellmind.com, 2023.

Chopra, Deepak, *The Seven Spiritual Laws of Success*, New World Library Amber-Allen Publishing, 1994

Chopra, Deepak, *What Are You Hungry For?*, New York, NY, Harmony Books, 2013.

Cole, Terri, *Boundary Boss*, Boulder, CO, Sounds True, 2021.

Daneman, R., & Alexandre Prat, "The Blood–Brain Barrier," *Cold Spring Harbor Perspectives in Biology, 7*(1), a020412, 2015.

Diek, Dina, Marten Piet Smidt, and Simone Mesman, "Molecular Organization and Patterning of the Medulla Oblongata in Health and Disease", *International Journal of Molecular Sciences* 23, no. 16: 9260, 2022.

Dirck, Sam, "Women Owned Businesses and Driving Economic Growth. Here's What Entrepreneurs Should Know," Wells Fargo www.stories.wf.com, January 9, 2024.

Eden, Donna, *Energy Medicine for Women*, New York, NY, Penguin Group, 2008.

Estes, Clarissa Pinkola, *Women Who Run With the Wolves*, New York, NY, Random House,1995.

Estes, Clarissa Pinkola, *The Creative Fire*, Boulder, CO, Sounds True, 1995.

Federici, Silvia, *Witches, Witch-Hunting and Women*, Oakland, CA, PM Press, 2018.

Finlay, Victoria, *Color: A Natural History of the Palette*, New York, Random House Trade Paperback, 2002.

Forbes, Nancy and Basil Mahon, *Faraday, Maxwell and the Electromagnetic Field How Two Men Revolutionized Physics*, Amherst, NY, Prometheus Books, 2014.

Flourish Ventures, "Groundbreaking Study Shows Links Between Founder Health And Performance in Brazil," www.flourishventures.com, March, 2024.

Greenhalgh, Tim, *Disrupting interior design*, D&AD, [web log post] Retrieved from http://www.dandad.org/en/disrupting-interior-design/, 2015.

Guidant Financial, "2024 Women in Business Trends: A look at women-owned small businesses in 2024," guidantfinancial.com, 2024.

Hallberg, Örjan, and Olle Johansson,"Increasing Melanoma—Too Many Skin Cell Damages or Too Few Repairs?" *Cancers* 5, no. 1: 184-204, 2013.

Hanh, Thich Nhat, *Teachings on Love*, Berkeley, CA, Parallax Press, 1997

Hawkins, David R., *Power vs. Force,* Hay House, Inc., 2002.

Hasirci, D., & Demirkan, H., "Understanding the effects of cognition in creative decision making: A creativity model for enhancing the design studio process," *Creativity Research Journal,* 19(2–3), 259–271, 2007.

Hathaway WR, Newton BW, *Neuroanatomy, Prefrontal Cortex,* [Updated 2023 May 29]. In: StatPearls [Internet]. Treasure Island (FL): StatPearls Publishing; 2025 Jan.

Henriksen, D., & Mishra, P., "Twisting knobs and connecting things: Rethinking Technology & Creativity in the 21st Century," *Techtrends: Linking Research & Practice To Improve Learning*, 58(1), 15-19, 2014.

Heidegger, Martin; trans. David Farrell Krell, The Origin of the Work of Art, Martin Heidegger:The Basic Writings, New York: HarperCollins. pp. 143–212, 2008.

Hoff, Benjamin, *The Tao of Pooh*, New York, NY, Penguin Group,1982.

Iliff, J. J., Wang, M., Liao, et al, "A Paravascular Pathway Facilitates CSF Flow Through the Brain Parenchyma and the Clearance of Interstitial Solutes, Including Amyloid β. Science," *Translational Medicine,* 2012.

Jones, Brandi, *Ghrelin and Leptin: Hormones,Hunger, Weight Changes*, www.verywellhealth.com, Updated on October 10, 2023.

Kang, H. J., et al, "Low salt and low calorie diet does not reduce more body fat than same calorie diet: A randomized controlled study," *Oncotarget, 9*(9), 8521, 2018.

Kaufman, J. C., & Beghetto, R. A., "Beyond big and little: The four c model of creativity," *Review of General Psychology,* 13(1), 1–12, 2009.

Kelly, Tom, *The Art of Innovation: Lessons in creativity from IDEO, America's   leading   design firm*. New York, NY, Random House, Inc., 2001.

Maisel, Eric, *The Coach's Way: The art and practice of powerful coaching in any field*, Novato, CA, New World Library, 2023.

Martins, Julia, *Paracelsus: Between Magic and Medicine in the Renaissance*, Living History YouTube Channel, 2024.

Mittal, D., Drummond, K. L., Blevins, D., Curran, G., Corrigan, P., & Sullivan, G. "Stigma associated with PTSD: Perceptions of treatment seeking combat veterans," *Psychiatric Rehabilitation Journal, 36*(2), 86–92, 2013.

Montag, T., Maertz, C. P., & Baer, M., "A Critical Analysis of the Workplace Creativity Criterion Space." *Journal of Management,* 38(4), 1362–1386, 2012.

Morter, Sue, *The Energy Codes*, Simon and Schuster, New York, NY, 2019

Nelson, Bradley, *The Emotion Code,* St Martin's Press, New York, NY, 2019.

New York State Comptrollers Office, "Economic and Policy Insights: New York State Business Owners," www.osc.state.ny.us, March, 2024.

Nguyen, Bao, *The Greatest Night in Pop*, Netflix, 2024

Nummenmaa, L., Glerean, E., Hari, R., & Hietanen, J. K., "Bodily maps of emotions," *Proceedings of the National Academy of Sciences of the United States of America, 111*(2), 646, 2013.

O'Neil, Sharon and Doris Shallcross. "Sensational Thinking A Teaching/Learning Model for Creativity." *The Journal of Creative Behavior 28*, no. 2, 1994.

Pfeiffer, S. *Serving the gifted: Evidence-based clinical and psychoeducational practice*, New York: Routledge, 2013.

Pludowski, P., et al, "Clinical Practice in the Prevention, Diagnosis and Treatment of Vitamin D Deficiency, A Central and Eastern European Expert Consensus Statement," *Nutrients, 14*(7), 1483, 2022.

Portillo, M., "Creativity defined: Implicit theories in the professions of interior design, architecture, landscape architecture, and engineering," *Journal of Interior Design,* 28(1),10–26, 2002.

Questlove, *Creative Quest*, New York, NY, Ecco, 2018.

Roberts, Jane and Robert Butts, *Seth Speaks: The Eternal Validity of the Soul*, San Rafael, CA, Amber-Allen Publishing,1994.

Roberts, Jane and Robert Butts, *The Nature of Personal Reality*, San Rafael, CA, Amber-Allen Publishing, 1994

Rovelli, Carlo, *Reality is not What it Seems*, New York, Riverhead Books, 2017

Rubik, Beverly, et al, "Biofield Science and Healing: History, Terminology and Concepts," *Global Adv Health Med,* 4(suppl):8-14, 2015.

Ruppert, S. S., "Creativity, Innovation and Arts Learning: Preparing All Students for Success in a Global Economy," *Arts Education Partnership* (NJ1), 2010.

Russel, J.S., "Idleness as Play and Leisure: A Reflection on Idleness: A Philosophical Essay by Brian O'Connor," *American Journal of Play,* Vol.14, no. 3, 2022.

Sawyer, R. K., & DeZutter, S. "Distributed creativity: How collective creations emerge from collaboration," *Psychology of Aesthetics, Creativity, and the Arts, 3*(2), 2009.

Sherrell, Zia, "Integumentary system: Function, parts, and conditions," MPH, medicalnewstoday.com, November 27, 2023.

Singh Khalsa, Dharma and Cameron Status, *Meditation as Medicine: Activate the Power of Your Natural Healing Force*, New York, NY, Fireside/ Simon and Schuster, 2001

Stella, D.; Kleisner, K., "Visible beyond Violet: How Butterflies Manage Ultraviolet," *Insects 2022*,13, 242, 2022.

Tarokh, Leila, Jared M. Saletin, and Mary A. Carskadon. "Sleep in Adolescence: Physiology, Cognition and Mental Health." *Neuroscience and Biobehavioral Reviews,* 2016.

Taylor, Mark and Julieanna Preston, *Intimus Interior Design Theory Reader*, John Wiley & Sons, Ltd., West Sussex. England, 2006.

Tau, Lao translated by Ursula K. LeGuin, *Tao Te Ching*, Shambhala Publications, Inc., Boulder, CO, 1997.

Trivedi MK, et al, "Effects of distant biofield energy healing on adults associated with psychological and mental health-related symptoms: a randomized, placebo-controlled, double-blind study," *Health Psychology Research,* 2024;12, 2024.

Tyson, Neil deGrasse, *Astrophysics for People in a Hurry*, New York, London, W.W. Norton and Co., 2017.

Voshell, Martin, *High Acceleration and the Human Body,* 2004

Wakim, Suzanne, Mandeep Grewal, Butte College, *Introduction to the Integumentary System*, Libre Texts Biology, January 24, 2023

Wattles, Wallace D., *The Science of Getting Rich*, Tarcher/ Penguin, 1910, 2007.

Water Science School, *Sublimation and the Water Cycle*, June 8, 2019, online resource: https://www.usgs.gov/special-topics/water-science-school/science/

Wells Fargo, "The 2024 Impact of Women-Owned Businesses, Core Woman, WIPP Education Institute," Ventureneer, www.wellsfargo.com, 2024.

Wittekind, D. A., Kratzsch, J., et al. "Leptin, but not ghrelin, is associated with food addiction scores in a population-based subject sample," *Frontiers in Psychiatry,* 14,1200021, 2023.

Wong, Y., & Siu, K. "A model of creative design process for fostering creativity of students in design education," International Journal of Technology & Design Education, 22(4), 437–450, 2012.

Zeisel, John, Inquiry by Design, New York, NY, W.W. Norton & Company, Inc., 2006.

Healing Protocols Template

Grounding and 'bubbling' statement: (Edited 10/26/24)
Be sure to do Source cord visualization with grounding cord.
"I place myself in an energy of requirement for the purpose of grounding and healing any and all past energies that are keeping me ungrounded. I uncreate detrimental (past life) energies and only allow the past to move forward if it benefits myself and healing others. I ask to fully connect to my Highest Self and align with True Source Energy through the energies of requirement."

Autonomic Response System:
Clears reverberation of detrimental and denied aspect energy, neutralizes discordant and dissonant energy, which almost always come up, causing wound to be re-enacted.
"I install the impulse in my mind to clear my body and energy systems when emotional overwhelm happens through the deepest love and the highest light."

System Reprogram: (Edited 10/26/24)
Energetically, your mind is more responsive than your body to understanding what's happening. The body is aligned with the divine but not at all times whereas the mind can detect energies outside its domain of influence.
"I uncreate all energies within me that no longer serve my highest and best. I install the impulse to release denigration from my body and release it with ease."

"I demand my mind to be forthright in releasing the past life behaviors that serve to repeat denigration patterns. I ask my heart center to transmute those energies back to True Source energy through my Source core connection to the Earth."

Clearing chakras and mycelia system: *(Edited 10-26-2024)*
Also any energies effecting Source connection through the Solar Plexus energy system, which is your Source core.
"I ask my mind as [state your full name] to install the grounded nature of my Source core connection to the Earth when I am feeling energetically challenged through the deepest love and highest light."

Meridians: (Edited 10-26-2024)
"I [state your full name] release all stuck energies in my body's meridians that are causing stress, anger, fear, grief and any entrapping frequencies from electronic media entertainment to overrun my systems. I ask my mind to immediately react to these energies through the deepest love and highest light to remove all blockages.

"I neutralize and harmonize any and all discordant and dissonant energies that are causing fear and anger to persist in my existence and I transmute those energies back to True Source energy through the deepest love and highest light."

Physical Systems: *Using metaphor to effect change (November 1, 2024)*
Time and memory form a solid through manifestation. Transform first so the power of love is already induced through your Source core. Now that it is not physical form, it moves out of the body naturally as an energy, be sure to transmute back to Source.

Grief Statements:
- "I sublimate the forces in my head that are causing me to shrink away from life."
- "I sublimate the pieces of time in my mind known as memory that cause me to believe I am not enough."
- "I sublimate the stuck energies in my heart that feel like a puncture wound."
- " I sublimate the stuck energies in my heart that feel like it's been ripped and torn to pieces." (Or sometimes both!)

Suffering Statement: A heavy heart is a heart under water.
- "I sublimate all stuck energies in my heart that make it feel like it's under water."

Fear and Anger Statements:
- "I sublimate the stuck energies in my gut that are causing me to feel like a gut punch or sucker punch has occurred.
- "I sublimate the stuck energies in my heart-gut connection that are causing my stomach to feel overfull.

General statement for sublimation clearing, because when you don't know, you don't know!
- "I demand my mind to sublimate all stuck energies in my body known and unknown. I transmute those energies back to True Source energy through the deepest love and highest light."

Unrequited Love Release: *fill the vacuum/hole after sublimation*
- If unrequited love exists in you, say: **"I request the requirement of love and joy to fill my heart and be requited and whole unto myself."** Say this incantation for yourself after sublimating energies.
- If the unrequited love exists in another person, you say: **"I request access to _____ [say the person's name] to require love and joy to be requited in his/her/their heart."**

Cortisol Release: (Edited 10/26/24, 11/15/24)
Meridians control the hormone release system because they are the energy or power source that connects all the systems together.
"I demand my mind and body to sublimate fat, fear and anger and all energies keeping me from releasing them through the deepest love and highest light now and forever more. I demand my body to release itself from all anger and fear and transmute it back to True Source energy through deepest love and highest light."

"I demand my mind as [state your full name] to clear and bless my body's fear response and keep it to a minimum through the deepest love and highest light now and forever more."

Fear of Fat Release:
Many energies in our bodies are in fear in terms of weight regulation. Fear of fat is like an anchor point, it will keep you down if you don't release it through love, joy and avasa.

"I release and uncreate any and all fear and anger towards fat in my body and I install joy and avasa through love and light."

Weight Gain Release: (edited 10-26-2024)
"I demand my mind to align the energy in my body to release weight gain and integrate being satiated and feeling full through deepest love and highest light."

Weight Loss Install: (edited 10-26-2024)
"I demand my mind to align with my body's energy related to weight loss through the deepest love and highest light so I can lose weight rapidly and with ease."

"I demand my mind to release any and all hidden energies and neutralize and harmonize any and all discordant and dissonant energies that are preventing me from losing weight rapidly and with ease."

Limbic System Response Release: (Edited 10/26/24 & 12/13/24)
Limbic system healing is through your Source core connection to the Earth and provides a balanced approach to healing past life and this life energy fears.

If you or the person you are clearing have PTSD or other traumatic stress, DO NOT clear the limbic system at this point!! Wait until after you have cleared everything else, just before 'Requirement Energy.'
"I [state your full name] release and understand the overwhelm of the past, present, and future as it moves through my limbic system and I transmute all my body's systems back to True Source energy through the deepest love and highest light."

Clear cranial rhythms: (Edited 11-3–2024)
As a part of speech patterns that affect the medulla. Cranial rhythms are part of the blood brain barrier connection to the medulla and nervous system.
"I demand my mind to change the rhythms of my behavior to be rhythms of care and concern for my own energies. I uncreate all non-beneficial energies all thought processes that are keeping me in a pattern of denigration and I transmute them back to Fully Source energy. I demand that all past and present energies be beneficial to my mind and thought processes within."

"I [state your full name] ask my mind to release the overwhelm of past life behaviors that are keeping me in the looping pattern of a Timefield. I uncreate all negative thought processes that are keeping me down and anchored to the past."

Clear and Release Medulla Oblongata: (August 29, 2024, Edited, 9/5/24,10/26/24) *Clear energy from the medulla as the source of energy resistance in the nervous system in terms of healing the vagus and aortic nerves and the autonomic nervous system.*
"I uncreate all energies that are holding me in a negative belief pattern in understanding the past. I ask my mind to release those energies from my medulla and transmute them back to Full Source Energy through the deepest love and highest light."

Integumentary System Clearing and Release: (Edited 10/26/24)
*If you or the person you are clearing have PTSD or other traumatic stress, DO NOT clear the integumentary system at this point!! Wait until after you have cleared everything else, just before 'Requirement Energy.'**

"I ask my mind as [state your full name] to release those energies from my integumentary system that are keeping me from my Divine Life Force Energy connection points. I ask my heart to transmute the non-benevolent energies back to True Source energy through my Source Core connection to the Earth and bring in love and light for further transformation in time and space."

Parasympathetic Nervous System: (July 27, 2024, edited 12/13/24)
"I release and uncreate any and all energy blocking and causing stress and anger to persist in my parasympathetic nervous system through overwhelm. I transmute all stress and anger in my body back to Full source energy through deepest love and highest light."

"I demand my body and mind to release frozen fear (and anger) so that I may find balance now and forever more through deepest love and highest light." (July 26, 2024, edited 12/13/24, 01/06/25)

Timeline Clearing for faster results: (Edited 10/26/24)
"I ask my mind to reveal any and all hidden lifetimes, discordant, and dissonant energies that are preventing me from [state the issue]. I demand those energies to be fully revealed in time and space to their highest levels so that I may release them quickly and easily."

"I [state your full name] demand all timelines that are slowing down the energies of change and transformation be transmuted back to True Source Energy. I ask for new guides if necessary to assist me with my choices so that I am empowered to make changes quickly and easily in my body, heart and mind."

"I release all timelines that are keeping me in a looping pattern of denigration and transmute them back to Full Source energy through the deepest love and highest light."

Clear your light: (June, 2024, Edited 10/26/24)
Your light is the most important aspect of clearing energy because it is energy in its purest form. Use this so you don't get reverbs when checking for Timefields and wounds.

"I ask my mind and body to emit my own light on Earth through the deepest love. All low vibrational energies who destroy my light are unwelcome. I maintain my own voice with my own light and my own light with my own voice and transmute lower vibrational energies back to Full Source energy."

Tidal Locking Statement for (past life) sequence breaking:
There are energies within us that are locked in place through a sequence of events that are part of our life now or as a past life imprint. Our nervous systems carry this forward

in time and the pressure of it, like a tidal wave, can feel insurmountable at times. When you break the sequence, you are unlocking it to release the past moment.

"I allow my sequence to be free of the energy of a (past life) tidal block. I release and uncreate all (past life) tidal sequences and energies that are keeping me tidally locked and transmute them back to Full Source energy through deepest love and highest light."

Timefield Statements:
For general malaise - works with cranial rhythms of behaviors
"I ask my mind to release the overwhelm of (past life) behaviors that are keeping me in the looping pattern of a Timefield. I uncreate all negative thought processes that are keeping me down and anchored to the past."

Check for Timefields: *Can also be released through body scan method.*
"I release and uncreate all negative (past life) Timefields anchor points (of_____) and I transmute them back to True Source energy through the deepest love and highest light."

Check for wounded behaviors (unseen forces or hidden behaviors): *Can also be released through body scan method.*
"I release and uncreate all (past life) wounds and wounded behavior hubs (of_____) and I transmute them back to True Source energy through the deepest love."

Prevent backdraft energy with install
"I install joy and avasa constantly and consistently into my mind, heart, and body through the deepest love and highest light."

"I allow myself to change all past life denigration behaviors that no longer serve my healing energy of the Earth's Source core and I transmute them back to True Source Energy."

Bifurcation Energy Release: (September 10, 2024)
"I no longer allow past interception energies to force my life. I maintain stillness in my mind and keep my life intact as an individual without pain and suffering. I no longer allow sorrow to emanate from my beingness and energy field and maintain a posture of love and understanding in my life, with others' actions held accountable for their own behaviors."

Wish Fulfillment with Bifurcation Install (February 11, 2025)
Reframing the bifurcation experience to be one of joy and love experience.
"I allow the swallow tail of my existence to [state your wish] and I allow the non-biased energy of love to bring in joy and light. I maintain my heart center energy in time and sync with my own behaviors and allow the energy of tomorrow to provide me with an energy of love, joy and avasa."

For PTSD and traumatic stress survivors, it is now safe to clear first the limbic system and then the integumentary system using the incantations above.

Unforgiveness Energy Release: (November 23, 2024)

There are other ways of releasing this energy like thought forms or other energies within you that are unwelcome in the vacuum of time and space.

"I sublimate all patterns of denigration known and unknown within me and transmute them back to true Source energy through deepest love and highest light."

"I sublimate all the denigration patterns of unrequited love known and unknown within me and transmute them back to true Source energy through deepest love and highest light."

"I sublimate all energies within me that are in unforgiveness and I ask for the requirement of forgiveness to replace the vacuum effect in my heart, mind, body, and energy field. I allow the feelings of being unwelcome to fall away in space and time. And I transmute all the sublimated and vacuum effect energy back to Full Source energy through deepest love and highest light."

Wish Fulfillment: Sublimated energies of time (November 27, 2024, Edited 12/13/24)

"I request access to my energy of love in my heart for wish fulfillment. I sublimate the energies of time in my mind to be in alignment with my wish fulfillment and I transmute all sublimated energy back to Full Source energy through deepest love and highest light."

Double-check your work!

End Notes

Amy Jo Ellis, Court of Atonement: www.courtofatonement.com
Medium and psychic who focuses on healing unrequited love and other energies with her version of energy healing.

Amanda Woodward: www.guardianones.com
Highly attuned healer with powerful modality. Works directly with land wounding all over the world, offers online classes and other guidance.

Brene Brown: www.brenebrown.com, *Unlocking Us* podcast. Also see bibliography for book reference.

Corinne Labita - *Witch Way from Here* podcast focusing on paranormal activity and how it interacts with people and places on Earth.

Dr. Michael Lennox: www.michaellennox.com
Astrologer and psychologist focusing on the symbolic aspects of astrology. *Conscious Embodiment* podcast with weekly transit astrology and dream interpretation.

Lee Harris - Lee Harris Energy, www.leeharrisenergy.com
For more instrumental ways to connect with your spiritual practice including healing through channeling and guides, mantra music, books, and other informative online classes.

Sapien Medicine - YouTube https://www.youtube.com/c/SapienMedicine/store or Spotify for sound healing frequencies that are powerful and effective. Be sure not to overdo it!

This is the end of the road for me, but if you are heartily ready to make changes in your creative life, help yourself to more energy healing through my grounded healing methods by scheduling a healing session.

Visit my website: www.klabitahealing.com to understand my methods and how I work with individuals. Also check out my blog posts where I've covered other topics, including how it feels to be guided by unseen forces. And I will continue to write posts to help fill in gaps on some of the topics in this book. I could have spent pages on some of them, but chose to edit it down to keep it short and sweet.

Thank you, Merci, Grazie, Danke, Mahalo, Gracias, Obrigado, Arigato, Gamsahabnida,
and all the ways around the world there are to give thanks to people outside your realm of influence. I hope that you will be happy and find joy in your creative process and believe in the love, light, and laughter that you deserve.

Believe in magic again.
Believe in all day rainbows, fairies, and nine-tailed foxes (or <i>kitsune, kumiho,</i> or <i>huli jing,</i> depending on your cultural background) for they are your (re)entry point into believing in yourself.</p>

~Begin Again~

www.ingramcontent.com/pod-product-compliance
Lightning Source LLC
Chambersburg PA
CBHW070614030426
42337CB00020B/3795